MOVING MODERNISMS

Moving Modernisms

Motion, Technology, and Modernity

Edited by
DAVID BRADSHAW
LAURA MARCUS
and
REBECCA ROACH

OXFORD
UNIVERSITY PRESS

OXFORD

UNIVERSITY PRESS

Great Clarendon Street, Oxford, OX2 6DP,
United Kingdom

Oxford University Press is a department of the University of Oxford.
It furthers the University's objective of excellence in research, scholarship,
and education by publishing worldwide. Oxford is a registered trade mark of
Oxford University Press in the UK and in certain other countries

© Open University Press 2016

The moral rights of the authors have been asserted

First published 2016

Published in the United States of America by Oxford University Press
198 Madison Avenue, New York, NY 10016, United States of America

British Library Cataloguing in Publication Data
Data available

ISBN 978–0–19–871417–0

Contents

List of Figures

List of Contributors

Tim Armstrong is Professor of Modern Literature and head of the Department of English at Royal Holloway, University of London. His publications include *Modernism, Technology and the Body* (1998), *Modernism: A Cultural Study* (2005), *Haunted Hardy: Poetry, History, Memory* (2000), and most recently *The Logic of Slavery: Debt, Technology and Pain in American Literature* (2012). He is co-editor of the Edinburgh University Press series, *Edinburgh Critical Studies in Modernist Culture*, and one of the organizers of the London Modernism Seminar.

David Ayers is Professor of Modernism and Critical Theory at the University of Kent. His published works include *Wyndham Lewis and Western Man* (1992), *English Literature of the 1920s* (1999), and *Literary Theory: A Reintroduction* (2008). His study of modernism, internationalism, and the Russian Revolution is forthcoming from Edinburgh University Press. He is the former chair of the European Network for Avant-Garde and Modernism Studies (EAM) and joint editor of the EAM book series.

David Bradshaw is Professor of English Literature at Oxford University and a Fellow of Worcester College. In addition to editing a range of modernist texts, including *Mrs Dalloway*, *To the Lighthouse*, *The Waves*, *A Room of One's Own* (with Stuart N. Clarke), and *The Good Soldier*, he has published numerous articles on modernist writing and culture, and edited *The Hidden Huxley* (1994), *A Concise Companion to Modernism* (2003), *A Companion to Modernist Literature and Culture* (2006; with Kevin J. H. Dettmar), *The Cambridge Companion to E. M. Forster* (2007), and *Prudes on the Prowl: Fiction and Obscenity in England, 1850 to the Present Day* (2013; with Rachel Potter).

Steven Connor is Grace 2 Professor of English in the University of Cambridge and Fellow of Peterhouse, Cambridge. His most recent books are *Paraphernalia: The Curious Lives of Magical Things* (2011), *A Philosophy of Sport* (2011), *Beyond Words: Sobs, Hums, Stutters and Other Vocalizations* (2014), *Beckett, Modernism and the Material Imagination* (2014), and *Living by Numbers: In Defence of Quality* (2016).

Wai Chee Dimock has written on every period of American literature, from Anne Bradstreet to *Star Trek*, in *Critical Inquiry*, *Chronicle of Higher Education*, *Los Angeles Review of Books*, and *Salon*. Her 2007 book, *Through Other Continents: American Literature Across Deep Time*, received Honorable Mention for the James Russell Lowell Prize of the Modern Language Association and the Harry Levin Prize of the American Comparative Literature Association. This was followed by a collaborative volume, *Shades of the Planet: American Literature as World Literature*. Her essay here is part of a new project, 'Weak Theory: Networks, Low Bar, Environmental Genres'.

Enda Duffy is Professor of English and Comparative Literature at the University of California, Santa Barbara. He is the author of *The Subaltern Ulysses* (1996) and *The Speed Handbook: Velocity, Pleasure, Modernism* (2009), which won the 2010 Modernist Studies Association Book Prize. With Maurizia Boscagli, he is co-editor of *Joyce, Benjamin and Magical Urbanism* (2011) and author of articles in such journals as *Modernism/Modernity*, *Modernist Cultures*, and the *James Joyce Quarterly*, as well as in many edited collections. At UC Santa Barbara, he is Co-director of COMMA, the Center for Modernism, Materialism, Aesthetics.

Ken Hirschkop is Associate Professor of English at the University of Waterloo. He is co-author of *Benjamin's Arcades: An unGuided tour* (2005) and the author of *Mikhail Bakhtin: An Aesthetic for Democracy* (1999) as well as many articles on Bakhtin, the philosophy of language, and twentieth-century cultural criticism. He is currently completing the study *Linguistic Turns, 1890–1950: Writing on Language as Social Theory* for Oxford University Press, from which the article in this collection is drawn.

Deborah Longworth is Senior Lecturer in Nineteenth- and Twentieth-Century English Literature at the University of Birmingham. She is the author of *Streetwalking the Metropolis* (2000), *Djuna Barnes* (2003), and *Theorists of the Modernist Novel: Joyce, Richardson, Woolf* (2007), and has published widely on modernism and modernist women writers. She is currently one of the editorial team on the AHRC-funded Dorothy Richardson Editions Project, and is also completing a monograph on Edith, Osbert, and Sacheverell Sitwell.

Laura Marcus, FBA, is Goldsmiths' Professor of English Literature at the University of Oxford, where she is Professorial Fellow of New College. Her book publications include *Auto/biographical Discourses: Theory, Criticism, Practice* (1994), *Virginia Woolf: Writers and their Work* (1997/2004), *The Tenth Muse: Writing about Cinema in the Modernist Period* (2007; awarded the 2008 James Russell Lowell Prize of the Modern Language Association), *Dreams of Modernity: Psychoanalysis, Literature, Cinema* (2015), and, as co-editor, *The Cambridge History of Twentieth-Century English Literature* (2004). Her current research project includes a study of the concept of 'rhythm' in the late nineteenth and early twentieth centuries, in a range of disciplinary contexts.

Julian Murphet is Scientia Professor in Modern Film and Literature in the School of the Arts and Media at the University of New South Wales, where he directs the Centre for Modernism Studies in Australia. He has written *Multimedia Modernism* (2009) and co-edited, among other things, *Modernism and Masculinity* (2014), and is preparing a book on Faulkner, media, and romance.

Marjorie Perloff's many books on modernist subjects include *The Poetics of Indeterminacy: Rimbaud to Cage* (1981), *The Futurist Moment: Avant-Garde, Avant-Guerre and the Language of Rupture* (1986), *Wittgenstein's Ladder* (1996), *Twenty-First Century Modernism* (2002), and '*Unoriginal Genius' Poetry by Other Means in the New Century* (2006). Her most recent book is *Edge of Irony: Modernism in the Shadow of the Habsburg Empire* published in 2016 by the University of Chicago Press. Perloff was, until her retirement in 2002, the Sadie D. Patek Professor of Humanities at Stanford University; she is also Florence R. Scott Professor of English at the University of Southern California.

Rachel Potter is Professor of Modern Literature at the University of East Anglia. She is the author of *Modernism and Democracy: Literary Culture 1900–1930* (2007), *Modernist Literature* (2012), and *Obscene Modernism: Literary Censorship and Experiment 1900–1940* (2013). She is also co-editor of *The Mina Loy Companion* (2010) and *Prudes on the Prowl: British Fiction, Censorship and Obscenity 1850—the Present Day* (2013). She is currently working on a new project about early twentieth-century literature, free speech, and International PEN.

Jean-Michel Rabaté, Professor of English and Comparative Literature at the University of Pennsylvania since 1992, is a curator of The Slought Foundation, an editor of the *Journal of Modern Literature*, and Fellow of the American Academy of Arts and Sciences. He has authored or edited more than thirty books on modernism, psychoanalysis, and philosophy. Recent books include *Crimes of the Future* (2014), *An Introduction to Literature and Psychoanalysis* (2014), the edited volume *1922: Literature, Culture, Politics* (2015), and in 2016 *The Pathos of Distance* and *Think, Pig! Samuel Beckett at the Limit of the Human*.

Rebecca Roach is a postdoctoral researcher on the ERC-funded project, 'Ego-Media: The Impact of New Media on Forms and Practices of Self-Presentation' (2014–19) at King's College London. Her current project draws on theories of life writing, the public sphere, linguistics, information theory, and history of the book/material culture to explore communication and collaboration in digital literature. Prior to joining King's, Rebecca completed her doctorate at Oxford University (2014). Her thesis, entitled 'Transatlantic Conversations: The Art of the Interview in Britain and America' assessed the role of the interview form within Anglophone literature from the late nineteenth century to the present day.

Paul K. Saint-Amour teaches in the English Department at the University of Pennsylvania. He wrote *The Copywrights: Intellectual Property and the Literary Imagination* (2003), which won the MLA Prize for a First Book, and edited the collection *Modernism and Copyright* (2011). Saint-Amour has been a fellow at the Stanford Humanities Center, the Society for the Humanities at Cornell, and the National Humanities Center. He co-edits, with Jessica Berman, the Modernist Latitudes series at Columbia University Press and served as President of the Modernist Studies Association in 2012–13. His latest book is *Tense Future: Modernism, Total War, Encyclopedic Form* (2015).

Garrett Stewart is James O. Freedman Professor of Letters at the University of Iowa and the author, among several books of literary and film criticism, of *Between Film and Screen: Modernism's Photo Synthesis* (1999) and its sequel, *Framed Time: Toward a Postfilmic Cinema* (2007). The larger context for his argument about Fritz Lang appears in *Closed Circuits: Screening Narrative Surveillance* (2015). He was elected in 2010 to the American Academy of Arts and Sciences and was a Leverhulme Visiting Professor at Queen Mary, University of London, in 2015.

Olga Taxidou is Professor of Drama at the University of Edinburgh. Her research interests lie mainly in the fields of theatre history and performance studies, with an emphasis on modernism. Her publications include *The Mask: a Periodical Performance by Edward Gordon Craig* (1998), *Tragedy, Modernity and Mourning* (2004), *Modernism and Performance: Jarry to Brecht* (2007), and the co-edited anthologies *Modernism: An Anthology of Sources and Documents* (1998) with Vassiliki Kolocotroni and Jane Goldman, and, with Vassiliki Kolocotroni, *Modernism: A Dictionary*. She is Series Editor of the *Edinburgh Critical Studies in Modernism, Drama and Performance*. Her current project, *Greek Tragedy and Modernist Performance*, results from a series of lectures delivered as part of the Onassis Foundation Senior Visiting Scholars series in 2010–11.

Andrew Thacker is Professor of Twentieth-Century Literature at Nottingham Trent University. He is the author or editor of several books on modernism, including the three volumes of *The Oxford Critical and Cultural History of Modernist Magazines* (2009–13) and *Moving Through Modernity: Space and Geography in Modernism* (2009). He is an editor of the journal *Literature & History* and was the first Chair of the British Association for Modernist Studies.

Patricia Waugh has been a professor in the Department of English Studies at Durham University since 1997. Her first book was *Metafiction: The Theory and Practice of Self-Conscious Fiction* (1984). She has since authored and edited many books and essays on modern fiction, modernism and postmodernism, feminism and fiction, contemporary fiction, and literary theory. She is completing a monograph entitled, *The Fragility of Mind*, examining the relationship between literary cultures and texts and theories and philosophies of mind since 1900. She is also completing a book with Marc Botha, *Critical Transitions: Genealogies of Intellectual Change*. She is planning a new monograph—part of a contribution to a Wellcome-funded collaborative research project at Durham University on Hearing the Voice—on Virginia Woolf and voices, examining Woolf's experiments with voice in relation to narratological and aesthetic, psychological, and philosophical theories of voice and hearing voices.

Robert J. C. Young, FBA, is Julius Silver Professor of English and Comparative Literature, New York University. His writing ranges across the fields of cultural and political history, literature, philosophy, photography, psychoanalysis, and translation studies, with a particular focus on colonial history and postcolonial theory. He is currently completing a book on the philosophy and theory of cultural translation. His publications include *White Mythologies: Writing History and the West* (1990), *Colonial Desire: Hybridity in Culture, Theory and Race* (1995), *Postcolonialism: An Historical Introduction* (2001), *Postcolonialism: A Very Short Introduction* (2003), *The Idea of English Ethnicity* (2008), and *Empire, Colony, Postcolony* (2015), and, edited with Jean Khalfa, *Frantz Fanon. Écrits inédits sur l'aliénation et la liberté* (2015). He is editor of the bimonthly journal *Interventions: International Journal of Postcolonial Studies*. His work has been translated into over twenty languages.

Acknowledgements

Some of the material in Olga Taxidou's chapter initially appeared in *Modernism and Performance: Jarry to Brecht* (Basingstoke: Palgrave Macmillan, 2007), pp. 104–16 (under the title 'Stages for Dancers').

A portion of the text in Jean-Michel Rabaté's chapter has been published in *Crimes of the Future* (New York: Bloomsbury, 2014), pp. 176–84.

A version of Marjorie Perloff's text was published in *Battersea Review* 1/1 (2012), www.batterseareview.com accessed 1 Feb. 2016.

1

Introduction

Modernism as 'a space that is filled with moving'

Laura Marcus and David Bradshaw

'Movement is reality itself', Henri Bergson wrote in *The Creative Mind*.[1] This volume of essays sets out to explore the realities, and the fantasies, of 'movement' in the context of the modernisms of the late nineteenth and early twentieth centuries. It seeks to open up the many dimensions and arenas of modernist movement and movements: spatial, geographical, and political; affective and physiological; temporal and epochal; technological, locomotive, and metropolitan; aesthetic and representational.

Individual chapters explore modernism's complex geographies, including those 'metageographies' and 'heterotopias' in which space is both real and imagined. While the principal focus of the volume is on Anglo-European modernism, including some discussion of the US, USSR, Australia, and New Zealand, many of the essays engage with the debates engendered by recent models of world literatures and global modernisms. They address issues of locality and regionalism, internationalism and transnationalism, borders and diaspora, and cosmopolitanism and translation. Further central issues include questions of periodization and the conceptual relationships between modernism and modernity. We also see a concern with the topic of scale, which has recently become a key concept in literary and cultural studies and, in modernist contexts in particular, has been explored in relation to the intense engagement with space and spatiality. For Andreas Huyssen, for example, scale is profoundly imbricated with the experience and perception of the modern metropolis. The textual 'miniature', of early twentieth-century German literature and critical theory in particular, is, he argues, 'grounded in the micrological experience of metropolitan space, time and life at that earlier stage of modernization when new shapes and scales of urban modernity emerged at accelerated speed but did not yet penetrate the totality of national social and political space'.[2] This is the era of the fragment. For contributors to *Moving Modernisms*, scale is understood in a number of contexts, cultural and aesthetic: the scale of the regional or the micro-scale of the modernist aphorism and phoneme.

'Movement' is also understood in relation to feeling and affect, as an aspect of the relationship between motion and emotion, as well as body and mind, that defined the 'physiological aesthetics' of the turn of the century and which has become central to contemporary neuroscience. Jean-Michel Rabaté, in his chapter in this volume, points to the 'amphibology' of the gerund or present participle in the phrase 'moving modernism', as in the concept of being 'touched' or 'moved' by a text. Physiology dominated 'the aesthetics of movement' that developed in the nineteenth century and helped shape modernist and avant-garde visual and performing arts: studies of animal and human locomotion and the mechanics of movement ran parallel to more expressivist explorations of the body's capacities for motion. 'Vitalism', as a theory of energy and animation, further influenced modernist arts and philosophies in the most powerful ways.

'Movement' indeed becomes definitional of modernity. The development of 'time and motion studies' in the America of the early 1920s had an unexpected outlet in the avant-garde prose of Gertrude Stein, whose Preface to *The Gradual Making of the Making of the Americans* closes with a discussion of 'the question of time', and 'the assembling of a thing to make a whole thing...everybody knows who is an American just how many seconds minutes or hours it is going to take to do a whole thing'. Stein continues: 'I am always trying to tell this thing that a space of time is a natural thing for an American to have always inside them as something in which they are continuously moving...it is something strictly American to conceive a space that is filled with moving, a space of time that is filled always filled with moving ...'.[3] Our contributors do not confine their discussions to the 'strictly American', but the broader concept of modernity as 'filled with moving' is central.

The modernist relationship to twentieth-century modernity, and in particular to new technologies of transportation, communication, and representation in the urban context, is the focus of a number of chapters in the volume. So, too, is a concentration on 'the moving image', also explored in its imbrications with the modernist city. Film possesses an unparalleled capacity to represent and replicate movement, while raising fundamental questions of the relationship between stasis and motion. 'The only real thing in the motion picture', the critic Alexander Bakshy wrote in 1927, 'is *movement* without which all its objects would appear as lifeless shadows...There are, therefore, clearly defined limits for the illusionist effects of real life and nature in the motion picture: the latter can be realistic only when its shadowy world is set in motion.' In Bakshy's account, as in Bergson's, 'movement' becomes 'reality itself': 'the only real thing'.[4]

We begin this volume, in the section on 'Times and Places', with the geographical and historical trajectories of modernism and modernity. In his 'Placing Modernism', Andrew Thacker points to some of the problems inherent in recent large-scale constructions of 'global', 'transnational', and 'planetary' modernisms. He strikes a warning note about cultural standpoints: 'the globe of a global modernism looks very different depending upon where you are positioned'. In offering alternative mappings, Thacker proposes, firstly, a re-evaluation of 'modernist internationalism'; secondly, following the lead of Jon Hegglund's recent study *World Views: Metageographies of Modernist Fiction*, an attentiveness both to the 'national dimensions and origins' of modernism and to 'intercultural encounters'; thirdly, a focus on the idea of *scale* and a non-hierarchical spatial layering, which was opened up, most influentially, in Henri Lefebvre's theory of the 'hypercomplexity of social space'.

Regionalism, Thacker suggests, is one of the overlooked dimensions of modernist scale. Region and locality are also taken up in Tim Armstrong's discussion of 'micro-modernism'. In his chapter, Armstrong suggests that a more dynamic picture of modernism emerges when we pay attention to it as 'a local effect which contests the power of any existing map'. 'Micromodernisms', in Armstrong's account, can be defined as involving '*sites, occasions, and trajectories*'. The first of these (exemplified for Armstrong in the 'Hammersmith modernism' of the late 1920s and 1930s) suggests a renewed attention to the localism of artistic formations and groupings, while the second points to an understanding of the particular publication or the specific literary event as a cultural crucible. In exploring 'trajectories', Armstrong looks to an Antipodean modernism, tracing the path of writers and artists from Australia and New Zealand, including Jack Lindsay, Len Lye, and Patrick White, who arrived in Britain in the early decades of the twentieth century. In the work they produced and the networks they formed we find 'a modernism of disconnection' which, Armstrong argues, characterizes the aesthetics of the 1930s and describes 'an angle of traversal across what we call modernism, impelled by a sense of dissidence'.

In 'Modernism's Missing Modernity', David Ayers addresses the fundamental issue of the relation between modernist culture and 'the periodization of a social modernity'. Noting that 'modernism', like the continental European conception of the avant-garde, is highly diffuse, he suggests that the only adequate response is to examine more closely the interrelation between modernist culture and its historical background. He calls attention, in this context, to the caesura of the Russian revolution and to reflections on technology both by Marxists such as Walter Benjamin and by Heidegger (in *Being and Time* and in his later essay on technology). The way in which these thinkers increasingly problematized the theory of history can be understood, Ayers suggests, as a response to a process of 'de-imperialization' in Europe and Asia which, among other things, reconfigures the artist as a 'transnational subject' in a 'globally redefined field'.

In our second section, 'Horizons', Wai Chee Dimock explores the concept of a 'networked modernism', which demands a reaching beyond the boundaries—biographical, historical, and geographical—of the corpus of a single author. Her discussion starts with a place—Gibraltar—, which plays a central role in Joyce's *Ulysses*. In its idealization, 'it is as much a concept as it is a physical locality', moving the reader eastward from twentieth-century Ireland to a mythic Mediterranean. In *Ulysses*, Gibraltar is aligned with the Atlas Mountains and, implicitly, with Atlas's daughter Calypso: 'the Calypso effect' identified by Dimock relates to the etymology of the nymph's name, which derives from the Greek for 'to cover, to conceal, or to hide'. The effect is, Dimock argues, a central aspect of modernist aesthetics: a superabundance of detail creates an 'atmospheric blur' through which we see mere glimpses of geopolitical, religious, and historical formations. In the writings of Ezra Pound and Paul Bowles on Gibraltar and Morocco, places are differently, but no less heavily 'mediated and refracted...subject to the constraints of partial illumination'.

Robert Young's chapter, 'Restless Modernisms: D. H. Lawrence Caught in the Shadow of Gramsci', also focuses on a specific place and its mediations: in this instance, Sardinia through the eyes of Lawrence. Young places Lawrence in a tradition of orientalist travel writing about Sardinia, while noting the modernity of his restlessness: 'Comes over one an absolutely necessity to move' is the opening line of *Sea and Sardinia*. In search of the primitive (though highly irascible in the face of the 'primitive' living conditions he encounters) Lawrence finds in the Sardinian people humanity 'before the soul became self-conscious: before the mentality of Greece appeared in the world'. For Young, Lawrence is not only blind to the politics, historical and contemporary, of place but seemingly unaware that his 'primitives' might be quite otherwise: both the economist Piero Sraffa and the Marxist thinker and activist Antonio Gramsci were native Sicilians. 'What', Young asks, 'if the instinctual dumb native actually happened to be one of the greatest intellectuals of the twentieth century?' Lawrence and Gramsci never met, but the terms of an imagined encounter break apart the assumptions on which the modernist conception of primitivism was grounded.

The third section of the volume moves away from the concerns of space and place to focus on movement and motion as questions of 'Energies and Quantities'. Enda Duffy's chapter, 'High-Energy Modernism' considers the ways in which modernist literature treats and transmits human energy. This newly discerned somatic economy is organized around the newly minted notion of 'stress'. In developing textual strategies to annotate the somatic reactions of its characters and elicit them in its readers, and in casting these myriad reactions into the modulations of often new, or newly public, gestures, modernist literature went well beyond the scientific discourse on stress in order to invent a new gestural repertoire. Modernist literary experimental styles, as in Joyce's *Ulysses* and Woolf's *Mrs Dalloway*, were adept at seismographically annotating even the slightest somatic change. The chapter reads modernist 'soma-textuality' as the measure of human energy expenditure at the moment when a new global politics, built around energy, was being born.

'Numbers It Is', the title of Steven Connor's essay, is a phrase taken from the 'Sirens' episode of *Ulysses*, as Leopold Bloom reflects on 'Musemathematics'. Modernity, Connor argues, is a matter of measurement. He notes the pull, in modernist thought and writing, between quality and quantity, intensity and measure, the continuous and the discontinuous, and observes the defining role of 'scale'. Numbers represent the possibility of absolute distinctiveness and a world of discontinuities, against which the philosophy of Henri Bergson was pitted. For Bergson, the opponent was divisibility itself: 'To a world of distinct objects, Bergson opposes a world of commingled vibrations.' In Virginia Woolf's writing, including her diaries, Connor finds a counterpoint between the attempts to capture ephemeral states and a preoccupation with 'the rendering of calendrical accounts'. The fluency and continuity which Woolf sought were only achievable 'against the background of resistance formed by the steady diminishment of the clock'. Similarly, in Samuel Beckett's work, we find a compulsive attention to levels, scales, and ratios, and the mathematization of modernist movement.

For Bergson, as Connor notes, music and dance were examples of absolute continuity. Olga Taxidou's chapter, '"Do Not Call Me a Dancer" (Isadora Duncan, 1929): Dance and Modernist Experimentation', examines the relationship between movement in modernist dance and experiments in narrative and poetry. 'I use my body as my medium just as a writer uses his words': Isadora Duncan's analogy between textuality and embodiment is one that is experimented with throughout modernist theatre and dance. The chapter explores modernist dance experimentation, as represented by the Ballets Russes production of *Les Noces* (1923), Jean Cocteau's *The Marriage on the Eiffel Tower* (1921), and W. B. Yeats's *Fighting the Waves* (1929). All three bring together and help to shape the idea of modern dance through the conspicuous presence of the female dancer, while thematically they all radically rework classical ballet's 'marriage plot'. At the same time, they are informed by theories of acting of the period, whereby the performing body is viewed as a machine for experimentation in modernist *ekphrasis,* itself a form of movement between different aesthetic or representational spheres. Taxidou examines both 'the word as flesh' and 'the flesh as word', as the creative interface between literary modernism and the moving modernisms of dance performance.

The two chapters in the next section of the volume, 'Avant-Gardes', turn to the connections between Gertrude Stein and Marcel Duchamp, James Joyce and Franz Kafka. They raise questions of 'movement' between art forms and issues of scale: for Jean-Michel Rabaté, Kafka generates 'a perpetual movement by using a very small textual surface'. In '"A Cessation of Resemblances": Stein/Picasso/Duchamp', Marjorie Perloff offers a radical rethinking of *ekphrasis,* as she turns from the more familiar pairing of Stein and Picasso to the relationship between Stein and Duchamp, and to the unexplored territory of the influence of Stein's verbal compositions on the visual artwork of her contemporaries. Perloff suggests that there is an intimate and intricate relationship between Stein and Duchamp's feminine alter ego, Rrose Sélavy. She also opens up, through an exploration of Stein's phonemic play, the embedding of the Stein/Duchamp relationship in Stein's portrait 'Next. Life and Letters of Marcel Duchamp' and in *Stanzas in Meditation,* her most abstract and her least 'retinal' work, which was translated by Duchamp. It is he, rather than Picasso, Perloff argues, who stands 'Next' to Stein.

In '"A Cage Went in Search of a Bird": How do Kafka's and Joyce's Aphorisms Move Us?', Jean-Michel Rabaté looks at the relationship between Joyce's epiphanies and Kafka's aphorisms. The compression of the form, which 'presents the shortest narrative form capable of capturing the dialectical intertwining of Self and Other', allows both writers to found their writing on a sense of the Real as an insuperable outside, whose violence moves and dislocates at the same time. This process allows them to be touched by the power of such an encounter while requiring specific forms so as to convey the shock to the reader. The main difference is that Joyce's career begins with these enigmatic fragments, whereas Kafka's career comes to a close with them. These short texts are to be understood less as keystones than as steles or tombstones. In their brush with radical otherness and mortality, they do not so much provide keys to a redemptive vision or to salvation as affirm the power of language to contain, within its folds, the dynamic ambivalence of an encounter with truth.

The chapters in our next section, 'Discourses/Voices', turn to cultural, political, and literary movements, and to a variety of 'voices': those of political fora, public opinion, and literary narration. Rachel Potter discusses the contribution made by modernists and others to the writers' organization PEN (Poets, Playwrights, Essayists, and Novelists), founded in 1921, and PEN's role in relation to the post-WW2 human rights agenda marked by the Universal Declaration of Human Rights in 1948. This contribution, she suggests, has been overlooked even in recent accounts which emphasize the global context of literature of that period. Modernism, in particular, has often been portrayed as remote from social and political concerns. Potter shows that even writers critical of PEN's universalism, whether for its lack of realism or for its Eurocentric limitations, were in fact substantially responding to these themes. In the early 1930s, with the Nazis in power and H. G. Wells succeeding Galsworthy as president of PEN, the organization spoke up more emphatically in defence of human rights and, for example, founded a library of books banned by the Nazis. With its open membership policy, PEN provided a focus for a wide range of writers in the interwar years.

Ken Hirschkop's chapter explores the notion of public opinion, discussed by the psychologist and sociologist Gabriel Tarde in 1898, and the role of myth as analysed by Ogden and Richards in *The Meaning of Meaning* (1923), by Mikhail Bakhtin in the Soviet Union, and by Saussure and, later, Barthes in Switzerland and France. Political myth, as theorized by Georges Sorel in the early years of the century, was a particular concern for Ogden and Richards and in the German refugee Ernst Cassirer's *Myth of the State* (1946). The chapter closes with a discussion of Gramsci's analysis of political language, metaphor, and myth, in which the idea of political myth is reappropriated for progressive politics. Gramsci was attempting, as Hirschkop shows, a similar but more effective combination of didactic and propagandistic motifs to the kind attempted in Bukharin's *Theory of Historical Materialism*. Bukharin, Gramsci argued, should have engaged more directly with the 'common sense' of his intended audience in attempting to transform its consciousness.

Patricia Waugh's chapter, 'Precarious Voices: Moderns, Moods, and Moving Epochs', takes up the question of 'voice' through an exploration of 'the strange reality of fictional illusion' and of 'moods and voices' in the modern British novel. In its focus on 'moving epochs' it also offers a critique of literary periodization and of approaches to modernist literature and culture which have rendered the rich and complex novels of the mid-twentieth century merely an 'after modernism': the texts of this period, Waugh argues, are too often misunderstood or diminished. She points in particular to the 'distributed' exposition of mind, through a broadly phenomenological grasp of the structures of experience, running throughout the fiction of the twentieth century from Kafka, Woolf, Proust, and Faulkner onwards. There was an extensive employment of expressionist techniques, born of phenomenological insights, in many of the most compelling novels of the 1950s (including work by Muriel Spark, William Sansom, William Golding, Elizabeth Bowen, and Samuel Beckett), which became a vehicle for imagining and opening up worlds that reflect disturbed minds and alienated outsiders. The 'precarious voices' of these texts have particular resonance with our present moment, in all its 'precarity'.

In our final section, 'Motion Studies', 'movement' and 'motion' are explored in relation both to the complex and paradoxical dimensions of the 'moving image' and to travel and transport in modernity. In 'Stillness and Altitude', Paul Saint-Amour offers a detailed reading of the French director René Clair's 1925 silent film *Paris qui dort*, which presents a narrative of frozen time amid modernity's ceaseless motion. The chapter explores *Paris qui dort* as a meditation less on stasis than on the repose that inheres at high speed, which Roland Barthes called the coenaesthesis (the internal, humoral swoon) of motionlessness. Speed, Saint-Amour notes, 'used to happen to the body. Now it happens *in* the body.' Clair's film identifies the leading edge of what Barthes would describe as a full-blown phenomenon, attempting to afflict its viewers with something like a coenaesthesis of motionlessness in its games with camera speed and its insistence that even stilled images in cinema are speed phenomena. But by making money and time functions of one another, *Paris qui dort* also links the dizzy stasis of both the flier and the filmgoer with the velocity of *capital*, a term that drops out of Barthes's analysis.

In his chapter, 'Frame-Advance Modernism: The Case of Fritz Lang's *M*', Garrett Stewart adopts a different approach to the question of stasis and motion in film. Extending his work on 'frame-advance modernism' and on the seriality of photomechanical succession as cinema's optical specificity, Stewart explores the allusions in *M* (Lang's first sound film) to the graphic arts, including the painting and photography of the Neue Sachlichkeit movement in Weimar Germany. He explores the ways in which the 'arrested visuals' of the film's still images 'break into the movement-image itself and derail its normal storytelling'. Other recent commentators on *M* (including Gilles Deleuze and Jacques Rancière) overlook the film's track and 'its deep engagement both with the general energies of a time-based (frame-advance) modernism and with the specific impedances to seamless narrative flow introduced by *M*'s repeated evocation of Weimar's objectivist still lifes'. *M* also offers, Stewart argues, a spectatorial logic fitted to a society of surveillance, and an instrumentalized vision which defines modernity. *M*, in this account, 'is a film about the participation of its own surveillance ethos in the wider spectrum of modernist visual culture', and the alphabetic character or integer *M* stands not only for 'murderer' but also for the Modern itself 'under the sign of the seen'.

What, Paul Saint-Amour asks in his chapter, 'is the *speed* of speed?', a question also explored by Enda Duffy in his book *The Speed Handbook*. Deborah Longworth, in her chapter in this volume, 'Perpetual Motion: Speed, Spectacle, and Cycle-Racing', examines the fascination of the bicycle, or more specifically bicycle racing, for the avant-garde in the first decades of the twentieth century. Jean Metzinger's Cubo-Futurist *At the Cycle-Race Track* (Au Vélodrome) (1912) represented at once the commercial world of the bike race and the cadence of the sprinting cyclist; Marcel Duchamp's spinning *Bicycle Wheel* (1913) exemplified the non-functionality of speed; while Umberto Boccioni, Enrico Prampolini, Gino Severini, and Mario Sironi aimed to realize in art the mutual dynamism of the human body and the bicycle. The velodrome with its heated and smoky interior, in which thousands of spectators at a time crowded to bet on the riders sprinting elbow to elbow around the banked wooden track, was a cosmopolitan phenomenon. It celebrated the conjunction of man and machine, and what Hemingway called 'the driving purity of speed'.

In the final chapter in this section and in the volume, 'A Desire Named Streetcar', Julian Murphet explores the literary figurations of another mode of transport, the streetcar, in its movement from the naturalism of the late nineteenth century to the modernism of the early twentieth. The streetcar gathered, into a single 'moving image', powerful cognitive signals (in relation to finance capital, urban transportation networks, 'public works', and the very structure of the modern city) without sacrificing dramatic and imaginative potential. In the shift to a dominant modernist aesthetic, different functions are discovered for what was by now a nostalgic image, in particular a rich web of phenomenological and perceptual intensities, and a free-floating discursive register. The chapter demonstrates the dialectical nature of the streetcar as an aesthetic image in the modern: it is, Murphet argues, simultaneously impressionist and realist, oscillating between a perceptual and a cognitive function. More broadly, Murphet's claim is that 'modernism can be understood as a clandestine fidelity to the cognitive achievement of the realists, such that, relatively ironized and muted, it can undergo a frenzy of formal experimentation with its figures'. Here we find movement in both space and time, as the nineteenth century transits into modernism.

Many of the chapters in the volume have developed out of papers given at the *Moving Modernisms* conference held at the University of Oxford in 2012. We thank all our speakers, chairs, and participants, as well as our conference helpers, Kevin Brazil, Angus Brown, and Laura Nelson, and, as contributors to the website and artwork, Dorothy Butchard and Maya Evans. We would also like to thank Oxford University Press, the Bodleian Library, Blackwell's Bookshop, Oxford, Garsington Manor, and the Ashmolean Museum. The conference and this volume were made possible by support from the Oxford English Faculty and the Ludwig Fund at New College, Oxford: we would like to express our gratitude to Eugene Ludwig for his invaluable contribution to work in the Humanities.

NOTES

1. Henri Bergson, *The Creative Mind: An Introduction to Metaphysics* (New York: Philosophical Library, 1946, rpt. New York: Dover, 2007), p. 119.
2. Andreas Huyssen, *Miniature Metropolis: Literature in an Age of Photography and Film* (Cambridge, MA: Harvard University Press, 2015), p. 10.
3. Gertrude Stein, 'The Making of the Making of Americans', in *Selected Writings of Gertrude Stein*, ed. Carl Van Vechten (New York: Viking, 1945), pp. 257–8.
4. Alexander Bakshy, 'The Road to Art in the Motion Picture', *Theatre Arts Monthly XI* (June 1927), p. 456.

TIMES AND PLACES

2

Placing Modernism

Andrew Thacker

Where today do we place modernism in the world? What has impelled the movement of modernism to multiple new territories around the globe? Will modernism ever stop moving and expanding? And how does modernism take root in these diverse new locations? It would be an interesting party game to try to locate somewhere on the globe to which modernism has *not* moved (the Arctic maybe?).[1] Sometimes, however, it seems as if modernism can be found just about everywhere and yet, paradoxically, located nowhere in particular. Rather than the sometimes abstract space of a 'global modernism' or a 'world republic of letters', then, this chapter considers the importance of thinking more particularized geographies of modernism, wherever they take root. Indeed, how modernism has taken root across the globe is a crucial question that must continue to be interrogated and explored via the material texts of specific geographical cultures. This chapter thus questions some of the current critical work in transnational and global modernist studies. Suggesting that there are problems with certain aspects of a shift to transnational or global modernisms should not be taken to be a nostalgic or conservative gesture: modernist studies is, thankfully, never going to return to the narrow model of the Anglo-American 'men of 1914'. But it is important to consider more carefully some of the implications—particularly in terms of a critical literary geography[2]—of a modernism that seemingly aligns itself with a transnational agenda and rejects internationalism. One unfortunate consequence of this agenda is that some of the calls for a globalized modernist studies tend to be rather myopic in their geographical gaze: yes, for important and necessary reasons, to Asia, Japan, China, Africa, sometimes South America and the Middle East, but rarely looking at those areas in Europe outside of Britain, Ireland, France, or Germany, in which modernist and avant-garde activity flourished—for example, the Nordic countries, the Baltic states, or the complex and shifting entity of Central Europe.[3] Examining the programmes of conferences mounted by the European Avant-Garde and Modernism Network (EAM) one glimpses a large European hinterland that appears somewhat opaque to some proponents of 'global modernism'.[4] This is rather unfortunate, given the complexity and range of modernist activity across Europe, work which should surely be viewed as part of a globalizing of what we study when we study modernism, as we thankfully move away from the restrictive canons of the past. This chapter will thus begin with a discussion of modernism and place, before moving on to consider some problems with global and transnational versions of modernism.

MODERNISM AND INTERNATIONALISM

Over the last decade or so we have witnessed a welcome broadening of where in the world we locate modernism; in addition we have also witnessed changes in the geographical imaginary of this expanded field. One significant tendency is a shift from the 'international' to the 'transnational' as a paradigm for understanding how modernism moves and becomes placed in the world. We can trace this shift if we look back to Malcolm Bradbury and Alan MacFarlane's classic 1976 study of *Modernism*, where we find that internationalism is the primary geographical descriptor:

> We took...as the period of concentration the years 1890–1930, and for our geographical map the international span of the Modern movement right across Europe and to the United States.
>
> The when and the where are crucial dimensions because much of the discussion of literary Modernism has stayed resolutely national or regionalized. Much English-language discussion of Modernism has, for instance, steadfastly held to the London-Paris-New York axis, an emphasis that has narrowed interpretation, simplified reading, and ignored the scale and interpenetration of a uniquely international and polyglot body of arts. Most of the interfusing movements and tendencies which made for the debates and directions of Modernism were pan-European (if differently rooted from place to place) and the product of an era of artistic migration and internationalism. They regularly came from those cities which were on, or were themselves, cultural frontiers—Paris, Rome, Vienna, Prague, Budapest, Munich, Berlin, Zurich, Oslo, Barcelona, Saint Petersburg, even Dublin and Trieste, where Joyce wrote much of *Ulysses*. At this time London was such a city; so, to an ever-growing degree, were New York and Chicago. They came, too, from the clustering of migrant artists, in a time when willing and unwilling expatriations and exiles were common. No single nation ever owned Modernism, even though many of the multiform movements of which it was made did have national dimensions and origins in specific regions of European culture. Many if not most of its chief creators crossed frontiers, cultures, languages and ideologies in order to achieve it.[5]

This is a fascinating and, in many ways, quite ambivalent argument. Although it stays very much within the tenor of the literary criticism of its time, several indications of a different problematic around the geography of modernism also surface. The periodization is now widely understood as too limited, overlooking earlier trends in France, for example, and ignoring the 'late modernism' of the 1930s and 1940s, let alone the abstract art or modernist tendencies, such as the Black Mountain group, that were only to take hold in America after World War II. The focus on Europe and North America also looks far too narrow from a postcolonial perspective: beyond Europe and America the map is blank. And, in relation to the United States itself, only the two cities mentioned here receive attention in the book, neglecting the notion that there might be interesting takes on modernism outside of New York and Chicago in places such as Nashville or New Orleans.[6] The authors are aware, however, of the dangers of constricting the focus to a London-Paris-New York axis and, quite rightly, point to other locations for modernism, primarily from Europe.[7]

However, the dominant geographical imaginary that operates here is that of internationalism, an epithet that is repeated three times in this short section. Elsewhere the editors claim that 'the essence of Modernism is its international character … Modernism, in short, is synonymous with internationalism.'[8] Modernism is here an international set of practices transported across 'frontiers' of various kinds (geographical, linguistic, and cultural) by a set of 'migrant artists' and exiles, taking root—an important word here—in many diverse locations. 'No single nation ever owned modernism,' write Bradbury and McFarlane, because in this conception it was a rootless form of expression that roamed across the globe. We are reminded here of the term 'international style' in architecture: precisely a form of building that was deemed transportable from one country to another.[9] An even stronger formulation of this paradigm was given in Hugh Kenner's 1984 article on 'The Making of the Modernist Canon', where Kenner suggested that works by a very limited number of writers such as Joyce, Eliot, and Pound are 'best located in a supranational movement called International Modernism'.[10] In Kenner's conception this is a modernism that is 'located' in a vacuum in terms of material geographical space. Kenner's shaky grasp of geography only seems confirmed in his dismissal of Virginia Woolf as a 'voice from a province' (along with William Faulkner and Wallace Stevens) (59), writing 'village gossip from a village called Bloomsbury' (57), an account that seems purblind to Woolf's persistent engagement with the city of London outside of the area of Bloomsbury in much of her fiction, as well as in essays such as 'The London Scene'.[11]

Many recent critics have, rightly, challenged these earlier accounts of how modernism has moved around the world. They have critiqued the 'international paradigm' developed here because, in Jahan Ramazani's words, its 'internationalism was not always particularized, its Eurocentrism made scant room for the developing world, and its supposed universalism tended to de-ethnicize writers'.[12] Susan Stanford Friedman, for example, describes critics such as Kenner or Bradbury and McFarlane as exhibiting a 'parochial internationalism'.[13] Jessica Berman, in developing a rapprochement between modernism and comparative literature, argues that 'comparative modernist studies must at last kill that old bogey, "international modernism", along with its homogenizing impulses and its insistence on a singular universal sphere of readership'.[14]

Such critiques are particularly valid in relation to Kenner's parochial view of modernism, but miss an important aspect of Bradbury and MacFarlane's argument. For here there are the inklings of a different geographical imaginary, one that views location not simply as the place where modernism, somewhat like a suitcase, ends up after its travels, but where location plays a dynamic role in the constitution of modernism in a way that does not seem that different from the model conceived here by certain proponents of transnationalism. For Bradbury and MacFarlane argue that modernism is not only 'differently rooted from place to place', but also has 'national dimensions and origins in specific regions of European culture'. Clearly the restricted European focus taken here is insufficient, but what is more significant are the theoretical implications of stating that modernism took 'root' in different places: how far are Bradbury and McFarlane here imagining that 'national dimensions' actively shaped *how* modernism took root, and thus produced its quite distinctive cultural forms? Is there a glimpse here of a modernism marked strongly and decisively by particular geographical locations rather than being seen as a set of aesthetic practices existing in the empty space of an 'International Modernism'?

One way to understand the conception of modernism being 'differently rooted' across the globe is thus through the lens of transnationalism. In a much-cited overview of new directions in modernist studies in 2008 Douglas Mao and Rebecca Walkowitz noted that there 'can be no doubt that modernist studies is undergoing a transnational turn'.[15] In this view modernism shifts from place to place, crossing continents, taking root at different times as well as in diverse locations. Importantly, the conception here is that in the encounter with new geographical spaces very different modernisms are formed and forged: modernism now is something more than a style begun in Paris and transported to London, then Stockholm, then Shanghai. Rather a transnational agenda stresses that an idea of 'being modern' travels across the globe and then, in the encounter with 'national dimensions', something fresh appears: a Shanghai Modernism, a Nordic Modernism, and so on.[16] Modernism is now an empty signifier whose signified is derived, to some extent, from that geographical location in which it takes root. Here we are exploring 'modernisms at large', to borrow Andreas Huyssen's adaptation of Arjun Appadurai's 'modernity at large', investigating what Huyssen calls 'the legacies of imported *and* indigenous modernisms'.[17]

The agents of change, in this case, are not the individual 'migrant artists' and exiles referred to by Bradbury and MacFarlane, heroic figures bringing the torch of modernism to illuminate the gloomy spaces of tradition: rather it is the places themselves that function dynamically, bending the idea of the modern, of experimentation, of 'making it new', to the social and cultural conditions of the particular geography in which it takes root. In this conception modernism is not 'differently rooted' in Chicago or Shanghai but, after taking root, the seed of modernism flowers and develops differently in these locations. Such instances of modernism taking root in a place after geographical movement have been described by Susan Stanford Friedman as a process of *indigenization*. Echoing an idea formulated in Edward Said's 'Traveling Theory', Friedman writes that all modernisms 'develop' as forms of 'cultural translation or transplantation produced through intercultural encounters', and that one version is that of indigenization, defined as:

> a form of making native or indigenous something from elsewhere. Indigenization presumes an affinity of some sort between the cultural practices from elsewhere and those in the indigenizing location. Hostile soil does not allow transplantation to take hold; conversely, the practices that take hold in their new location are changed in the process.[18]

In some ways, therefore, we are not that far from Bradbury and McFarlane's idea of modernism being differently rooted from place to place. However, in Friedman there is clearly a much stronger emphasis upon the dynamism of place: a German-born modernism, for instance, that finds a home in Calcutta is transformed in that process of transplantation.

Just such an example is given in Partha Mitter's account of modernism and the visual arts in the last decades of colonial India. For Mitter, the first phase of the rooting of modernism in the visual arts in India began in 1922, with an exhibition in Calcutta of European avant-garde figures such as Paul Klee, Wassily Kandinsky, and other artists of the Bauhaus, as well as, somewhat unexpectedly, a painting by Wyndham Lewis. This exhibition was prompted by the visit of the Indian Nobel Laureate Rabindranath Tagore to the Bauhaus in 1921. As this imported modernism took root in India, its 'radical formalist language' offered artists such as Tagore and Jamini Roy 'a new weapon of anti-colonial resistance' as they forged an aesthetic drawing upon Cubism and then complex notions of primitivism.[19] Hence, modernism as produced by travel and indigenization. However, a more radical interpretation of a transnational perspective posits that the seed that produces a specifically located modernism is *native* and not imported: thus, there not only exist 'imported' modernisms, or syncretic versions that emerge out of contact with 'foreign' cultural forms, but also thoroughly '*indigenous* modernisms'. In other words, these are modernisms that not only display 'national dimensions', but also 'national *origins*', where the dynamics of place produce specific cultural forms seemingly prior to any engagement with a 'Western' or 'European' model of aesthetic or cultural modernism.

How then to explain the flourishing of the seeds of native modernisms? In a series of recent essays Friedman has pursued the implications of the idea of 'indigenous modernisms' in what she calls 'a planetary approach to modernism that breaks the Anglo-European hold on the field'.[20] Friedman argues that not only are there forms of modernism still to be understood in other geographical locations on the planet, but also 'modernisms' hidden in the 'deep time' of the planet's history. Friedman thus posits the idea of 'modernisms' and 'modernities' existing considerably before the nineteenth century, citing the Tang Dynasty China, the Mughal Empire in India, or the Muslim Empire of Al-Andalus, as possible examples.[21] Friedman defines her 'planetary modernism' as follows:

A planetary aesthetics of modernism needs to be transformative rather than merely additive. It is worthwhile to identify texts—visual, verbal, auditory—outside the West that exhibit the aesthetics of so-called 'high-modernism', but a fully planetary approach should aim to detect the different forms that representational rupture take in connection with different modernities. We need to let go of the familiar laundry list of aesthetic properties drawn from the Western culture capitals of the early twentieth century as the definitional core of modernism. . . . we need to provincialize it, that is to see 'high' or 'avant-garde' modernism as ONE articulation of a particularly situated modernism—an important modernism but not the measure by which all others are judged and to which all others must be compared. Instead, we must look across the planet, through deep time, and vertically within each location to identify sites of the slash—modernity/modernism—and then focus our attention on the nature of the particular modernity in question, explore the shapes and forms of creative expressivities engaging that modernity, and ask what cultural and political work those aesthetic practices perform as an important domain within it.[22]

Friedman's argument, and the challenge it poses to the future of modernist studies, is a provocative and exciting one, although it is not without problems, as she herself acknowledges at various points. There are, for instance, some thorny theoretical difficulties with the claim that multiple modernities produce multiple modernisms: for example, the definition of modernism as 'the expressive domain of modernity',[23] or 'the creative and expressive domain within' modernity,[24] appears rather vague in formulation and, more or less, resembles Marshall Berman's more elaborated theory of modernism as an aesthetic response to the social and political changes of modernity and modernization, a model critiqued by Friedman.[25] Equally, while we might have sympathy with the idea of moving away from a 'definitional core' for modernism drawn from a Western 'laundry list of aesthetic properties', it seems contradictory to utilize one item familiar from that list—'representational rupture'—as a way of detecting non-Anglo-European modernisms. Friedman writes that a 'planetary modernist poetics must be plural, opening up the concept of formal ruptures to a wide array of representational engagements with modernity'.[26] *Formal, representational rupture* seems to be precisely the ways in which we have long theorized writers such as Joyce or Pound. It should be noted that the difficulties of identifying non-Western modernisms without using Western modernist categories is something that Friedman is acutely aware of, but does not entirely resolve.[27] As Huyssen argues, 'it may well turn out that, despite the best of intentions, [the] de-Westernization of modernism/ modernity will remain limited because of the Western genealogy of the concepts themselves'.[28]

Friedman's project, with its claim that a 'planetary modernist poetics must be plural', thus sets itself firmly against those interpretations of modernity and modernism that align themselves with Frederic Jameson's notion of a 'singular modernity', identified with worldwide capitalism and with 'central' and 'peripheral' forms of modernist practice that are homologous with the uneven spread of capitalist development across the globe.[29] Jameson himself dismisses talk of 'alternative modernities' (and by implication 'alternative' or multiple modernisms) as merely 'pious hopes for cultural variety in a future world colonized by a universal market order'.[30] From a slightly different perspective, Pascale Casanova's *World Republic of Letters* draws upon a globalized version of Pierre Bourdieu's literary field in order to chart the struggles in 'world literary space' between modern national literatures occupying a position close to the 'Greenwich Meridian of literature' (Paris) and those on the margins of this literary world system.[31] From Friedman's point of view such arguments are deeply problematic: she is critical of a 'center/periphery binary that ignores the often long histories of aesthetic production among the colonized', asserting that the 'danger for modernist studies of the center/periphery model of world literature should be self-evident: at its heart lies the reassertion of the "old" internationalism'. Frustratingly, Friedman does not here explain why such conceptions reinstate an 'old' and problematic internationalism, or explicitly clarify what is problematic about internationalism per se. Instead she turns to Homi Bhabha and then Jahan Ramazani for an alternative 'circulation model' for how modernism moves around the globe: in Ramazani's 'transnational poetics' there are no centres and peripheries, and thus it 'breaks open the Eurocentric frameworks that have dominated the field of modernist studies'.[32] Though wary, therefore, of the 'core/periphery' binary, Friedman's argument does rely upon another, equally troubling, binary: that between (bad old) internationalism and (good new) transnationalism.

This transnational or global perspective on modernism thus has far-reaching and radical implications for how we understand modernism. It also raises some crucial problems when considered from the point of view of a critical literary geography; these include the use of the binary transnational/international and a neglect of geographical scale. To pursue this critique I will now pose three questions of transnational and global modernism.

THREE QUESTIONS FOR TRANSNATIONALISM AND GLOBAL MODERNISM

Question One: what is so wrong with internationalism?

It is crucial to distinguish between the apparent 'parochial internationalism' of some post-World War II critical constructions of modernism, and what we might term the more 'worldly' internationalism of many of the traditional protagonists of Anglo-European modernism in the early twentieth century. For such writers—enduring two world wars in the first half of the century—modernist internationalism was anything but parochial. Woolf's famous proclamation in *Three Guineas* that 'as a woman, I have no country.... As a woman my country is the whole world'[33] can be read as just one instance of a 'good' internationalism to be found in Anglo-European modernism. Melba Cuddy-Keane has, for example, traced something of this 'global consciousness' in modernism, indicating how for a writer such as Woolf—and even more so for her husband, Leonard, and his work in founding the League of Nations—the internationalism of modern artists and writers promised a way to push past the violent nationalisms that produced the First World War and which had underpinned imperialism.[34] The work of the PEN Club (Poets, Playwrights, Publishers, Essayists, Editors and Novelists) from the 1920s onwards, as recently discussed by Rachel Potter, illustrates an organization committed to internationalism as a form of liberal cultural politics.[35] With its origins in London in 1921, there were soon many branches of PEN across Europe, followed by groups in Iraq, Egypt, and Argentina in the 1920s, and India, China, and Japan in the 1930s (156). Though initially apolitical, PEN's stance came under pressure during the late 1930s and early 1940s, with the novelist Storm Jameson, a president of PEN, instrumental in shifting the organization towards a greater awareness of how the wider world political situation affected the individual writer.[36] Or we might point to Ezra Pound's early articles for the *New Age*, entitled 'Provincialism the Enemy', in which he championed internationalism in literature, citing Galdos in Spain, Turgenev in Russia, Flaubert in France, and Henry James in England as exemplars of writers combating prejudice, conformity, and the narrowness of nationalism.[37] Pound, of course, for all his manifest political failings, was often prepared to champion writers from around the globe, as seen in his initial support for Tagore and, later on, for new writers in Japan.[38]

Simply setting internationalism against transnationalism, then, is something of a false binary and works to simplify a considerably complex series of discourses around national and international geographies. It might also be said that it is precisely the shared *international* political and aesthetic aspirations of certain aspects of the early twentieth-century avant-garde that it is worth turning to today as contemporary globalization moves hand in hand with the recrudescence across Europe and beyond with many deeply unpleasant forms of *nationalist* thought. Which prompts the next question.

> **Question Two:** why does the discourse of transnationalism often seem to take the concept of a *nation* as an a priori given?[39]

For instance, the category of the 'nation' in Ireland, for many centuries and, crucially, since partition in 1921, is precisely not a clearly defined a priori entity, even geographically, let alone culturally or politically. Or, to turn to Spain, is Catalonia a region or a nation? It depends very much on where you ask the question: in Madrid or Barcelona. Attending more closely to the geopolitical implications of terms such as 'transnational' and the spatial histories implied here is important. Jahan Ramazani, an influential proponent of a transnational approach to modernist poetry, is acutely aware of this issue, arguing that 'in a transnational reframing of modern and contemporary poetic history, nationality and ethnicity still need to play important roles', as even in a globalized world to say that 'the nation-state is a tolerated anachronism understates the centripetal force of location and the undertow of national cultures'.[40] However, Ramazani also notes that 'overly nationalized and ethnicized narratives of cultural history' run the risk of ignoring 'the energy of…intercultural transfer…of translocal or interethnic negotiation',[41] citing a range of such examples, including the influence of the anti-Semitic Pound upon a number of Jewish-American poets from Louis Zukofsky to Charles Bernstein, and the influence of T. S. Eliot upon the Barbadian poet, Edward Kamau Brathwaite. Ramazani concludes by stressing that such 'transnational and cross-ethnic ironies' could result in a reassertion of 'the very national and ethnic categories of identity that a cross-cultural poetics is meant to outstrip'.[42] Ramazani is thus aware of, but unable to resolve, this dilemma, for it appears that the transnational relies upon the category of the nation (for a discourse to cross nations relies, logically, upon some stable sense of a national entity being crossed) and that there is something of an intrinsic or host/parasite relationship between the two terms. To move across nations, or to conceive of a transnational poetic practice or identity formation, rests upon some notion of a national identity against which the transnational can be defined. Much as proponents of the transnational might seek to escape the perceived constrictions of national affiliations, a transnational modernism does not float above such categories: indeed, in a kind of Derridean fashion, we might note that at the heart of the transnational is actually the national.

One possible way to address this problematic is by reframing it; that is, by thinking with more geographical precision about modernism and the 'transnational'. A sophisticated critique of how the discourse of global modernism views the nation is offered by Jon Hegglund in his superb book, *World Views*, which argues that in a 'laudable desire to open up modernism to transnational approaches...critics of modernism have at times idealized the "trans-" without fully considering the implications of the "national"'.[43] Hegglund explores how a range of modernist texts by writers such as E. M. Forster, Graham Greene, James Joyce, Jamaica Kincaid, and Jean Rhys mediate in their texts between differing geographical scales, between the 'national' and 'outside' the national, or between the national and the regional. Interestingly, Hegglund is hesitant to call such an approach 'global' or 'transnational' because,

> [t]hese terms imply a point of view at another geographical scale, one that simply moves beyond the nation towards a wider, encompassing realm. What I am interested in, however, is not so much another geographical scale that encircles and contains the nation, but rather an enunciative space within literary discourse that ironizes the notion of geographical space itself.[44]

Hegglund calls such an approach 'metageographical', drawing upon the work of cultural geographers Martin Lewis and Kären Wigen, a term which describes a complex geographical self-consciousness about the employment of spatial terms in our descriptions of the world: metageography thus 'defines the very orders and categories of space that we use to plot locations, itineraries, and distances in the world'[45] and in such fiction space is foregrounded in the narrative such that the 'reader's attention...is drawn to the production of geographical space'.[46] Hegglund's work (which I have drastically summarized here) thus demonstrates the advantages in adopting a more sophisticated approach to the geographies of modernism, paying close attention to the way that modernism is *rooted* in particular locations in the world, as well as the *routes* by which modernism travels around the globe; 'national dimensions and origins', then, as well as 'intercultural encounters' and indigenization.

Another key aspect of such an approach to the geographies of modernism, which prompts my third question, is to be more attentive to geographical notions of *scale*, rather than simply shifting to what might be called the 'abstract space', in Henri Lefebvre's terms, of a globalized modernism.[47]

Question Three: what happens, therefore, to 'global modernism' when we introduce the concept of scale?

In the course of sketching a critique of certain contemporary conceptions of 'world literature' Andreas Huyssen also raises something of a question mark over the notion of 'global modernism'. 'What, if anything', asserts Huyssen, 'was global about modernism?', given that 'transnational phenomena rarely if ever encompass the whole globe', since the 'travelling and distribution of cultural products is always specific and particular, never homogenously global'.[48] Huyssen concludes 'that the current debate pays far too little attention to the multiple layers and hierarchies within transnational cultural exchange. Isn't "global" far too global a term to capture processes of cultural intermingling, appropriations and reciprocal mimicry?'[49]

The worry articulated here, which echoes Hegglund's own concerns, is that the discourse of globalized modernism has a tendency to ignore the complex spatial layering represented by the idea of *scale*. Body, house, street, neighbourhood, city, region, nation, international, transnational, global—it would be more productive for modernist studies to pay closer attention to the material specificities of such spatial categories and to how scale makes a difference. Thinking in terms of differing yet interrelated scales is, therefore, one way of adding nuance to the analysis of modernist spaces and to movements across and within them. If we jettison internationalism for its supposedly homogenizing tendencies, do we necessarily gain more geographical precision in viewing modernism through the lens of 'transnationalism' or 'global modernism'?

To invoke the category of scale is not, however, to reach for a fixed hierarchy of discrete spatial entities, but to use different notions of scale as a way to ground materially more abstract notions of the geographies of modernism. As the cultural geographer Neil Smith notes in an influential article, 'the construction of geographical scale is a primary means through which spatial differentiation "takes place"' and is itself a set of key social practices.[50] Thus, the separation of the national from the local or regional, or the transnational from the national, should be seen as a complex social process rather than a simple hermeneutic differentiation. Smith here follows Henri Lefebvre's influential theory of the 'hypercomplexity of social space':

> The national and regional levels take in innumerable 'places'; national space embraces the regions; and world space does not merely subsume national spaces, but even … precipitates the formation of new national spaces through a remarkable process of fission. All these spaces, meanwhile, are traversed by myriad currents. The hypercomplexity of social space should by now be apparent, embracing as it does individual entities and peculiarities, relatively fixed points, movements, and flows and waves—some interpenetrating, others in conflict, and so on.[51]

Smith thus adapts Lefebvre's view of the interlayering of different spatial scales, arguing that it is 'the active social connectedness of scales that is vital' rather than some hierarchical organization of different scalar elements.[52]

We thus need to be able to discuss different scales within a literary geography of modernism, whilst also interrogating how these scales interpenetrate, conflict, and fissure. A vocabulary too easily tied to the transnational or the global runs the risk of overlooking other geographical scales and what I have called elsewhere 'the polytopic quality of modernist writing'.[53] One such overlooked modernist scale is that of *regionalism,* something that is evident, for instance, if we consider the locations of many modernist magazines and, in particular, the differences between the magazines of Britain and Ireland, where metropolitan centres dominated, and those of North America, where regional magazines thrived in many locations.[54] Even in the case of British magazines (let alone those published in the national spaces of Wales, Scotland, and Ireland), regional affiliations marked certain modernist magazines quite strongly. The *New Age*, for example, was influenced greatly by its origins in the Leeds Art Club founded by the two editors of the magazine, A. R. Orage and Holbrook Jackson. Orage and Jackson, along with later contributors such as Edwin Muir, Storm Jameson, and Herbert Read, were all figures who, in Jameson's words, made the 'journey from the north' of Britain to London, but who retained an affective relationship—in complex ways—to their regional origins.[55] The Orcadian

Muir, for example, wrote that on arriving in the metropolis one felt differently both about one's regional origins and one's own identity in that city: such responses could also include disgust and dislike of one's 'provincial' origins.[56] It seems important to explore further how these forms of regional attachment (and disavowal) work within modernism, without necessarily separating this local or regional scale from other larger scales (the national, the international).[57]

Certain critics who have proposed a transnational agenda do demonstrate an awareness of geographical scales other than that of the nation. Jessica Berman's careful and stimulating critique of some proponents of world literature, such as Casanova, draws attention to the binary *local / international*, and the ways in which the local or regional is often seen as the 'weaker' term in the binary. Berman thus calls for a cosmopolitan or 'nodal model of worldwide modernism' where 'interlocking circles of affiliation would allow specific local modes to coexist with a dynamic and varied global interconnection.... [and] the fear of the taint of the local would also disappear, along with the binary of local/international'.[58] Laura Doyle, in an article outlining the philosophical underpinning of transnationalism, stresses the importance of 'regional transnational networks of culture and economy' in areas such as the Mediterranean or South East Asia.[59] However, within such work it is often the larger geographical scale that tends to dominate the smaller, so that the regional or local becomes merely a staging post on the transnational journey around the globe. And while we hear the term 'transnational' used frequently, we notice the related term, 'transregional', far less frequently.[60] Closer attention is thus required to national and regional 'origins', and to the spatial processes whereby modernism becomes rooted in particular regions, in addition to focusing upon its routes and reroutings around the globe. Perceiving modernism through the lens of scale thus brings a much sharper focus to the spatial issues of conflict, fissure, and connectedness raised by Lefebvre and Smith.

Other critics have, therefore, begun to explore in more detail the regional scale of modernism, as in Hegglund's chapter on Patrick Geddes and E. M. Forster in his *World Views*, and more extensively, in the recent volume, *Regional Modernisms*, edited by Neal Alexander and James Moran. In this book the editors stress 'the variety of spatial scales at which modernism takes place, emphasizing the pervasive significance of local and regional attachments for modernist writing'.[61] One of the contributors, David James, also warns that we need to continue to 'test and refine the framework' of the turn to the transnational in modernist studies by engaging with regional writers (he discusses Sylvia Townsend Warner and Storm Jameson) who 'after being recovered from relative neglect, might now suffer the ironic fate of becoming consigned to the margins of critical interest once more as the new modernist studies goes global'.[62] Tellingly, perhaps, there is no index entry for regionalism in the recent *Oxford Handbook of Global Modernisms*.[63]

Thinking through modernism with a focus on the multiple geographies of scale and their interconnections is thus one way to embed a more precise consideration of the interaction between spatiality and literature and to understand the active role played by the dynamics of location in shaping modernism. In the course of a critique of 'distance' in certain theorists of world literature Nirvana Tanoukhi makes a similar case for a renewed attention to scale in literature: 'We are at a juncture where we must pursue directly a literary phenomenology of the production of scale, which can begin to elucidate the diverse forms of entanglement between literary history and the history of the production of space'; this approach, Tanoukhi concludes, would 'conceptualize scale as the social condition of a landscape's utility'.[64] Such a strategy, in other words, would produce more detailed spatial histories of modernism(s), exploring how scale is a key component in the geographical production of literary and cultural texts.

CONCLUSION: 'NO SINGLE NATION'

A proper genealogy of the impact of the idea of transnationalism upon contemporary modernist studies—especially as it has taken root in the United States—would commence with an investigation into Randolph Bourne's foundational text of modern American cultural criticism, 'Trans-national America', published first in the *Atlantic Monthly* in 1916.[65] In this famous article, a key text in the modernist cultural formation of 'Young America', Bourne argued against the assimilationist model of America as a melting pot of individual national identities forced into a singular American national identity; instead, Bourne stated that America is 'coming to be, not a nationality but a transnationality, a weaving back and forth, with the other lands, of many threads'. Only America, argued Bourne, can lead in this 'higher cosmopolitan ideal', and in a world 'which has dreamed of internationalism, we find that we have all unawares been building up the first international nation'.[66] Interestingly, Bourne's essay here relies upon another rather problematic binary, between an internationalism that reaches across geographical borders (the world that has 'dreamed of internationalism'), and a transnationalism that remains within one country (America as the first 'international nation').

Arguably, the radicalism of Bourne's vision of America's role as the upholder of this 'cosmopolitan ideal' is, nearly a century later, somewhat compromised by the historical and political events of the last hundred years. We need further scrutiny of whether, or how far, the term 'transnational' is still, in some sense, tied umbilically to this specific American conception of national identity, a conception whose radical aims have perhaps been fatally compromised. Perhaps we need to deconstruct fully such a term, tracing how its 'national origins and dimensions', in Bradbury and MacFarlane's terms, might affect its current sense and continuing value, and consider more carefully whether the 'transnational' (and also the 'cosmopolitan') is conceived differently in other geographical locations around the globe.[67] Transnationalism, we might say, is experienced very differently in Nairobi than in New York City, Lahore rather than London. Simply put, the globe of a global modernism looks very different depending upon where you are positioned: this is a key question for contemporary modernist studies, involving meticulous attention to scale, to locality, and to regionalism. Rejecting the international for a supposedly more cosmopolitan transnationalism in our discussions of modernism thus demands much further, and more critical, examination.

Placing modernism requires us, then, to think more about complex geographies of modernism, reintegrating debates on the national, the regional, and the local alongside those of the transnational and international, exploring in more detail how multiple scales of modernist space interact and inform these debates. Only in this way will we be better able to understand how modernism moves around the globe, while also becoming rooted in particular places in it, and be better equipped to consider further the implications of the idea that 'no single nation ever owned Modernism'.

NOTES

1. Recent work representing these developments can be found in many of the chapters in *The Oxford Handbook of Modernisms*, edited by Peter Brooker, Andrzej Gasiorek, Deborah Longworth, and Andrew Thacker (Oxford: Oxford University Press, 2010), and also in *The Oxford Handbook of Global Modernisms*, edited by Mark Wollaeger with Matt Eatough (New York: Oxford University Press, 2012).
2. See Andrew Thacker, 'The Idea of a Critical Literary Geography', *New Formations*, 57 (Winter 2005–6), pp. 56–73.
3. Sascha Bru and Dirk de Geest, for example, note how critiques of the 'Euromodernist' canon tend to neglect the minorities and differences that exist within and across the modernisms of Central Europe. See 'What Modernism Was and Is', in *Modernism Today*, edited by Sjef Houppermans, Peter Liebregts, Jan Baetens, and Otto Boele (Amsterdam: Rodopi, 2013), pp. 1–10; 5–6.
4. See http://www.eam-europe.be/ for information on EAM.
5. Malcolm Bradbury and Alan McFarlane, eds., *Modernism: A Guide to European Literature* (Harmondsworth: Penguin, 1976), p. 13. Interestingly enough this quotation is from the reprint edition of 1991, showing how the paradigm of modernism as internationalism lasted for some time.
6. For example, see the accounts of modernist little magazines, *The Fugitive* and *The Double Dealer*, in these two cities in chapters 21 and 22 of *The Oxford Critical and Cultural History of Modernist Magazines: Volume II, North America 1894–1960*, edited by Peter Brooker and Andrew Thacker (Oxford: Oxford University Press, 2012).
7. One reason for the focus on Europe in this volume—the subtitle in one edition is *A Guide to European Literature*—is the genealogy of the volume in the English, American, and European comparative literature departments of the University of East Anglia (UEA) in the 1970s. Out of twenty contributors to the volume, eleven, including the editors had a UEA connection.
8. Bradbury and McFarlane, *Modernism*, p. 31.
9. *The International Style* was the title of an influential exhibition held at MOMA, New York, in 1932 which promoted European modernist buildings devoid of the social and political ideas that underpinned architects such as Le Corbusier or Walter Gropius. See Christopher Crouch, 'Architecture, Design, and Modern Living', in *The Oxford Handbook of Modernisms*, pp. 618–36; 631, and Tim Benton, 'Building Utopia', in *Modernism 1914–1939: Designing a New World*, edited by Christopher Wilk (London: V&A Publications, 2006), pp. 149–223; 164–5.
10. Hugh Kenner, 'The Making of the Modernist Canon', *Chicago Review*, 34:2 (1984): pp. 49–61; 53.

11. See Virginia Woolf, *The London Scene* (London: Snowbooks, 2004); for a discussion of this and other aspects of Woolf's interest in geography, see Anna Snaith and Michael H. Whitworth, 'Approaches to Space and Place in Woolf', in *Locating Woolf: The Politics of Space and Place*, edited by Anna Snaith and Michael H. Whitworth (Basingstoke: Palgrave Macmillan, 2007), pp. 1–28.
12. See Jahan Ramazani, 'A Transnational Poetics', *American Literary History*, 18:2 (Summer 2006): pp. 332–59; 350.
13. Susan Stanford Friedman, 'World Modernisms, World Literature, and Comparativity', in Wollaeger with Eatough, *The Oxford Handbook of Global Modernisms*, pp. 499–524; 500.
14. Jessica Berman, 'Imagining World Literature', in *Disciplining Modernism*, edited by Pamela L. Caughie (Basingstoke: Palgrave Macmillan, 2009), pp. 53–70; 68–9.
15. Douglas Mao and Rebecca L. Walkowitz, 'The New Modernist Studies', *PMLA* 123:3 (2009): pp. 737–48; 738. See also the special issue of *Modernism/Modernity* on this topic in 2006.
16. See various chapters in *The Oxford Handbook of Modernisms*.
17. Andreas Huyssen, 'Geographies of modernism in a globalizing world', in *Geographies of Modernism: Literature, Cultures, Spaces*, edited by Peter Brooker and Andrew Thacker (London: Routledge, 2005), pp. 6–18; 12; Arjun Appadurai, *Modernity at Large: Cultural Dimensions of Globalization* (Minneapolis, MN: University of Minnesota Press, 1996).
18. Susan Stanford Friedman, 'Periodizing Modernism: Postcolonial Modernities and the Space/Time Borders of Modernist Studies', *Modernism/Modernity* 13:3 (2006): pp. 425–43; 430–1. Edward Said, 'Traveling Theory', in his *The World, the Text, and the Critic* (Cambridge, MA: Harvard University Press, 1983).
19. Partha Mitter, *The Triumph of Modernism: India's Artists and the Avant-garde, 1922–1947* (London: Reaktion Books, 2007), p. 10. And for an overview of the modernist arts in India, see Supriya Chaudhuri in *The Oxford Handbook of Modernisms*. From the other direction, an exhibition of Bengali art was held in Berlin in the early 1920s.
20. Susan Stanford Friedman, 'Planetarity: Musing Modernist Studies', *Modernism/Modernity* 17:3 (2010): pp. 471–99; 475. This and other essays form the basis of Friedman's book, *Planetary Modernism: Provocations on Modernity Across Time* (New York: Columbia University Press, 2015).
21. Friedman, 'Planetarity', p. 481. For a slightly different account of such an argument, see Laura Doyle and Laura Winkiel's idea of 'geomodernism', in their edited volume, *Geomodernism: Race, Modernism, Modernity* (Bloomington, IN: Indiana University Press, 2005), pp. 3–4.
22. Friedman, 'Planetarity', pp. 487–8.
23. Friedman, 'Planetarity', p. 476.
24. Friedman, 'Planetarity', p. 492.
25. See Marshall Berman, *All That Is Solid Melts Into Air: The Experience of Modernity* (London: Verso, 1983). Berman's and Friedman's theoretical model for the operation of modernism/modernity is thus similar, although the historical and geographical range they have in mind for the concepts differs greatly. For Friedman on Berman, see her 'Definitional Excursions: the Meanings of Modern/Modernity/Modernism', *Modernism/Modernity*, 8:3 (Sept. 2001): pp. 493–513; 497.
26. Friedman, 'Planetarity', p. 489.
27. For the comments on the difficulty of moving outside her own 'epistemological frame', see Friedman, 'Planetarity', p. 480.

28. Huyssens, 'Geographies of Modernism', p. 13.
29. Such work often draws upon Wallerstein's world systems model; see, for example, Neil Lazarus, 'Modernism and African Literature', in Wollaeger with Eatough, *Global Modernisms*, pp. 228–48; and Benita Parry, 'Aspects of Peripheral Modernism', *Ariel* 40:1 (2009): pp. 27–55. For an overall assessment of Wallerstein for literary and cultural studies, see *Immanuel Wallerstein and the Problem of the World: System, Scale, Culture*, edited by David Palumbo-Liu, Bruce Robbins, and Nirvana Tanoukhi (Durham, NC: Duke University Press, 2011)
30. Fredric Jameson, *A Singular Modernity: Essay on the Ontology of the Present* (London and New York: Verso, 2002), pp. 12–13.
31. Pascale Casanova, *The World Republic of Letters*, translated by M. B. DeBevoise (Cambridge, MA.: Harvard University Press, 2004).
32. Friedman, 'World Modernisms', p. 502–3.
33. Virginia Woolf, *Three Guineas*, in *A Room of One's Own* and *Three Guineas* (Oxford: Oxford University Press, 1992), p. 313.
34. See Melba Cuddy-Keane, 'Modernism, Geopolitics, Globalization', *Modernism/Modernity* 10:3 (2003): pp. 539–58.
35. See Rachel Potter, *Obscene Modernism: Literary Censorship and Experiment 1900–1940* (Oxford: Oxford University Press, 2013).
36. See R. A. Wilford, 'The PEN Club, 1930–50', *Journal of Contemporary History* 14 (1979): pp. 99–116; 108.
37. See Pound's essay series, 'Provincialism the Enemy', commencing 12 July 1917 in *The New Age*.
38. See Pound, 'Rabindranath Tagore', *Fortnightly Review*, March 1913: pp. 571–9. Pound, however, did revise his opinion of Tagore: see Harold Hurwitz, 'Ezra Pound and Rabindranath Tagore', in *American Literature*, 36:1 (1964): pp. 53–63. For Pound's support for contemporary Japanese poetry, see *Ezra Pound and Japan: Letters and Essays*, edited by Sanehide Kodama (Redeling Ridge, CT: Black Swan Books, 1987).
39. A point made by Christopher Prendergast in his critique of Casanova's *World Republic of Letters*. See Christopher Prendergast, 'The World Republic of Letters', in *Debating World Literature*, edited by Christopher Prendergast (London: Verso, 2004), pp. 1–25; 14, 21.
40. Ramazani, 'A Transnational Poetics', p. 350.
41. Ramazani, 'A Transnational Poetics', p. 352.
42. Ramazani, 'A Transnational Poetics', p. 353.
43. Jon Hegglund, *World Views: Metageographies of Modernist Fiction* (New York: Oxford University Press, 2012), p. 5.
44. Hegglund, *World Views*, p. 6.
45. Hegglund, *World Views*, p. 6.
46. Hegglund, *World Views*, p. 11.
47. For the concept of 'abstract space', see Henri Lefebvre, *The Production of Space* (Oxford: Blackwell, 1991).
48. Huyssen, 'Geographies of Modernism', p. 15.
49. Huyssen, 'Geographies of Modernism', p. 10.
50. Neil Smith, 'Homeless/global: Scaling places', in *Mapping the Futures: Local Cultures, Global Change*, edited by Jon Bird, Barry Curtis, Tim Putnam, George Robertson, and Lisa Tickner (London: Routledge, 1993), pp. 87–119; 97. A very similar version of this essay was first published in *Social Text* 33 (1992): pp. 54–81. For discussions of scale in geographical theory, see Eric Sheppard and Robert B. McMaster, eds., *Scale and*

Geographical Inquiry: Nature, Society, and Method (Oxford: Blackwell, 2004) and Andrew Herod, *Scale* (London: Routledge, 2011).

51. Lefebvre, *Production of Space*, p. 88.
52. Smith, 'Homeless/global', p. 101.
53. Andrew Thacker, *Moving Through Modernity: Space and Geography in Modernism* (Manchester: Manchester University Press, 2003), p. 7.
54. On this point, see the 'General Introduction' to *The Oxford Critical and Cultural History of Modernist Magazines: Volume II, North America*, pp. 2–12.
55. See Storm Jameson, *Journey from the North: Autobiography of Storm Jameson* (New York: Harper and Row, 1970).
56. See the series of articles by Muir under the pseudonym 'Hengist', entitled, 'Epistles to the Provincials', published in *The New Age* from 18 March 1920 onwards.
57. For more on *The New Age*, see my essay, '"that trouble": Regional Modernism and "Little Magazines"', in *Regional Modernisms*, edited by Neal Alexander and James Moran (Edinburgh: Edinburgh University Press, 2013), pp. 22–43.
58. Berman, 'Imagining World Literature', in *Disciplining Modernism*, p. 69. See also her book, *Modernist Commitments: Ethics, Politics, and Transnational Modernism* (New York: Columbia University Press, 2011).
59. Laura Doyle, 'Toward a Philosophy of Transnationalism', *The Journal of Transnational American Studies* 1:1 (2009), http://escholarship.org/uc/item/9vr1k8hk accessed 1 Feb. 2016.
60. Though Doyle refers to the importance of a 'regional transnationalism', this perhaps runs the risk of blurring the scalar differences and complex relationships between the regional and the national. See Doyle, 'Toward a Philosophy of Transnationalism', pp. 3–5.
61. 'Introduction: Regional Modernism', in Alexander and Moran, *Regional Modernisms*, p. 18.
62. David James, 'Capturing the Scale of Fiction at Mid-Century', in Alexander and Moran, *Regional Modernism*, p. 120.
63. See Wollaeger with Eatough, *Global Modernisms*.
64. Nirvana Tanoukhi, 'The Scale of World Literature', in *Immanuel Wallerstein and the Problem of the World*, pp. 78–98; 95.
65. Randolph Bourne, 'Trans-national America', *Atlantic Monthly*, 118 (July 1916): pp. 86–97. For a discussion of the importance of Bourne's essay, see Casey Nelson Blake, *Beloved Community: The Cultural Criticism of Randolph Bourne, Van Wyck Brooks, Waldo Frank, and Lewis Mumford* (Chapel Hill: University of North Carolina Press, 1990).
66. Bourne, 'Trans-national America', p. 97.
67. For a discussion of modernism and 'critical cosmopolitanism', see Rebecca L. Walkowitz, *Cosmopolitan Style: Modernism Beyond the Nation* (New York: Columbia University Press, 2006), pp. 1–32.

3

Micromodernism
Towards a Modernism of Disconnection

Tim Armstrong

We often speak of mapping modernism, and are accustomed to those diagrams of interrelated groupings that appear in the work of Steve Watson, Bonnie Kime Scott, and others.[1] But there are reasons to be suspicious of the idea of mapping, with its adherence to established names and a known terrain. It takes us too close to the fixities of the modernist canon, which, for all that we congratulate ourselves on its 'opening up' in the last three decades, seems remarkably persistent. It has been modified, to be sure, in terms of race and gender; but our sense of its core has remained relatively stable at the level of the course, anthology, survey, and even monograph. Canons have an inbuilt conservativism, one might conclude (though there are of course honourable exceptions, like the capacious survey of Chris Baldick's 2004 Oxford history[2]).

I have come to think this a particular problem in relation to the period after 1926, when the established reputations of the first-generation modernists were, as Rodney Rosenquist has shown, already creating problems of mapping and remapping the field of the 'modern' for those that followed.[3] The map of London pubs you see below (**Fig. 3.1**) may be a joke, but it was issued by the publishers of *Life and Letters Today*—one of the British journals of the 1930s most concerned with modernism's inheritance—and in that context evokes a world of debate—about film; about the possibilities of an English surrealism; about class and war. The second half of the 1930s is a period of particular anxiety, reflected in a rash of publications stressing some element of the contemporary or the inaugural: today; seeding; new signatures; proems.[4]

What alternatives are there to the map? Early explorers often worked from the portulan: the seafarer's chart including entry points into land via rivers and inlets. In this spirit, I think we can propose a more *dynamic* picture of modernism in which it is a shifting field traversed by different actors, all of whom have their own sense of its existing configurations, of their literary aims, and of the localities where their version of modernism is enacted. Modernism, that is to say, is in movement across the open period of its production, and is often produced as a local effect which contests the power of any existing map. That effect might be a barrier to be defended or removed; a work of art; a letter; or a conversation in a pub. Hence the term I use in this chapter for a modernism defined in terms of its localisms: *micromodernism*.

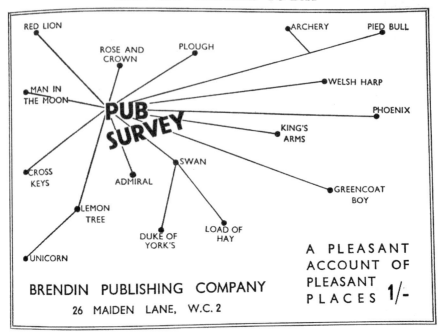

Figure 3.1. Advertisement, *Life and Letters Today* 18:2 (1938), p. 209.

Within that field, we might see particular micromodernisms as definable in tripartite terms: as involving *sites*, *occasions*, and *trajectories*. These three terms are fairly self-explanatory—in fact they are deliberately a form of weak thinking, suggestive entry points rather than intended to be fully analytic—but I will briefly illustrate what I mean by the first two before moving to a more extended example of the third.

SITES AND OCCASIONS

The places in which a particular understanding of late modernism might be located are varied; they include both micro-sites—say, J. B. S. Haldane's garden in Cambridge in the early 1930s, the gathering place for a group of poets fascinated by the new biology—and more permanent areas, like the New York of wartime émigrés.

Here is a localized version of modernism I have become interested in. In the period between 1927 and 1931, 35A St. Peter's Square, London is the centre of what I think of as 'Hammersmith modernism', an important staging post between high modernism and later abstract art in the UK. At the centre of this grouping are Laura Riding and Robert Graves, both concerned with the possibilities of a modernist inheritance, and around them a range of places—flats; barges on the Thames; studios; pubs—and various people, including writers, artists, film-makers, critics, and scientists. What characterizes Hammersmith modernism—and its work continued from Riding's and Graves' base in Mallorca—is a range of linked concerns: writing as a form of direct personal exchange (especially the letter); the technologies of reproduction, including film and sound recording; a stress on the practice of art as an engagement with its materials. The letter is represented in publications like Riding's *Four Unposted Letters to Catherine* (1930); Len Lye's free-form surrealist letters in *No Trouble* (1930); Robert Graves's *To Whom Else*; Riding's novel in letters, *Everybody's Letters* (1933); and *The World and Ourselves* (1938), a set of responses to her own letter about political crisis—with appended essays on the value of epistolary exchange in producing a localized version of the public sphere of the kind figured in miniature in the circle's in-house journal *Focus* (1935). One might even include Lye's films for the Post Office—with their bouncing, stylized letters and injunctions about posting early—as a lateralization of this epistolary imagination.

My second term is the *occasion*, and my necessarily brief example is the publication of a collection of poems in 1939, entitled *Proems*. Its contributors were Patrick Evans, Lawrence Durrell, Ruthven Todd, Edgar Foxall, Oswell Blakeston, and Rayner Heppenstall. The brief Prefatory Note states that only Heppenstall's work had previously appeared 'in book form'.[5] So given its title, *Proems* might *look* like a modernist vehicle, launching a new generation. It was published by a private press with reasonably high production values, with illustrations by Heppenstall.

In fact, the Fortune Press was the entrepreneurial vehicle of the eccentric pornographer and slum landlord Reginald Caton, famous for his combination of pirated material, authors who were seldom paid or for whom he acted as a vanity press, and gay erotica.[6] He only turned to poetry as a commercial proposition after his prosecution for obscene libel in 1934. Nevertheless, he published Dylan Thomas, Philip Larkin, Elizabeth Jennings, Nicholas Moore, Ted Hughes, and many others, including the first, unauthorized selection of Wallace Stevens in the UK.[7] His enterprise is in an important sense an indicator of where poetry was in the late 1930s, outside the security of the Faber list. With Moore as his advisor, Caton suggests an avant-garde which is shadowed by its own marginality.

If we ask to what extent the authors in *Proems* were a cohesive or programmatic grouping, the answer is not very closely: I have no evidence that they ever gathered. But they were loosely linked and appeared in the same magazines in the period. Patrick Evans, who was to have less of a poetic career than any of the others, has a poem entitled 'Proem' and poems dedicated to Durrell and Blakeston; he visited Durrell in Corfu in 1936.[8] Heppenstall, in many ways the least connected to the group, knew Blakeston and had some contact with Durrell.[9] Nicholas Moore, whose contacts with Durrell went back to *Seven* magazine at Cambridge, is an implicit presence. Durrell took the opportunity to publish some of his satirical 'Unkebunck' sequence, which Eliot had turned down at Faber; Foxall also had links with Eliot. Blakeston, Foxall, and Todd were later published individually by the Fortune Press.

What we can see in *Proems* is an attempt to 'sort' the inheritance of the 1920s. Different affiliations are present: to Eliot, to Auden, Lawrence; to surrealism and the (largely Scottish) grouping known as the 'New Apocalypse'. Evans's letters, some of which are in the papers of Durrell's friend Alan Thomas at the British Library, show him reading Yeats, Pound, Auden, and MacNeice in search of models: 'shall I add a new gasometer/To literary history [?]', as he puts it in a poem which conveys tentativeness amidst a field of Audenesque cliché.[10] *Proems*, in all its serendipity, is an anthology which captures a group of poets in trajectory; between position and alliance on the one hand and divergence on the other. That the poets of *Proems* leave no very clear inheritance—only one of them, Foxall, is remembered primarily for his career as a poet—is surely in part a product of the forces at play in the collection, and tells us quite a lot about the uncertainties of late modernism as war approached.[11]

TRAJECTORIES: ANTIPODEANS AND THE MODERNISM OF DISCONNECTION

I want to spend the bulk of this essay looking at my third term, tracing a *trajectory* across the uncertain field of modernism in this period, with a few thoughts on its implications. It involves a particular example: Antipodeans: writers and artists who travelled from New Zealand and Sydney to London in the decade between the General Strike and the 1936 surrealism exhibition, seeking a metropolitan modernism.

They followed a range of authors arriving in the UK who were born in or traversed the Antipodes: George Egerton, Havelock Ellis, Anna Wickham, Katherine Mansfield, Henry Handel Richardson; then a later generation including Christina Stead, Robin Hyde, A. R. D. Fairburn, and others. Many brought with them an outsider's perspective; many only appear in national literary histories or are lost. What is modernism, one can only wonder, from the perspective of Hal Collins, otherwise known as Te Akau, Maori manservant of the composer Peter Warlock—Soho barman, illustrator, nightclub painter, and songwriter?[12] I will begin with Jack Lindsay and Len Lye, who moved through interlocking circles in Sydney in the mid-1920s and in London in around 1930, and then move on to the Nobel Laureate Patrick White, a younger writer—still at school in Cheltenham when Lindsay arrived in London—but nevertheless one of a generation responding to modernism.

Here is an anecdote from the first volume of Jack Lindsay's reminiscences, *The Roaring Twenties*. It is Sydney, early in modernism's year:

> It must have been in April 1922 that Frank told me that I had just missed D. H. Lawrence, who had come into the shop [Dymock's bookshop], and asked if I'd like him to arrange a meeting. I said no. For D.H.L. was one of the writers on N.L.'s index of art-villains. I had read little of his work...Later I was sorry.[13]

Lindsay, in thrall to the Nietzscheanism of his famous father, the artist Norman Lindsay, refuses Lawrence—and Pound as well, whose work his father mocks.

There is of course a colonial chippiness here. The introduction to the *Vision* anthology which Lindsay edited in Sydney insisted that 'If English poetry collapses, all that England stood for would also collapse – unless Australia took over.'[14] 'All copies sent to England were strictly ignored,'[15] he notes sardonically. In early 1926 Lindsay put that programme to work: he moved his publishing enterprise, the Franfrolico Press, to the UK, setting up in Bloomsbury Square. His subsequent pilgrimage through the London avant-garde and English socialism saw him emerge in the post-war period as a prolific man of letters, novelist, historian, and classicist, as well as a leading Marxist critic; Lindsay was one of those authors who, dangerously, wrote more than his height in books. He never returned to Australia.

The flagship of the Franfrolico Press was its bimonthly journal *The London Aphrodite*, its title a tilt at Squire's *London Mercury*. The *Aphrodite* ran for a planned six issues from August 1928 to June 1929.[16] The editors claimed the first issue sold 2,000 copies; bound copies of the run were later issued as a book. It began with work by Lindsay and his Sydney circle—his co-editor P. R. ('Inky') Stephenson, Kenneth Slessor, Hugh McCrae, his brother Philip, and Lindsay himself, in person and using pseudonyms—then gathered Antipodean connections including Anna Wickham, and broadened to take in Aldous Huxley, Robert Nichols, Karel Čapek, Ivan Goll, Norman Douglas, and Edgell Rickword, among others. In the few years he spent in London before moving to the country, Lindsay was an assiduous networker: he met—often at The Plough in Museum Street—Nina Hamnett, Liam O'Flaherty, Yeats, Basil Bunting, Mary Butts, Robert Graves and Laura Riding, Dylan Thomas, and Peter Warlock. He also knew Mulk Raj Anand, publishing the first major study of him in 1948.[17]

The *Aphrodite*'s editorials promoted a renewal of letters through a Nietzschean vitalism. That project had two fronts: an attack on Eliot, a few hundred yards up the road at Faber; and engagement with Lawrence. Lindsay's 'Waste of Time' (*Aphrodite* 3, Dec. 1928) describes Eliot and the Georgians as locked in conflict with the 1890s, with, in Eliot's case, a curate's fastidiousness about the materials of disillusion:

> Eliot is not modern. He has no sense of the problems of this age. The new impulse into Tragedy, the new delicate sense of subjective values, the new passionate scepticism, which hold the creative potentialities of the post-war epoch, are altogether unknown to him. He is the last remnant of the pre-war generation… He is the tincan tied to the tail of the disillusioned Nineties.[18]

The piece ends with a squib directed at Eliot for his origins as, of all things, a *provincial* turned gatekeeper. This critique of Eliot is sustained through to the sixth and final issue, where his work is dismissed as 'utterly devoid of any poetic identity'.[19]

Lawrence was another matter. Lindsay's co-editor Stephenson stayed with Lawrence and Frieda in late 1928, and they formed the plan of publishing Lawrence's paintings in London. Stephenson became the private publisher of the unexpurgated edition of Lawrence's *Pansies*, after the Secker edition was seized, as well as of an unofficial first English edition of *Chatterley*, typeset in a Bloomsbury basement.[20] Then:

> In March [1930] D.H.L. died. I wrote a *Letter to his Spirit*, which I sent to Charley Lahrs [*sic*], who said he'd print it; but it never appeared...I felt the need to make a summing-up statement, to round off the strange process that had been the dialogue of D.H.L. with us all throughout the twenties.[21]

Indeed, one could say that it is around Lawrence that Lindsay's literary community forms. He described joining Mudie's Library:

> The first book I took out was the first volume of *Scrutinies* [the volume of essays edited by Edgell Rickword], which exited me very much, especially the long essay by D. H. L. on Galsworthy. Almost all the essays won my hearty assent and for the first time since I landed I felt that I was not alone; somewhere there was developing a body of critical opinion with which I felt a considerable kinship.[22]

Lindsay contacted Rickword and appeared in the second *Scrutinies*, writing on Joyce. In the same volume his friend Brian Penton wrote a 'Note on Form in the Novel' which even-handedly attacks Joyce's 'dunghill', the bloodlessness of Huxley, and the externality of Dreiser. The essay is textbook Franfrolico: '[T]he only voice...that commands attention to-day', he trumpets, is Lawrence. Class animus is 'a refined pain sublimated in a dynamic frenzy that fecundates his mind and gathers every energy of every fibre to a concentrated shriek of anger', creating 'a real world'. The 'novel form is a projection from the blood of the creator not a convention—not an external form as the ode is a form'.[23]

The attack on Eliot is matched by an attack on modernist academicism. Issue 3 has a parodic exercise in 'Modernistic Annotation' by 'Willie Wagstaff' (Lindsay), under the heading: 'If e.e. cummings had written a verse of the psalm of life and Laura Riding and Robert Graves had annotated it'.[24] A pompous epigram on Life is broken up typographically and mockingly explicated in the manner of Graves and Riding's *Survey*. The 'Ex Cathedra' blast just over the page, ending the issue, declares that 'The Moderns are getting old now', including even *transition* (founded a whole year earlier). Instead, the Aphrodite group have 'taken a return ticket backwards in time in order to get ahead of the ghastly modern epoch', back to the Renaissance, Rabelais, the classics.[25]

These are all familiar—indeed, time-worn—modernist gestures of modernist adherence to the past that matters. What is distinctive in Lindsay's version is the absence of uncertainty; a refusal of the lapse into silence which afflicted many second-generation modernists; and a bustling entrepreneurship which in his later career becomes an adherence to the profession of writer—he was a stalwart of PEN and of left writing groups. But I think the attempt to explore modernism's legacy helps explain Lindsay's hyperactivity. This is a brief period in late 1929:

> I was also doing a lot of writing for myself. *Hereward*, in which I tried to define my divided condition between Betty and Eliza, was finished in June; I asked Gough to devise some simple drum-rhythms to go between the scenes...I also wrote a full-length

play on Wycherley's marriage; and shorter plays on Rembrandt and Paracelsus...as well as an experimental play based on Tuareg traditional songs. At the same time I had a shot in prose at a surrealist novel...In *Hereward* I carried on with the method of *Love*, adding a rapid kaleidoscopic effect of short scenes organized on a cinematic system, with snatches of song in darkness between ...[26]

Expressionism, Yeats, primitivism, and classicism contend with surrealism and the new visual technology, as if he were sorting through available modernisms. 'Each novel...will exhaust its method,' Penton had said in his Lawrence piece, an apt comment on the restlessness here.[27] Lindsay's project anticipates many of the debates of the 1930s, visible in groups like the New Apocalypse and the English Surrealists. But for all that, as Lindsay himself later noted, the Franfrolico Press and *The London Aphrodite* remain absent from official histories of modernism. In retrospect, he characterized his project as the retention of a revolutionary impulse present within early modernism and obscured by Eliot and his tradition.

Lindsay had an impoverished thirties, wandering England with a rather disturbed woman called Elsa. He turned to Marxism, and his later work is characterized by a progressive engagement with English history and the classics, finding links with such writers as Graves and Mary Butts.[28] But it retains traces of experimentalism in his use of embedded documents, multiple points of view, and stylistic shifts. A strong view of the modernist period is articulated in his autobiographies and *Meetings with Poets* (1968), which recalls Thomas, Aragon, Tzara, Eluard, and Edith Sitwell, whom he came to see both as the great lost modernist and as the only real reader of his unpublished critical synthesis on the revolutionary tradition, *The Starfish Road*.

LEN LYE: FENDING OFF SURREALISM

In the same year that Lindsay refused Lawrence, 1922, Len Lye arrived in Sydney from Auckland. In New Zealand, he had experienced modernism at a distance, poring over Ezra Pound's *Gaudier-Brzeska* and magazines from the UK, and relating those works to Maori and Island art in his notebooks.[29] In Sydney he quickly became a part of the bohemian artistic scene. In 1924 he spent several months in Samoa before being ejected for consorting too closely with the locals. He worked his way to London as a stoker, arriving in November 1926, six months after Lindsay. He quickly attached himself to various groupings—firstly by simply ringing up artists in the phone book, until Eric Kennington gave him a space in his Hammersmith studio. He was drawn into the circle of Riding and Graves, for whose Seizin press he wrote a book of 'Letters' and designed covers, and also the London Surrealists and the Seven and Five Society—the grouping which included Ben Nicholson, Henry Moore, and Barbara Hepworth. His batiks were reproduced in *transition*, and his film *Tusalava* was shown at the London Film Society in 1929 and praised by Oswell Blakeston in *Close Up*, among others. Roger Fry wrote of his capacity for thinking 'not of forms in themselves but of them as moments in time', adding 'I suspect it will need a new kind of imagination to seize this.'[30] Eventually

Lye found a home in the GPO film unit, where he worked as a pioneering direct-animator for a number of years. He moved to the USA in 1944, filming a project on Basic English for I. A. Richards; later he was a pioneering kinetic sculptor.

Lye contrasts with Lindsay in his rather distant engagement with modernist movements; he was not temperamentally a joiner, and largely eschewed theory. In *Life and Letters Today* in 1937 he wrote:

> I am mere Len Lye with my own rationalization antagonistic to all theory and all painting up to now with buckets of sense more Lennie than Lyzze. The less theory with optic the more eye truth in the psyche the better.[31]

His most sustained polemic in these years—shared with Riding in her short book on his work—was against the importation of literary values into the visual field. Here, too, Lye is involved in a moment of conscious disconnection. In a 1978 interview with Wystan Curnow he recalled that it was other authors who stimulated him:

> L. L.: And it wasn't until, having met Robert, that I started to get interested—and Riding—again in poetry because here were these two sensible people immersed in poetry. And that I'd overlooked something and I'd better find out what it was. Then I came across Hopkins, and some other stuff. And sat back and realised there was something really going on.
>
> W. C.: T. S. Eliot at all?
>
> L. L.: No, he was too intellectual for me. No, I needed the Hopkins magic-stuff. I'm trying to think now of all the people I settled for. Yeats I thought was pretty good. But the greatest thing—set me back—was Norman Cameron's translation of Rimbaud. Boy! By Hogarth Press. Were they the something that I could reach! You know, Rimbaud is a visual – his images are all visual.[32]

Despite his anti-theoretical statements, Lye's writings of the 1930s suggest a fairly sustained dialogue with surrealism in particular. He criticizes surrealist films for their 'literary' qualities; they have not given themselves fully to an automatism founded in the body. His 'Notes on a Short Colour Film', published in *Life and Letters Today* in 1936, contrast the 'realistic imagery' of dream-depiction—he is thinking of Dali, Ernst—with 'the pure visual impulse' of the mind (Miró).[33] In a series of pieces labelled 'Song Time Stuff', published in *Life and Letters Today*, he uses the term 'eyecheck' for a looking which simply registers the object with all its pre-existing meanings—here again surrealism is guilty:

> Apart from mind content at least hooray my mind is made up on why go into an aesthetics taste built up swoon over eyecheck subjects tastefully composed in paint or planes. And surrealism is some of the thresh of this same fish landed. Thresh and swoon on both your cultures in lards in the glow of cathedral chimes and village belles. Such a pun on living is not really on my brow. Your façade sir is not either. Perhaps I was born in a cowl.[34]

'The surreals' filter what they see through the 'eye-check sieve'.[35] Seeking an antidote, Lye turns to an idiom rooted in New Zealand life: his reference to 'mind dags'

(dags are dried shit on a sheep's backside). Or even more brazenly, 'Toot re Root', with its rejection of any homeopathic distance from the real:

> Mind thy sting is rooted where my mind is and not in fancy dilutions from it. Come from the roots then a statement in their visual terms without justification whatever in eyewashing eyecheck[36]

—a thought one can only follow, if at all, knowing that Toot or Tutu is a highly poisonous New Zealand plant. In contrast it is the art of the 'sensation stimulus' he aims for in his abstract films, 'a sort of pulsation'[37] akin to jazz; a version of what Pound had called the primal pigment—'colour marks and values'.[38] He departs from surrealism towards a vitalism founded less in the unconscious than in biomechanics more generally. This, for Lye, is the happiness of the body, expressed and externalized in his later kinetic work.

Did Lye and Lindsay meet? They walked the same ground. Both knew Graves and Riding (Lye intimately); both knew Dylan Thomas, Nancy Cunard, and others. Lindsay describes drinking with Graves and an Australian musician who would have been Lye's friend Jack Ellitt.[39] And in Lindsay's autobiography, he describes visiting Graves: 'After the meal we walked down to see some friends who lived in a houseboat on the Thames.'[40] This might well be Lye, I think, as he was living on the *Avoca* at Hammersmith in some of this period. But his name is never mentioned. Ships in the night.

PATRICK WHITE'S ANATOMY OF MODERNISM

Finally, we can turn to Patrick White. His contacts with the avant-garde were less extensive; his time in London between 1935 and 1939 was conditioned by money and an English education; by homosexuality and by mainstream theatrical ambitions. In a letter to James Stern—whose *New York Times* review of *The Tree of Man* did so much to cement White's reputation—White wrote:

> How lucky the Irish are, and the American Jews, in having those rich tormented backgrounds to draw on; here we are, the bloody Australians, with nothing, having to conjure rabbits out of the air.[41]

This provides a keynote to White's denial of influence. I can think of few other writers who say so little about their literary affiliations: no essays or reviewing; a relentlessly personal autobiography. There are passing comments in his letters about Joyce, George Moore, Thomas Mann, and others; but even his palpable debt to Lawrence is marked more by his pilgrimage to Taos than anything he wrote. In Maine, writing his second novel *The Living and the Dead* (1941), he says, 'I don't know why a jug and a basin should remind me of Auden, but they do,'[42] adding, 'Never met him myself,' before praising his work tepidly and adding that he was told to look him up in New York but didn't. The jug and the basin might nevertheless be said to make their way into the novel, in the 'wash-basin on the rickety stand' at the Essex beach house where Eden and Joe first spend a night together.

And Auden's famous poem might provide the motto for this interlude as Eden watches Joe's 'sleeping face': 'Lay your sleeping head, my love,/Human on my faithless arm ...'[43] It is this sense of the power of the political held at bay which energizes the novel's romance, and Auden is one name for that.

For all that he refuses to formalize influence, then, White's early novels do emerge from a dialogue with context. His first, the suppressed *Happy Valley* (1939), has an adultery plot and hinges on a fatal, serio-comic accident in the manner of Hardy's novels.[44] The next two novels, I will suggest, involve a dialogue with modernism. I'll begin with *The Living and the Dead* (1941). In its depiction of London, it displays the tropes of thirties fiction: a decaying bourgeoisie; the mixing of classes and cultures, jazz and Mozart; the war in Spain as a call to action; even gasometers. But what is interesting to me is the way that in working out its own modernism it contains a generational debate *within* modernism. More than one reader has compared the endlessly tentative 'Elyot Standish' in the novel to Prufrock, and indeed the novel's opening is suffused with references to 'yellow fog', shirtsleeves, the question of forcing a 'moment' to its crisis, and a self addressed as 'you'.[45] Compare Elyot's later reflections on his maturity:

> You ceased to be the dumb self sitting on the edge of other people's conversations, stammering on the telephone, avoiding familiar faces in the street. To be the creature of your work, which anyway was a highly detached, synthetic product, to which you were related as an instrument.[46]

Not only does this echo 'Prufrock', but Elyot's passivity is a product of that expanded sense of timeless time. One could compare the collocation of Eliot and the Spanish Civil War in Edgar Foxall's 'Poem' from *Proems*:

> Where are those isles? Oh, the war in Spain,
> and torrents waiting to fall from the sky;
> the pressed trousers and the perfect part
> in the thin hair of the a.m. nuisance.
> All the blonde typists with hot legs
> and minds like turkeys, birds with mean eyes.[47]

The poem ends with the 'white/gangrene of uncertainty'—a death-in-life White's novel associates with aestheticism. In terms of modernism it centres on the figure of Muriel Raphael, the Jewish gallery owner who is comprehensively up on the latest art.[48] Muriel's status as modernist icon is reinforced by her shape and clothing—she is 'steel-plated', kin to Wyndham Lewis's tyros. But more profoundly, her modernism is articulated by her angular language:

> Her smile remained a symbol of emotion, not emotion. You accepted it, the hieroglyph. It was like Adelaide reading off the success of her party, knowing by the right reactions. This consoled Adelaide. Just the equation. But Elyot Standish, watching what became back, buttocks, the splintering of steel, regretted the dimensionless. Even the hand of Muriel Raphael and all it offered. The sloping belly, the dress where it shaped the thighs. The whole physical Muriel, which was still the hieroglyph.[49]

Muriel and Elyot, briefly lovers, are contrasted with Elyot's sister Eden and her working-class boyfriend Joe. Where Eden's face is withdrawn but readable, Muriel's is all surface; where Eden and Joe seek to find a vaguely delineated 'substance' behind the symbolic—the reality of flesh, of appetite; an identification with others productive of action—Muriel remains locked in narcissism.

The final major figure in the novels is Mrs Standish, the mother who embodies a *fin-de-siècle* modernity founded on relaxation, sexual freedom and the worship of art. Meeting Muriel, she is confronted with a modernism which seeks tension rather than relaxation, friction rather than dialogue. Mrs Standish fails to contain herself: her emotions 'escaped from the body and flowed round the room'[50] as she encounters her own supercession:

> You began to feel sentimental, a little bit out of it, in a world of Picasso and Contemporary Movements. As a girl Mrs Standish had never realised she was contemporary with her period. She suspected that contemporaneity was an invention of the thirties, a term coined by your children to keep you out....And the Movements. By middle age, these had become either incomprehensible or irrelevant—Communism, Surrealism, the Oxford Group.[51]

This defines a particular fracture, but one in which White cannot himself be contemporary, I would suggest. Indeed, something of his own sense of displacement is registered in the semi-autobiographical description of a dinner party:

> And the figures that moved in Adelaide's landscape, her husband Gerald, the uncle who had the horses, the Spanish attaché, they walked with their faces averted from Eden Standish, the way the characters do, the characters you'll never meet, in somebody else's narrative.[52]

The novel's end gestures towards Spain; but with little conviction, as if bemused by the tropes of the 1930s; its strongest impulse is towards flight and extinction. If the novel opens with a fog out of Prufrock, it also eventually elaborates the fog—in an episode by the sea—as a metaphor for distance and disconnection which might be overcome:

> You took the evidence of a finite world on trust, from newspapers read in public houses, the apparent fact of Spain or China. Fog and the floating banks of mud denied such evidence. And the woman at the bar, unwinding her thoughtful skein of mist out of the pint glass.[53]

The real is a dead dog or a map of Spain; mouth on mouth and direct confrontation rather than the distance of the telephone; death rather than art.

We can turn briefly to White's *The Aunt's Story* (1948), where debates within modernism continue. In the opening Australian section Theodora—the aunt of the title—is compared to a polished tree, but represses an inner vitality expressed in a wild dance she performs. Her sculptural self-protection contrasts with the dissolution signalled by the epigraph to the second section, 'Jardin Exotique', set in a hotel in France. The epigraph is taken from Henry Miller: 'Henceforward we walk split into myriad fragments, like an insect with a hundred feet.' This is what the novel calls 'The great fragmentation of maturity'.[54]

The shift in gear between the first two parts of *The Aunt's Story* can be read as, among other things, a move between varieties of modernism. The first or Australian section represents a high modernism predicated on refusal, distance, and negation— emblematized by Theodora's prowess as a shooter, which she flaunts as an abstract and alienating gesture, as well as the abstract description of her body as sculpture, and a suspicion of both social life and language: 'But words, whether written or spoken, were at most frail slat bridges over chasms.'[55] The Picasso-esque cover of the first UK edition reinforced this modernism. The second section, set at the Hôtel du Midi, displays both the traces of expressionism in the mode of Strindberg's *A Dream Play* and a surrealism predicated on automaticity, in which flows of language as well as flows between people open up: 'Skin is after all no protection against communicating bedrooms.'[56] The rapid move between these sections, and the accompanying shift of linguistic gears, as well as abrupt temporal jumps and syntactical elisions, all discomfort readers entering the 'Jardin Exotique'. (In relation to this, I think the description sometimes offered of Theodora as insane in the hotel section is misleading: this is not her consciousness, but rather a world like that of *Alice in Wonderland*, through which she wanders.) Thus we have language like the following: 'Mrs Rapallo laughed, or rather she set in motion the mechanism of her laughter, letting fall a shower of serious teaspoons on to the pavement.'[57]

But the dreamworld of the Hotel ends in chaos and conflagration: the fate of Europe. This poses a particular question: after the angular satire of the Australian section, and the dreamworld of the European, what remains to return to Australia with? (This is a question which has an oblique relation to the novel's notoriously poor reception in Australia.) The impassable distance between Theodora and Australian understanding is signalled by her sister's decision that she is mad, on the basis of a letter saying she will 'return to Abyssinia'. Theodora's reference is to *Rasselas*, with its lesson about the pleasures of what one knows (White's play *Return to Abyssinia* was produced in London in 1947). But in the 1930s, Abyssinia is also the call of others: the London International Surrealist Exhibition of 1936 took place against the background of the Second Italo-Abyssinian War. In this context, the hotel and its dreamworld become the ruins of modernism.

That is not the end, however: the novel's structure is triadic. In the cryptic final section, Theodora wanders off a train into the American heartland and seems to meet a ghost, Holstius, in an abandoned shack on a mountainside. If this is dialectic—modernism as critique of Australian conservatism; surrealism as the nightmare of Europe—then the final section seems like an evocation of the space of pure being, only minimally constrained by social life. The flow of being is most clearly seen in the growth of corn and the 'time of crumbling hills',[58] but also in the shredding of tickets purchased 'for the purpose of prolonging herself through many fresh phrases of what was accepted as Theodora Goodman'. She enters a world defined less by human classification than by biology: 'She was walking between pines or firs, anyway some kind of small coniferous tree, stunted and dark, which possessed that part of the earth. Animal life was moving in the undergrowth of dark, dead twigs and needles, and stiff, thistly things, and yellow grass.' This is close to Lawrence's vision of the animal: 'Theodora could smell the dust. She could smell the expanding odour of her own body, which was no longer the sour, mean smell of the human body in enclosed spaces.'[59]

What is noticeable about her alter ego Holstius is the 'whole' suggested by his name: he offers a unified consciousness in which the contents of dream no longer threaten and fragment; he accepts and heals the 'discord' of Theodora's personality, asserting that 'true permanence is a state of multiplication and division'.[60] Theodora's stepping off the train also involves a move into a different language, into a simpler style in which the trailing forms of White's free indirect discourse no longer present the untidiness of thought. Beyond this is the world of White's later artists and mystics, who open themselves to experience without compromise, and a realism which no longer works under the sign of self-protection—which constantly reaches towards the dangers of plenitude and epic fulfilment, both in terms of White's characters and in terms of the risks of writing.

CONCLUSION: THE THIRTIES AND A MODERNISM OF DISCONNECTION

What I am proposing in examining this 'Antipodean trajectory' is a modernism of disconnection; that is, a modernism which seeks to bring an end to modernism, to borrow Rosenquist's phase again. It is striking that all three writers fly from their initial point of entry in both geographical and aesthetic terms—Lindsay to Communism, Essex, and the historical novel; Lye to New York and kinetic sculpture; and White back to Australia and a transfigured realism. While their motivations are partly personal, and the war is a major factor, one can't help thinking that what these artists had in common was an angle of traversal across what we call modernism, impelled by a sense of dissidence in which an underlying problematic energizing their career only slowly emerges. What draws them to the metropolis is bound up with modernist identifications—with Lawrence, Joyce, Gaudier, surrealism—but that prior identification also involves an impulse to discriminate, sort, establish another, less agonistic version of the new.

But in the name of what values is this flight from modernism articulated? What is implied is often something less formally defined than the discourse of modernism, but nevertheless rescued from its disasters. As we have seen, one need that seemed particularly pressing in the 1930s was keeping the memory of Lawrence alive; and countering Eliot's hegemony. Another was configured by the pressure of the political, though that is hardly news. The agonies involved are particularly intense, I think, for White, even if the result sometimes borders on the uncertainties of kitsch as he schematizes literary history for his own ends, and drives towards his own version of a Lawrentian plenitude.

I'll conclude by returning to the programme of Slessor and Lindsay's *Vision*, back in Sydney in 1923, because it seems to me kin to White's *The Living and the Dead*:

> If you are tired of glutinous chatter about Chelsea artists—or reports from passionate spinsters on their souls—or studies in the rectangular nude by futurist tradesmen—or the poetic dropsy of the weekly Celts—or the smacking honesty of the monthly sea-dogs—or the album-cleverness of the young ladies and gentlemen who wrote *vers libre*—
> In short if you are tired of being modern and want to be alive.
> Then take heart. *Vision* may help you yet.[61]

In its refusal at least, this aesthetic programme may have been truer than it knew, for all that Lindsay never claimed the inheritance he had imagined, or returned to the place from where it came.

NOTES

1. Bonnie Kime Scott, *Refiguring Modernism, Vol. 1: The Women of 1928* (Bloomington, IN: Indiana University Press, 1995), pp. xxiii; Steve Watson, *Strange Bedfellows: The First American Avant-garde* (New York: Abbeville Press, 1991), pp. 16–17, 42–3, *passim*.
2. Chris Baldick, *The Modern Movement*, vol. 10 of *The Oxford English Literary History* (Oxford: Oxford University Press, 2004).
3. Rodney Rosenquist, *Modernism, the Market and the Institution of the New* (Cambridge: Cambridge University Press, 2009).
4. See Oswell Blakeston and Herbert Jones's magazine *Seed* (1933); *Proems* (1938); and Michael Robert's anthology *New Signatures* (1932).
5. Patrick Evans, Lawrence Durrell, Ruthven Todd, Edgar Foxall, Oswell Blakeston, and Rayner Heppenstall, *Proems* (London: Fortune Press, 1938).
6. On Caton, see Timothy D'Arch Smith, *R. A. Caton and the Fortune Press* (London: Bertrand Rota, 1983).
7. Mark Ford, 'Nicholas Moore, Stevens and the Fortune Press', in *Wallace Stevens across the Atlantic*, edited by Bart Eeckhout and Edward Ragg (Basingstoke: Palgrave, 2008), pp. 165–85.
8. Evans Letters, Lawrence Durrell Collection, Vol. LII, British Library Add MS 73143.
9. See Heppenstall's autobiography *The Intellectual Part* (London: Barrie and Rockliff, 1963), p. 38; *Master Eccentric: The Journals of Rayner Heppenstall*, edited by Jonathan Goodman (London: Allison and Busby, 1986), p. 206.
10. *Proems*, p. 22.
11. A great deal more could be said about the careers of Heppenstall and Durrell as novelists: each negotiates in a complex manner with modernist inheritances, Heppenstall in a disconnected picaresque, and Durrell in a radical perspectivism.
12. Frank Callaway, 'Hal Collins and the Warlock Connection', *Peter Warlock: A Centenary Celebration*, edited by David Cox and John Bishop (London: Thames, 1994), pp. 242–7.
13. Jack Lindsay, *The Roaring Twenties* (London: Bodley Head, 1960), p. 65.
14. Lindsay, *The Roaring Twenties*, p. 89.

15. Lindsay, *The Roaring Twenties*, p. 87.
16. *The London Aphrodite*, edited by Jack Lindsay and P. R. Stephensen (London: Franfrolico Press, 1928–9). This is the collected volume, subsequently cited by volume and page number. One of the few discussions of the journal is Lawrence Coupe, 'Jack Lindsay: From the Aphrodite to Arena', in *Jack Lindsay: The Thirties and Forties*, edited by Robert Mackie (London: Institute of Commonwealth Studies, 1984), pp. 46–60.
17. See Jack Lindsay, *Franfrolico and After* (London: Bodley Head, 1962).
18. *The London Aphrodite*, vol. 3, p. 227.
19. *The London Aphrodite*, vol. 6, p. 464.
20. Craig Monro, *Inky Stephenson: Wild Man of Letters* (Melbourne: University of Melbourne Press, 1984), pp. 82.
21. Lindsay, *Franfrolico and After*, p. 179.
22. Lindsay, *Franfrolico and After*, p. 10.
23. Brian Penton, 'Note on the Form of the Novel', *Scrutinies* II, edited by Edgell Rickword (London: Wishart, 1931), pp. 255, 257.
24. *The London Aphrodite*, vol. 3, p. 230.
25. *The London Aphrodite*, vol. 3, p. 232.
26. Lindsay, *Franfrolico and After*, p. 162.
27. Penton, 'Note on the Form', p. 258.
28. Lindsay, *Franfrolico and After*, p. 249.
29. Details from Roger Horrocks, *Len Lye: A Biography* (Auckland: Auckland University Press, 2001).
30. Roger Fry to Len Lye, 3 Dec. 1929, Len Lye Archive, Govett-Brewster Art Gallery, New Plymouth.
31. Len Lye, *Figures of Motion: Selected Writings*, edited by Wystan Curnow and Roger Horrocks (Auckland: Auckland University Press, 1984), p. 115.
32. Wystan Curnow, An Interview with Len Lye', *Art New Zealand*, 17 (Spring 1980), http://www.art-newzealand.com/Issues11to20/Lye09.htm accessed 1 Feb. 2016.
33. Lye, *Figures of Motion*, p. 50.
34. Lye, *Figures of Motion*, p. 117.
35. Lye, *Figures of Motion*, p. 118.
36. Lye, *Figures of Motion*, p. 117.
37. Lye, *Figures of Motion*, p. 50.
38. Lye, *Figures of Motion*, p. 118.
39. Lindsay, *Franfrolico and After*, p. 80.
40. Lindsay, *Franfrolico and After*, p. 79.
41. *The Letters of Patrick White*, edited by David Marr (Chicago: University of Chicago Press, 1996), p. 359.
42. White, *Letters*, p. 20.
43. W. H. Auden, *The English Auden*, edited by Edward Mendelson (London: Faber, 1977), p. 207.
44. Patrick White, *Happy Valley* (London: Harrap, 1939). The novel was supressed by White in his lifetime.
45. Patrick White, *The Living and the Dead* (1941) (Harmondsworth: Penguin, 1967).
46. White, *The Living and the Dead*, p. 176.
47. *Proems*, p. 70.
48. White, *The Living and the Dead*, p. 216.
49. White, *The Living and the Dead*, p. 213.
50. White, *The Living and the Dead*, p. 349.

51. White, *The Living and the Dead*, p. 216.
52. White, *The Living and the Dead*, p. 182.
53. White, *The Living and the Dead*, p. 270.
54. Patrick White, *The Aunt's Story* (London: Vintage, 1994), p. 139.
55. White, *The Aunt's Story*, p. 133.
56. White, *The Aunt's Story*, p. 254.
57. White, *The Aunt's Story*, p. 191.
58. White, *The Aunt's Story*, p. 286.
59. White, *The Aunt's Story*, pp. 273–4.
60. White, *The Aunt's Story*, p. 295.
61. Lindsay, *The Roaring Twenties*, pp. 87–8.

4

Modernism's Missing Modernity

David Ayers

This essay examines the reasons that the scholarship and—such as it is—theory of 'modernism' seem constitutionally to lack the very theory of modernity which the term 'modernism' might be thought by any innocent outsider to imply and to require. One reason that modernism lacks a corresponding theory of modernity is straightforward and probably widely understood. There is no reason to assume any strong connection between a modernist literature or art and the periodization of a social modernity. Moreover, the creation of a loosely bounded modernist period which corresponds to one or other periodization of high modernist literature, but is assumed to include all cultural production of the 'period', is an accidental construction that is grounded in the moment of aesthetic innovation rather than in the identification of any particular social-historical change affecting groups outside the small coteries that generate high art. This creation of a modernist period serves the needs of scholars for whom work of any detail tends to require period boundaries that set realistic limits to the scope of their projects.

There is, of course, an asymmetry when the Anglophone notion of modernism is contrasted with the 'Continental' notion of the avant-garde. While this would require a certain working-out, I do not propose to offer that here. Indeed, such a contrast, if given too much substance, begins to reify histories that are quite fluid. It makes too much of the fact that avant-garde movements in the style of Futurism, Dada and surrealism found only partial and relatively less important reflections in the Anglophone literature of the 1920s, which generated works of a different type and generally with goals that the avant-garde would not in the main have endorsed. All we should note here, though, is that the contingency of the term 'modernism'—very infrequently used in the modernist period, just as the notion of 'avant-garde' is very infrequently found in the manifestos of the historical avant-garde—points in fact less towards the supposed isolation, or combined and uneven development (to maladapt Marxist economic theory) of Anglophone literature at this time, than to a contingency in the materials rather than the scholarship. By this I mean that the issue of 'modernism' is already tightly governed, less by a supposed developmental strand in the literary materials than by the discipline of Anglophone literary studies itself. To say this is not to suggest that we should indulge in disciplinary guilt, but rather to note that there is a 'we' which tends to have been historically and institutionally shaped, and indeed to caution the opposite. Rather than become absorbed in the guilt as to our own historical limits—more simply, our finitude as researchers and thinkers—we learn to think openly and creatively about where we are in modernist studies and how that no doubt various locatedness is bound to our current world circumstance. That circumstance is in fact quite closely linked to the modernist history we commonly examine as if it were a set of remote and completed actions, a misapprehension of reality and process perhaps inevitable among scholars for whom adherence to the actuality of objects is a condition of our practice. The early twentieth century is not the eighteenth century, I was about to write, but in a way it is, as that eighteenth-century world, with its developing apparatus of the public sphere, its juxtapositions of journalism and literature, its professionalism of authorship, rationalization of language and of publication, above all in its address to opinion and resistance to any authority but that of the individual, is so closely related to the world of 'modernism' and of our own, that it is hard really not to grasp 'modernity' as a 300-year stretch.

What scholar could grasp a 300-year modernity? And what theorist could do other than worry away at what would begin to appear as an arbitrary starting point? Modernism as the product of scholarly finitude and modernity as the product of any theoretical attempt, after Hegel, to map the present epoch, sit uneasily alongside each other. As long as Marxism retained explicit and implicit sway in literary studies during the Cold War, the notion of modern society as capitalist, according to a model of periodization established by Marx and Engels, could be almost unquestioningly invoked in the context of English literary studies, which were struggling at that time to reach their intellectual potential. Elsewhere, Marxist theorists debated whether the 'Third World' should be seen as simply catching up with the inevitable development of the 'West', and wrangled too over the nature of the Soviet Union and China, where capitalism in the form of some sort of state capitalism seemed to deny liberties even more thoroughly than the 'free world', whose oppressions had to be thought through in increasingly nuanced ways (sexual repression as an aspect of capitalism) or in ways that increasingly dispensed with the Marxist theory of historical development (race, sexual orientation, and those feminisms which disaggregated themselves entirely from socialist and Marxist models). The dominance of a theory of history that assumed progressive movement from dependence to freedom was not only interdicted by the complexities of experience and debate in the context of Third World and First World liberation struggles, but also by those developments in theory which hammered away not only at progressive theories of history but at most of the philosophical pillars of that theory, with exceptions in the main for those thinkers who sat most awkwardly in relation to the Hegelian inheritance, Nietzsche and Heidegger.

I use the term 'weak theory' to designate in general the state of critical thought in the wake of the demise of the philosophy of history.[1] What I offer here is, first, a generalized account of what that means in terms that we probably already commonly understand, followed by some close analysis of the key modernist topic of technology in Heidegger and Benjamin, intended to identify some of the theoretical lacunae of the theory of modernity in its implication for modernist studies.

The theory of history is the theory of the future. In our own time literary or critical theory, while infrequently explicitly prescriptive, is generally framed around a question concerning usually implicit desiderata for the human future. It was the philosophy of history which gave shape to the predictive or utopian desire of modern theory, even though it no longer directly governs it. The names associated with the development of the theory of history in the eighteenth century are Giambattista Vico, Johann Gottfried Herder, and the Marquis de Condorcet. The eighteenth century sought to see history in terms of observable regularities rather than as the mere accidental succession of events which the ancients had taken it to be. One objective of the theory of history was to give an account of the emergence of modernity and of its essence. It was Hegel who capped these efforts with his synthesis of the ontogenetic and phylogenetic elements of the development of spirit and whose philosophy has stood over modernity even where that philosophy is rejected. Since Hegel in *Philosophy of Right* argued that the modern state was in effect an achieved and final form—a view which subsequent events have arguably done nothing to correct—his theory of history remained descriptive rather than prescriptive. It was Hegel's view of the state which so irked Marx and Engels, who not alone in the nineteenth century sought to predict a future which would be more logical, harmonious, and just, and which would properly harness the productive forces of humanity, catapult humankind from the realm of necessity to the realm of freedom, and thus provide the real end of history which Hegel had prematurely announced—or, in other terms, begin a human history of which all that had passed before was merely the prehistory.

This is the point at which the theory of history is brought to bear on the utopian imaginary, which speculatively suggested alternative forms of social existence. It is also at the point where the strain of using a theory of history, based on the observation of regularities in what has passed, begins to show. How might it be possible to base a theory of the future on the notion that history is governed by laws? Marx and Engels, of course, advocated communism, though we should grasp 'communism' not as a specific social arrangement but as the name under which the actuality of a liberated humanity could begin to appear—in other words, 'communism' designates human liberation as such. Marx and Engels were convinced of the need for a scientific socialism as opposed to the utopian socialism of Saint-Simon, Fourier, and Owen. In *Socialism: Utopian or Scientific* (1880), a late and influential text, Engels declared the ideas of the utopists to be a 'mish-mash', since their invented systems bore no relation to a theory of history which could explain their possible coming-into-being.[2] More dialectics—to repeat Adorno's admonition of Benjamin—were required to explain the necessary and law-governed emergence of this future. The paradox of Marx and Engels' thought was that this future was indiscernible.[3] This is visible in the famous formulation in *The German Ideology* (1846), which is found in the context of the analysis of the division of labour which Marx and Engels considered so objectionable: 'in communist society...society regulates the general production and thus makes it possible for me to do one thing today and another tomorrow, to hunt in the morning, fish in the afternoon, rear cattle in the evening, criticise after dinner, just as I have a mind'.[4]

The Eighteenth Brumaire of Louis Napoleon (1852) indicates a similar aporia: 'The social revolution of the nineteenth century can only create its poetry from the future, not from the past.'[5]

The aporetic nature of the theory of history—that it cannot plausibly present or represent the future to which it believes it inevitably points came crashing out of the realm of the speculative in the wake of the Bolshevik revolution. Lenin did not believe that a communist revolution could come about in Russia, although the theory of permanent revolution adopted by the impatient Trotsky had suggested it might. That their revolution did not meet scientific criteria troubled Lenin, who sat in his Moscow office receiving his numerous British guests with the same question—would the revolution come in Britain as Marxist theory predicted? How to approach and in what way to implement communism when the theory of history which they had attempted to fulfil appeared, in the same movement, to have left the rails was not their only problem. Writers and artists under the Bolsheviks began the clamour for theory in the arts which has echoed down to the present day. The theory they sought was prescriptive, not descriptive. Trotsky's attempt in *Literature and Revolution* (1924) to bring this debate to a head resulted merely in paradox. Formalists, he argued, offered a necessary science but were weak on content (and, of course, we know that the primary consequence of his attack on formalism arrived in the West via Prague and Paris in a history that there is no need to repeat). According to Trotsky, the writers of the present could not discern the forces of history which shaped their current reality, let alone the future. They could not produce the art of the future since they did not belong to it and could not anticipate it. The proletarian writers could not write the literature of the future since the whole point of communism was that the proletariat as a class would disappear. The proletariat was transitional, as indeed was the whole revolutionary situation which Trotsky thought might entail a further fifty years of struggle in Europe. The question they confronted, we now see, was one of the imaginary of the future. What the Bolshevik situation highlights is that the call for theory rested on the theory of history, but it became increasingly apparent that it could not draw on that theory in the moment of its actualization.

The anti-Hegelian movement of later French thought only confirmed intellectually the practical outcome of the Russian Revolution. However much emphasis is put on the Nietzschean component of modern anti-systematic thought, it would probably be correct to say that it is the influence of the history of science which has had the greatest intellectual bearing on the abandonment of the theory of history. Via Foucault, the fashion developed for models of history as discontinuity in terms of the 'epistemic break' proposed by Bachelard, which is in turn akin to the 'paradigm shifts' in the natural sciences analysed by Thomas Kuhn in *The Structure of Scientific Revolutions* (1962).

This is a sketch of the situation of theory, intended to indicate that theory was consigned to weakness not simply by the incoherence of the theory of history itself, but in the very moment when the bearers of that theory, the Bolsheviks, created the conditions under which theory itself in it its politically and scientifically grounded form could be called into being and given a platform. In case we have missed the point of this imbrication of theory with the failure of communism, it is notable that Alain Badiou, perhaps the pre-eminent living philosopher of communism, has entirely dispensed with the theory of history. In his work, communism is a hypothesis, and events—such as revolutions—are discontinuous with what has gone before and do not depend for their instantiation on any prior process or on any collective subject, whether the subject of history or the subject of the social movements.[6]

This sketch of the progress of the progression of the theory of history serves as a reminder of what is at stake in the attempt to think through the question of modernism's modernity. Modernism in some way abuts on a narrative concerning the qualitative change in human life, whether conceived as progress (Hegel, Marx) or indeed regression (Adorno). The theory of modernity implies both the marked differentiation from the premodern, and implies also a possible movement towards a future which will be markedly differentiated from the modern once again. One difficulty for modernist studies has been the weakening of all theories of modernity, and a consequence of this has been the manner in which the topics of the theory of modernity recur frequently in modernist studies, independently of the attendant theory, recurring as motifs which are presented as the seeming marks of the modern but which are cut adrift of any viable theory of modernity. So we may find ourselves tracing elements of the modern in order to examine the components of what the theory of history has alerted us to, and which may be historical-qualitative changes in human existence. We may, however, also find ourselves locked into kinds of micro-narrative documentation which gesture to a broader epochal process, without having at hand any theory which would account for that epoch, and which might then retroactively shape our more local decisions as to our research objects and methods.

This can be seen if we look at the theme of technology. Technology—or rather, multiple aspects of the technological—is an established topos of modernist studies, as witnessed by the exemplary work of Tim Armstrong in *Modernism, Technology and the Body* (1998). While we concentrate on technologies, and on their various effects in cultural and social life, in modernist studies we seem less focused on the question of technology as such which, in creating this grouping or set of the 'technological', we would appear to imply and draw on. The notion of technology-as-such appears to require a register other than the observational and lies adjacent to, indeed athwart of, the theory of history. Perhaps the first and clearest articulation of the theory of history which attempted to map the role of technology in the qualitative change of human existence came in the work of Marx and Engels. While it is hardly necessary to summarize the basic ideas of Marx here, we should remind ourselves that in Marx's argument it is changes in the technology of production that are the drivers of social change. Changes in the means of production which enhance human productivity decrease the dependence on nature and move humans as a species towards the realm of freedom. Increase in productivity requires changes in social forms to enable the new increases in productivity to be realized. The inevitable movement from feudalism to capitalism to communism allows for a qualitative alteration in human existence as the division of labour is outmoded and overcome and all can participate in a new history which might render existing history a mere prehistory—a new modality of history which would correspond to the emergence of a newly free and unconstrained humanity. As we have noted, the utopian projection of Marx and Engels is strangely aporetic but, viewed broadly, their argument makes the connection between developments in technology and an existential change.

Modernist studies commonly take as a kind of foundational text Walter Benjamin's famous essay on 'The Work of Art in the Age of its Technological Reproducibility' (1939). Before turning to that text in order to consider the lacunae which its apparent centrality indicates and exemplifies, it is useful to take a detour through Heidegger's equally celebrated essay, 'The Question Concerning Technology' (1954).[7] For all that Heidegger has proved such a dominant modernist voice, his influence on modernist studies is only an indirect one, principally realized in the Francophone and subsequent Anglophone adaptation of his much-vaunted deconstruction of metaphysics rather than in any more direct engagement. Yet on this question of the role of technology in relation to any apparent qualitative change in the collective life of modernity, elements of Heidegger's thought prove illuminating even if we are likely to wish to disaggregate those elements from the existential tenor of his thought more globally.

The first part of Heidegger's essay is salutary for any attempt to consider the role of technology in modernity, since it obliges us to consider what is meant by the term 'technology'. 'Technology', Heidegger cautions, 'is not equivalent to the essence of technology', so no single exemplum will serve as a guide. The essence of technology 'is by no means anything technological'.[8] The dominant conception of technology regards it as a means to an end, but this notion does not yet yield the essence of technology. Using the example of a sacrificial chalice—in one of those evocations of Greek mystery which often cause materialist readers of Heidegger to avert their gaze—Heidegger argues that the Greeks identified four forms of causality and that, in the example of the chalice, these are identified in four ways: the matter, silver, of which the chalice is made, to which the chalice is indebted; the aspect of its chaliceness, without which it would have no form; the *telos* (aim or purpose) of the chalice, to which both its matter and aspect are subordinated; finally, the silversmith, who is not simply the maker or producer, but who is 'co-responsible' with the other three causes for causing the chalice to appear.[9] The unison of these four ways of 'occasioning' lets 'what is not present arrive into presencing'. This 'bringing forth' is *poiesis*, a term which incorporates *physis*, the 'arising of something out of itself'.[10] This 'bringing forth' is unconcealment, revealing, *aletheia*. Consequently, Heidegger argues:

> Technology is therefore no mere means. Technology is a way of revealing. If we give heed to this, then another whole realm for the essence of technology will open itself up to us. It is the realm of revealing, i.e. of truth.[11]

Heidegger reminds us that 'technology' is derived from *techne*, which 'is the name not only for the activities and skills of the craftsman, but also for the arts of the mind and the fine arts. *Techne* belongs to bringing-forth, to *poesis*; it is something poetic.' Moreover, *techne* is linked to *episteme*, 'knowing in the widest sense'. He concludes:

Thus what is decisive in *techne* does not lie at all in making and manipulating nor in the using of means, but rather in the revealing mentioned before. It is as revealing, and not as manufacturing, that *techne* is a bringing-forth.... Technology is a mode of revealing.[12]

While the general tenor of Heidegger's thinking to this point may be familiar, it is useful for our purposes to have briefly examined the workings simply in order to show that the notion of technology cannot simply be read off as, for example, machinery, and that technology *tout court* must probably in some way be grasped ontologically.

This returns us then to the question for a theory of history of the possibility of an existential or ontological change brought about by technology. If the essence of technology embraces all manner of *poiesis* as the presencing of truth, what space is left to argue for any fundamental ontological difference belonging to 'modern' technology, however defined? Here we recall that Heidegger, after Marx and Engels, and in parallel with Adorno and the Frankfurt School, is one of the principal theorists of a modernity grasped in terms of the role of technology. The second part of his 1954 essay occupies some of the same ground, much more familiar to modernist studies, as Adorno and Horkheimer's pessimistic *Dialectic of Enlightenment* (1944). Modern technology, asserts Heidegger, 'does not unfold into a bringing-forth in the sense of *poiesis*'. Instead, modern technology is 'a challenging, which puts to nature the unreasonable demand that it supply energy which can be extracted and stored as such'.[13] The result of this is a transformation of nature such that

> the energy concealed in nature is unlocked, what is unlocked is transformed, what is transformed is stored up, what is stored up is, in turn, distributed and what is distributed is switched about ever anew. Unlocking, transforming, storing, distributing, and switching about are ways of revealing. But the revealing never simply comes to an end.... Everything is ordered to stand by, to be immediately on hand, indeed to stand there just so it can be on call for a further ordering.[14]

It would require too much space, and be in the end unwelcome, to elaborate every element of the thesis Heidegger develops regarding what he labels as 'enframing', being the particular modality of the revealing of truth in the context of the mode of ordering entailed by modern technology. We should note first, in a general way, the motif of the transformation of nature, as familiar to us from Wordsworth as from Adorno and Horkheimer. Within that, we should note the attention paid to the ends–means metaphor, very squarely present in *Dialectic of Enlightenment*, but carefully (if contentiously) here rebutted by Heidegger as a misprision of the essence of technology. One element of his case worth noting is his distinction between mathematical science and the technology which postdated it by almost two centuries:

> Chronologically speaking, modern physical science begins in the seventeenth century. In contrast, machine-power technology develops only in the second half of the eighteenth century. But modern technology, which for chronological reckoning is the later, is, from the point of view of the essence holding sway within it, historically earlier.
>
> ...
>
> Modern technology must employ exact physical science. Through its so doing the deceptive illusion arises that modern technology is applied physical science.[15]

Physics moves away from the object to a 'realm of representation incapable of being visualised' and retreats from 'the kind of representation which turns only to objects'; nature for physics is 'identifiable through calculation' and remains 'orderable as a system of information'.[16] This truism Heidegger shares with Adorno and Horkheimer. The existential danger of this—although Heidegger does not here use the term 'existential'—is that man in the 'midst of objectlessness is nothing but the orderer of the standing reserve...he comes to the point where he himself will have to be taken as standing reserve'. Again, Heidegger's general idea resembles the tenor of the opening chapter of *Dialectic of Enlightenment*. Despite this evident convergence, Heidegger's careful bracketing of the ends–means interpretation of technology allows for a different conclusion:

> The coming to presence of technology threatens revealing, threatens it with the possibility that all revealing will be consumed in ordering and that everything will present itself only in the unconcealedness of standing-reserve.[17]

There may, however, be allowed to humanity 'a more primally granted revealing'. Since '*techne*' once did not indicate merely technology but 'the *poiesis* of the fine arts', and since 'the essence of technology is nothing technological', perhaps an 'essential reflection' on technology can take place in the 'realm of art'.[18]

While this constitutes a theory of modernism in itself, albeit one that draws on Hölderlin rather than Joyce, the objective here is not to endorse Heidegger's conclusions or even vocabulary, but to note the careful deconstruction of the essence of technology which Heidegger brings to what might seem by now an almost orthodox periodizing account of the modernity governed first by the exact sciences and then by technology, an account of the kind familiar to Adorno and Horkheimer from their reading of Weber. At the centre of this account is an ontological thesis concerning the loss and possible restoration of nature which reminds us that the question of modernity will in general be not simply qualitative but existential. It is from this platform that we can now turn back to Benjamin's 1939 essay.

Heidegger's essay works as a kind of obstacle to 'The Work of Art in the Age of its Technological Reproducibility'.[19] Benjamin's essay has quietly assumed an influence in modernist studies even where it is not cited. This is in some ways curious, not least because it seems it can easily be read either as a pessimistic account of modernity, in which the essential 'aura' of the object is lost in a maze of mechanical iterability, or as an optimistic account in which subjects are liberated from the tyranny of the particular by the demystifying effects of photography and the shock-effect of film. I rather suspect that it is a piece of Brechtian optimism underpinned by a melancholy countercurrent of nostalgia but, however it is taken, its peculiar indeterminacy is a sign that it belongs to that realm of 'weak theory' in which, I have indicated, theoretical motifs flourish, apparently under the umbrella of some overarching theory of modernity, but the theory of history on which they seem to depend, and of which they are supposedly the coarticulation, can never appear.

Benjamin's essay begins by evoking Marx, yet Marx is quietly obliterated. The ostensible theme is the manifestation of the 'conditions of production' which Marx had found only in their 'infancy' but which have now taken effect 'in all areas of culture'.[20] That part of Marx which is quietly bracketed is the thesis, which I will label ontological, of the loss of true consciousness of the commodity as use value, to be replaced by a false consciousness of it as exchange value. More routinely, perhaps, Benjamin is clearly presenting a version of the theory of ideology, in which the demystification of 'aura' corresponds to the attack on the false consciousness of religion in Marx and Engels, but where, more ambivalently, the loss of aura corresponds to a loss of 'authenticity' that allows for a new form of 'actualization',[21] without any sense being clearly established that the loss of auratic distance and authenticity is compensated in this new regime driven by the 'desire of the present-day masses to "get closer" to things spatially and humanly'. The shift, which is barely announced, is from the question of the total organization of society according to the relations of production, to a question of 'perception': 'Just as the entire mode of existence of human collectives changes over long historical periods, so too does their mode of perception.'[22] Benjamin posits as a juxtaposition what Marxism should more probably posit as a dialectical relationship in which on the one hand consciousness is determined by the existing relations of production (not exactly what is indicated by Benjamin's phrase 'mode of existence of human collectives'), and on the other hand the consciousness of the proletariat (not exactly the same thing as the masses) must forge itself in struggle as the instrument which will bring about a fundamental alteration in the existing relations of production. This shift to 'mode of perception' based in technologies of art is one with which many versions of modernist and cultural studies are quite comfortable, not necessarily because of any scholarly betrayal or bourgeoisification of intellectual life, but because in general the weakening of theory which Benjamin's essay marks is an objective one: that is, his essay responds both to the failure of Soviet Communism and to the failure of communism to take effective hold in Germany, as well as to the framing limits set by his nineteenth-century predecessors. These limits cannot be surmounted by will or decision.

Though the moment which Benjamin's essay marks, after the Stalin terror and the coming to power of Hitler, constitutes the objective moment in which it becomes necessary to re-examine all questions of consciousness, whether of the proletariat or the mass, or even of consciousness-as-such, it is also a moment in which the questionable basis of the theory of history—a theory to which Benjamin alludes but apparently does not adhere—becomes visible. With Heidegger's questioning of the nature of the object in mind,[23] it becomes easier to see that the question of the artwork abuts directly on the broader question of authentic perception, which in turn opens onto the question of authentic experience. We can note, without completely dissecting, the difference between Heidegger's conception of technology in its essence as 'revealing' and Benjamin's notion of getting 'hold of an object at close range'.[24] It is surely this strain of Benjamin's thought that leads some readers of his essay to regard it as a lament for the loss of aura. His famous analogy of the bringing-closer of the landscape in an overcoming of distance seems to indicate a simple incoherence in the demand of the masses for 'proximity'. If 'to follow with the eye – while resting on a summer afternoon – a mountain range on the horizon or a branch that casts its shadow on the beholder is to breathe the aura of those mountains, of that branch' is supposed to help us 'grasp the basis of the aura's present decay',[25] then the whole dynamic of Benjamin's essay takes a wild turn from which it can never recover. Is nature to be grasped through the senses as landscape in the manner of the British Romantic poets, who celebrated these relaxed and contemplative moments as the grounding of an authentic way of being denied by social modernity? If so, why does Benjamin's essay appear to celebrate the overcoming of aura? Are we being asked, almost in an aside, to affirm auratic distance as the very mode of authentic inwardness? And therefore implicitly to repel the call to bring things nearer for purposes of demystification, with all that implies for the liberation of consciousness, as an undesirable feature of visual tech-nology which will prevail even if social forms change? It has always appeared to me that Benjamin knowingly introduces this incoherence into his own account, as if to signal dissent from the Marxist discourse with which he seems otherwise to be in some sort of conformity. What this passage marks most clearly is the weakening of the theory of history. Marx and Engels were confident in what must increasingly appear as a badly thought attempt to ground the potential of human futurity in a restoration of the thing as use value. Benjamin implicitly asks what the use of a landscape can be, and by extension the use of any object. Heidegger shows that the manufactured object cannot be simply read off in terms of its use according to an ends–means model. Read in the light of Heidegger's essay, Benjamin's essay seems to demonstrate, without arguing it, not that technology can liberate consciousness, but that technology—in the single aspect of visual culture in which he considers it—is indeed something like the enframing which Heidegger describes. In other words that, to repeat the sentence we have already quoted from Heidegger, 'The coming to presence of technology threatens revealing . . . with the possibility . . . that everything will present itself only in the unconcealedness of standing-reserve.'[26]

We have concentrated here on only one aspect of the weakening of theory, that aspect of the theory of history which becomes philosophically incoherent once we realize that received forms of the theory of history rest on notions of existential authenticity in one manner or another. Here we have peeked a little through Benjamin at Hegel and Marx at the notion of the restoration to perception of things in their authentic mode, with Benjamin dissenting from the notion of thing-as-use-value implicit in the notion of bringing closer.[27] This philosophical question of the mode of availability of the real, in whatever jargon it might be expressed, lies most certainly in the domain of ontology.[28] This is the interpretation, notably, of Michel Henry, who comments in his extensive analysis of Marx that 'reality consid-ered in itself is not at all economic', denouncing the 'monumental error' which finds in Marx a theory of reality as fundamentally economic and arguing that Marx seg-regates absolutely an ontology of the real—of use value and praxis—from the realm of economic exchange value.[29] This ontological fundamental, which we have seen constitutes an aporia in Benjamin's work simply because the premises regarding authentic apperception of the real cannot be made coherent, is linked directly to the question of periodization which, we have already stated, is at the root of any attempt to peg 'modernism' to something which can be labelled modernity.

Benjamin's periodization in the 1939 essay is determined more by ontological desire than by any objectivity in the treatment of technological reproduction. Too many obvious objections to his framing claims are ignored in the drive to peg the technology of art to industrial technology in such a way that a convergence might be found in the nineteenth century with the development of photography. We could note that really any reproduction is technological—and we can say this without evoking Heidegger's account of *techne* as *poiesis*—since even manual reproduction is a technology. We could note too that what Benjamin calls reproduction is already relatively impoverished when set against the Marxist notion of economic reproduction (i.e. the reproduction of the conditions required for production) and is really a theory of *replication*.[30] We can also note the strange privileging of the visual over the verbal or over the understanding, so that print as the most obvious example of *mechanical* replication is sidelined in the essay. From this we can further note that while photography is presented as the mode of replication in which images can be made to proliferate before the eyes of the masses, it is actually the mechanical reproduction of print, rather than the artisanal work of photography, which achieves this task of mass distribution. Benjamin's essay is not unaware of at least some of these dilemmas. We note them here simply in order to indicate that this essay marks that moment in which the theory of history is breached and the attempted theory of modernity casts around for period markers in terms of apperceptive authenticity, on the one hand, and technological developments in the field of what is still referred to, undisturbed, as art. Benjamin's account lacks the confidence to rest on the nineteenth-century machinery supplied by Hegel and Marx, now strongly in doubt, yet is also unable to produce any alternative unifying narrative which could bridge the gap between ontology and technology.

To identify Benjamin's essay as a moment or marker of 'weak theory' is not to say that weak theory is not theory, but to begin to identify the thinking that must be brought to this weakness, to thematize it, and to recognize its place in the necessarily finite and discipline-bound field of modernist studies. Modernism implies period. It therefore implicitly calls for a theory of modernity. Fredric Jameson, in *A Singular Modernity* (2002), identifies fourteen conventional models of modernity as some kind of beginning, which date it variously to the Protestant Reformation, Descartes, the conquest of the Americas, the Enlightenment, the French Revolution, Galileo, capitalism, secularization, Weberian rationalization, 'aesthetic modernism itself with the reification of language', and 'last but not least, the Soviet Revolution'.[31] Jameson goes on to propose a 'formal analysis of the uses of the word "modernity" that explicitly rejects any presupposition that there is a correct use of the word',[32] but for the purposes of an already roughly periodized modernist studies I suggest that we reject Jameson's formalist approach and seek another more immanent weak-theoretical solution, one that will incorporate the moment of the weakening of theory and recognize that this moment is constitutive of our field.

That periodization which should be key for modernist studies, at least for as long as it takes to remind ourselves of its centrality, is geopolitical. The approach

I suggest would locate the crisis of the theory of history not in the intellectual assaults of Nietzsche, Heidegger, and subsequently poststructuralism, but in the demolition of old Europe after 1917 (with the Russian Revolution, the destruction of the Ottoman Empire, and the consequent reterritorialization of much of the Eastern Hemisphere, of which the Versailles Treaty is the most clearly visible historical manifestation). Key to this theoretical-practical approach is the interpretation of the entry into history as a historical actor of the theory of history itself, in the form of Bolshevism. This cannot, however, be narrativized in terms of any inherited model of the theory of history on the grounds that the entry into history of that theory as the Bolshevik Revolution in effect ruined that theory by arriving at its limit in the very moment when it was supposed to be implemented.

I suggest a renarrativization of the period from the Revolution and the Great War under the rubric *de-imperialization*, which I take to be a global process that has taken place in the Eastern hemisphere since 1917. This process has not reached any proper conclusion, and the term de-imperialization incorporates a notion of modernity as a certain kind of *moving away*, rather than a moving towards the synthesis suggested by the term globalization. The term de-imperialization also avoids the suggestion of a move towards capitalist domination or victory, but rather allows capitalism to appear as one of the components in the field which it loosely outlines. However, the notion of de-imperialization has the advantage of grouping histories which in terms of a narrative of capitalist/communist or empire/colony might otherwise not be imagined in terms of any continuity.

Under this rubric, which can be no further developed here, many tendencies in the thought and scholarship of the arts can appear and be reconfigured—the artist conceived of as a 'transnational' subject (in the new modernist studies) can now appear as an actor in a field viewed from a presumption of internationality on which that very 'subjectivity' and the already ideological preference for the 'subjective' over the world-historical 'objective' process can themselves appear as components in the globally redefined field. The attempts of artists to negotiate time and history now appear in a de-imperializing world in which the very notions of time and history have been set at stake by the Bolsheviks as bearers of those ideas, ideas which therefore are in the process of being contested and written throughout all modes of discourse and all social practices. The nationalist or internationalist postures of individual artists or of national or international coteries can appear in a context of changes in the frameworks of global security which shape their fields of action.

These, then, briefly indicated, are the ambitions of a weak-theoretical periodization that might sit inside and across what we now with impossible looseness consider to be a modernist period. It retains a historicity and a periodizing value in that it attaches itself to the most substantial changes to the international order since the Congress of Vienna (1815), while it specifically avoids a narrativization in terms of social progress, in whatever historicist guise that might appear. While currently much work on modernism makes highly fragmentary reference to the remains of the theory, *as if* to build on a theory of modernity without actually being in possession of any such theory of history, there is scope to develop a structured but nevertheless weak-theoretical account of a modernity which does not date that modernity from any technological, intellectual, or even social-organizational rupture, but from the specific shifts in political geography which have taken place since 1917.

NOTES

1. I draw on the term, but none of the conceptions, given currency by Vattimo and Rovatti in *Weak Thought*. See *Il pensiero debole*, edited by Gianni Vattimo and Pier Aldo Rovatti (Milan: Feltrinelli, 1987).
2. Friedrich Engels, *Selected Writings*, edited and introduced by W. O. Henderson (Harmondsworh: Penguin, 1967), p. 197.
3. I adopt the term 'indiscernible' from Alain Badiou. See Alain Badiou, *L'Etre et l'événement* (Paris: Seuil, 1988), pp. 361–77.
4. Karl Marx and Friedrich Engels, *The German Ideology*, including *Theses on Feuerbach* and *Introduction to the Critique of Political Economy* (Amherst, NY: Prometheus, 1998), p. 53.
5. Karl Marx, *Surveys from Exile. Political Writings: Volume 2*, edited and introduced by David Fernbach (Harmondsworth: Penguin, 1973), p. 149.
6. For one summary of Badiou's shifting position, see Alain Badiou, *L'Hypothèse communiste* (Paris: Lignes, 2009), pp. 179–205.
7. Martin Heidegger, *Basic Writings: from Being and Time (1927) to The Task of Thinking (1964)*, edited and introduced by David Farrell Krell (London and Henley: Routledge and Kegan Paul, 1978), pp. 287–317.
8. Heidegger, *Basic Writings*, p. 287.
9. Heidegger, *Basic Writings*, pp. 290–1.
10. Heidegger, *Basic Writings*, p. 293.
11. Heidegger, *Basic Writings*, p. 294.
12. Heidegger, *Basic Writings*, p. 295.
13. Heidegger, *Basic Writings*, p. 296.
14. Heidegger, *Basic Writings*, pp. 297–8.
15. Heidegger, *Basic Writings*, p. 304.
16. Heidegger, *Basic Writings*, p. 304.
17. Heidegger, *Basic Writings*, p. 315.
18. Heidegger, *Basic Writings*, pp. 315, 317.
19. Walter Benjamin, *Selected Writings: Volume 4. 1938–40*, translated by Edmund Jephcott et al., edited by Howard Eiland and Michael W. Jennings (Cambridge, MA, and London: Harvard University Press, 2003), pp. 251–70.
20. Benjamin, *Selected Writings: Volume 4*, pp. 251–2.
21. 'In permitting the reproduction to reach the recipient in his or her own situation, it actualizes that which is reproduced', Benjamin, *Selected Writings: Volume 4*, p. 254.
22. Benjamin, *Selected Writings: Volume 4*, p. 255.
23. I have in mind also Heidegger's essay 'The Thing', though there is no space to discuss that here. See Martin Heidegger, *Poetry, Language, Thought*, translated and introduced Albert Hofstadter (New York, Hagerstown, MD, San Francisco, and London: Harper and Row, 1975), pp. 163–86.
24. Benjamin, *Selected Writings: Volume 4*, p. 255.

25. Benjamin, *Selected Writings: Volume 4*, p. 255.
26. Heidegger, *Basic Writings*, p. 315.
27. I allude, without following through, to Heidegger's repeated invocation of 'proximity', not least, but not only, in 'The Thing'.
28. We take note, here, of the interdiction of this 'jargon' in Theodor Adorno, *The Jargon of Authenticity*, translated by Knut Tarnowski and Frederic Will (London: Routledge and Kegan Paul, 1973). Adorno identifies a connection between Heideggerian language and Benjaminian 'aura': 'The fact that the words of the jargon sound as if they said something higher than what they mean suggests the term "aura". It is hardly an accident that Benjamin introduced the term at the same moment when, according to his own theory, what he understood by "aura" became impossible to experience,' p. 9.
29. See Michel Henry, *Marx: II. Une Philosphie de l'économie* (Paris: Gallimard, 1976), pp. 189–280; 208.
30. 'Whatever the social form of the production process, it has to be continuous, it must periodically repeat the same phases. A society can no more cease to produce than it can cease to consume. When viewed, therefore, as a connected whole, and in the constant flux of its incessant renewal, every social process of production is at the same time a process of reproduction. The conditions of production are also those of reproduction.' Karl Marx, *Capital: A Critique of Political Economy. Volume 1*, introduced by Ernest Mandel and translated by Ben Fowkes (Harmondsworth; Penguin, 1976), p. 711.
31. Fredric Jameson, *A Singular Modernity: Essay on the Ontology of the Present* (London and New York: Verso, 2002), pp. 31–2.
32. Jameson, *A Singular Modernity*, p. 13.

HORIZONS

5

Gibraltar and Beyond
James Joyce, Ezra Pound, Paul Bowles

Wai Chee Dimock

I would like to begin by exploring the concept of 'network'—to my mind a way to think about forms of movement that require multiple entries, perhaps multiple tangents, without resorting to the concepts of design, intentionality, or genealogy. What I have in mind is a form of connectivity that is occasional, variously mediated, transpiring at a distance and often at a low intensity, and, for that very reason, likely to expand and multiply indefinitely. A 'networked modernism', then, rather than featuring works beginning and ending at some discrete point, takes the form instead of a work in progress, a field still in the making: long-drawn-out, with many participants, many fits and starts, emerging more or less unpredictably, with no necessary direction with no necessary terminus. It is less an event, or even a set of events, than a vector, an outbound orientation, one that says: 'to be continued'. It can be taken in any number of ways, elaborated in any number of ways. Different authors add different legs to it; these legs don't always move in unison, and perhaps that is the point.

What this suggests about literary history is that the existing corpus of any one author is bound to be 'incomplete'—in the sense that it cannot be its own sequel, or its own end point—precisely because it is singular, the work of one pair of hands, and arrested at one particular moment in time. This isn't necessarily a shortcoming, a sign of commission or omission. Rather, it is what we might expect: a condition not only inescapable but in many ways beneficial, a constitutive limit that generates an inverse forward momentum, turning literature into an input-accepting and therefore continually unfolding drama, unsupervised, unforeseeable, a collaboration open to many players. Empty spaces subsequently filled, roads not taken subsequently visited—such reparative doubling and redoubling are the lifelines of this 'networked modernism'. Through these long-distance, not necessarily targeted, though sometimes surprisingly meaningful associations, happening as much by chance as by design, traces of the unactualized past can be carried into the future, and ill-defined shadows can be given alternate outlines.

With that in mind, I'd like to turn to Gibraltar, and to James Joyce, the first of the three-author network that I hope to explore. Gibraltar is, of course, impossible to miss in *Ulysses*. As Richard Brown points out, in quantitative terms roughly 'a fifth to a quarter' of the 'Penelope' episode is material set in Gibraltar or revolving around Gibraltar, making this the novel's significant 'other' locale.[1] It is strange that, in a novel so focused on Dublin and so circumscribed by Dublin, the last chapter should have this conspicuous foray, vaulting to a place so obviously outside that orbit. Robert Martin Adams shows that Joyce had done his research with his usual thoroughness, reading up on details of streets and names of shops in the *Gibraltar Directory*, just as he had done with *Thom's Dublin Directory*.[2] He also drew heavily on Henry Field's *Gibraltar*, published in 1888, and repeated some of its errors, including its tendency to make too much of a good thing. Field emphasizes, for instance, the magnificent views and great distances that one can see from Gibraltar. An officer on duty can 'with his field-glasses, sweep the whole horizon, north and south, from the Sierra Nevada in Spain, to the long chain of the Atlas Mountains in Africa'.[3] Joyce repeats this error by equipping Molly with a borrowed spyglass, so that she too 'could see over to Morocco almost the bay of Tangier white and the Atlas mountain with snow on it'.[4] As Don Gifford drily observes, 'On a clear day, Molly could easily see Morocco, but Tangiers, 35 miles through the straits to the southwest, would be masked by headlands, and the snowcapped Saharan Atlas Mountains in Algeria, 375 miles to the southeast, are clearly out of range.'[5]

Joyce's account of Gibraltar is not only heavily mediated, dependent on the prior writing of others, but it is also highly idealized, giving us a Gibraltar that is as much a concept as it is a physical locality. This idealization no doubt has something to do with Joyce's desire, as Andrew Gibson and others have argued, to present Gibraltar as a utopia of sorts: open, vibrant, multi-ethnic, with warring populations elsewhere coexisting more or less in peace here.[6] Molly tells us about 'the Spanish girls laughing in their shawls and their tall combs and the auctions in the morning the Greeks and the jews and the Arabs and the devil knows who else from all the ends of Europe'.[7] Such a place would indeed be a significant alternative to the insular world of Dublin. And, by aligning Gibraltar with the Atlas Mountains, Joyce also seems to be aligning it implicitly with Calypso, daughter of Atlas, the nymph who, true to the etymology of her name (from καλύπτω, meaning 'to cover', 'to conceal', 'to hide'), keeps Odysseus spirited away for seven years on her island, Ogygia. A networked modernism here is clearly moving east, away from the contentious modernity of twentieth-century Ireland and into a mythic Mediterranean, a Homeric landscape defined by the epic form rather than by the disgraced spectacle of Charles Stewart Parnell, or the economic reification and postcolonial subalternity that Fredric Jameson and Enda Duffy associate with the city of Dublin.[8] That eastward movement would have the effect of idealizing Gibraltar as well, extracting it from the ongoing reality of its militarization, which would otherwise have been hard to overlook in that garrison town.

And yet Joyce is anything but ignorant of militarization and the shadow it casts. As several critics have pointed out, in 1921 he had made a point of asking Frank Budgen to get him a book on the sieges of Gibraltar.[9] What he did with that knowledge, however, is not so simple. I would argue that this knowledge is in fact muted and refracted, into something like a Calypso effect, a 'veil of ignorance' not unlike the hypothetical one proposed by John Rawls,[10] a suspending of any information deemed too narrowly determining, too much weighted toward one particular outcome. What emerges here instead is a deliberately wide-open, off-focus image of a world that would otherwise have been sharply and starkly marred by conflict.

I suggest that this Calypso effect is an important part of modernist aesthetics, and that its deployment with various degrees of insistence and at various distances from its subject is one of the most interesting differential axes within a fraught compositional field. With Fredric Jameson, we could call it a 'crisis of detail', a process by which salience and blurriness go hand in hand, by which the supera-bundance of cascading minutiae is inseparable from its dissolution.[11] I will have more to say about this in the context of other authors, but staying with *Ulysses* for the moment, I want to look at one particular passage from 'Penelope', in which 'the Atlas mountain' is embedded in a sensory and mnemonic overload:

> I went up windmill hill to the flats that Sunday morning with Captain Rubios that was dead spyglass like the sentry had he said hed have one or two from on board I wore that frock from the B Marche Paris and the coral necklace the straits shining I could see over to Morocco almost the bay of Tangier white and the Atlas mountain with snow on it and the straits like a river so clear Harry Molly Darling I was thinking of him on the sea all the time after at mass when my petticoat began to slip down at the elevation weeks and weeks I kept the handkerchief under my pillow for the smell of him there was no decent perfume to be got in that Gibraltar only that cheap peau despagne that faded and left a stink on you more than anything else I wanted to give him a memento he gave me that clumsy Claddagh ring for luck that I gave Gardner going to South Africa where those Boers killed him with their war and fever but they were well beaten all the same.[12]

Gibraltar does seem to be the place where the entire world converges. Already we're seeing a global consumer culture: the Paris department store, the hope for better perfumes imported from abroad. Equally global are the footprints of colonialism: its far-flung bases, its constant deployment of troops, its significant casualties. And not just British colonialism but also French, with Morocco in plain view just across the Strait. This is the moment when we have a glimpse of the hard facts of geopol-itics. But it is just a glimpse, fleeting, quickly suspended, because it happens to be mediated and circumscribed by the consciousness of Molly, who isn't thinking about geopolitics at all, but about the various men from various points in her life: Harry Mulvey, her first love, the one who gave her the Claddagh ring, now lost; Captain Gardner, who received the ring from her and was then killed in the Boer War; Captain Rubios, her beau for the occasion who loaned her the spyglass, who is now also dead; and of course, Leopold Bloom, thankfully still alive, but mixed up with all the others.

This tangle of men, whose distance from one another is deliberately not specified, not measured with any numerical precision, collapses space and time into the same undulating fabric, putting events both large and small on the same plane, magnify-ing some and diminishing others, in an all-encompassing scalar indeterminacy, amorphous and chimerical. It's not just that the Boer War is now roughly the same size as the Claddagh ring, but the concentrated attention given to this ring—the initial gift of it, and the death of its final bearer—creates a significant degree of foreshortening, so much so that everything between those two points, Gibraltar and South Africa, is either emptied out or converted into a kind of atmospheric blur. Morocco, in this off-focus mapping, is simply the place on the other side of the Strait of Gibraltar. It isn't exactly depopulated, but it is relieved of much of the historical data that usually comes with human populations.

Of course, Molly wouldn't be the one to tell us that there was a long and fraught history between North Africa and Spain, that the word 'Moor' still conjured up unquiet spectres long after the Reconquista of 1492. And, even though she herself is probably of Jewish descent from her mother Lunita Laredo (as Phillip Herring, Marilyn Reizbaum, and others have argued),[13] she probably wouldn't know that the 1712 Treaty of Utrecht, by which Spain formally ceded Gibraltar to Britain, carried an explicit clause prohibiting Jews as well as Arabs from settling in the city. Leopold Bloom, of course, in the 'Cyclops' episode, has famously lamented the fate of Jews: 'Plundered. Insulted. Persecuted.... Sold by auction in Morocco like slaves or cattle',[14] but since Molly is spending time with Blazes Boylan at just that moment, she isn't on hand to hear that remark. And, since the present for her is the Dublin of 1904, and she is thinking back to her girlhood in Gibraltar in 1884–5, the 1905 Tangier Crisis and the 1911 Agadir Crisis are both in the future, out of reach for her, as well as the fact that, in 1912, the Treaty of Fez would effectively divide Morocco into a French and a Spanish protectorate. She wouldn't know about any of these things. But Joyce most certainly would.

In fact, not only had he done his research on the sieges of Gibraltar, he was also exceptionally well informed about the long background to this faith-torn environment. The Protestant/Catholic divide, second nature to any Irish author, would not be the only fault line here. Joyce was fully aware of the indelible, incendiary presence of another religion. When he went on to write *Finnegans Wake*, Islam would be there, front and centre: with the Koran serving as one of the overlapping templates for the new novel. James Atherton writes: 'Joyce was probably talking about himself when he made his Shaun say of his Shem: "I have his quoram of images all on my retinue, Mohammadhawn Mike" (443.1). On one level of meaning this can be taking as saying that Joyce, who is jokingly calling himself a Mohammedan Irishman – and a homadhaun, which is Irish for a lout – has all the images from the Koran on his retina. This last word is also telling us that the first European translation of the Koran was a Latin version by an Englishman, "Robert of Retina"—a fact which Joyce may have learned from Hughes's *History of Islam*...where the Koran is always given its Arabic spelling, *Qur-an*.'[15]

Joyce's knowledge of Islam would put all of us to shame. Granted, his knowledge might not have been quite as extensive when he was writing *Ulysses*, but given the level of microscopic detail characteristic of all of his readings, I think we can say that the atmospheric haze in 'Penelope' is probably deliberate, the result of a narration that is meant to relieve the world of all the historical data that would otherwise have been too incapacitating. When Molly absentmindedly mentions the 'Greeks and the Jews and the Arabs' and 'those handsome Moors all in white and turbans like kings asking you to sit down in their bit of a shop',[16] what Joyce is creating is effectively a veil, replacing flood-lit information with a barely illuminated fuzzy sketch. I've been calling this a Calypso effect; it is very much a utopian effect, one that sacrifices sharpness of resolution in order to preserve the uncrystallized condition of possibility just prior to it. This is what Joyce wants in this particular moment and what, I would argue, serves as a productively underdeveloped and meant-to-be-continued modernist signature.

Since fuzziness signifies aspiration as well as a self-imposed limit, I think this is also the moment when it makes sense to speak of supplementarity as a non-intentional effect of networking among authors. The two candidates I have in mind are Ezra Pound and Paul Bowles. With the former, the tie to Joyce is, of course, widely known and thoroughly documented; with the latter, much less so. I would like to make a case for each of these as a low-grade, low-threshold, but nonetheless non-trivial connection, each taking up where Joyce leaves off, adding not only specificity but also new contextual pressure to the eastward and south-ward trajectory that he is just beginning to gesture toward.

With Pound, there might even be some degree of intentionality at play. In fact, Joyce and Gibraltar would be strangely intertwined for him twenty years down the road—in 1945—probably the darkest moment in his life. In Canto 74, the first of the *Pisan Cantos*, while talking about his first visit to Spain in 1898 (during which he had travelled to Granada with his aunt and also paid a visit to Morocco), Pound abruptly brings both Joyce and Gibraltar into the picture:

> And thence to Al Hambra, the lion court and el
>   mirador de la reina Lindaraja
> orient reaching to Tangier, the cliffs the villa of Perdicaris
> Rais Uli, periplum
> Mr Joyce also preoccupied with Gibraltar
>   And the pillars of Hercules[17]

The word that leaps out at me here is a word that ordinarily connotes secondari-ness, but here priority: 'also'—'Mr Joyce also preoccupied with Gibraltar'. Pound has company, it seems. As far as writing about Gibraltar is concerned, Joyce was there first. But, as the laid-backness of 'also' suggests, Joyce's priority is not much of a concern here, and we will soon see why. Whereas Joyce's Gibraltar is heavily Spanish, with hardly any mention of Islam, this is not the case with Pound. His nodes and coordinates are entirely different.

Pound's Gibraltar is linked to two geographical compass points: on the one hand, the Alhambra in Granada, and, on the other hand, the Villa of Perdicaris in Tangier. Granada was the last Moorish stronghold to fall to Ferdinand and Isabella in 1492, shortly after which both Jews and Arabs were banished from the city. But Pound's reference is not to that fateful year. Rather, it is to an earlier time, before the Reconquista, when the great Islamic cities, Granada and Cordoba, were cities of unsurpassed beauty and refinement. The Court of Lions (**Fig. 5.1**) and

Figure 5.1. J. Laurent, 'Granada. El Patio de los Leones desde la Sala de los Escudos (Alhambra)' (*c*.1860–80). Courtesy of Library of Congress.

el mirador de la reina Lindaraja (**Fig. 5.2**), in particular, are enduring testimonies to the magnificence of that period. This medieval Islam would have been familiar to Pound, in part through his lifelong dedication to the work of Guido Cavalcanti, whose sonnets he translated in 1912, and who, in 1931, would be the subject of

Figure 5.2. J. Laurent. 'Granada. Interior de Generalife (Alhambra)' (*c.*1860–80). Courtesy of Library of Congress.

one of the three radio operas he wrote, commissioned by the BBC. In his essay on Cavalcanti, Pound specifically cites the inspiration from two Islamic philosophers, Avicenna and Averroes, referred to here by their Arabic names, Ibn Sina and Ibn Rachd:

> From this poem and from passages elsewhere it would seem that Guido had derived certain notions from the Aristotelian commentators, the *'filosofica famiglia,'* Ibn Sina, for the *spiriti, spiriti* of the eyes, of the senses; Ibn Rachd, *che il gran comento feo,* for the demand for intelligence on the part of the recipients.[18]

This is what Islam means to Pound: intellectual labour and intellectual dedication, a symbol of enlightened reason that Cavalcanti embraced in the thirteenth century, and that Pound himself would love to have available to himself in the twentieth, especially now that he was locked up at the American Disciplinary Training Center at Pisa, awaiting trial for his pro-Fascist radio broadcasts. It is fair to say, then, that, for Pound, the outbound trajectory that leads from Gibraltar is largely a temporal trajectory, one that goes backward to various glorified and idealized locales in the past. This is the 'beyond' that he yearns for: Spain under Islam, China under Confucius, the seven-walled city of Dioce, the Aegean Sea of Homer—these are the receded temporal and spatial coordinates that offer him hope and solace.

Of course, even in Canto 74, there is another trajectory as well, one that goes in the other direction, heading south from Gibraltar, ending up in Tangier. In Tangier, it finds itself face to face with this character, Mulai Ahmed el Raisuni (**Fig. 5.3**), a Berber bandit who kidnapped Ion Perdicaris and his nephew Cromwell Varley to collect $80,000 ransom. For Pound, this is a quintessential twentieth-century story, and Morocco, as the setting for that story, is the emblem of a century that is synonymous with greed, chaos, and violence, a century more destructive and inhospitable than any other on record.

All of which is to suggest that Gibraltar and what lies beyond it are as heavily mediated and refracted for Pound as for Joyce. If anything, the Calypso effect is even more powerful here, because it is filtered, not through the erotic life of one woman but through the cumulative and fantasized splendour of the whole of human civilization. Against that composite utopia, modern Morocco must look very dark indeed.

Could there be a Morocco present on its own terms, not refracted to stand for something else or to stand against something else? In conclusion, and as a provisional resting place, I would like to turn very briefly to Paul Bowles's *The Spider's House.* Morocco is front and centre in this novel; there is no other contrasting frame superimposed upon it. But it remains just as mediated as the others, as subject to the constraints of partial illumination, if only because this North African Islamic nation, seen through the eyes of an American, is itself a veil, a Calypso effect deployed not at a distance, but at the closest possible range. The scene that unfolds is this: a boy takes off his shoes and wades into the pool to fish out a large, drowning insect. He holds the insect in his hand. Then the insect flies away. And the boy seems satisfied. One of the spectators, Stenham, turns to his companion, Polly, and says:

Figure 5.3. Rosita Forbes, 'El Raisuni, outside the author's tent at Tazrut' in *El Raisuni: The Sultan of the Mountains, his life story as told to Rosita Forbes* (London: Thornton Butterworth, 1924), facing p. 68. Rosita Forbes © 1924. Courtesy of Cambridge University Library.

'Now, that was a strange bit of behavior. The boy made a special trip into the water just to pull out some kind of insect.'

'Well, he's kind-hearted.'

'I know, but they're not. That's the whole point. In all my time here I've never seen anyone do a thing like that.'

He looked at the boy's round face, heavy, regular features, and curly black hair.

'He could be a Sicilian, or a Greek,' he said as if to himself. 'If he's not a Moroccan, there's nothing surprising about his deed. But if he is, then I give up. Moroccans just don't do things like that.'[19]

The young boy is in fact Moroccan. Why is he behaving in this particular way? Is he as un-Moroccan as Stenham says he is? We'll never know. We'll never know—for the simple reason that, even though Stenham is Arab-speaking and knowledgeable about North Africa, its inhabitants are anything but transparent to him. Instead, their opaqueness is, if anything, even more intractable and bewildering up close. What is 'beyond' Gibraltar isn't a place, a reachable or legible destination. It is the blur that greets us when we get there, a blur that tells us that there is more, a great deal more, to follow.

NOTES

1. Richard Brown, 'Molly's Gibraltar: The Other Location in Joyce's *Ulysses*', in *A Companion to James Joyce*, edited by Richard Brown (Oxford: Blackwell, 2008), pp. 157–73; 158.

2. Robert Martin Adams, *Surface and Symbol: The Consistency of James Joyce's Ulysses* (New York: Oxford University Press, 1962), pp. 231–3.

3. Henry M. Field, *Gibraltar* (New York: Scribner's, 1888), quoted in Brown, 'Molly's Gibraltar', p. 166.

4. James Joyce, *Ulysses*, edited by Hans Walter Gabler, Wolfhard Steppe, and Claus Melchior (New York: Vintage, 1986), 18.859–60.

5. Don Gifford and Robert J. Seidman, *Notes for Joyce: An Annotation of James Joyce's Ulysses* (New York: Dutton, 1974), p. 509.

6. Andrew Gibson, *Joyce's Revenge: History, Politics, and Aesthetics in Joyce's Ulysses* (Oxford: Oxford University Press, 2002).

7. Joyce, *Ulysses*, 18.1586–9.

8. Michael Seidel, *Epic Geography* (Princeton, NJ: Princeton University Press, 1976); Fredric Jameson, '*Ulysses* in History', in *James Joyce and Modern Literature*, edited by W. J. McCormack and Alistair Stead (London: Routledge and Kegan Paul, 1982), pp. 126–41; Enda Duffy, *The Subaltern Ulysses* (Minneapolis, MN: University of Minnesota Press, 1994).

9. James Joyce to Frank Budgen, 16 August 1921, in *Letters of James Joyce*, edited by Stuart Gilbert and Richard Ellmann, 3 vols. (London: Faber, 1957–66), vol. 1, p. 169.

10. John Rawls, *A Theory of Justice* (Cambridge, MA: Harvard University Press, 1971).

11. Fredric Jameson, '*Ulysses* in History', pp. 126–41.

12. Joyce, *Ulysses*, 18.855–68.

13. Phillip Herring, *Joyce's Uncertainty Principle* (Princeton, NJ: Princeton University Press, 1987), pp. 117–40; Marilyn Reizbaum, *James Joyce's Judaic Others* (Stanford, CA: Stanford University Press, 1999), pp. 130–2.

14. Joyce, *Ulysses*, 12.1470–2.

15. James Atherton, *The Books at the Wake* (Mamaroneck, NY: Paul P. Appel, 1974), pp. 201–17.

16. Joyce, *Ulysses*, 18.1593–4.

17. Ezra Pound, *Pisan Cantos*, edited by Richard Sieburth (New York: New Directions, 2003), 74.785–90.

18. Ezra Pound, 'Cavalcanti', in *Literary Essays of Ezra Pound*, edited by T. S. Eliot (New York: New Directions, 1934), pp. 149–200; 158.

19. Paul Bowles, *The Spider's House* (New York: Random House, 1955), p. 251.

6

Restless Modernisms
D. H. Lawrence Caught in the Shadow of Gramsci

Robert J. C. Young

TAORMINA

D. H. Lawrence just can't sit still. In that sense he is, it could be said, constitutively modern, driven by modernity's impatience with stasis. In Picinisco, Lazio, he writes: 'My feet itch, and a seat burns my posterior if I sit too long. What ails me I don't know, but it's on and on.'[1] And so too the constitutional restlessness that marks the opening of *Sea and Sardinia*:

> Comes over one an absolute necessity to move. And what is more, to move in some particular direction. A double necessity then: to get on the move, and to know whither.
> Why can't one sit still? Here in Sicily it is so pleasant.[2]

Sicily may be agreeable, but Mount Etna, which towers unmoving over him, is, we are told, a beautiful torturer. So Lawrence must flee from her.

> Where then? Spain or Sardinia, Spain or Sardinia. Sardinia, which is like nowhere. Sardinia, which has no history, no date, no race, no offering. Let it be Sardinia. They say neither Romans nor Phoenicians, Greeks or Arabs ever subdued Sardinia. It lies outside; outside the circuit of civilisation....Sure enough, it is Italian now, with its railways and its motor-omnibuses. But there is an uncaptured Sardinia still. It lies within the net of this European civilisation, but it isn't landed yet.[3]

So, Sardinia then. Somewhere that is nowhere, a wild beast that remains at large un-netted, uncaptured, uncaught, a blank on the map, with no history, date, or race, or so he says. Outside the circuit of modern, degenerate European civilization that turns Lawrence into a fidgety fugitive, flitting away from 'these maddening, exasperating, impossible Sicilians, who never knew what truth was and have long lost all notion of what a human being is....*Andiamo!*'[4]

Although Lawrence seems to know next to nothing about Sardinia, pronouncing that it has no culture or history, he nevertheless subscribes unquestioningly to the orientalist tradition of travel writing about Sardinia, particularly its contemporary realization in the romantic fiction of Grazia Deledda, which portrays it as remote and untouched, populated by fiercely independent peasants and macho lawless bandits, a 'primitive populace' who still live 'the old, blind life of instinct', of 'savage individualism':

An island of rigid conventions, the rigid conventions of barbarism, and at the same time the fierce violence of the instinctive passions. A savage tradition of chastity, with a savage lust of the flesh. A barbaric overlordship of the gentry, with a fierce indomitableness of the servile classes. A lack of public opinion, a lack of belonging to any other part of the world, a lack of mental awakening, which makes inland Sardinia almost as savage as Benin.[5]

The civilization which has produced him and which Lawrence, faithful to a line of Romantics going back to Rousseau and Wordsworth, Victorians such as Robert Louis Stevenson or Paul Gauguin, or later modernists such as Bronislaw Malinowski or Alejo Carpentier, then seeks to escape, keeps him permanently on the move, trying to translate himself into something he is not, something that he has lost, left behind, a homosocial longing (Lawrence's favourite words in *Sea and Sardinia* are 'manly' and 'naked') for something fixed, steadfast, primeval, and above all unselfconscious. In Sardinia, he hopes to land that uncaptured savage primitivism that he seeks and with which he identifies. He will be disappointed, of course, and to a certain degree Lawrence himself drapes his hopeless pursuit of escape from his own excruciating self-consciousness within a comic self-mockery. But what if instead Sardinia were to translate the literary modernist out of his insatiable quest into the realm of the political? Lawrence translates Sardinia according to the needs of his own restless desires. What if Sardinia were to look at Lawrence and translate him instead?

Sea and Sardinia, seeing Sardinia, an account of a ten-day trip that Lawrence and Frieda took in early 1921, 'one of the most delightful of Lawrence's books' according to his biographer Mark Kinkead-Weekes, was written in the six weeks following his return to Taormina in Sicily.[6] For all of the five days actually spent in Sardinia, from January 6 to 10, they kept continually on the move, never staying more than a night anywhere, journeying on trains, boats, buses. The Lawrences went to Sardinia because the lease was expiring on their house and they had thought of moving on. There were too many foreigners like them in Sicily, particularly in Taormina, while Lawrence also found the natives there too culturally mixed or even 'over-cultured' for his taste.[7] Before he came to its final title, Lawrence thought of calling the book 'Sketches of Sardinia', 'Sardinian Snaps', or even 'Sardinian Films', and this is how it is conceived: a montage of incidents, separated by a line—a kind of frame—drawn in the middle of the page, written as if in diary form, switching randomly between a continuous present and past tense, with verbs propelling the continual movement by being placed subjectless at the start of the sentence, beginning with the opening line, 'Comes over one...'. 'Sardinian Snaps' would perhaps have been the most accurate title, for it would have described not only Lawrence's sequences of distance and close-up representations snapped while they were on the move, but also the way in which the book is structured according to a series of Lawrentian rages, which leads him habitually to snap at his challenging or disrespectful interlocutors. The Sardinian is a romantic figure, just so long as the subaltern does not speak, and reveal him or herself as annoying, crass, pretentious, irritating, rapacious, surly, insolent—or politicized or an intellectual. Like children, primitives should be seen and not heard, and, above all, not answer back.

CAGLIARI

Arrive the Lawrences at the southern port of Cagliari. He is immediately satisfied by its apparent defiance of modernity: 'Strange, stony Cagliari....Our mechanical age tries to override it. But it does not succeed. In the end the strange, sinister spirit of place...will smash our mechanical oneness into smithereens, and all that we think the real thing will go off with a pop, and we shall be left staring.'[8] Things go off pop fairly quickly and soon Frieda is left staring. It is carnival time, and Lawrence and Frieda ('the queen-bee' or simply the 'q-b'), terrified of the maskers, hasten down the street only to run up against a man dressed up as a peasant woman: 'the q-b hovers in the distance, half-fascinated, and watches'.[9] They join the evening *passeggiata*, or *passillada* as it is locally known,[10] on the Via Roma by the sea, where carriages 'spank along' and the maskers 'dance and prance'. They pass men seated at the cafes whose insouciance immediately suggests to Lawrence that they are 'without the modern self-consciousness'.[11] Then he gets really excited: 'And I see my first peasant in costume.' He is apparently a very different thing from the man dressed up in a woman's peasant costume. The peasant's traditional dress involves 'a short kilt or frill...a band of which goes between the legs, between the full, loose drawers of coarse linen'. 'How handsome he is,' exclaims Lawrence 'and so beautifully male!',[12] adding:

> How fascinating it is, after the soft Italians, to see these limbs in their close knee-breeches, so definite, so manly, with the old fierceness in them still. One realises, with horror, that the race of men is almost extinct in Europe. Only Christ-like heroes and woman-worshipping Don Juans, and rabid equality-mongrels. The last sparks are dying out in Sardinia and Spain. Nothing left but the herd-proletariat and the herd-equality mongrelism, and the wistful poisonous self-sacrificial cultured soul. How detestable.

> But that curious, flashing, black-and-white costume! I seem to have known it before: to have worn it even: to have dreamed it. To have dreamed it: to have had actual contact with it. It belongs in some way to something in me—to my past, perhaps. I don't know. But the uneasy sense of blood-familiarity haunts me. I *know* I have known it before.[13]

Our English Nietzsche, abhorring the mixed-race mongrels of modernity, calls up a haunting *revenant* from elsewhere, from the deep past of blood consciousness. The traditionally dressed Sardinian peasant takes him back to his own primal being. And he experiences all this, within a few hours of landing on the island.

> One sees a few fascinating faces in Cagliari: those great, dark unlighted eyes....here one sees eyes of soft blank darkness, all velvet, with no imp looking out of them. And they strike a stranger, older note: before the soul became self-conscious: before the mentality of Greece appeared in the world. Remote, always remote, as if the intelligence lay deep within the cave, and never came forward. One searches into the gloom for one second, while the glance lasts. But without being able to penetrate to the reality. It recedes, like some unknown creature deeper into its lair. There *is* a creature, dark and potent. But what?[14]

The mysterious eyes of the Sardinian native, which do not reflect the light self-consciously, bearing an unenlightened pre-Hellenic intelligence deep within Plato's cave of illusion, manifest a dark and potent creature untouched by civilization. So Lawrence reflects as he stares into the eyes of a Cagliari face. Who might this dark and potent creature have been? Perhaps it was the famous Marxist economist Piero Sraffa, who would become professor of economics at the University of Cagliari just a few years later in 1926 before he went directly to King's College, Cambridge, and then on to Trinity. What if the instinctual dumb native actually happened to be one of the greatest intellectuals of the twentieth century?

SORGONO

January 8. Arrive the Lawrences in Sorgono, high in the interior, 'nestling beautifully among the wooded slopes in front. Oh magic little town. Ah, you terminus and gan-glion of island roads, we hope in you for a pleasant inn and happy company. Perhaps we will stay a day or two at Sorgono.' They almost seem to have come to a little town in Hardy's Wessex, Lawrence enthuses. But as always, his high hopes translate into a very different reality: in a Joycean trope, reminiscent of the continual descents into bathos in *A Portrait of the Artist as a Young Man,* the sublimity that Lawrence conjures up when the village lies at an aesthetic distance, is translated when he gets close up into the bathos of sordid poverty. The Albergo d'Italia, which his Baedeker recommends, is now no more. Instead, he is taken to a building where 'labelled in huge letters: RISTORAͶTE RISVEGLIO: the letter N being printed backwards. *Risveglio* if you please: which means waking up, or rousing, like the word *reveille*.'[15] 'If you please': Lawrence is fond of this gossipy aside with which English people put down the pre-tensions of others, usually in terms of a social pretension that is seen as going beyond its proper class station, or here used alternatively where he is himself not treated with the proper respect for his class by the natives.[16] So too, seeing a family taking drinks while the nurse sits separately down the table away from them, he writes approvingly of the 'invisible salt',[17] that is, the class distinction that is still being upheld.

But there is nothing for it. There is nowhere else to stay, so they will have to submit.

> Risveglio or nothing. In we go. We pass into a big, dreary bar....At length appears mine host, a youngish fellow of the esquimo type, but rather bigger, in a dreary black suit and a cutaway waistcoat suggesting a dinner-waistcoat, and innumerable wine-stains on his shirt front. I instantly hated him for the filthy appearance he made.[18]

The esquimo type, as Lawrence likes to characterize 'one brand of Sardinian',[19] shows them to their filthy room and leaves. '"Dirty, disgusting swine!" said I, and I was in a rage.'[20] The Lawrences stay in a rage for most of their short stay in Sorgono: 'A dreary hole! A cold, hopeless, lifeless, Saturday afternoon-weary vil-lage, rather sordid, with nothing to say for itself. No real shops at all.'[21] The pov-erty and backwardness of 'this vile village' appals him. It is 'weary-dreary'. They wander into a little lane and to their horror find themselves 'in the thick of a public lavatory'.[22] When he encounters real primitivism, Lawrence is not amused. Despite seeing a Wordsworthian shepherd who had been standing in the distance like a stone utterly motionless, Lawrence stays in a foul rage. Even Frieda remonstrates with him. Why is he so angry with the Sardinians? Is it simply because they are the wrong sort of primitive? Poor instead of manly, dark and potent?

> But no, my rage is black, black, black. . . . I cursed the degenerate aborigines, the dirty-breasted host who *dared* to keep such an inn, the sordid villagers who had the baseness to squat their beastly human nastiness in this upland valley.[23]

As he leaves, he remonstrates angrily with the innkeeper, finally demanding 'Why do you have the impudence to take in travellers? What does it mean, that this is an inn? What, say, what does it mean? Say then—what does it mean? What does it mean, your Ristorante Risveglio, written so large?'[24]

Lawrence's Italian is good, but his disinterest in Italian politics—'it always makes me sick to hear people chewing over newspaper pulp'[25]—means that he misses the signs of everyday politics around him. The backwards printed N gives the hotel name a Russian look, as if a Cyrillic И. '*Risveglio* if you please: which means waking up, or rousing', Lawrence has informed us. But *Risveglio* was also the name of Sardinia's proletarian weekly, *Il Risveglio dell'Isola* ('Island Awakening'), which had been published from Cagliari since before the war.[26] At the heart of the primitive, Lawrence has run into a nest of surly Sardinian socialists. In fact, to his dismay, he will keep encountering 'a downright, smack-out belief in Socialism'[27] wherever he goes. He pays his bill in disgust, 'picks up every farthing of the change', leaves no tip, makes tea for his thermos and his way out of the Risveglio, his knapsack over his shoulder:

> to the wider space where the bus stands: I hope they haven't the impudence to call it a Piazza.
>
> 'Is this the Nuoro bus?', I ask of a bunch of urchins.
>
> And even they begin to jeer.[28]

Lawrence's fury and his unbearable self-consciousness always go together. They keep him on the move. Until this moment, in fact it has been Lawrence who has been jeering at the pretensions of the natives. Call this an inn! Call this a Piazza? Their insolence is something that he himself has created.

When the restless Lawrence goes to Sardinia in search of the primitive as a cure for his own existential self-consciousness, for the burden of modernity, he carries that burden on his back in the form of a knapsack, while Frieda carries the 'kitchenino' which contains their machines of modernity, a Primus stove and thermos flask.[29] Some natives are suitably amazed when they see the steaming liquid pouring from the thermos as if by magic,[30] but it also makes a spectacle of them whereby the reaction of others staring at him throws Lawrence into paroxysms of rage and self-consciousness.

> Be it remembered that I have on my back the brown knapsack, and the q-b carries the kitchenino. This is enough to make a travelling menagerie of us. If I had my shirt sticking out behind, and if the q-b had happened merely to catch up the table-cloth and wrap it round her as she came out, all well and good. But a big brown knapsack! And a basket with thermos flask etc! No, one could not expect such a thing to pass in a southern capital.[31]

Everywhere he goes, the natives seem to mock the irascible red-haired Lawrence in an actual or metaphorical carnivalesque inversion of authority, observing the observer. The problem with these Sardinian subalterns is that they speak, and even taunt their English and German betters, leaving Lawrence wriggling in embarrassment, furious, wounded, spiteful, unbearably self-conscious. David Ellis and Howard Mills have written of Lawrence's 'sensitivity to what others would make of him' in *Sea and Sardinia*. He is always seeing himself through the imagined hostile gaze of others: 'The knapsack', they go on, 'continues to figure in the book like some kind of physical deformity, drawing attention to the narrator and making him feel that he is always disappointing other people's expectations of how he should travel.'[32]

With the conspicuous knapsack on his back, Lawrence walks through Sardinia looking like a hunchback. Curiously this turns him into a ghostly revenant resembling a local inhabitant of Sorgono who had left some years before his visit. Had he passed by twenty-five years earlier, Lawrence might well have encountered a young boy, with thick curly hair and blue eyes, rather short for his age with a large hump on his back—a *gobbo*, a hunchback child whom Lawrence would no doubt have instantly characterized as one of the 'degenerate aborigines' who lived in that vile town. The boy's name: Antonio Gramsci. Sorgono was the village where the Gramsci family spent their happiest years (1892–8), for at that time their father had a job there as a registrar. It was also at Sorgono that Gramsci the boy first showed the signs of developing Pott's disease, a form of extrapulmonary tuberculosis that affects the spine, which left him humpbacked like the hunchback of Notre Dame. As the disease developed, he too developed an excruciating self-consciousness, not existential as in the case of Lawrence but because of his physical condition:

> For a very long time, I have believed it was absolutely, fatally impossible that I should ever be loved.... When I was a ten-year-old boy I began to feel this way about my own parents. My physical condition was so feeble, I was forced to make so many sacrifices, that I became convinced I was a burden, an intruder in my own family.[33]

In Sorgono, the Gramscis were not poor, by village standards. But in 1898, when Gramsci was seven, they suffered a Dickensian reversal of fortune: having supported a losing candidate in an election, Gramsci's father was then accused of embezzlement and sent to prison for five years. Giuseppina Gramsci, with her seven children, was left penniless, and had to return to their family village of Ghilarza, some twenty-five miles to the west. There Gramsci went to primary school, but at the age of twelve, despite getting top marks, he had to give up his education since there was no money to send him to secondary school. At this point, any similarity with Lawrence, a miner's son from Eastwood, Nottinghamshire, ceases: when he completed Primary School, Lawrence won a County Council scholarship to Nottingham High School. Gramsci, on the other hand, went immediately to work, for ten hours a day, seven days a week, lugging folios at the local Land Registry. His pay: nine lire a month. Years later he wrote:

> What saved me from becoming a complete stuffed shirt? An instinct of rebellion, that from a child I had against the rich, because I was unable to continue my studies, I who had scored a 10 in all my elementary school subjects, while the sons of the butcher, the chemist, the clothing store merchant, could.[34]

A hunchback already struggling at the fringes of society, one of the *emarginazione* surviving, as he later wrote, by hiding 'behind a mask of hardness or an ironic smile', the experience of being taken out of school when he was top of the class because he was too poor to continue left Gramsci embittered, more isolated than ever.[35] It sowed the seeds of political rebelliousness that took him in the opposite direction to Lawrence. Gramsci's poverty in Ghilarza, however, was to be surpassed by the deprivations that he suffered later when he moved to Cagliari with his brother.

Let's rerun the Lawrences' arrival in Cagliari, putting the English novelist in proximity with the Sardinian politician. They climb the hill and survey the city from the vantage point of the Citadella. 'We go down the steep streets, smelly, dark, dank and very cold.... People live in one room. Men are combing their hair or fastening their collars in the doorways.'[36] Had they turned right on their descent to the Corso Vittorio Emanuele rather than retreated to the Viale Regina Margherita where their hotel, the Scala di Ferro, was (and still is), they would have come to the street where Antonio Gramsci lived in 1909, and at the time of Lawrence's visit still the home of Gennaro Gramsci, Gramsci's elder brother, a militant socialist who had returned to Cagliari after the war to run a consumer cooperative.[37] While he looked for primitive peasants lost in time, paradoxically asserting their fierce individuality, according to Lawrence, by wearing the uniform black-and-white peasant dress, one of those ordinary natives that he saw walking the *passillada* that January evening could well have been Gramsci's elder brother.

Gramsci himself, after several years out of school, went on to study at the Liceo Dettòri in Cagliari, from 1908 to 1911, living at first with his brother at no 24, Via Principe Amedeo, not more than a hundred metres from Lawrences' hotel on the Viale Regina Margherita. The two brothers survived on Gennaro's salary of 100 lire per month. They had so little money Gramsci had only one set of clothes, lived on one meal a day, and ended his third year at the lycée in a state of severe malnutrition.[38] In January 1921, when the Lawrences chance upon the market during their walk around Cagliari, Frieda exclaims that she must come to live there, for everything is so cheap. Ham is only thirty-five lire a kilo![39]

LIRAS LIRAS LIRAS

Lawrence often fulminates against contemporary materialism that has ruined Italy: 'Liras—liras—liras—nothing else. Romantic, poetic, cypress-and-orange tree Italy is gone. Remains an Italy smothered in the filthy smother of innumerable lira notes: ragged, unsavoury paper money so thick upon the air one breathes it like some greasy fog.'[40] Yet Lawrence himself also seems obsessed with money. He tells us the price of everything, not just in the market. Every ticket (their first-class tickets on the bus, cost: twenty-seven lire each[41]), every meal (cost: fifteen francs for them both at Siniscola[42]), every hotel bill (their night in Cagliari with three meals each, cost: sixty lire[43]), even a round of drinks with a commercial traveller ('the bounder' who offers him cigarettes, 'Murattis if you please'[44]) on the boat back to the mainland (cost: sixty lire[45])—each time we are solemnly informed how much he spent. You could work out the total cost of his holiday exactly. Lawrence does not, though, tell us that a field labourer in Sardinia earns just one and a half lire a day. To be fair, he probably never knew.

Lawrence usually travels first-class, though he still remarks when he gets back that 'My wife and I are poor people.' Poverty is relative. While he is counting his pennies, solemn materialist that he is, what really gets his goat is that everyone he meets complains to him about the exchange rate that puts English people at such an advantage. A schoolmistress complains:

> You English, with your money exchange, you come here and buy everything for noth-
> ing, you take the best of everything, and with your money you pay nothing for it… .
>
> I felt angry. Am I always to have the exchange flung in my teeth, as if I were a personal
> thief?'[46]

When he tells us that he gets 'a hundred and three lira for each pound note',[47] Lawrence does not mention that just a year before, the exchange rate had dropped from thirty to 103 lire to the pound, making Italy absurdly cheap for the English.[48] And not only do people keep complaining to him about the exchange rate, but also about all the advantages that England and France took from Versailles in 1919, when Italy got almost nothing. The book ends with Lawrence getting in more and more of a rage that people keep taking him for an Englishman enjoying all the material advantages of being English—'Ten francs don't matter to you,' the girovago twice remarks[49]—and not as an individual: 'I must insist that I am a single human being, an individual, not a mere national unit, a mere chip of d'Ing-hilterra or la Germania. I am not a chip of any nasty old block. I am myself.'[50]

But his protest against being taken for the national or ethnic type rather than a free individual, 'I am myself', does not work both ways: 'I hate Jews,' he writes to his friend Robert Mountsier, in the very same month as he is writing this passage in *Sea and Sardinia*.[51] And he does this not just in private letters: his complaint in the book that he is not so much an Englishman as himself does not stop him from writing about seeing some Sardinian miners get on the train and immediately characterizing them as primitives with 'their splendid, animal-bright stupidity':[52]

> But there is a gulf between oneself and them. They have no inkling of our crucifixion,
> our universal consciousness. Each of them is pivoted and limited to himself, as wild
> animals are.…. The fascination of what is beyond them has not seized them. Their
> neighbour is a mere external. Their life is centripetal, pivoted inside itself, and does
> not run out towards others and mankind.…. Coarse, vigorous, determined, they will
> stick to their own coarse, dark stupidity and let the big world find its own way to its
> own enlightened hell. Their hell is their own hell, they prefer it unenlightened.[53]

How does he know all this? Just by looking at them? Or because they reminded him too uncomfortably of his own father, also a miner? Lawrence is secure in his knowledge of their 'dark stupidity' and his assertion of the gulf between them as long as the subaltern does not speak to him, or speak out. Gramsci's protest against state censorship of just a couple of years before could apply equally well to Lawrence:

Why is it prohibited to recall [he wrote after an article on Sardinia had been banned by the censor] that Sardinian miners are paid starvation wages...? Why should it be prohibited to recall that two-thirds of the inhabitants of Sardinia (especially women and children) go without shoes winter and summer, through the thorns and the river-beds that take the place of roads, because the price of leather has gone prohibitively high as a result of the protective tariffs that enrich the Turin industrial leather manu-facturers...? Why is it prohibited to recall that in the Italian state, Sardinian peasants, shepherds and artisans are treated worse than in the colony of Eritrea...?[54]

On 15 January 1921, the day after the Lawrences returned to Taormina in Sicily, the seventeenth national congress of the Italian Socialist Party opened in Livorno. Six days later, Gramsci and his comrades split from the Socialist Party and founded the Partito Comunista d'Italia. It would not, however, be until he was imprisoned many years later that Gramsci, sustained by books sent by his friend Piero Sraffa, would invent the concept of subaltern classes as a comprehensive term for all those disadvantaged by capitalism and feudalism, for all those who have to struggle to survive.

CONVICTS ON THE TRAIN

On 4 January, at 'horrible' Messina on the way to Palermo and the pursuit of 'uncaptured Sardinia', Lawrence sees on the platform 'two convicts chained together among the crowd'.[55] He feels no compassion for these fellow travellers on the move—the reverse in fact: 'No, but convicts are horrible creatures.... Something cold, sightless.... I should loathe to have to touch him.... No, evil is horrible. I used to think there was no absolute evil. Now I know there is a great deal.' The men are bound, he speculates, for the penal colony of Lipari, a nearby island in the Tyrrhenian Sea that his boat will pass by on its way to Cagliari.

But then he suddenly thinks of Oscar Wilde, being taunted as he stands a con-vict on a platform at Reading station, and imagines being in that situation himself. 'What a terrible mistake, to let oneself be martyred by a lot of canaille,' Lawrence muses. 'A man must say his say. But *noli me tangere*.'[56] Lawrence's choice of the term '*canaille*' is interesting, for the word means 'the lowest class of people, the rabble, the vulgar',[57] hardly the people who in fact martyred Wilde. Moreover, he was not so much martyred for what he said, as for what he did. Odder still is Lawrence's sudden unexpected self-identification with the risen Christ, telling Mary Magdalene, who has recognized him, not to touch him. For a brief moment, recalling perhaps the repression of *The Rainbow* on grounds of obscenity, and his time in Zennor during the war when he and Frieda were accused of spying and sending signals to German submarines, he has allowed himself the horrifying thought—what if that convict were *him*, standing there ignominiously on the plat-form with his knapsack hunched on his back?

Five years later, in December 1926, another convict would be sent handcuffed on a train via Messina and Palermo to a prison on another Tyrrhenian island, Ustica, that Lawrence's boat would also have passed by, a parliamentary deputy whose arrest had been ordered personally by the by-then dictator Mussolini. The journey took twelve days, including the prison stops on the way. On such a journey, wrote Gramsci philosophically, oblivious to Lawrence's characterization of Italian prisoners of five years before, 'it is not very comfortable, even for a robust man, to travel for hour after hour on local trains and boat in handcuffs that are tied in turn to a chain that attached you to the wrists of your travel companions'.[58] But the journey to Ustica was nothing like his trip back, two months later, when he was transferred all the way to a prison in Milan, slowly moved on from one stop to another along the way:

> In general the trip has been for me a very long cinematic event.... .

> Let me give you an impression of my transfer as a whole. Just imagine that an immense worm slithers from Palermo to Milan, a worm that continually breaks up and comes together again, leaving part of its rings in each prison, reforming new ones, tossing the same parts to right and left and then reincorporating the extractions. This worm has lairs in each prison, which accumulate the dirt and misery of generations, clotting them together. You arrive tired, dirty, your wrists hurting because of the long hours in manacles, and on your face a long stubble, your hair dishevelled, eyes sunk deep and glittering both from the excitation of strained fatigue and sleeplessness, you fling yourself on the pallets that are who knows how old, fully dressed so as not to come into contact with the filth, wrapping your face and hands in your towels, covering yourself with the skimpy blankets just to avoid freezing. Then you leave again dirtier and wearier for the next transit, and your wrists are even more bruised because of the cold irons and the weight of the chains.[59]

As Lawrence gazes on the tiny, hunched Gramsci-like figure standing in chains on the platform, as so often, his own self-loathing is projected outwards on to others:

> That ghastly abstractness of criminals. They don't *know* any more what other people feel. Yet some horrible force drives them.

> It is a great mistake to abolish the death penalty. If I were a dictator, I should order the old one to be hung [*sic*] at once.... I would have that man destroyed. Quickly.[60]

Though not ordered to be hanged at once by a dictator, Gramsci would indeed die, but slowly,[61] just as Lawrence wished for his fellow prisoner of five years before. It was not only the Sicilians, as Lawrence claimed, who had 'long lost all notion of what a human being is'.

NOTES

1. D. H. Lawrence, *The Letters of D. H. Lawrence*, vol. 3: Oct. 1916–June 1921, edited by James T. Boulton and Andrew Robertson (Cambridge: Cambridge University Press, 1984) p. 435, cited in Mark Kinkead-Weekes, *D. H. Lawrence: Triumph to Exile, 1912–1922* (Cambridge: Cambridge University Press, 1996), p. 623.
2. D. H. Lawrence, *Sea and Sardinia*, edited by Mara Kalnins, introduction and notes by Jill Franks (London: Penguin, 1999), p. 7.
3. Lawrence, *Sea and Sardinia*, p. 9.

4. Lawrence, *Sea and Sardinia,* p. 9.
5. D. H. Lawrence, Preface to *The Mother* by Grazia Deledda in *Phoenix: The Posthumous Papers of D. H. Lawrence* (New York: Viking Press, 1972), pp. 1, 263–4.
6. Lawrence, *Sea and Sardinia,* p. xxviii n. 8; Harry T. Moore, *Poste Restante: A Lawrence Travel Calendar* (Berkeley: University of California Press, 1956), pp. 61–2. Kinkead-Weekes, *D. H. Lawrence*, p. 622, cited in Neil Roberts, *D. H. Lawrence: Travel and Cultural Difference* (Basingstoke: Palgrave, 2004), p. 51.
7. Lawrence, *Sea and Sardinia*, p. 79.
8. Lawrence, *Sea and Sardinia*, pp. 56–7.
9. Lawrence, *Sea and Sardinia,* p. 60.
10. Giuseppe Fiori, *Antonio Gramsci: Life of a Revolutionary*, translated by Tom Nairn (New York: Schocken Books, 1973), p. 53.
11. Lawrence, *Sea and Sardinia*, p. 61.
12. Lawrence, *Sea and Sardinia*, p. 62.
13. Lawrence, *Sea and Sardinia*, p. 63.
14. Lawrence, *Sea and Sardinia*, pp. 67–8.
15. Lawrence, *Sea and Sardinia*, p. 92.
16. At the hotel in Cagliari: 'And thus we are led off, if you please, to the bagnio …', Lawrence, *Sea and Sardinia*, p. 55.
17. Lawrence, *Sea and Sardinia*, p. 62.
18. Lawrence, *Sea and Sardinia*, p. 92.
19. Lawrence, *Sea and Sardinia*, p. 55.
20. Lawrence, *Sea and Sardinia*, p. 93.
21. Lawrence, *Sea and Sardinia*, pp. 93–4.
22. Lawrence, *Sea and Sardinia*, p. 94.
23. Lawrence, *Sea and Sardinia*, p. 96.
24. Lawrence, *Sea and Sardinia*, p. 112.
25. Lawrence, *Sea and Sardinia*, p. 174.
26. Fiori, *Antonio Gramsci*, p. 85. It is possible that the reversed N in 'Ristorante' was simply Art Deco lettering, which sometimes employed this form, rather than an implied link to the USSR, but either way the association of the restaurant's name with the *Risveglio dell'Isola* remains relevant.
27. Lawrence, *Sea and Sardinia*, p. 79.
28. Lawrence, *Sea and Sardinia*, p. 113.
29. The thermos flask was first manufactured in 1904.
30. Lawrence, *Sea and Sardinia*, p. 70.
31. Lawrence, *Sea and Sardinia*, p. 23.
32. David Ellis and Howard Mills, *D. H. Lawrence's Non-Fiction: Art, Thought and Genre* (Cambridge: Cambridge University Press, 1988), pp. 99–100.
33. Fiori, *Antonio Gramsci*, p. 26.
34. Gramsci, letter to Giulia, 6 March 1924, cited in Fiori, *Antonio Gramsci,* note on p. 26; Antonio Gramsci, *Lettere 1908–1926*, edited by Antonio A. Santucci (Turin: Einaudi, 1992), p. 271.
35. To Giulia Schucht, 6 March 1924, in Antonio Gramsci, *Cara compagna: Lettere amorose a Giulia Schucht*, edited by Emma Chimenti (Milan: Kaos edizioni, 2012), p. 47; See also Dante Germino, *Antonio Gramsci: Architect of a New Politics* (Baton Rouge, LA: Louisiana University Press, 1990), pp. 1–5.
36. Lawrence, *Sea and Sardinia*, p. 60.
37. Fiori, *Antonio Gramsci*, p. 115.

38. Fiori, *Antonio Gramsci*, pp. 51, 66.
39. Lawrence, *Sea and Sardinia*, pp. 64–5. For the most part, Lawrence refers to lire as francs, which had been equivalents since the institution of the Sardinian lira in 1816 as the Piedmontese version of the franc.
40. Lawrence, *Sea and Sardinia*, p. 32.
41. Lawrence, *Sea and Sardinia*, p. 123.
42. Lawrence, *Sea and Sardinia*, p. 155.
43. Lawrence, *Sea and Sardinia*, p. 69.
44. Lawrence, *Sea and Sardinia*, p. 181.
45. Lawrence, *Sea and Sardinia*, p. 184.
46. Lawrence, *Sea and Sardinia*, p. 175.
47. Lawrence, *Sea and Sardinia*, p. 171.
48. Michael Squires and Lynn K. Talbot, *Living at the Edge: A Biography of D. H. Lawrence and Frieda von Richthofen* (Madison: University of Wisconsin Press, 2002), p. 233.
49. Lawrence, *Sea and Sardinia*, p. 105.
50. Lawrence, *Sea and Sardinia*, p. 186.
51. 3 March 1921, Lawrence, *The Letters*, vol. 3, p. 678.
52. Lawrence, *Sea and Sardinia*, p. 89.
53. Lawrence, *Sea and Sardinia*, p. 88.
54. Antonio Gramsci, 'I dolori della Sardegna', *Avanti*, 16 April 1919, in *Scritti sulla Sardegna*, edited by Guido Melia (Nuoro: Illiso edizioni, 2008), pp. 74–5 (my translation). For a more extended discussion of Gramsci and the Southern Question, see my 'Il Gramsci meridionale', in *The Postcolonial Gramsci*, edited by Neelam Srivastava and Baidik Bhattacharya (New York: Routledge, 2012), pp. 17–33.
55. Lawrence, *Sea and Sardinia*, p. 15.
56. Lawrence, *Sea and Sardinia*, p. 16.
57. Literally, a pack of dogs.
58. Antonio Gramsci, *Letters from Prison*, edited by Frank Rosengarten, translated by Raymond Rosenthal (New York: Columbia University Press, 1994), pp. 1, 39.
59. Fiori, *Antonio Gramsci*, p. 222; Gramsci, *Letters from Prison*, pp. 1, 70–1.
60. Lawrence, *Sea and Sardinia*, pp. 15–16.
61. Gramsci died in the Quisisana clinic, six days after being given full freedom.

ENERGIES AND QUANTITIES

7

High-Energy Modernism

Enda Duffy

What matters most to modern man is no longer pleasure or displeasure, but
excitement.

Friedrich Nietzsche, *Ecce Homo*, 1888.[1]

Imagine, to begin, a modern history of the smile. In that history, the smile turns out
to be something of a modernist invention. Scrutinize photographs from the interwar years: it is as if, somewhere around 1930, a switch was pulled, and people
everywhere in the West agreed to rejig the complicated musculature of their faces in
order to make the smile the default public mode.[2] 'Unsmiling' became a pejorative
term. The staid stares that had been a staple of Victorian portrait photography gave
way to grins and laughter. If, for example, you take the photographs month by
month of American presidents from 1900 onwards, it is in the early thirties—
especially with F. D. Roosevelt—that the smile at last emerges. Literature registered
it too. As early as 1892, the Sherlock Holmes story 'The Man with the Twisted Lip'
offers a veiled, politically unconscious allegory of the role of the smile in modernity,
through a story about a man who skilfully makes up his face into a fearful grin and
thereby becomes a persuasive and highly successful London beggar. W. B. Yeats,
born in 1865, was old enough to be embarrassed by his own smile in the twenties,
when he describes himself ruefully as 'a sixty-year old smiling public man'.[3] James
Joyce in *Ulysses* registers with perfect pitch the modernist ambivalence about the
smile—and, indirectly, the way it can flit across one's face—when he asks of Bloom,
who is entering into bed beside Molly, in the dark, and realizing that Boylan has
been there before him: 'If he had smiled, why would he have smiled?'[4] Modernism's
new medium, film, became a vast field for experimenting with smiles. In *Pandora's
Box* (1929), starring Louise Brooks, the smiles of the heroine and her patron
Schigloch seem tentative, even experimental; in *The Blue Angel* (1930), the repertoire of smiles, smirks, and laughter of Marlene Dietrich strikes the viewer as natural. Why was smiling naturalized in the modernist period? Not, surely, because
people were happier; the smile's arrival coincides with the Depression. The early
twentieth-century smile was one aspect of a new importance accorded to human
somatic reaction in the West in the modernist period, a change which, this chapter
claims, propelled much of what is revolutionary in modernism itself.

Giorgio Agamben has written: 'By the end of the nineteenth century, the western bourgeoisie had definitely lost its gestures.'[5] The temptation is to think of the smile and associated embodied expressions of emotional states as signs of a new, progressive regime of what Foucault calls 'the care of the self', one now characterized by relaxation and openness. The smile is only one of a range of such expressions, many of them expressive of modernist anomie: consider the shock-horror on the face of the figure in Munch's 'The Scream', the worried eyes of the human figures Picasso painted in his 'Blue Period', or the grotesque, sated expressions of the haut-bourgeois figures in German expressionist painting. It is difficult to tell if people truly were more 'expressive' in the new century; what is certain is that modernist art was intensely interested in these manifestations of human affect. The first claim of this essay is this: modernist art, and in particular modernist literature, is arresting and experimental in the first place because it generates new ways of annotating, with an absolutely unprecedented and delicate accuracy, the somatic reactions, the symptoms of nervous energy, of its subjects. The smile, the grimace, the blush, the batting eyelids, the beating heart: these are not gestures, but physical reactions to external stimuli. They are somatic, haptic, visceral. Modernist style, to a striking degree, is a matter of absolutely scrupulous attention to the minute-by-minute changes in these somatic signs of affect. Modernist literature, page by page, offers a vast symptomology of fidgets, rates of breathing, grimaces, blushes and heartbeats of its characters.

Here is a summary of this essay's claims. First, modernist literature is a somatic literature. Its defamiliarizing effects are in this regard a function of its effort to annotate with an unprecedented exactitude the smiles and breath rates, the twitches and the modulations of the gait, of its characters. Modernist art's impact, however, comes not only from the strategies its practitioners developed to annotate with precision the somatic reactions of the people it portrayed, but from its effectiveness in transmitting these modulations of soma to the reader or viewer. Modernist writing, as it developed forms (each writer in her or his own way) to transmit this somatic data to the reader or viewer, itself became elastic and reverberative. Hence the act of reading or perceiving the modernist artwork stops being contemplative and judgemental; stops being a matter of becoming still, of taking a position at a distance as a Cartesian, thinking subject and, instead, generates visceral, somatic response effects in the reader herself. (In this sense modernist writing strives for the condition of cinema, not in how it paints visual images, but in its capacity, with its own jump cuts, fast editing, close-ups, and so on, to evoke an ongoing series of visceral reactions in the reader as the pleasure of the text.) The famous 'shock' of the modernist new is only the first and most crude of these reactions elicited by the modernist soma text. This, in turn, means that, when modernist writing is centrally concerned with annotating somatic affect and inducing corresponding somatic affects in the reader too, it is now less concerned with larger narrative arcs of emotion, motivation, and any readerly work of moral judgement. The reader is no longer invited to be concerned with, or even to believe in the possibility of, a grander, overarching story that follows the grooves of a well-worn ideology ('love', 'honour', 'fate'), but is induced to be excited by the character's minute-by-minute, page-by-page tremulations of affect. The modernist soma text surrenders culture's formerly assumed concern with 'feeling' (as emotion readable within an ideological framework) and, instead, takes as its concern what might be called human 'intensity', which is a value ascribed to the expenditure of human energy. Human energy expenditure, then, becomes the central topic and value of the modernist text. In particular, 'stress', a term theorized in the 1930s and one of the great modernist conceptualizations in the field of medicine, became a modernist literary obsession. 'Stress', which quickly migrated from medical terminology to become a byword of modern living, is an account of human energy dynamics in daily life. Bloom, Mrs Dalloway, Gregor Samsa, Prufrock: all of the great modernist characters are case studies of stress. Modernist literature's interest in somatic reaction and human energy expenditure was paralleled in the same years by a huge interest on the part of medicine in human energy and its role as evidence of life. Finally, in both medicine and modernist art, the new focus on energy was symptomatic of a new awareness in the West that the post-imperial world order would devolve around a new global economy of energy. Modernism began with the widespread use of oil and ended with the mass use of nuclear power. Modernism's task was to re-evaluate the place of human energy in that enormously expanded global energy economy.

To grasp how the representation of minute-by-minute somatic change matters to the aesthetic experience of modernist prose, consider a single example, the ending of the 'Lestrygonians' episode of *Ulysses*. Bloom sees, after he has eaten lunch, coming towards him in Kildare street, Blazes Boylan, the man who he knows is going to go and sleep with his—Bloom's—wife, that very afternoon. Bloom, as Franco Moretti points out,[6] could have stood his ground and confronted Boylan—and thus granted the novel a conventional love-triangle plot. But he doesn't; he scuttles away, and Joyce, writing like a zealous cameraman who wants to capture every tremble and inflection of a victim's body and face, gives us not deep thoughts on Bloom's cowardice, not a report on Bloom's own feelings, certainly not a wistful hymn to Bloom's lost love, but rather a second-by-second account of the exact symptoms of bodily changes Bloom exhibits—his reddening face, his shortening, panting breaths, his faster-beating heart, and the exact movements of his fluttering hands:

> Mr Bloom came into Kildare street. First I must. Library.
> Straw hat in sunlight. Tan shoes. Turnedup trousers. It is. It is.
> His heart quopped softly. To the right. Museum. Goddesses. He
> swerved to the right.
> Is it? Almost certain. Won't look. Wine in my face. Why did I?
> Too heady.
> Yes, it is. The walk. Not see. Get on.
> Making for the museum gate with long windy steps he lifted his
> eyes. Handsome building. Sir Thomas Deane designed. Not
> following me.
> Didn't see me perhaps. Light in his eyes.
> The flutter of his breath came forth in short sighs. Quick. Cold statues:
> Quiet there. Safe in a minute.
> No. Didn't see me. After two. Just at the gate.
> My heart![7]

The key line: 'His heart quopped softly'—the accuracy of 'quopped' is stunning here. It is flanked by mention of Bloom's sudden blush ('Wine in my face'), his altered gait ('swerved'), his shortened breadth ('with long windy steps'), and his now pounding heart ('My heart!'), all transmitted in telegraphically brief sentence fragments. The pace of these sentence bits matches the jagged rhythm of Bloom's speeded-up somatic state. Bloom here has an adrenaline surge—and adrenaline was first synthesized in 1903. The telegraphese transmits itself instantly to the reader; her own heart rate accelerates. Joyce went to Paris in 1903 to enrol in medical school; there is an almost medical attention to human somatic reaction here— as everywhere in his texts.

Joyce is the practitioner par excellence of a modernist adrenaline aesthetics. Yet all of the great modernists, each working in a distinctive style, practise with equal or greater effectiveness this seismographically accurate writing that tracks somatic variation as evidence in changes of intensity. Virginia Woolf, annotating what she called the 'semi-transparent envelope'[8] around each character, pursued a textual sensitivity to physical well-being even more nuanced than that of Joyce. Consider too the slow-motion sentence arcs of Joseph Conrad, Eliot's languorous 'streamline moderne' rhythms, the electricity metaphors and vitalist purposefulness of D. H. Lawrence, and the symbolist telegraphese of Djuna Barnes; all these styles limn, with an unprecedented, experimental exactitude, the affective symptoms of their characters, their nervous stimulation, their haptic lives. All prove that to register this fluctuation requires new kinds of prose. The characteristic technical innovations of cinema, likewise, were developed to enhance the viewer's appreciation of character's emotions as readable upon their bodies: the close-up maps embodied tension in the changing architecture of the star's face; slow motion attends scrupulously to each physical change, magnifying the somatic. Film, as an education of the gaze upon the bodies of others, may have pioneered the assumption, then grasped by modernist prose, that for culture as well as medicine only subtle body movement, minutely observed, can signify emotional change. Both modernist prose and film imply that only human energy outlays are true indices of feeling. The literary texts outdo the filmic ones, however, in that for them (as in the case of *Ulysses*) the translation of the energetic evidence back into a narrative of feeling ceases to be of interest. The modernist novel about human energy emerges from the shell of the Victorian novel about love. This moved the writers or film-makers to be closer to the fields of medicine and scientific observation: we will see in a moment how, before modernism, these fields investigated human energetics with paradigms the modernists followed. First, however, to underline how revolutionary was this modernist move from human feeling to energy, consider how crucial energy has become in our sense of modern selfhood since.

If, in the modernist moment, human energy came to replace emotion as focus of culture, then an energetics must be theorized. In brief: what is human energy? What is human fatigue? How do these relate to the place of any given human subject in modernity? Once, in the days when Baden-Powell lamented the 'weaklings' who had not been energetic enough to fight the Boer War more effectively for Britain, this effect was named by now unfashionable words, like 'vim' and 'mettle'.

A century later, well-being is explained as energy: one might say 'I feel full of energy' or 'I feel drained'. Or 'I'm hyper', or 'I'm stressed'. Clearly, energy is, first, a capacity for more, and faster, physical movement. It is also a matter of the power of attentiveness and the ability to sustain concentration. It implies the perceived stimulation of the physiological body as well as of one's mental capacity: you might say, referring to your heightened blood pressure, or to the adrenaline coursing through your veins, 'I was excited', or 'It was an intense experience.' What exactly is this intensity? It suggests the extreme exposure of each of the senses to stimuli: 'heightened awareness' of eye, nose, tongue, ear, skin. To be energized is to be excited: the physical body, the nervous system, the capacity for alertness, what is called the will, collude. Lord Henry Wotton speaks of this already in 1890–1 in *The Picture of Dorian Gray* when he says that 'Life is a question of nerves and fibers, slowly built-up cells in which thought hides itself and passion has its dream.'[9]— Wotton's mixing of medicine and Nietzscheanism marks him as an early adapter of the now commonplace notion that energy is the prime attribute by which we know and name nothing less than life. By now, to be alive is to be full of energy.

SCIENCES OF HUMAN ENERGY

If modernist literature made human energy its central concern, it was merely one component of a vast new interest in energy, including but by no means limited to human energy, that grew up in the late nineteenth and early twentieth century. In part, this was the result of a plethora of new technologies invented and popularized in these years, from the internal combustion engine to electric light, with which human energy had to compete.[10] It was profoundly related to the fact that the sciences were discovering new energies in matter. In Einstein's terms, the key discovery was that matter could no longer be thought of as static; rather, matter was energy; his 1905 essay outlining his Special Theory of Relativity was entitled 'The Electrodynamics of Moving Bodies'; his famous equation of the same year, $E=mc^2$, which posits that the mass of an object is equivalent to its energy content, may represent the most important discovery of twentieth-century physics. Third, the modernist energy focus followed a new interest in human movement that had emerged in medicine in the second half of the nineteenth century. The interest in somatic and quick-reaction emotion reflected the shift to service work by the newly minted middle-class citizens of the West during this period: members of many of the new professions, from flight attendant to salesman, had to show affect (to 'emote', or at least to fake the motions of emotion) in order to earn a living. Finally, it followed the dawning sense that while in geopolitical terms the imperialism of geographic, static space had reached its limits, a new imperial power struggle over finite energy resources on the planet had just begun. Energy, then, now mattered in striking new ways, and even human energy became part of matter's new visibility. Everywhere, science's insight was coming true: static matter was turning out to be energetic—and the extraction of energy from static matter of every form became a fundamental goal of every modernist project.

The issue of human energy has emerged at nodal points of modernity, and in the history of medicine and science, as an almost strange obsession. As Georges Canguilhem, pioneer of 'biopower' and teacher of Foucault, has noted,[11] it was raised by Descartes in his short essay 'La Description du corps humain' in 1648, in which Descartes describes how man's movements are antecedent to, and allow the possibilities for the expression of, man's soul. Descartes decides that as human energy can only be known through human movement, this movement should be minutely observed. This modus operandi became the byword for subsequent studies.

It is appropriate that Lord Henry Wotton sounds modern with his talk of nerves, fibres, cells, as science—medicine, but also the engineering involved in new technologies such as the camera—was edging into the field of 'feeling', which had been the concern of art at least since the arrival of one model of emotion for modernity in Goethe's *The Sorrows of Young Werther* of 1774. This turn of medical attention to the living, moving, active human occurred, I suggest, in two phases. First, in the second half of the nineteenth century, scientists scrutinized the human body as a mechanism of variously efficient moving parts, their accuracy increasing as they developed new mechanical measuring devices. Eadweard Muybridge in the US and Jules-Étienne Marey in France famously pioneered this collusion of new machines and medical surveillance when each took a series of photographs of the human body in motion. Soon scientists began to develop machines to make measurements of human locomotion, machines with esoteric names: the myograph, the odograph, the ergonomic monocycle of Jules Amor, the ergograph developed by Angelo Mosso in 1884, to take precise measurements of even the twitching of a finger. To record modulations of human gait, Gilles de la Tourette, who would give his name to Tourette's syndrome, laid out rolls of marked white wallpaper, on which patients, their feet smeared with sesquioxide powder, were made to walk, so that the paper was stained red. 'While the left leg acts as a fulcrum', he wrote, 'the right foot is raised from the ground with a coiling motion that starts at the heel and reaches the tip of the toes, which leave the ground last.'[12] His obsessive annotating of human movement was then related to efficient physical work, in an age when physical labour was still, along with the engine, the basis of wealth production. This culminated in the work of Frederick Taylor, and the Gilbreths, pioneers of 'Taylorism' and 'scientific management', which analysed workers' physical movements in order to design workplaces where motor movement could be more efficient. Henry Ford adopted Taylorism systematically in the factory assembly line, which marshalled the masses to become more efficient manual workers. The machine was in this science the measure of man; the body was thought of mechanically, that is, as composed of interrelated mechanical components, and the governing assumption was that the human subject needed to be as efficient as the machine, if he could not equal its power.

This boom in the scientific study of human (and animal) physical energy, innovative in its ties to public health and in its use of machineries of measurement, which attempted to understand the minutest human movement through mass observation, was, however, as Anson Rabinbach has written,[13] only the first phase of the medical discourse on the 'human motor'. The next phase, the counterpoint to the first on human motion, developed around human fatigue. There was, as Rabinbach shows, an obsession with fatigue at the end of the nineteenth century, which devolved into an examination of such deviations from the action model as listlessness, nervousness, agitation, so called 'mental fatigue', and sheer laziness. The New York doctor George Beard wrote *American Nervousness: Its Causes and Consequences*[14] in 1881; he was also co-author of the standard textbook on electro-shock therapy. Ever more sensitive measuring machines continued to be developed, such as Herman Greisbach's aesthesiometer, which measured perceived sensations upon the surface of the skin. What had been called 'Beard's disease' in the 1870s became known as 'neurasthenia' by the 1890s. Many investigators, such as Adrien Proust, father of the twentieth century's most famous neurasthenic of all, were quick to connect the ailment, as a failure of energy, to the pressures of the modern world, so that the new field of sociology was quick to take it up: Émile Durkheim's book *Suicide* of 1897, for example, describes how 'Every impression is a source of discomfort for the neuropath.'[15] From all of this ferment there developed, at sites such as at Charcot's Paris laboratory, the basis of modern Freudian psychiatry. Yet the flourishing psycho-physiological tradition continued, with an influence possibly more pervasive for the modern sense of subjecthood than Freudism itself.

At this point the story shifts from the Paris–Vienna–Turin axis of Charcot, Freud, and Mosso back to the US. (Mosso's book *La paura* of 1884, translated into English as *Fear*[16] in 1891, might be seen as the turning point.) In William James's famous essay, 'What is an Emotion?' of 1884, he sided with the physiologists by insisting that an emotion was first experienced upon the body, and that it was our sensation of that experience that constitutes the emotion. In his words, 'we feel sorry because we cry, angry because we strike, afraid because we tremble, and [it is] not that we cry, strike, or tremble, because we are sorry, angry, or fearful, as the case may be'.[17] Despite his use of the term 'emotion', in other words, attention was shifting to sensory reactions, reflexes, and the rawest 'visceral' sensations. A key inspiration for this was Darwin's *The Expression of Emotion in Man and Animals*,[18] in which he wrote of such facial expressions as the frown, suggesting again how visual readings enabled by new technologies were what made attention to the most subtle somatic reactions possible. (Darwin's was one of the first books to include photographs, in this case heliotype plates.) William James's work was continued by Walter Cannon, whose *Bodily Changes in Pain, Hunger, Fear and Rage*[19] appeared in 1915, in which he wrote about such sensations as dry mouth, hunger, and increase in body heat, and whose key chapter was entitled 'The Energizing Influence of Emotional Excitement', a rousing endorsement of the uses of wild excitement in increasing physical energy. The work explored the physiology of emotions by testing the function of newly discovered glands. Whereas the nineteenth-century scientists had been concerned with the muscles, the new focus was the glands and their secretions, especially the adrenal gland.

Whereas the previous generation, in taking the measure of man as machine, had thought in terms of mechanics, now the governing analogy of energetic man was electricity. Electricity was the new, omnipresent, invisible, hygienic and dangerous form of energy in the early twentieth century, so its use as explicit and implicit issue in this branch of physiology was more or less inevitable: electricity's pulses, after all, might explain the body's own distribution of energy. (Marcel Duchamp may have been alluding to this, for example, when in 1914 he wrote the caption 'Portrait of a Young Woman in a State of Nudity' and placed it above a drawing of a spark plug.) Finally, if fatigue had been the counter-interest of nineteenth-century human energetics, by 1934 the twentieth century had found its version. This was *stress*, named by Cannon and brought into use as we all now know it colloquially by the Hungarian-Canadian doctor Hans Seyle in the 1930s. Stress was more than fatigue or even neurasthenia: its symptoms ranged from inability to concentrate to agitation, rapid heartbeat, overeating, nervous habits. In this condition, the energized human body cannot quite control its energies, is turned against its own efficiency, is stressed.

HUMAN ENERGY AND MODERNIST CULTURE

This, in brief, is an account of how mostly male scientists colonized a new field of research, a terrain which had previously been left to culture, and cast as a concern of women. Notice that with the arrival of science, the zone previously designated 'feeling' and cast mostly as an issue of leisure, was now rethought as energy and recast as work. In this way too the model of artistic feeling that valorized depth, and that suggested that deep feeling was more meaningful, was forsaken for a model of energetic reaction which valorized intensity. Further, these scientific categories did not remain within science: it is remarkable how many of the books by scientists, from Beard's *American Nervousness* to Seyle's *The Stress of Life* of 1956,[20] became international bestsellers, and how many of the scientists set out to popularize their findings, with great success. This science developed in conjunction with both the new public health systems and the new mass media. Culminating with stress, it rapidly turned its scientific concepts into widely adapted and culturally pervasive social categories, which in turn were then available to be judged in ethical terms. To take one example, one of the best known cultural judgements of the twentieth-century *fin de siècle* was that made by Fredric Jameson, in *Postmodernism, or the Cultural Logic of Late-Capitalism*, that modern Western subjects suffer from the 'death of affect'. What Jameson suggests is that we have lost our capacity for deep feeling, which he blames, following Baudrillard and Debord, on the rise of a culture of simulation under the late capitalist consumer society of the spectacle. This is convincing in its own terms, but what has happened on the ground is more accurately the process which I've outlined above: the cultural model of deep emotion has been ditched, with the connivance of science, in favour of categories developed by the scientists' physiological investigations: energy, intensity, exhaustion, stimulation, excitement, stress.

It is not simply that modernism deploys 'the shock of the new' to jolt us into seeing some reality; it's rather that, the medium being the message, the shock it gives is simply what we require in a culture which values intense sensation. Stimulation, rather than simulation, is primary. Simulation can be grasped in Jamesonian terms, as the sign of the late-capitalist inauthentic; stimulation, as critics such as Jonathan Crary have shown,[21] can certainly be read suspiciously as the glorification of modern overwork, but it can equally be considered an attempt to reclaim tactility, embodied sensation, and all of the excitements of struggle in a society in which one is denied them by the airless sweetness of the simulative pseudo-culture proffered by capital. Just as it is fascinating to wonder whether people's actual somatic lives changed, or whether it was merely that representations of them in literature, cinema, and all the arts grew much more attentive to the intensities of somatic lives, we as critics must ask whether the new scientific investigations, or the new art forms, precipitated the change, acted as an avant-garde that, rather, demanded it, or whether the new art and science were merely reflective of changes—the adaption of new technologies such as electricity, mass embourgeoisification in the West, the rise of the global energy economy—that were put in train by social, economic, and political forces antecedent to the interventions of art and science.

What we can surmise is that modernism represented the attempt by culture to seize the initiative back from science, but only after the scientists had completely colonized the field and recast its terms, categories, and assumptions. What we witness at the turn of the twentieth century is a terrific amount of disturbance, casting up strange and ghostly cultural formations, at the borderlands where science, the various high art forms and newly hegemonic forces such as public health and other bureaucratic state discourses, the newly energized and fast-proliferating forms of mass popular culture, and even early twentieth-century philosophy meet. On the one hand in literature of that moment there was an often remarked-upon interest in ghosts, spiritualism, and unseen or vaguely seen forces of all kinds, which produced work from Bram Stoker's *Dracula* to Yeats's weird spiritualism. In science itself there was a resurgence of interest in vitalism, for example in Hans Driesch's theory of entelechy, outlined in his Gifford Lectures at the University of Aberdeen in 1906–8. This was taken up in philosophy by the enormously popular neo-vitalism of Henri Bergson, whose brother-in-law was McGregor Mathers, the founder of the thoroughly spiritualist and occult Order of the Golden Dawn. At the same moment, popular novelettes, penny dreadfuls, railway novels, and the new form of the comic book all popularized sensation fiction, lurid tales that promised to make your flesh creep. In mass advertising fantastic claims were made for the energizing—and sexually reviving—powers of the newly available force that was electricity. The newly invented cinema played up a number of these elements—from ghostliness to sensationalism—in portraying the enormous faces of stars in the close-up. The strange somatic activity that is laughter (and it is a human somatic activity only, as humans alone laugh) got put to new uses in another new modernist art form, the cartoon film. (Bergson went on to write *On Laughter* in 1924, a bookend of sorts to Mosso's *Fear* of forty years earlier.)

This returns us to the emergence of the smile, and its implication that, far from being the literature of anomie, angst, and anguish in the face of stress as it is usually imagined to be, modernism can be thought of either as a compensation for a life of stress, a crash course in how to handle or profit from it, or an education in stress's excitements and pleasures. All of this excitable cultural activity, even to the point of throwing up new popular art forms, can be read as part of the disturbance around the shifting of the focus on how to characterize the rhythms of human life and what to value in such lives: a shift from the valorization of deep feeling, which arcs over a time span that could be developed in, for example, the leisurely time world of a realist novel, to a dream of high energy, as intensity, stimulation, and somatic overload. Paul Virilio, in *The Art of the Motor*, in a chapter called 'From Superman to Active Man' notes that 'For the biologist, excitability is the fundamental property of living tissue.'[22] He adds: 'If to be alive is to be excited, then to be alive is to be at speed, a metabolic speed that technology is compelled to increase and improve.' Modernist art, with its battery of estranging effects designed to viscerally shock, upset, excite and make us empathize, set itself up as varieties of such a technology, to underline, show up, and enact for its audience, and if possible induce in that audience, this experience of excitable speed. Given that the novel was the literary genre of the experience of the Western bourgeoisie, it was inevitable that, with the early twentieth-century expansion of that class (Eliot's army of black-coated workers 'flowing over London Bridge'), the everyday texture of the new kind of work many of them did—service work—would be taken seriously by novels. Here the somatic turn proved opportune.

   This energy discourse—which has become a dominant one in the rhythm of our lives—was first articulated by a branch of medical science, seized upon by the luridness of the new sensational writing, of yellow journalism, true crime stories, and the whole range of new mass culture writing, and even the vivid tales beloved of *fin de siècle* opera, and advanced by the new and characteristically modernist medium of film, a medium expert at showing the somatic signs of energy on the body's surface. Only at that point was it taken up by high modernist literature. Because, in the era of mass factory work, which culminated in the Fordist production line, the scientific investigations which imagined human life as the capacity for efficient machine-modelled movement were closely tied to state-sponsored interest in the efficient use of human physical labour, they made efficient labour power their investigative goal. The continuation of this work, into studies of exhaustion, then neurasthenia, and then into the minutest somatic and affective reactions, represented not only a progression to more minutely observed physical responses, but corresponded to a new kind of work then becoming general, so-called white-collar work. This emergence of white-collar work and the 'service economy', expanding the bourgeoisie, meant that those workers' lives were available as a new kind of fictional subject. Service work is labour at which one somatizes for a living: thus the soma—of Gregor Samsa in Kafka's 'Metamorphosis', of the ad-salesman Leopold Bloom, even of Dr O'Connor in Djuna Barnes's *Nightwood*, service workers all—became a phenomenon in the field of vision of the literary. Now a key swathe of the workforce found that for them emoting and somatizing was a major part of their role in capital, and the expression of their place in the new energy economy.

One reason service work became more common for all classes was factory automation, which meant that human physical energy was less needed in labour, so that the employed now did not have to 'use their hands'. Automation meant that more energetic labour was performed by machines, so that the relation of humans and machines changed also, and the old 'human motor' analogy of body and machine was now inadequate. Victorian science might have seen humans as machinic; modernist novels now saw them as nodes of energy concentration and expenditure. At the same time, the machines had to be fed energy in one form to produce it in another. The spread of new machineries using energy meant that there was a huge new need for energy, so that energy procurement quickly emerged as a political and, soon, a geopolitical issue. This happened very much at the same moment as the European empires had colonized the whole of the globe, the 'Mackinder moment', named after Halford Mackinder, an Oxford geographer and director of the London School of Economics, who began to imagine the implications of the fact that by 1904 the whole of the world had been mapped and even the remotest regions colonized.[23] If the *geos* in the age of Empire had been imagined as a set of static administered territories, contacted by ocean-going vessels, and lately traversed by railway and telegraph lines, post-Mackinder this was replaced by a new awareness of the finitude of the earth itself, and of the finitude of the resources in it. This happened at the same moment as it became clear that these resources would be needed for energy. (The history of Royal Dutch Shell, founded after the discovery of oil in Sumatra in the 1880s, and BP, which began as the Anglo-Persian Oil Company in 1909 to extract oil from Iran, is illustrative here: energy-extracting multinational companies grew up as the old territorial empires wound down.) The aggregate amount of available energy in circulation at this stage of modernity, in other words, vastly increased. Whereas for centuries human power had only had to compete with horsepower, and a few limited turbines such as the water wheel at a mill, human physical energy as a percentage of the whole was now almost negligible in the vast new energy economy of modernity. In one sense, this liberated human energy into all kinds of new experiments about its dispersal and dissemination, and modernist literature was a pioneer of such experimentation. Further, the fact that human energy was now less needed as raw labour power meant more leisure, so that people had more opportunities to spend their energy outside productive labour. Carnivalesque modernism, in particular, examines energy expenditure that could be sacrificial, scandalously wasteful, or dispersed for reasons entirely symbolic. The various modernist styles emerge from the nexus of a medical discourse blessed with soma as a reading of human energy from Darwin to Cannon to Seyle, a new global political focus on energy resources such as oil and hydro-electric power, and a new kind of soma-as-labour service work. Finally, there were new possibilities for masses of people to imagine how they might somatize outside the cycle of production altogether, at leisure. Operating at this nexus, modernist literature showed soma as symptomatic of the human subject's place in the new energy economy. Annotating these symptoms are all the new forms of modernist text.

How then did modernist art read these symptoms? A small subset of that art revelled in the new energy technologies, and declared vehemently that humans should try to join the booming new energy economy. In the hall of the Palais de Tokyo in Paris, consider Raoul Dufy's vast mural 'La Fée Électricité', a celebratory history of electricity as magical force painted for the 1937 Paris International Exposition, and hailed at the time as possibly the largest mural ever painted. The Futurists are the most notorious bearers of the pro-speed message. A more diffuse group, among them the Georgian poets, set themselves up as a bulwark against the new dynamics, celebrating pastoral as stasis to counter the rush of modernity. Most modernist artworks however, unconsciously or not, refracted the new rhythms of energy in their work. These are the writers who produced the often jagged, almost always ambivalent modernist soma text. Joyce's heart-throbbing, nervous Bloom, Woolf's Clarissa Dalloway, of whom we are told, when she heard of the suicide of Septimus Smith, 'Always her body went through it first...Her body burnt',[24] Eliot's woman in a pub who tells her friend 'Its them pills I took...I've never felt the same',[25] Huxley's characters who, when they feel glum in *Brave New World* are actually told that 'What you need is a gram of soma'[26] and drug themselves to gain energy: the most famous modernist characters are all brought to life on the page as they have their somatic reactions narrated, and are all struggling to come to terms with their bursts of energy, their stretches of sluggishness, their fleeting senses of intense experience, their sense of the embodied physical tangibility of their lives. In film, slow motion was invented in 1904 by an Austrian priest, August Musger, who appeared to slow time with a mirrored drum, even as the number of images run through the frame per second in early cinema made every human appear to scuttle, and defamiliarized what may be the most unselfconscious of all human movements, the gait. Modernist literature and film focused on soma as the terrain on which its anxieties and anticipations about the human subject's participation in the new energy economy could be openly explored.

How does the soma text do energy? When it shows it in its characters, it delivers an acute mimeticism in the wake of nineteenth-century naturalism. D. H. Lawrence wrote disparagingly, but accurately, of this style when he said of his fellow writers:

> 'Did I feel a twinge in my little toe, or didn't I?' asks every character of Mr. Joyce, or of Miss Richardson or M. Proust....Through thousands and thousands of pages Mr. Joyce and Miss Richardson tear themselves to pieces, strip their smallest emotions to their finest threads.[27]

Obviously, such mimeticism can suggest energy as pleasurable: an excitement and intensity. Or it can cast it as stress. The late Theresa Brennan's important book, *Exhausting Modernity*,[28] which she opens by asserting that modernity itself is literally exhausting, that modern life imposes impossible conditions of existence even on its winners, suggests one way to judge the uses of modernist soma textuality. At the same time, the representation of pleasurable somatic states suggests that these texts may be utopian, that is, developing new models of tactility, experience, and sheer physical sensation that would counter such conditions as the alienation, that is the numbing tendency, generated by consumerism, labour which is not your own, and reification generally. In most modernist texts there is a dialectic between the pleasures and the torments of somaticity. For example the *flâneur*, staple figure in so many modernist novels, moves at a rhythm that can hardly be said to embody the speed thrust of techno-modernity. Yet the percussive rhythms of modernist forms themselves, rather than any issue in the representation of a character, are key to invoking somatic energy not only in modernist texts, but in their readers. The modernist soma text is an immersive one; that is, it works to have the reader experience sensations in response to the character. As the protocols of an art that relies on perspectival, contemplative distance are broken down, the soma text touches the reader's sensations. Modern art, in other words, wants to approach the condition of the video game: to make your stomach clench and your hands sweat. Its shocks want to be real before they are 'epiphanic' or cognitive. Following very much the terms in which William James theorized emotion, it wants you to experience the work of art viscerally, on your body. It wants your adrenaline to pump, and for you to fight, not fly, as you experience yourself experiencing the artwork. This immersion is the condition to which modernist art strives, and this in turn implies that, whether its producers in any given case approved of the new somaticity or not, and hence had an opinion on the place of the human subject in the new energy economy, escape from this economy for the artwork itself is impossible. Given this, the modernist text begs to be read as a kind of escape manual: it shows how to take an intensely surveillance-oriented biopolitical regime, in which our every movement to show our somatic reactions, our energy expenditure, is observed, and not only suggests how to make this bearable, even pleasurable, but—revamping the pleasure as a politics—offers some blueprint for people under cover of this pleasure to recast their roles in the energy economy.

In such a recasting, movement is key. Contemplate again the enormous, devastating poignancy of the original scene where all this began, with Muybridge's and Marey's film sequences of a man throwing a javelin, a woman lifting an urn. Both naked. This is bare life. Remember Agamben's provocative declaration: 'By the end of the nineteenth century, the Western bourgeoisie had definitely lost its gestures.' It may be true that the Victorians had a repertoire of gestures that went with supposedly deep feelings, what we now think of as the incongruously grandiloquent emotional gestures of late nineteenth-century Italian grand opera, for example. In the wake of all that, the modernist artwork becomes a documentary of the moment when those gestures seemed hollow, and the somatic scene displays people who are at a loss for gestures. (Agamben goes on to claim that cinema was invented to teach us a new gestural repertoire.) The claim of this essay, however, is that most art, with the possible exception of dance, is more than a matter of gesture as art form. Rather, modernist art shows people trying to recreate themselves as energetic, and to imagine the material world energized, at the moment of the birth of the new economy of energy. The key years may be 1904–5. Think of this congruence: in 1904 Mackinder writes that the available space of the world has run out as the whole of the globe is mapped and colonized. In 1905, Einstein publishes his proofs that all matter is really energy, slow motion is invented in film, and 1904, aptly, is the year in which *Ulysses* is set. The age of materialism is over; the era of energetics has begun. From that juncture onwards, art had to become an energy evaluator, and every artist an energy-meter reader. Now every artwork was a kind of fuse, like Duchamp's nude girl as spark plug, a transmission point between different flows and strengths of energy currents. Regulating this flow through human subjects, modernism invented the soma text. Watch the subject squirm, watch her heart beat. Induce the same squirm and blood-pressure rate in the reader now unsure of the nineteenth-century's accepted gestures, and already exhausted by modernity. Modernist artworks are machines for generating soma in controlled experiments. We receive modernist art as a pleasurable stress.

NOTES

1. Friedrich Nietzsche, *Ecce Homo*, in *Basic Writings of Nietzsche,* translated by Walter Kaufmann (New York: Random House, 1968), p. 693.
2. On the history of laughter, see Anca Parvulescu, *Laughter: Notes on a Passion* (Cambridge, MA: MIT Press, 2010).
3. W. B. Yeats, 'Among School Children', in *Selected Poems and Two Plays of W. B. Yeats*, edited by M. L. Rosenthal (New York: Macmillan, 1962), p. 115.
4. James Joyce, *Ulysses* (New York: Modern Library, 1961), 17:731.
5. Giorgio Agamben, 'Notes on Gesture', in *Means Without Ends: Notes on Politics* (Minneapolis, MN: University of Minnesota Press, 2000), pp. 49–62; 49.
6. Franco Moretti, 'The Long Goodbye: *Ulysses* and the End of Liberal Capitalism' in *Signs Taken For Wonders* (London: Verso, 1988), pp. 182–208.
7. Joyce, *Ulysses*, 8:183.
8. Virginia Woolf, *The Essays of Virginia Woolf*, vol. 3. 1919–1924, edited by Andrew McNeillie (New York: Harcourt Brace Jovanovich, 1988), p. 33.
9. Oscar Wilde, *The Picture of Dorian Gray*, in *The Portable Oscar Wilde*, edited by Stanley Weintraub (New York: Viking Penguin, 1977), pp. 225–6.
10. See, among others, Stephen Kern, *The Culture of Time and Space, 1880–1918* (Cambridge, MA: Harvard University Press, new edition, 2003), Cecelia Tichi, *Shifting Gears: Technology, Literature, Culture in Modernist America* (Chapel Hill, NC: University of North Carolina Press, 1987), and Enda Duffy, *The Speed Handbook: Velocity, Pleasure, Modernism* (Durham, NC: Duke University Press, 2009).
11. Georges Cangueilhem, *Knowledge of Life* (New York: Fordham University Press, 1988), p. 86.
12. Gilles de la Tourette, *Études cliniques et physiologiques sur la marche* (Paris: Bureaux de progrès, 1886), quoted in Agamben, 'Notes on Gesture,' p. 49.
13. Anson Rabinbach, *The Human Motor: Energy, Fatigue, and the Origins of Modernity* (Berkeley, CA: University of California Press, 1992).
14. G. M. Beard, *American Nervousness, Its Causes and Consequences* (New York: G. P. Putnam's Sons, 1881).
15. Émile Durkheim, *Suicide: A Study in Sociology* (1897) (London: Routledge Classics, 2002), p. 14, and cited in Rabinbach, *The Human Motor*, p. 154.
16. Angelo Mosso, *Fear* (London: Longmans, Green, and Company, 1896).
17. William James, 'What is an Emotion?' *Mind*, 9 (1884): pp. 188–205; 190.

18. Charles Darwin, *The Expression of the Emotions in Man and Animals* (London: John Murray, 1872).

19. Walter Bradford Cannon, *Bodily Changes in Pain, Hunger, Fear and Rage: An Account of Recent Researches into the Function of Emotional Excitement* (New York: Appleton, 1915).

20. Hans Selye, *The Stress of Life* (New York: McGraw-Hill, 1956).

21. Jonathan Crary, *24/7: Late Capitalism and the Ends of Sleep* (London: Verso, 2013).

22. Paul Virilio, *The Art of the Motor*, translated by Julie Rose (Minneapolis, MN: University of Minnesota Press, 1995), p. 123.

23. Halford Mackinder, 'The Geographical Pivot of History', *The Geographic Journal*, 4:23 (April 1904), pp. 421–37.

24. Virginia Woolf, *Mrs Dalloway* (New York: Vintage, 1982), p. 184.

25. T. S. Eliot, *The Wasteland* (1922) in *Collected Poems 1909–1935* (New York: Harcourt, Brace and Company, 1936), pp. 67–98.

26. Aldous Huxley, *Brave New World* (1932) (New York: Harper Perennial, 2006), p. 52.

27. D. H. Lawrence, *Selected Literary Criticism*, edited by Anthony Beal (New York: Viking, 1956), pp. 114–15.

28. Teresa Brennan, *Exhausting Modernity: Grounds for a New Economy* (London: Routledge, 2000).

8

Numbers It Is
The Musemathematics of Modernism

Steven Connor

There can be no doubt of what we have so often been told, that the modern world experiences itself in terms of speed and flux, of a glissade that outruns perception. But it is also, coincidentally and consequentially, the case that modernity is a matter of measurement. This is often represented as a conflict between the quality of 'pure' movement, announced (Bergson) and denounced (Lewis) throughout modern literature and culture, and efforts to measure and calibrate that movement. As with many dichotomies, these two alternatives provoke and perpetuate each other. Modernity is expressed and experienced as fluent speed, to be sure; but it is also embodied and epitomized in the speedometer—a word that is recorded in print for the first time in *The Times* in 1904; a speedometer was offered as an optional extra on the Ford Model T, first produced in 1908. Modern thinking is toned and textured by the pull between quality and quantity, intensity and measure—in short, between the continuous and the discontinuous. We might associate the speedometer, as emblematic modernist device, with the switch, which gave to the modern world its characteristic capacity for abrupt and absolute transitions between on and off, slow and fast. It is striking that Samuel Beckett, who had devoted so much attention in his work to slow diminishments and gradual fadings-out should have left, as the final words of the last play he ever completed, 'Make sense who may. I switch off.'[1]

This tension expresses itself in a heightened awareness of the defining role of scale in resolving molecular or corpuscular aggregates into lines or series. We might pause to recall what Michel Serres repeatedly notes, that the derivation of 'tension' and allied words like 'tone' and 'tune' is uncertain: perhaps from *teino*, to stretch, but perhaps also from *temno*, to cut or dissect. The same ambiguity attaches to the word 'rhythm', which comes from the Greek word which means 'to flow', even as rhythm is precisely that which chops duration into measures.[2] Modernist movement quakes with these tremors of minimality. Beneath or within the blur of persistence of vision, there is the 'dynamite of the tenth of a second',[3] splitting or atomizing every apparent continuity. We may note, as a prelude to the ideas laid out here, the primal preoccupation of cinema with the fact of explosion. Moving image was not just employed to analyse into its components the gestures and movements of human bodies; it was also employed to restore or rearticulate the temporal contour of an action that seemed to consist of nothing but dissolution.

Leopold Bloom puzzles over one version of this dichotomy in the 'Sirens' episode of *Ulysses*.

> Numbers it is. All music when you come to think. Two multiplied by two divided by half is twice one. Vibrations: chords those are. One plus two plus six is seven. Do anything you like with figures juggling. Always find out this equal to that. Symmetry under a cemetery wall. He doesn't see my mourning. Callous: all for his own gut. Musemathematics. And you think you're listening to the etherial. But suppose you said it like: Martha, seven times nine minus x is thirtyfive thousand. Fall quite flat. It's on account of the sounds it is.[4]

Students continue to be subject to headshaking reproof for calling this kind of thing 'stream of consciousness', and with Bloom indeed, there is very little quality of the stream, with his typically staccato shunts of thought from one idea to the next, sometimes juddering forward along a more or less intelligible straight line, sometimes slicing aside, as in the sudden reflections on Richie Goulding's purblind appetite. The only example of streaming in his choppy discourse is the coinage 'Musemathematics', and even this lacks the collideorscape inventiveness of many of Joyce's word blends. 'Musemathematics' is a slight improvement on 'mathematical music', since it seems to activate the idea of musing, anticipating the 'museyroom' of *Finnegans Wake*,[5] but the improvement is minimal. The word wobbles slightly between the singular of 'music' and the plural of 'mathematics', recalling the slight incongruity of the phrase 'Numbers it is', an incongruity precisely of what is known grammatically as 'number'.

Indeed, we might view all the 'music' of the 'Sirens' episode as the kind of mathematization about which Bloom speculates here, involving as it does the addition, subtraction, and transposition of letters and words, considered as quanta. 'Sirens' is full of lyric lengthenings of vowels which may appear to make the words croon and yearn ('Seabloom, greaseabloom'),[6] but it also has reduction to musical elements, like the scale picked out in relaying the actions of the deaf waiter: 'Bald deaf Pat brought quite flat pad ink. Pat set with ink pen quite flat pad. Pat took plate dish knife fork. Pat went.'[7] At times, the writing of the chapter itself seems to adopt Bloom's mathematical reading of music, in which the mimicry of musical form actually bleaches out musical effect from the words, which are reduced to what Garrett Stewart has called 'alphabetic integers'.[8] In this respect, the chapter itself can seem as tone-deaf as Pat the waiter. An example would be Anthony Burgess's reading of the phrase 'Blmstdp' for 'Bloom stood up' as a mimicry of a 'hollow fifth', a chord in which the thirds are suppressed.[9] This identification benefits from the mathematical pun which makes the (notoriously ugly or unmusical) fifth the result of the removal of the vowels, of which there are five, both because there are five vowels and because five of them (o, o, o, o, u) have been removed.

But we should note that Bloom's musings go in opposite directions. 'Numbers it is. All music when you come to think' could mean both 'Music is just a matter of numbers when it comes down to it', or the more Pythagorean 'All mathematical relations are a kind of music'. The reference to 'the etherial' might also evoke Pythagoras, as well as the coalescence of matter and movement in the magical, all-pervading pseudo-substance, the ether, which Lord Salisbury, in an address to the British Association for the Advancement of Science, described as 'the substantive case of the verb "to undulate"'.[10]

Bloom's apprehension of music as mathematics is embodied in the bit of apparatus that Lambert demonstrates for indicating which turn is on in the music hall. Joyce reminds us of this apparatus in a wonderful conjoining of letters and numbers, as we briefly glimpse Blazes Boylan's secretary putting aside her book at work:

> Miss Dunne hid the Capel street library copy of *The Woman in White* far back in her drawer and rolled a sheet of gaudy notepaper into her typewriter.

> Too much mystery business in it. Is he in love with that one, Marion? Change it and get another by Mary Cecil Haye.

> The disk shot down the groove, wobbled a while, ceased and ogled them: six.

> Miss Dunne clicked on the keyboard:

> — 16 June 1904.

> Five tallwhitehatted sandwichmen between Monypeny's corner and the slab where Wolfe Tone's statue was not, eeled themselves turning H. E. L. Y.'S and plodded back as they had come.[11]

Bloom's mathematical musings recall Helmholtz's demonstrations of the compound nature of sound vibrations in *On the Sensations of Tone*, and come at the end of a long period of reflections on the atomistic components of composite forms. The nineteenth century had seen the invention and popularization of the idea of the mathematical curve, in the characteristic bell shape of Gaussian or normal distribution. More generally, it had made familiar the idea that the movement or transmission of messages or information was most conveniently effected by decomposing and then reassembling the information to be transmitted. The ideal of maximal convertibility and maximum communicability that was developed in the nineteenth century—which might be seen as an ideal of maximal continuity, or minimized discontinuity—required the intervention of a discontinuous medium. As many have noted, the seance and later on the telepathic soirée were a kind of parallel to technological forms of transmission like the telegraph, for they employed precisely the same logic of decomposition followed by synthesis. Table-rapping was a sort of slow typewriting. In this sense, all the allegedly analogue technologies of the nineteenth century, were in fact digital, or protodigital, in that they involved the translation of a continuously variable wave into a discontinuous set of variations. The epitome of the protodigital medium was the cinema, with its dramatic slicing and dicing into the continuity of the visible for the purposes of capturing and reproducing motion. But the most widespread digital code in the nineteenth century was, of course, Morse, which makes its appearance in *Ulysses* in Stephen's evocation of the dog on the shore of Sandymount:

> His snout lifted barked at the wavenoise, herds of seamorse. They serpented towards his feet, curling, unfurling many crests, every ninth, breaking, plashing, from far, from farther out, waves and waves.[12]

The passage indicates not only the oscillations of position that make up each individual wave, but also, at a higher level, the alternating current of the waves, which allows them to be distinguished and enumerated. These are oscillations that are not only measurable in terms of number, but are also oscillations in and out of the condition of number.

ZENO

A simple way of summarizing this concern is to say that modernity encounters in a series of strikingly practical ways the paradoxes of Zeno regarding movement. In accounts of modernism, Bergson has carried the day against Zeno. This is partly because the Bergsonian critique of the conjoined values of calculation, quantity, and intellect and correlative praise of pure becoming have become sovereign in our ways of thinking about art and its relation to time and meaning; for it is surely Bergson rather than Nietzsche who has powered thinking about language, form, and force in France, most notably in the work of Gilles Deleuze. If there is one rock to which we can cling amid the flux and foam of approximations, it is that the realm of Being, against which life, becoming, difference, etc., are pitted, is characterized by number. Numbers represent the possibility of absolute and exact distinctness, and a world of inert discontinuities which we teach ourselves ever and again to fear and abhor. Ultimately, numbers are death, death being what comes when your number is up. The time philosophy of Bergson drew together into one current the preference for the power of intuition, which was able to apprehend the complex persistingness in fluidity and fluidity in persistingness of things, and the power of intellect, which divides the world up into static objects. Bertrand Russell characterizes this attitude neatly in his essay 'The Philosophy of Bergson' of 1912: 'Thus logic and mathematics do not represent a positive spiritual effort . . . but mere somnambulism, in which the will is suspended, and the mind is no longer active. Incapacity for mathematics is therefore a sign of grace—fortunately a very common one.'[13] We have taught ourselves to prefer motion conceived, not as the magical and, for Zeno, inconceivable passage from one fixed condition to another, but as the pulsive current of becoming, in which nothing is ever entirely left behind, and all is a continuous commingling of retention and protention.

For Bergson, the force of 'life' was not only immeasurable; it was also inexhaustible. This was good news for the allies in the First World War, who Bergson assured in 1914 were fighting an enemy fuelled only by its own barbarous mechanism, whereas the allies were on the undefeatable side of life: 'to the force which feeds only on its own brutality we are opposing that which seeks outside and above itself a principle of life and renovation. While the one is gradually spending itself, the other is continually remaking itself.'[14] It is not just that Germany will gradually run out of nitrates and international credit; it is that they have blunderingly pledged themselves to measurability itself.

Measurability, and, in particular, the infinite divisibility proposed in Zeno's paradoxes, belongs to an order of discontinuity to which Bergson opposes an absolute continuity. Ultimately, Bergson's opponent is divisibility itself. To a world of distinct objects, Bergson opposes a world of commingled vibrations. The distinction between two colours is a distinction between two frequencies, which seems absolute only because of 'the narrow duration into which are contracted the billions of vibrations which they execute in one of our moments'.[15] Slow down our perceptions so that we can 'live it out at a slower rhythm' and we are synchronized with those vibrations, and the colours blur together, or become simply vibrations, as when one pushes one's nose right up to a Seurat or a pixellated video screen, which, oddly enough, Bergson refers to, not as pure quantity, but as 'quality itself',[16] the blending of sensation and perception. Like many others, Bergson finds in the new physics, and especially atomic physics, a contradiction of the fundamental discontinuity in nature announced by Democritus, in his announcement that all that exists are atoms and the spaces between them. 'We see force more and more materialized, the atom more and more idealized, the two terms converging towards a common limit and the universe thus recovering its continuity.... [T]he nearer we draw to the ultimate elements of matter the better we note the vanishing of that discontinuity which our senses perceived on the surface.'[17] Bergsonism amounts to the demand for 'the idea of an universal continuity'[18]—the smooth enjambement effected by that 'n' before 'universal' being a little phono-philosophical rhyme offered by Bergson's translator. The same action of magnification and deceleration is involved in Benjamin's decimal and decimating dynamite, the effect of which was to explode the seeming integrity of forms. Dance and music provide Bergson with examples of absolute continuity, in which before and after are indisseverable:

> If jerky movements are wanting in grace, the reason is that each of them is self-sufficient and does not announce those which are to follow. If curves are more graceful than broken lines, the reason is that, while a curved line changes its direction at every moment, every new direction is indicated in the preceding one. Thus the perception of ease in motion passes over into the pleasure of mastering the flow of time and of holding the future in the present.[19]

But there is something strange and logically irksome about this systematic preference. Benjamin's evocation of the Angel of History can help us understand why. The Angel is being blown backwards out of Paradise. Presumably because the Angel is history, rather than a creature in or of it, the wind that is blowing out of Paradise can never budge him because history is in itself movement; it cannot itself move. Rather the Angel is suspended, like a windhover 'riding the rolling level underneath him steady air', buffeted by the agitations that it is. For the Angel, there is only emergence without decay, an absolute continuity that never allows for the opening-up of distance, or the lengthening-out of time that Bergson calls 'extensity' because nothing ever dies away. Hence, history is all of a piece, and appears to be just an accumulating heap of debris. There is no movement, no becoming. Or, rather, there is only becoming, with no ceasing.

At the end of the third chapter of his *Creative Evolution*, Bergson provides us with another image of the movement of history, as an immense and all-inclusive push of life through matter:

> As the smallest grain of dust is bound up with our entire solar system, drawn along with it in that undivided movement of descent which is materiality itself, so all organized

beings, from the humblest to the highest, from the first origins of life to the time in which we are, and in all places as in all times, do but evidence a single impulsion, the inverse of the movement of matter, and in itself indivisible. All the living hold together, and all yield to the same tremendous push. The animal takes its stand on the plant, man bestrides animality, and the whole of humanity, in space and in time, is one immense army gallop-ing beside and before and behind each of us in an overwhelming charge able to beat down every resistance and clear the most formidable obstacles, perhaps even death.[20]

Bertrand Russell comments that:

a cool critic, who feels himself a mere spectator, perhaps an unsympathetic spectator, of the charge in which man is mounted upon animality, may be inclined to think that calm and careful thought is hardly compatible with this form of exercise. When he is told that thought is a mere means of action, the mere impulse to avoid obstacles in the field, he may feel that such a view is becoming in a cavalry officer, but not in a philos-opher, whose business, after all, is with thought.[21]

For Bergson, intellect does violence to the world by fragmenting it; for Russell, Bergsonian intuition does violence to the world by forcing distinctness into unity.

This would in fact be the result of Bergson's absolute continuity without discon-tinuity, in which time only ever thickened. Without the possibility of discontinuity, in fact, without the numerable divisions insisted on by Zeno, there would be conti-nuity, but no movement; there would be, we may suppose, movement, but no internal spacing or differentiation, no movement away, no self-distancing of time, which would merely convolute and coagulate, like the weirdly 'smeared' state of matter known as the Bose-Einstein condensate that can occur at temperatures close to zero, which was predicted in 1924–5 and experimentally produced in 1995.

There is no absolute discontinuity between continuity and discontinuity. Zeno shows, not that movement is impossible, but rather that it may not be possible to make movement fully intelligible. He is right, not that there is no movement, but that move-ment is not intelligible without dependence on a principle of discontinuity that seems to make it impossible. The problem posed by the Eleatic paradoxes is not how to explain movement, but how to explain the fact that movement has these two incom-patible but indispensable dimensions, one merely aggregative, the other integral. Perhaps the reason why the mind is so exercised by the question of motion is because, in considering it, it must itself alternate, itself thus 'mined with a motion', between the plenitude of the continuous and the ration of the discontinuous. Readings of the par-adoxes like Bergson's are an attempt to create an absolute discontinuity between the discontinuity of intellect and the continuity revealed to intuition. Meanwhile the con-ditions of modern life continued to confirm the existence of Zeno's paradox, confirm-ing that there was no discontinuity between continuity and discontinuity.

ALTERNATING CURRENTS

Continuity and discontinuity are the two polarities between which much mod-ern writing alternates. Indeed, we might say that it is enacted in the principle of alternation itself, as this became more and more apparent in the machineries of the modern world. This is the period in which the concepts of periodicity and frequency enter powerfully, if also subliminally, into general awareness, uniting the discontinuous and the continuous at a higher level, since, in the repeating wave, the continuously variable curve forms a series of distinguishable oscillations. The movements of modernism are as much pulsations as propulsions. They are also movements of active, but immobile agitation. In a sense, modernity comes into being with the defeat of Edison's direct current and the adoption of the Tesla-Westinghouse system of alternating current. From now on, vectors would be indissolubly joined to oscillations, those inner atoms, or elementary particles of movement. Modern movement was the movement of fans, flywheels, propellers, dynamos, escalators, revolving doors (patented by Theophilus van Kannel in 1888) and rotary engines of all kinds, Gatling guns, cranked cameras and projectors, the tank, which propelled itself forward by means of repeated rotations of a single repeating loop, and helical instruments such as the phonograph and, later, the tape recorder. Their operation brought into being a whole new dinning tinnitus of sounds—hummings, whirrings, rattlings, hissings, whizzings, and buzzings. Cinema turned the binary alternations of instruments like the thaumatrope into a progressive form, but this happened by degrees, and Lynda Nead has observed how common it was for early films, especially striptease films, to be shown repeatedly backwards and forwards.[22]

If it is true that modernism has a defining attraction to the continuously varying waveform and indeed to curves of all kinds, it is also often drawn to the exposure of the blocky elements of those curves, through slowings or close-ups that reveal the elements of which they are aggregated. Garrett Stewart has pointed to what he calls the 'flicker effect' of modernism,[23] in which the spool seems to get caught or to judder, suddenly revealing the individual components of which film or narrative is composed, moments at which the numberless becomes suddenly numerable. A literary parallel to this is to be found in Conrad's *Secret Agent*, in which we read that Winnie Verloc is perplexed by the fact that her mother suddenly starts spending half-crowns and five shillingses on cab fares. Her mother's unaccustomed 'mania for locomotion' is explained when she reveals that she has secured new accommodation in an almshouse 'founded by a wealthy innkeeper for the destitute widows of the trade'.[24] Conrad renders her last cab journey as an extraordinary kind of agitation on the spot:

> Winnie followed her mother into the cab. Stevie climbed on the box. His vacant mouth and distressed eyes depicted the state of his mind in regard to the transactions which were taking place. In the narrow streets the progress of the journey was made sensible to those within by the near fronts of the houses gliding past slowly and shakily, with a great rattle and jingling of glass, as if about to collapse behind the cab; and the infirm horse, with the harness hung over his sharp backbone flapping very loose about his thighs, appeared to be dancing mincingly on his toes with infinite patience. Later on, in the wider space of Whitehall, all visual evidences of motion became imperceptible. The rattle and jingle of glass went on indefinitely in front of the long Treasury building – and time itself seemed to stand still.[25]

TELLING

A writer is often most palpably and painfully quartered between quantity and quality during the process of writing. Even before the days of automatic word counts, writers were driven to keep count of what they were writing, in words, paragraphs, chapters, and pages, and, later, print runs, sales figures, and revenues, for all that they might struggle to forge more fluent and organic forms of unity. Few writers have documented this process as evocatively as Virginia Woolf in her diaries, a form of writing which is cast between the uncaring ordinality of the clock and the more fluctuant and approximate graphings of thought and feeling. There is a sometimes bathetic counterpoint in her diaries between the attempts to capture fleeting insights and states of feeling and the rendering of calendrical accounts, through the recording of times, dates, birthdays. She begins her first entry for 1919 explaining that she is restricted by a hand injury to one hour's writing a day, but that 'having hoarded it this morning I may spend part of it now, since L. is out and I am much behindhand with the month of January'.[26] With her thirty-seventh birthday a few days away, on 25 January 1919, she imagines what will be her attitude at the age of fifty to what she will find written there: 'If Virginia Woolf at the age of 50, when she sits down to build her memoirs out of these books, is unable to make a phrase as it should be made, I can only condole with her.'[27] She undertakes, for the benefit of the 'elderly lady' she will be at fifty, to provide a full account of her friends, their achievements, and a forecast of their future works, concluding that '[t]he lady of 50 will be able to say how near to the truth I come; but I have written enough for tonight (only 15 minutes I see)'.[28] A week short of thirteen years later, with *The Waves* behind her and her fiftieth birthday in sight, she rationed out for herself, alas too generously, a prospectus of the two decades of work still in front of her:

> I shall be fifty on 25th, Monday week that is: and sometimes I feel I have lived 250 years already, and sometimes that I am still the youngest person on the omnibus. (Nessa says that she still always thinks this as she sits down.) And I want to write another four novels: *Waves*, I mean; and *The Tap on the Door*; and to go through English literature like a string through cheese, or rather like some industrious insect, eating its way from book to book, from Chaucer to Lawrence. This is a programme, considering my slowness, and how I get slower, thicker, more intolerant of the fling and the rush, to last out my 20 years, if I have them.[29]

There are interferences in these periodic cycles (later, she notes that it would have been her father's ninety-sixth birthday, and that, if he were still alive, she would never have written anything). Even her mood is given an implicit calibration, with her references to the fluctuations of her 'spiritual temperature'.[30] While she was writing, she oscillated between the desire for fluency, or continuity, and the desire for a kind of compacted integrity. Her sense of the book she is writing is alternately light, floating, fluent, dashing, and also 'tense and packed',[31] 'a hard muscular book'.[32] Time and again, she speaks of her desire to smooth out 'chop and change',[33] to create a kind of unity. These two conditions are imaged in the move from handwriting to typescript. She struggles to find the right kind of composite image for her own composition. Often, this image is of some entity made up of oscillation itself, for example *The Moths*, the idea of which 'hovers somewhere at the back of my brain'.[34] The title of the book itself shuttles for a few weeks between *The Moths* and *The Waves*, which we can read as a kind of alternation between different alternating frequencies, the rapid whirr of the moth's wing, and the slow, booming or thudding pulse of the waves—in '*the concussion of the waves breaking… with muffled thuds, like logs falling, on the shore*'.[35] Throughout the diaries, the activity of thought is rendered in the quasi-mechanical whirrings and flutterings of insects: 'The mind is the most capricious of insects—flitting, fluttering.'[36] Woolf strives to achieve fluency, but also is brought repeatedly to the recognition that this continuity is only achievable against the background of resistance formed by the steady diminishments of the clock: 'I find myself in the old driving whirlwind of writing against time. Have I ever written with it?'[37]

This sensation of mobility achieved against resistance precipitates a marvellous, self-referring image of rooks suspended, windhover- or angel-like, in the blustery air:

> I have to watch the rooks beating up against the wind, which is high, and still I say to myself instinctively, 'What's the phrase for that?' and try to make more and more vivid the roughness of the air current and the tremor of the rook's wing slicing as if the air were full of ridges and ripples and roughness. They rise and sink, up and down, as if the exercise rubbed and braced them like swimmers in rough water.[38]

Woolf's diaries are full of actions of counting up, counting out, and counting off, and they provide an energizing metre throughout her novels too. There is Susan grimly counting down the days to the end of the school term: 'I count each step as I mount, counting each step something done with. So each night I tear off the old day from the calendar, and screw it tight into a ball.'[39] Then there is the tense counting-off of the seconds to track the progress of the German air raid in *The Years*:

> Nicholas looked at his watch as if he were timing the guns. There was something queer about him, Eleanor thought; medical, priestly? He wore a seal that hung down from his watch-chain. The number on the box opposite was 1397. She noticed everything. The Germans must be overhead now. She felt a curious heaviness on top of her head. One, two, three, four, she counted, looking up at the greenish-grey stone. Then there was a violent crack of sound, like the split of lightning in the sky. The spider's web oscillated.
>
> 'On top of us,' said Nicholas, looking up. They all looked up. At any moment a bomb might fall. There was dead silence. In the silence they heard Maggie's voice in the kitchen.
>
> 'That was nothing. Turn round and go to sleep.' She spoke very calmly and soothingly.
>
> One, two, three four, Eleanor counted. The spider's web was swaying. That stone may fall, she thought, fixing a certain stone with her eyes. Then a gun boomed again. It was fainter—further away.
>
> 'That's over,' said Nicholas. He shut his watch with a click.[40]

As Joyce's washerwomen in 'Anna Livia Plurabelle' assert, 'every telling has a tal-ing',[41] and there is no writer in whose work the actions of telling, telling off, and tailing off are more entrained with each other than Samuel Beckett. Molloy's account of his laborious communication with his deaf and blind mother brings Stogether sequence and repetition, cardinality and ordinality, in telling fashion:

> I got into communication with her by rapping on her skull. One knock meant yes, two no, three I don't know, four, money, five goodbye. I was hard put to ram this code into her ruined and frantic understanding, but I did it, in the end. That she should confuse yes, no, I don't know and goodbye was all the same to me, I confused them myself. But that she should associate the four knocks with anything but money was something to be avoided at all costs. During the period of training therefore, at the same time as I administered the four knocks on her skull, I stuck a bank-note under her nose or in her mouth. In the innocence of my heart! For she seemed to have lost, if not absolutely all notion of mensuration, at least the faculty of counting beyond two. It was too far for her, yes, the distance was too great, from one to four. By the time she came to the fourth knock she imagined she was only at the second, the first two having been erased from her memory as completely as if they had never been felt.[42]

The counterposed orders of narrative and re-counting, of narrative and counting, here give the passage its characteristically syncopated or, to use a more Beckettian word, spavined movement. The fling and lingering of the writing are cross-cut with the table-rapping of the seance and the clopping of Clever Hans's hooves. We can perhaps think of the knocking on Mag's skull as the whirrings of Woolf's inspi-rational moths or waves slowed down to a frequency at which the cycles become countable. Just when it appears we are about to be allowed to break out of Mag's own autistic binarism, and the unintelligible knockings and bangings are about to build into a kind of narrative *durée*, we are dragged back to the order of elementary bodily percussion—the solution to Molloy's difficulty being not the invention of another code, but the simple amplification of the old one: 'I looked for and finally found a more effective way of putting the idea of money into her head. This con-sisted in replacing the four knocks of my index knuckle by one or more (according to my needs) thumps of the fist, on her skull. That she understood.'[43] Like the fabled monoglot Englishman whose method of getting a foreigner to understand him is to Speak More Loudly, this is the introversion of sense (in the double French sense of meaning and direction), the turning of movement on and into itself, to form a standing wave, a thrumming, mobile matter of pure pulsation.

It would be oxymoronic of an essay like this to have gone very far in a particular direction, or to claim to have got anywhere in particular. But it would be wholly consistent for it to turn back on itself in review. I have wanted to show that math-ematics, and in particular number, far from being the adversary of grace and intu-ition, is in fact a lever and accelerator of the modernist evocations of speed, flux, and the desire for 'universal continuity'.[44] Number is important because it forms part of the alternation between the principles of continuity and discontinuity, mel-ody and percussion, principles which come together in the heightened awareness of states of flicker, fluctuation, and alternation, and in a focus on the atomistic divisibility of forms of modern movement, depending as they often do on mechanical operations involving multitudinous but innumerable repeated process. Modernist movement is mathematized: in it, matter is riddled with motion, and motion condensed and accelerated into a tensely shivering kind of matter. Modernity may be characterized by the multiplicity of the gearing mechanisms needed to effect these transpositions between levels, scales, and ratios. The epistemological apparatus required for this might be given the same name as that invented at the beginning of his career by the poet, Marxist literary critic, and sometime engineer, Christopher Caudwell—the automatic infinitely variable gear.

NOTES

1. Samuel Beckett, *Complete Dramatic Works* (London: Faber and Faber, 1984), p. 476.
2. Michel Serres, *Récits d'humanisme* (Paris: Le Pommier, 2006), p. 41.
3. Walter Benjamin, *Illuminations: Essays and Reflections*, edited by Hannah Arendt, translated by Harry Zohn (New York: Schocken, 1969), p. 236.
4. James Joyce, *Ulysses*, edited by Jeri Johnson (Oxford: Oxford University Press, 1993), p. 267.
5. James Joyce, *Finnegans Wake* (London: Faber and Faber, 1971), p. 8.
6. Joyce, *Ulysses*, p. 279.
7. Joyce, *Ulysses*, p. 267.
8. Garrett Stewart, 'Cinécriture: Modernism's Flicker Effect,' *New Literary History*, 299 (1998): pp. 727–68; 729.
9. Anthony Burgess, *Re Joyce* (New York: W.W. Norton, 1965), p. 69.
10. Quoted, Oliver Lodge, *The Ether of Space* (New York and London: Harper and Brothers, 1909), p. 113.
11. Joyce, *Ulysses*, p. 220.
12. Joyce, *Ulysses*, p. 46.
13. Bertrand Russell, 'The Philosophy of Bergson.' *Monist*, 22 (1912): pp. 321–47; 326.
14. Henri Bergson, *The Meaning of the War: Life and Matter in Conflict* (London and Edinburgh: Ballantyne Press, 1915), pp. 46–7.
15. Henri Bergson, *Matter and Memory*, translated by Nancy Margaret Paul and W. Scott Palmer (London: Swan Sonnenschein; New York: Macmillan, 1911), p. 268.
16. Bergson, *Matter and Memory*, p. 268.
17. Bergson, *Matter and Memory*, pp. 265–6.
18. Bergson, *Matter and Memory*, p. 260.
19. Henri Bergson, *Time and Free Will: An Essay on the Immediate Data of Consciousness*, translated by F. L. Pogson (London: George Allen and Unwin, 1910), p. 12.
20. Henri Bergson, *Creative Evolution*, translated by Arthur Mitchell (New York: Henry Holt, 1911), pp. 270–1.
21. Russell, 'The Philosophy of Bergson, p. 333.
22. Lynda Nead, *The Haunted Gallery: Painting, Photography, Film c.1900* (New Haven, CT and London: Yale University Press, 2007), p. 194.
23. Stewart, 'Cinécriture', p. 731.
24. Joseph Conrad, *The Secret Agent: A Simple Tale* (Harmondsworth: Penguin, 1980), p. 127.
25. Conrad, *Secret Agent*, p. 131.

26. Virginia Woolf, *A Writer's Diary: Being Extracts from the Diary of Virginia Woolf*, edited by Leonard Woolf (London: Triad/Granada, 1981), p. 17.
27. Woolf, *A Writer's Diary*, p. 17.
28. Woolf, *A Writer's Diary*, pp. 17, 18.
29. Woolf, *A Writer's Diary*, p. 174.
30. Woolf, *A Writer's Diary*, p. 265.
31. Virginia Woolf, *The Waves* (London: Triad/Granada, 1980), p. 170.
32. Woolf, *A Writer's Diary*, p. 106
33. Woolf, *The Waves*, p. 102.
34. Woolf, *A Writer's Diary*, p. 131.
35. Woolf, *The Waves*, p. 20.
36. Woolf, *A Writer's Diary*, p. 124.
37. Woolf, *A Writer's Diary*, p. 127.
38. Woolf, *A Writer's Diary*, p. 131.
39. Woolf, *The Waves*, p. 27.
40. Virginia Woolf, *The Years*, edited by Susan Hill and Steven Connor (London: Vintage, 2000), p. 254.
41. Joyce, *Finnegans Wake*, p. 213.
42. Samuel Beckett, *Molloy, Malone Dies, The Unnamable* (London: Calder and Boyars, 1973), p. 18.
43. Beckett, *Molloy, Malone Dies, The Unnamable*, p. 18.
44. Bergson, *Matter and Memory*, p. 260.

9

'Do Not Call Me a Dancer'
(Isadora Duncan, 1929)
Dance and Modernist Experimentation

Olga Taxidou

Isadora Duncan's aphoristic proclamation not to call her a dancer makes both a thematic and a formal demand. 'I use my body as my medium just as a writer uses his words,'[1] she states in a conflation of textuality and embodiment that was to have a huge impact on experimentation in both modernist dance and literary modernism. T. S. Eliot expresses a similar formal quest when he states, as a response to the phenomenal success of the Ballets Russes in Paris (1909–29), that dance offers an *askesis* and poses the rhetorical question, 'If there is a future for drama and particularly for poetic drama, will it not be in the direction indicated by the ballet?'[2] For many of the literary modernists, the encounter with the theatre poses the question of how to present poetry on stage. For Eliot, Pound, and Yeats this quest in Cocteau's words for both 'poetry in the theatre' and 'poetry of theatre' is in many ways addressed through recourse to the dance experiments of the period.[3] Dance offers a laboratory where the discourses of Hellenism, Orientalism, Primitivism, technology, and gender interact, fuse with, and contradict each other, creating the movement that has come to be known as Modern Dance, but also inflecting the broader aesthetics of modernism.

One could claim that Duncan's entire 'project' acts as an appropriate precursor for the experiments in Modern Dance. However, it is a precursor that at once creates a historical genealogy *and* propels these experiments into the future. Her early training in the Delsarte system, her fascination with Nietzsche's *The Birth of Tragedy* (which she called her bible during her Berlin tour) and her direct attempts to be inspired by Greek statues (the Tanagra figures) create a distinct Hellenist dimension to her work. This form of Hellenism, which oscillates between embodiment and monumentalization (something that H. D. would later partake in), rather than being viewed as anti-modern,[4] can be seen as part of what Jacques Rancière calls the 'archeo-modern turn',[5] looking both backwards and forwards. It engages discourses of technology while also enacting a type of modernist primitivism. For Duncan this fusion also had a vitalist, feminist dimension, one that was to inspire many aspects of Sapphic modernism.

Her first appearance on the London stage (16 March 1900) at the New Gallery was accompanied by a reading of Theocritus by Jane Harrison, with Andrew Lang amongst others in the select audience. Harrison was yet to write her monumental *Themis* (1912) and Duncan herself would deliver her manifesto, *The Dance of the Future*, three years later in Berlin. The presence of Andrew Lang, the pioneer of the so-called British School of Anthropology, is also crucial. Part of a group of charismatic and radical thinkers, as Robert Ackerman claims, he 'made possible the work of Frazer and the Cambridge Ritualists'.[6] This was a project that merged classicism, sociology, and anthropology in a heady cocktail that proposed an evolutionary model for the study of human culture. Opposed to reading myth and religion simply through philology and narrative, the principles of ritual and rhythm became central. Indeed, it was these very principles that seem to have been embodied by Isadora Duncan's dance and punctuated by Jane Harrison's text. This fusion of texuality, visuality, and movement through the figures of the two iconic women brings together the scholarly and the aesthetic in a manner that at once pays homage to the past and points towards the future.

It also underlines the significance of gender for the experiments in modern dance. As Ramsey Burt writes in *The Male Dancer*:

> The label 'modern dance' generally refers to the work of the pioneer dance reformers (nearly all of whom were women) who developed styles other than ballet, including Ruth St Denis (1879–1968), Isadora Duncan (1877–1927), Doris Humphrey (1895–1958), Martha Graham (1894–1991), Rudolph Laban (1879–1958), Ted Shawn (1891–1972) and Mary Wigman (1886–1973) during the first half of the twentieth century.[7]

Most of these 'modern dancers', as many dance historians agree, had to substantially recreate the language of dance before they could find their place in it. Interestingly, one of the accusations against Duncan in this context is that her dance lacks formal awareness,[8] is impossible to recreate, and does not bequeath a pedagogy. On the contrary, her legacy, rather than being concerned with creating specific choreographies, places more emphasis on rewriting the language of dance itself and the role of the female performer. It is interested in negotiating the presence and absence of this performer, its debt to both the past and the future. In a similar chord to the aphorism in the title she claims, that she wants to create 'a school of life' not merely of dance.[9]

It is this *gestus* that makes Duncan an appropriate figurehead or mask for this chapter, providing a framework for the debates between texuality, embodiment, visuality, movement, narrative, and rhythm. And this pose that Duncan enacts allows her at once to act as direct, historical reference, but also to formally inspire modernist experimentation. Her impact is felt on writing about dance and gender, but also becomes part of a formal quest for synaesthesia, totality, part of what we may call modernist *ekphrasis*. In this sense, Duncan's dancer becomes a type of *ekphrastic* machine, a bodily enactment that transcribes itself ('just as the writer uses his words', as she claims above) from one medium to another, exploring the process of mediation itself. A paradigmatic example could be Gertrude Stein's rendition of Duncan in 'Orta or One Dancing':

This one is the one being dancing. This one is one thinking in believing in dancing having meaning. This one is one believing in thinking. This one is one thinking in dancing having meaning. This one is one believing in dancing having meaning. This one is one dancing. This one is one being that one. This one is one being in being one being dancing. This one is one being in being one who is dancing. This one is one being one. This one is one being in being one.[10]

Indeed, one can here see Stein's writing as a dance while reading it, again enacting the principle of modernist *ekphrasis*. This is almost a type of writing *as* dancing notation where the words and the ideas surrounding them—thinking, believing, meaning, dancing, being—are engaged not simply syntactically or semantically but in a dance. Characteristically the agent of this dance is not marked with a gendered pronoun but with the all-encompassing 'one'. It might not be coincidental that while Duncan's dances proved very difficult to notate, they nevertheless acted a source of inspiration for literary and visual modernism. Edward Gordon Craig, despite his difficulties with the female performer, could not resist drawing Duncan (**Fig. 9.1**). And perhaps the most famous drawings of her are those by fellow American Abraham Walkowitz, who drew over 5,000 versions of Duncan, in an attempt visually to capture her dance.

The fascination that Duncan inspired in her fellow modernists, particularly in the plastic and visual arts, was immense. In many ways, this fascination could also be read as an attempt to capture and notate her experiments. Drawing as it did on a variety of sources, and filtering them through the female body, Duncan's dance placed demands on systems of notation; demands that could perhaps only be addressed by recourse to other artistic media. And the crucial impact that she had on these other modernist arts, textual and visual, need not necessarily be read as a short-coming or a failure of her art form—its inability to have its own metalanguage—but can be seen as part of its radical potential. Its ability to transform and morph into other forms again underlines its *ekphrastic* dimension, at once located but permeable and utopian. The dance critic, Walter Terry, writes about this quality of her dance:

> Although her dance inarguably sprang from her inner sources and resources of motor power and emotional desire, the overt aspects of her dance were clearly coloured by Greek art and the sculptor's concept of the body in arrested gesture promising further action. These influences may be seen clearly in photographs of her and in the art works she inspired.[11]

Interestingly, Terry's phrase 'arrested gesture promising further action' and his fusion 'of motor power and emotional desire' point towards this utopian quality of Duncan's dance, but also somewhat incongruously can also be read as drawing parallels with the phantasmic qualities of Craig's *Übermarionette*. Again the mechanical and the vitalist seem to morph into each other. The image and imagistic trope that transpires throughout most of these attempts is probably most clearly exemplified in Walkowitz's many sketches of Duncan. And that is the trope of the *hieroglyph*. Used throughout modernist experiment as that mode that attempts to graphically notate a particular kind of kinetic and poetic sensibility, the hieroglyph becomes a type of *gestus* of writing that brings together movement and stasis, writing and image, the

Figure 9.1. Edward Gordon Craig, *Isadora Duncan Dancing* (1908). Published with the Consent of The Edward Gordon Craig Estate.

present and the future; and, of course, the hieroglyph also inflects the model of Hellenism, making it no longer pure and classical, but hybrid and Alexandrian.

For all these reasons Duncan's project can be read as enacting, staging many a modernist debate about the relationships between textuality and embodiment, movement and stasis, tradition and innovation, the fragment and the monument.

This analysis will now focus on three instances of modern dance that all engage with the demands created and posed by Duncan herself, some more directly influenced by her than others, but all in many ways under her spell. These are the Ballets Russes production of *Les Noces* (1923) choreographed by Bronislava Nijinska and designed by Natalia Goncharova; Jean Cocteau's *The Marriage on the Eiffel Tower* (1921), choreographed by Rolf de Maré and produced by the Swedish Ballet; and W. B. Yeats's *Fighting the Waves* (1929)—originally *The Only Jealousy of Emer*— produced by the Abbey Theatre with Ninette de Valois. All three bring together and help to shape the idea of modern dance through the conspicuous presence of the female dancer, while thematically they all radically rework what the dance theorist Sally Banes calls classical ballet's 'marriage plot'.[12] At the same time, they are informed by theories of acting of the period where the performing body is viewed as a machine for experimentation in modernist *ekphrasis*. Nijinska's work with the Ballets Russes was greatly influenced by Meyerhold's *biomechanics*; Cocteau formulates his notion of the actor as a 'universal athlete' in his notes to *The Marriage on the Eiffel Tower*; and Yeats's ideas about acting and movement were influenced not just by Ninette de Valois, but also by Edward Gordon Craig and Isadora Duncan.

The triumph of the Ballets Russes in Paris over the twenty-year period of Serge Diaghilev's inspirational direction posed a formidable challenge to any form of experimentation taking place on the stage at the time. Indeed, Eliot himself, as quoted above, writes in 'A Dialogue on Dramatic Poetry' in 1928:

> But I blame Mr Diaghilev, not the ballet in principle. If there is a future for drama and particularly for poetic drama, will it not be in the direction indicated by the ballet? Is it not a question of form rather than ethics? And is not the question of verse drama versus prose drama a question of degree of form?[13]

This formal imperative is mainly aimed at the physicality of the actor's body. According to Eliot, the theatrical performer could learn much from the dancer. As Eliot himself concedes, however, this formal training carries with it a moral/ethical dimension as well. He continues:

> Apart from Stravinskii, who is a real musician, and from Cocteau, who is a real playwright, what is the strength of the ballet?

> It is in a tradition, a training, an askesis, which to be fair, is not of Russian but of Italian origin, and which ascends for several centuries. Sufficient to say that any efficient dancer has undergone a training, which is like a moral training. Has any successful actor of our time undergone anything similar?[14]

The 'moral training' of the modernist performer informs most schools of actor training developed throughout modernism, from naturalism to epic. The Ballets Russes, however, apart from the 'ethics' implied by the strict formal training of its dancers, also introduced a new image of the dancer's body with its own 'moral system'. The early productions with the central femmes fatales figures and their decadent *fin de siècle* sensibility (*Cléopâtre*, 1909; *Schéhérazade*, 1910; *La Tragédie de Salomé*, 1913) all fed into a particular strand of orientalism, already prevalent in nineteenth-century French visual arts. This combined with the daring choreography of Michel Fokine and scenography by artists such as Léon Bakst, made the

Ballets Russes a fine example of the 'total work of art' on stage, and according to recent scholarship was itself partly inspired by Isadora Duncan's early tours of Russia.[15] And it was a totality that was centred largely around and carried through the body of the dancer. The dancers of the Ballets Russes combined the 'ethics' of strict training, their *askesis*, as Eliot called it, with the 'ethics' of the heavily eroticized and orientalized body of the dancer. Additionally, as dance historians today stress, Diaghilev's ballets centred primarily around the presentation of the male body.[16] The heavily eroticized and sometimes orientalized male body, especially in the figure of Diaghilev's primary dancer, Vaslav Nijinsky, becomes the main focus of many of these early ballets. This spotlight on the male dancer has sometimes been read, especially in the early pieces, as constituent of their overall misogyny. The gallery of decadent femmes fatales that people the early productions would certainly invite such a reading. However, as Sally Banes has shown, this reading might be slightly too schematic and does not take into account the totality of works spread over twenty years. In particular, she claims that the Stravinsky scores—*Firebird* (1910), *The Rite of Spring* (1913), and especially *Les Noces* (1923)—present an image of the female that is more ambiguous, sometimes fusing primitivism, orientalism, and traditions borrowed from Russian folklore. Either way, the issue of gender is central to the overall aesthetic proposed by the Ballets Russes. And the 'ethics' proposed by its dancers is highly eroticized, sometimes androgynous, always centred on the physicality of the body of the dancer.

As Edward Gordon Craig was quick to point out (in the following quotation), the phenomenon of the Ballets Russes also fed into the existing experimentation of the period, much of which was pioneered by these 'dancing women', as Banes calls them. Despite his usual patronizing and slightly competitive tone, Craig rightly underlines the influence of 'the American'. One wonders why he doesn't name Isadora Duncan in his review of the Ballets Russes. He writes in an article entitled 'Kleptomania, or The Russian Ballet':

> But the Russians have done a clever thing: they have increased the value of their French Ballet by adding to it a few tricks stolen from other lands and other arts. This was clever of them, ... and highly reprehensible.
>
> ... While doing so they stole an idea or two from the only original dancer of the age, the American, and another idea or two from the most advanced scene designers of Europe and superimposed all these upon the wiery artificial framework of the old French Ballet.[17]

The eclecticism of the Ballets Russes is frowned upon in favour of the 'originality' of Duncan's work. It is fascinating to note that even at this early stage, Isadora Duncan is hailed as the 'original dancer of the age'.

In many ways, Duncan's emphasis on the representational efficacy of the female dancer can also be seen in the fascination that modern dance portrays with what Banes calls the 'marriage plot', as mentioned above. In turn we could read this as the equivalent of naturalism's obsession with the 'woman question'. For Banes, this 'marriage plot' provides the themes, formal conventions, and interpretive frameworks for classical ballet, all categories that are radically reworked by the experiments in modern dance. And this is a trope to which the Ballets Russes also made a valuable contribution. *Les Noces (The Wedding)* premiered at the Théâtre de la Gaîté-Lyrique in Paris on 13 June 1923.

It was the third of the Ballets Russes works set to Stravinsky scores, and came after *The Firebird* (1910) and *The Rite of Spring* (1913). Choreographed by Bronislava Nijinska, Nijinsky's sister, and designed by Natalia Goncharova this formidable piece was to radically rework the marriage plot (**Fig. 9.2**). Like *The Rite of Spring* it results from Stravinsky's fascination with Russian folklore and for that reason has been mainly read as a companion piece to it. However, as Banes claims,

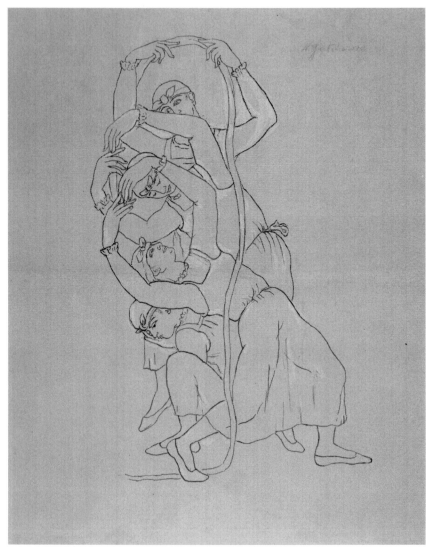

Figure 9.2. Natalia Goncharova, A Group of Female Dancers, set design for *Les Noces* © ADAGP, Paris and DACS, London 2015. Image courtesy of Victoria and Albert Museum, London.

it is a crucial piece for the development of modern dance, not least for the central position it accords to women. *Les Noces* is not simply a dramatization of a Russian Orthodox wedding; it is a complex piece that brings together the folk tradition, modernist experiment, the Orthodox liturgy, and Marxist utopia, and filters all these through the 'marriage plot'. Stravinsky himself draws parallels between this work and another central text of modernism: James Joyce's *Ulysses*:

> As a collection of clichés and quotations of typical wedding sayings [*Les Noces*] might be compared to one of those scenes in *Ulysses* in which the reader seems to be overhearing scraps of conversation without the connecting thread of discourse. But *Les Noces* might also be compared to *Ulysses* in the larger sense that both works are trying to *present* rather than to *describe*.[18]

Joyce's interest in dance, particularly through his daughter Lucia, would substantiate Stravinsky's parallels. Indeed, Molly Bloom's closing monologue could itself be read as a variation on the 'marriage plot'. Either way, it would be interesting to read *Les Noces* as occupying a similar position to *Ulysses* in the critical reception of modern dance and modernist performance.

Les Noces took over ten years to arrive on the stage. The period between 1912 and 1928 saw great changes in Russia, not least in the ways marriage, sex, and the rights of women were viewed. Although Nijinska had lived in Paris most of her life, she returned to Russia during the revolution and the civil war and finally emigrated to Paris in 1921. While in the Soviet Union she too shared in the initial utopian faith that the Russian avant-garde had in the possibilities presented by the Revolution. She ran her own ballet school in Kiev until 1919 and only left after suffering permanent hearing loss following a bombardment. While working on *Les Noces* she claims she 'was still breathing the air of Russia, Russia throbbing with excitement and intense feeling'.[19] This excitement included encounters with the revolutionary Russian avant-garde, particularly the constructivists. To this she added the fascination with folklore and an equal fascination with the 'woman question', high on both the political and artistic agenda at the time. However, Nijinska's reading of the 'marriage plot', through the peasant Russian wedding, radically rereads it more in the tradition of radical feminists like Alexandra Kollontai, who saw in the Russian Revolution not only the end of the class system, but also the potential end of patriarchy and the traditional family. Drawing on the analogies between the marriage liturgy and the funeral rites that exist in the Christian Orthodox liturgy, and in the lyrics of folk songs that Stravinsky used, she creates a piece that is bleak and melancholy. It has been characterized by the dance historian André Levinson, disdainfully, as a 'Marxist choreography' and he also describes the ending as 'a sort of practicable stage property constructed with flesh and blood or an apotheosis of exhibition gymnastics'.[20] The debt to constructivism (and probably directly to biomechanics) becomes clear. At the same time, the piece exhibits a particular 'Marxist aesthetic' that arose out of the early period of the revolution and the ways that utopian project was interpreted by artists all over Europe at the time. Although *Les Noces* was in some ways quintessentially Russian, like the Ballets Russes, it found a stage in Paris (not Moscow) and, through an aesthetic that was now beginning to be recognized as cosmopolitan modernism, presented the most radical and challenging reading of the 'marriage plot' that had appeared on the stages of Europe.

The choreography pays tribute to the tradition of folk dance but also to the new constructivist techniques being formulated in the Soviet Union at the time. The movements are strictly symmetrical, each dancer is almost always part of a group (the men or the women), and the only thing that separates the bride from the group is the impending wedding. David Drew, who worked with Nijinska in the 1966 revival of *Les Noces*[21] for the Royal Ballet in London, comments that Nijinska cast the bride by asking the female dancers of the company to strike a particular pose, not by auditioning their dance skills. This formal emphasis on order, repetition, and homogeneity is underscored by what Drew, in the same interview, called 'radically asymmetrical movements'. Similarly, and despite the charge of 'exhibition gymnastics', the end result also aspires to a kind of spirituality. This is also apparent in the famous image of the pyramid of brides' heads, woven together with the new bride's braids. Nijinska famously wanted all the dancers' eyes (tilted sideways as the heads rest on the shoulders) to form a clear vertical line through the centre of this pyramid. This was formal comment, 'stage property constructed in flesh and blood', as Levinson claims, but, standing back, the final image could also be read as a version of the Russian Orthodox marriage headdress or even as a mound of human skulls in a still picture that conflates the fertility rite of marriage with death ritual. It is this combination of formal and thematic experiment, energized by the radical sexual politics of the time, that makes *Les Noces* an 'iconic' modernist ballet, where the term also alludes to the connections with the Orthodox tradition of iconography.

In pointing towards the ballet (and the Ballets Russes in particular) for potential models for 'the successful actor of our time', Eliot is engaging with a complex experimental tradition, one that was undergoing its own radical modernist reshuffling. As always, this involved a reconfiguration of the dancer/performer on stage and almost invariably by engaging the discourses of gender and sexuality. What begins to emerge from this process is something we would today understand as dance theatre, as seen in the work of Pina Bausch, for example (who in 1975 choreographed and danced in her own version of *The Rite of Spring*). Eliot's reference to Stravinsky and Cocteau shows that he is aware that the ballet's strength lies in this very coexistence of music and poetry on stage. Crucially, what brings everything together on the stage is the performer. It is, however, a specific dancer/performer who embodies the possibility of a 'poetic drama' for Eliot in this context.

The Ballets Russes also had a huge impact on Cocteau, as Eliot knew well and as documented in the many drawings of the ballets Cocteau made throughout the height of the dance company's fame. Cocteau's *Les Mariés de la Tour Eiffel* (*The Marriage on the Eiffel Tower*), first produced in 1921, presents yet another take on the 'marriage plot', while introducing onto the stage Cocteau's idea of the actor as 'universal athlete'. This small piece combined poetry, dance, and music—indeed no fewer than five prominent composers collaborated on this project: Georges Auric, Darius Milhaud, Francis Poulenc, Germaine Tailleferre, and Arthur

Honegger—and acts as a fine example of Cocteau's attempt at substituting 'poetry in the theatre' with 'poetry of the theatre'. The publication of *Les Mariés* in 1922 was prefaced by his own manifesto for a poetic drama:

> Poetry in the theatre is a delicate lace, impossible to see at any distance. Poetry of the theatre should be a coarse lace, a lace of ropes, a ship at sea. *Les mariés* can have the frightening appearance of a drop of poetry seen under a microscope. The scenes are linked like the words of a poem.[22]

For Cocteau this poetry of the theatre is not simply a matter of transferring the poetic word onto the stage. It is more the case of the word itself becoming part of the stage properties. 'Under the microscope' it is spatialized, physicalized, no longer able to provide the narrative place of metaphor or even plot. Crucially this poetry of the theatre requires a new type of performer. Cocteau, again, acknowledges the contribution of Diaghilev and Rolf de Maré (the choreographer) in the creation of this dancer/actor. He states that the experiments with 'the fantastic, the dance, acrobatics, mime, drama, satire, music, and the spoken word combine to produce a new form; . . . the plastic expression and embodiment of poetry itself'.[23] *Les Mariés de la Tour Eiffel* was to be his contribution to this experiment. It is also the work that prompted him to formulate his notion of the performer as a 'universal athlete':

> A theatrical piece ought to be written, presented, costumed, furnished with musical accompaniment, played, and danced, by a single individual. This universal athlete does not exist. It is therefore important to replace the individual by what resembles an individual most: a friendly group.[24]

This fascinating formulation nods towards the constructivist manifestations of the actor as athlete, as acrobat, even as labourer (something that Cocteau would have been aware of through his connections with Nijinska and the preparations for *Les Noces*). This 'friendly group' working in a studio space (equally championed by Cocteau) is for him the best vehicle for poetry of the theatre. It is no longer a matter of maintaining the clarity and integrity of the poet's voice, which constitutes Eliot's main concern. The poet himself is transcribed into this 'friendly group', which in turn stands in for the ideal of the 'universal athlete'.

In *Les Mariés* Cocteau experiments with this idea of dispersal of poetry and the poet himself in the work of the 'friendly group'. Furthermore, this aesthetic is mirrored in the way the notion of dramatic character or even the individual human actor dissolves in favour of a fragmented representation, where the stage properties, animate or inanimate, happily occupy each other's place. The action is narrated or recited by two actors dressed as phonographs on either side of the stage 'half-hidden behind the proscenium arch'. This image of the phonograph, at once alluding to the uniqueness of the human voice (or the voice of poetry) and to a technology of reproducibility was to become very conspicuous on the modernist stage. The characters enter and exit through a camera that 'opens like a door', and also helps to structure the action. This wedding party is trying to celebrate a marriage at the Eiffel Tower, which should culminate in a group photo, commemorating and monumentalizing the event. However, every time one of the Phonographs shouts 'Watch the birdie', strange people and things appear out of the camera—A Bathing Beauty, A Fat Boy who proceeds to massacre the guests, A Lion. The movement is choreographed while the phonographs provide the narration and the voices of the actors, who wear masks. After a series of interruptions the wedding party manages to constitute itself as such and poses for the final photo. In the end, what creates the image of this marriage, what allows it to come together without further intrusions from the technological apparatus is the fact that it is turned into a work of art:

SECOND PHONOGRAPH: Look. The wedding party and The Photographer
    freeze. The entire wedding party is motionless. Don't you think they're a little …
FIRST PHONOGRAPH: A little wedding cake.
SECOND PHONOGRAPH: A little bouquet.
FIRST PHONOGRAPH: A little Mona Lisa.
SECOND PHONOGRAPH: A little masterpiece.
FIRST PHONOGRAPH: The Dealer in modern paintings and The Collector of
    modern paintings stop before the wedding party. What does The Dealer say?
SECOND PHONOGRAPH: I've brought you to the Eiffel Tower to show you
    before anyone else, a truly unique piece: 'The Wedding Party.'
FIRST PHONOGRAPH: And The Collector answers:
SECOND PHONOGRAPH: I follow you blindly.
FIRST PHONOGRAPH: Well? Isn't it lovely? It's a kind of primitive.
…
SECOND PHONOGRAPH: … But look at that paint! What texture!
Look at that style, that nobility, that 'joie de vivre!' It might almost be a funeral.
SECOND PHONOGRAPH: I see a wedding party.
FIRST PHONOGRAPH: Your vision is limited. It's more than a wedding. It's all
    weddings. More than all weddings: it's a cathedral.[25]

The wedding party, and indeed the 'marriage plot' itself, is initially redeemed by turning itself into an 'experimental' work of art. However, in an almost Dadaist manner this greatness is also what turns it into a commodity. In the process the rituals of marriage and funeral become interchangeable (as in Stravinsky's use of a similar analogy in *Les Noces*). It is this fragmented, comic, but also bleak image of the wedding party that the camera finally manages to capture. Even language starts to behave properly again. The final 'Watch the birdie' produces a dove from the camera. The metaphor is literally enacted rather than yielding strange and wonderful objects. With 'the camera working' and 'peace achieved' the characters all 'disappear into the camera'.

Cocteau rightly claimed that with this small piece he had 'already contributed a good deal' to the creation of 'a kind of poetic spirit' on stage.[26] Equally intriguing is the footnote following that declaration which states that he is also 'perhaps' seeking to 'rehabilitate Wagner'. The hesitation and the use of the term 'rehabilitate' show exactly how aware Cocteau was of the overall political dimensions of this debate. Cocteau approaches Wagner with caution. His poetry of the theatre was actively intervening in, or even correcting (rehabilitating), the Wagnerian ideal of the 'total work of art'. His version, with its emphasis on 'the friendly group', stylized through the 'universal athlete', and narrativized through the fragment, is, I believe, a direct attempt at containing the totalizing dimension of the Wagnerian aesthetic, while trying to maintain the radicalism of its formal experimentation. This critical engagement with the *Gesamtkunstwerk* is very consciously continued by Brecht, who, in equally deliberately Wagnerian terms, proposes the notion of a 'total work of art' that is based on the fragment.

In 1950, when Eliot was writing one of his final 'manifestos' on poetic theatre, it was Yeats's late play *Purgatory* that he put forward as the paradigm of poetic drama. This small play, he claims, has 'laid all his successors under obligation to him'.[27] The impact of the Ballets Russes and Cocteau seems to fade away, as in the end, for Eliot, it is primarily a matter of solving the 'problem of speech in verse'. However, this was not always the case for Yeats, as his so-called middle-period of *Plays for Dancers* clearly exhibits. Between 1915 and 1921 Yeats wrote four plays for dancers, which were based on the Japanese kyogen. Equally important is Yeats's fascination with the possibilities of dance on the stage. When he comes to stage one of these plays, *The Only Jealousy of Emer*, rewritten as *Fighting the Waves*, in 1929 at the Abbey Theatre, he too very directly draws on the experimentation with dance taking place at the time. In his experiments throughout the previous decade he had enlisted the talents of the Japanese dancer, Mitchio Ito;[28] however, here he was working with actors, not dancers. Following Eliot's plea (of 1928) for the ballet to provide an *askesis* for the actor, he set about creating the Abbey School of Acting (September 1927) *and* the Abbey School of Ballet (November 1927). This was run by Ninette de Valois, whose work as a choreographer Yeats had witnessed the previous year (1926) in a production of his own *On Baile's Strand*, directed by Norman Marshall at the Festival Theatre, Cambridge. Interestingly, the Festival itself had been inaugurated in 1926 with a production of *The Oresteia*, where Dame Ninette had eclectically used a number of avant-garde abstract approaches to choreograph the chorus of the Furies. Dame Ninette writes in her memoirs, *Come Dance with Me* (1957):

> The mind of Yeats was made up; he would have a small school of Ballet at the Abbey and I would send over a teacher. I would visit Dublin every three months and produce his *Plays for Dancers* and perform in them myself; thus, he said, the poetic drama in Ireland would live again and take its rightful place in the Nation's own Theatre, and the oblivion imposed on it by the popularity of peasant drama would become a thing of the past.[29]

The presence of Ninette de Valois and her group of dancers, as some contemporary scholars agree, forced Yeats to rewrite *The Only Jealousy of Emer* as a prose play.[30] For example, Ninette de Valois had great difficulty speaking on stage, especially when this involved verse. The end result could be compared to the production of Cocteau's *Les Mariés*, which also used masks. Famously, Cuchulain mimes a battle against a corps de ballet who represent the waves of the title. Even the mythological battle between the two 'brides' Emer and Fand, each claiming Cuchulain, could be read as a variation on the all-conspicuous 'marriage plot'. This is how Lady Gregory recorded the event:

> I went to Dublin and saw *The Fighting of the Waves*—wild, beautiful, the motion of the dancers, the rhythm of the music, the scene. The words lost, the masks hideous—yet added to the strange unreality. We might all have been at the bottom of the sea.[31]

The 'strange unreality' that Lady Gregory experienced could have partly resulted from what she laments as 'words lost'. As mentioned above, Yeats had agreed to rewrite *The Only Jealousy of Emer* as a prose play to accommodate the demands placed on the actors by dance. Indeed, the sense of estrangement that Lady Gregory invokes may result less from the opposition between words and movement and more from a forging of a kind of theatricality that brings together words, performing bodies, 'hideous masks', the presence of the audience, and her own experience of the event. Lady Gregory's sense of wonder, but also unease, underlines the constitutive relationship between words and bodies on the stage.

The quest for poetry in, of, or through the theatre almost always involves a similar quest for a poetics of physicality and embodiment. The experiments in physical movement that dance inspires also quite smoothly and, we may claim, *ekphrastically*, translate into experiments in narrative and poetry. From the pulse and heartbeat of the body as organic entity, as dancer, to the repetitive movement of the machine (or indeed of the body-as-machine), the concept of rhythm becomes a key trope that brings together and helps bridge the binaries between texuality and embodiment, viewing *both* 'the flesh as word' *and* 'the word as flesh', as this creative interface between literary modernism and these legacies of *moving modernisms* clearly exhibits.

Perhaps the final word should go to Isadora Duncan, whose posture or *gestus* shows how even this intense concern with movement can morph into its opposite, stasis, but a stillness that engages the body as present *and* absent, as nature *and* machine, and—as this was recorded in her autobiography—as experience *and* word:

> For hours I would stand completely still, my two hands folded between my breasts, covering the solar plexus. My mother often became alarmed to see me remain for such long intervals quite motionless as if in a trance—but I was searching, and finally discovered the central spring of all movement, the crater of motor power.[32]

NOTES

1. Irma Duncan and Allen Ross MacDougall, *Isadora Duncan's Russian Days* (New York: Covici-Friede Publishers, 1929), p. 168.
2. T. S. Eliot, *Selected Essays* (London: Faber, 1951), p. 46.
3. Jean Cocteau, 'Preface: 1922' to *The Wedding on the Eiffel Tower* (1921), translated by Michael Benedikt, in *Modern French Plays: An Anthology from Jarry to Ionesco* (London: Faber, 1964), pp. 96–7.
4. See Carrie Preston, *Modernism's Mythic Pose: Gender, Genre and Solo Performance* (Oxford: Oxford University Press, 2011).

5. Jacques Rancière, 'The Archaeomodern Turn', in *Walter Benjamin and the Demands of History*, edited by Michael P. Steinberg (Ithaca, NY: Cornell University Press, 1996), pp. 24–40; 28–9.

6. Robert Ackerman, *The Myth and Ritual School: J. G. Frazer and the Cambridge Ritualists* (London and New York: Routledge, 2002), pp. 29–30.

7. Ramsay Burt, *The Male Dancer* (London and New York: Routledge, 1995), p. 3.

8. See Arnold Rood, ed., *Gordon Craig on Movement and Dance* (London: Dance Books, 1977), p. xvii.

9. See Isadora Duncan, *Art of the Dance* (New York: Theatre Arts Books, 1928), p. 141.

10. Gertrude Stein, *A Stein Reader*, edited and introduction by Ulla E. Dydo (Evanston, IL: Northwestern University Press, 1993), pp. 123–4.

11. Walter Terry, *Isadora Duncan: Her Life, Her Art, Her Legacy* (New York: Dodd and Meade Company, 1963), p. 115.

12. See Sally Banes, *Dancing Women: Female Bodies on Stage* (London and New York: Routledge, 1998), pp. 5–7.

13. Eliot, *Selected Essays*, p. 46.

14. Eliot, *Selected Essays*, p. 46.

15. See Michelle Potter, 'Designed for Dance: The Costumes of Léon Bakst and the Art of Isadora Duncan', in *Dance Chronicle*, vol. 13, No. 2 (1990): pp. 154–9.

16. See Burt, *The Male Dancer*, pp. 3–5.

17. Edward Gordon Craig, *The Mask*, Vol. 4 (Florence, 1911), p. 98. Craig had also designed a ballet, *Psyche*, for Diaghilev in 1906–7, which was turned down. See Edward Gordon Craig, *Designs for the Theatre* (London: Heinemann, 1948), pp. 8, 18.

18. Igor Stravinsky and Robert Craft, *Expositions and Developments* (London: Faber, 1962), pp. 130–1. For the reception of *Les Noces* in London in 1926, see Susan Jones, *Literature, Modernism and Dance* (Oxford: Oxford University Press, 2013), pp. 117–27.

19. Quoted in Sally Banes, *Dancing Women*, p. 119.

20. Quoted in Joan Acocella and Lynn Garafola, eds., *André Levinson on Dance* (Hanover, NH: Wesleyan University Press, 1991), p. 41.

21. See Igor Stravinsky, *The Firebird* and *Les Noces*, directed by Ross MacGibbon, performed by the Royal Ballet (London: BBC/Opus Arte, 2001). DVD.

22. See Jean Cocteau, 'Preface: 1922', to *The Wedding on the Eiffel Tower*, p. 97.

23. Jean Cocteau, 'Preface: 1922', p. 98.

24. Jean Cocteau, 'Preface: 1922', p. 99.

25. Jean Cocteau, *The Wedding on the Eiffel Tower*, in *Modern French Plays*, pp. 101–15; 112–13.

26. Jean Cocteau, 'Preface: 1922', p. 99.

27. T. S. Eliot, *Poetry and Drama* (London: Faber and Faber, 1950), p. 20.

28. For a detailed analysis of the impact of Noh theatre and Michio Ito on the theatre of W. B. Yeats see Olga Taxidou, 'Sada Yakko, Michio Ito and Mei Lan-fang: Orientalism, Interculturalism and the Performance Event', in *Modernism and Performance: Jarry to Brecht* (Houndmills, Basingstoke: Palgrave Macmillan, 2007), pp. 118–47.

29. Ninette de Valois, *Come Dance with Me* (London: Faber and Faber, 1957), p. 88.

30. See Richard Taylor, *The Drama of W.B. Yeats: Irish Myth and the Japanese No* (London and New Haven: Yale University Press, 1976), pp. 162–70.

31. Quoted in Taylor, *The Drama of W.B. Yeats*, p. 170.

32. Isadora Duncan, *My Life* (New York: Liveright, 1927, reprinted 1996), p. 58.

AVANT-GARDES

10

'A Cessation of Resemblances'
Stein/Picasso/Duchamp

Marjorie Perloff

In 1935, as Gertrude Stein recalls it,[1] Picasso was suffering from what we might call painter's block.* Finding himself at an impasse in his personal life, for two years he stopped painting altogether, taking up writing instead. 'He commenced to write poems', Stein remarks, 'but this writing was never his writing. After all the egoism of a painter is not at all the egoism of a writer, there is nothing to say about it, it is not. No.'[2] And in *Everybody's Autobiography* (1937), Stein recalls telling the great painter, perhaps her closest friend:

> Your poetry...is more offensive than just bad poetry I do not know why it is but it just is, somebody who can really do something very well when he does something else which he cannot do and in which he cannot live it is particularly repellent, now you I said to him, you never read a book in your life that was not written by a friend and then not then and you never had any feelings about any words, words annoy you more than they do anything else so how can you write you know better....all right go on doing it but don't go on trying to make me tell you it is poetry.[3]

Stein's almost visceral reaction here was prompted, not just, as is often assumed, by Picasso's invasion of her territory or by her surprisingly traditional insistence on the separation of the arts. The deeper reason is that Picasso had never so much as pretended to *read* Stein's writing. For him, Gertrude was a wonderful patron and *copain*—he loved coming to her salon and gossiping with her on a daily basis—but her writing, especially given that it was in English—a language he couldn't, after all, read—was hardly within the radius of his discourse. Not surprisingly, when he did take on 'poetry' in the mid-1930s, his models were the then prominent French surrealists, beginning with his good friend André Breton. Here, for example, is the opening of a typical Picasso prose poem from 1935, as translated from the Spanish by Jerome Rothenberg:

> I mean a dish a cup a nest a knife a tree a frying pan a nasty spill while strolling on the sharp edge of a cornice breaking up into a thousand pieces screaming like a madwoman and lying down to sleep stark naked legs spread wide over the odor from a knife that just

---

* The images by Duchamp and others discussed in this essay are easily available in the longer online version for The Battersea Review, 1/1 (2012), www.batterseareview.com accessed 1 March 2016. The Duchamp figures are also readily available on Google Images. They are not reproduced here due to estate reproduction fees.

beheaded the wine froth and nothing bleeds from it except for lips like butterflies and asks you for no handouts for a visit to the bulls with a cicada like a feather in the wind.[4]

This passage is characteristically surrealist in its mysterious juxtaposition of seemingly unrelated images—'a tree a frying pan', a 'cornice...screaming like a madwoman'—its emphasis on violence—'stark naked legs spread wide over the odor from a knife'—and its collocation of elaborate metaphor and simple syntax. A passionate advocate of Picasso's early cubism, which, as has been frequently observed,[5] is a technique Stein herself adapted in such compositions as *Tender Buttons* (1914), Picasso's surrealist poetic mode is antithetical to Stein's own, with its avoidance of concrete nouns, its syntactic ambiguity, and its reliance on inde-terminate pronouns, articles, and prepositions to produce a poetic construct she took to be appropriate to the twentieth century. 'The surrealists', Stein remarks dismissively in her discussion of Picasso's painting of the early 1930s, 'still see things as everyone sees them, they complicate them in a different way but the vision is that of everyone else, in short the complication is the complication of the twentieth century but the vision is that of the nineteenth century.'[6]

This critique of surrealism, whether just or unjust, is echoed by another of Stein's contemporaries. In describing his *Box of 1913–14* (the *Green Box*) to Pierre Cabanne, Marcel Duchamp explains that his assemblage of miscellaneous notes placed inside the box was designed as an art object 'not to be "looked at" in the aesthetic sense of the word'—indeed, to 'remove the retinal aspect' which had dominated painting from Courbet to the present:

> Before, painting had other functions: it could be religious, philosophical, moral. If I had the chance to take an antiretinal attitude, it unfortunately hasn't changed much; our whole century is completely retinal, except for the Surrealists, who tried to go outside it somewhat. And still, they didn't go so far! In spite of the fact that [André] Breton says he believes in judging from a Surrealist point of view, deep down he's still really interested in painting in the retinal sense. It's absolutely ridiculous. It must change.[7]

Duchamp's critique of the retinal has its counterpart in Stein's writing, but the two artists have rarely been linked. For all the critical studies devoted to the relation-ship of Stein and Picasso (or, as in the exhibition *The Steins Collect*,[8] on Stein's debt to Cézanne or Matisse or to the cubism of Juan Gris), what has been curiously ignored is the reverse situation: the influence, if any, of Stein's verbal composition on the visual artwork of her contemporaries. And here Duchamp, whose move to New York in 1915 necessitated the acquisition of English, even as Stein's expatria-tion to Paris meant that her 'art discourse' (especially with the Spaniard Picasso) was to be conducted in French, is the pivotal figure.

The two first met, according to the *Autobiography of Alice B. Toklas*, in Paris in 1913:

> It was not long after this [the winter of 1913] that Mabel Dodge went to America and it was the winter of the armory show which was the first time the general public had a chance to see any of these pictures. It was there that Marcel Duchamp's Nude Descending the Staircase was shown.

> It was about this time that Picabia and Gertrude Stein met. I remember going to dinner at the Picabias' and a pleasant dinner it was, Gabrielle Picabia full of life and gaiety, Picabia dark and lively, and Marcel Duchamp looking like a young Norman crusader.

I was always perfectly able to understand the enthusiasm that Marcel Duchamp aroused in New York when he went there in the early years of the war. His brother had just died from the effect of his wounds, his other brother was still at the front and he himself was inapt for military service. He was very depressed and he went to America. Everyone loved him. So much so that it was a joke in Paris when any American arrived in Paris the first thing he said was, and how is Marcel.[9]

'The young Duchamp', she wrote a few days later to Mabel Dodge, 'looks like a young Englishman and talks very urgently about the fourth dimension.'[10] We know that Stein at this time was keenly interested in questions relating to mathematics and so this was a compliment.[11]

Indeed, Stein's account in *Alice B. Toklas* is unusually flattering and without her usual malice—quite unlike, say, her references to Matisse or Pound or Hemingway. The 'young Norman crusader': Duchamp was the son of a notary in the little Normandy town of Blainville, a fact Stein refers to with amusement in *Everybody's Autobiography*, where she remarks how many artists—Cocteau, Bernard Faÿ, Dali—were the sons of notaries.[12] Duchamp was handsome and charming. And in 1917, Stein was made aware of the brouhaha over *Fountain* by a letter from her friend Carl Van Vechten:

> This porcelain tribute was bought cold in some plumber shop (where it awaited the call to join some bath room trinity) and sent in.... When it was rejected [by the Salon of Independents], Marcel Duchamp at once resigned from the board. Stieglitz is exhibiting the object at '291'. And has made some wonderful photographs of it. The photographs make it look like anything from a Madonna to a Buddha.[13]

Did the readymades influence Stein's writing? Yes and no.[14] Her compositions resemble Duchamp's 'objects' in their wholesale rejection of the mimetic contract—a rejection that goes well beyond Cubist distortion and dislocation of what are, after all, still recognizable objects and bodies. In this sense, Duchamp's dismissal of the 'retinal' is also hers. Such prose poems as 'A Substance in a Cushion' and 'A Box' in *Tender Buttons*, for example, can be related to Duchamp's *Green Box* and the later *boîtes en valise* in their emphasis on what cannot be seen or inferred from the outside. More important, as different as their artistic productions were—Stein, after all, did not use 'readymade' or found text—they drew on each other's work in striking ways—ways that have largely been ignored.

The key text here is *Geography and Plays*, published in 1922. After the war, when Duchamp, having returned to Paris, called on Stein with their mutual friend Henri-Pierre Roché (the writer who had introduced Gertrude and Leo to Picasso and was the subject of a 1909 Portrait),[15] the discussion was evidently about Stein's desire to publish a collection of the shorter experimental texts—poems, prose pieces, portraits, and plays—she had been writing since 1908—for example, her masterpiece 'Miss Furr and Miss Skeene'.[16] Walter Arensberg and Henry McBride were enlisted, and Sherwood Anderson, newly arrived in Paris in 1921, offered to write a preface. After a number of rejections, Edmund F. Brown's Four Seas Company agreed to publish *Geography and Plays*, surely one of Stein's most seminal collections.

Geography and Plays contains the well-known early portraits of Harry Phelan Webb, Constance Fletcher, Georges Braque, Carl Van Vechten ('One'), and Mrs Whitehead; the rhyming musical pieces like 'Susie Asado', 'Pink Melon Joy', and 'Accents in Alsace'; and the plays 'Ladies Voices' and 'What Happened'. Roughly at the centre of the volume, Stein placed 'Sacred Emily' (1913), a ten-page poem Duchamp is quite likely to have known, which contains the first instance of what is probably her most famous line: 'Rose is a rose is a rose is a rose.'[17]

The rose as a proper name has already appeared in the opening section:

> Compose compose beds.
> Wives of great men rest tranquil.
> Come go stay philip philip.
> Egg be takers.
> Parts of place nuts.
> Suppose twenty for cent.
> It is rose in hen[18]

This passage recalls 'Susie Asado' in its punning and rhyming short and seemingly quite unrelated phrases. 'Compose' rhymes with 'rose', 'philip philip' sounds like a bird call, 'Egg be takers' puns on 'egg beaters', 'place nuts' seems to be a misheard reference to 'placements' or 'place names', just as 'twenty for cent' should be 'twenty percent', but, then again, since 'per' means 'for', 'twenty for cent' is oddly accurate. By the time we come to line 7, what might have conventionally been a 'rose in bloom' becomes a 'rose in hen' (the eggs have already been laid), with its sound allusion to Rosinante, as well as its erotic reference of the verb form 'rose' which functions here.

Then too Rose as a high-frequency proper name is contrasted to the 'Sacred Emily' of the title. The reference is probably to Émile Zola, a sacred cow indeed in turn-of-the century France. The second line, 'Wives of great men rest tranquil', surely refers to the great author's death, while asleep in his bed, from carbon monoxide poisoning from a blocked chimney, even as his wife, 'composed' in the bed beside him, miraculously survived. And the sculptor of Zola's tomb was Philippe Solari—the 'philip philip' invoked in line 3.[19]

I do not mean to suggest that 'Sacred Emily' is 'about' Zola. Stein does not operate in this way; rather, 'So great so great Emily./Sew grate sew grate Emily' becomes the occasion for the celebration of Stein's own domestic happiness with Alice. The sentence 'Rose is a rose is a rose is a rose' is followed by these lines:

> Rose is a rose is a rose is a rose.
> Loveliness extreme.
> Extra gaiters.
> Loveliness extreme.
> Sweetest ice-cream.
> Page ages page ages page ages.
> Wiped Wiped wire wire.
> Sweeter than peaches and pears and cream.
> Wiped wire wiped wire.[20]

'Loveliness extreme', with its allusion to Edmund Waller's famous 'Go Lovely Rose', jostles in Dadaesque fashion with those 'Extra gaiters' evidently needed for protection, or again 'extricators' from difficult situations, and with the 'Sweetest ice-cream' that echoes that other 1913 poem 'Preciosilla'. The lines that follow introduce the phonemic play that, in these years, became one of Stein's signatures: 'Page ages page ages page ages', where the words (nouns or verbs?) merge with one another and also call up 'passages'; and the echolalia in 'Wiped Wiped wire wire', where a single phoneme makes all the difference. The ugly monosyllables of 'Wiped wire wiped wire' are in turn undercut by the cloying sing-songy simile 'Sweeter than peaches and pears and cream'.

Cyrena Pondrom remarks that 'Sacred Emily' 'proceeds as an interplay of three extensive sets of reference—the sexual, the domestic, and the aesthetic'.[21] I think this is accurate: the poem begins, after all, with 'compose'—composition—of 'beds', followed by the observation that 'Wives of great men rest tranquil'—a reference to Stein's own 'wife' as well as Zola's. Indeed, like 'Ada' or 'Susie Asado', 'Sacred Emily' is an erotic love poem for Alice. A rose is a rose is a rose: a rose is eros. By line 18 of its opening page, the erotic theme is distinctly audible in:

> Murmur pet murmur pet murmur.
> Push sea push sea push sea push sea push sea push sea push
> sea push sea
> Sweet and good and kind to all.[22]

And eros is the dominant motif of the entire book, coming to a kind of crescendo in 'Accents in Alsace', which culminates in the passage;

> Sweeter than water or cream or ice. Sweeter than bells of roses. Sweeter than winter or summer or spring. Sweeter than pretty posies. Sweeter than anything is my queen and loving is her nature.
> Loving and good and delighted and best is her little King and Sire whose devotion is entire who has but one desire to express the love which is hers to inspire.
> In the photograph the Rhine hardly showed
> In what way do chimes remind you of singing. In what way do birds sing. In what way are forests black or white.
> We saw them blue.
> With for get me nots.
> In the midst of our happiness we were very pleased.[23]

'Accents in Alsace' (1919) is followed by a portrait that was the last piece written for inclusion in *Geography & Plays*: namely, 'Next. Life and Letters of Marcel Duchamp'.[24] Its 'nextness' can, I think, be related to the fact that the year of its composition (1920), Duchamp, back in New York, had given birth to his female alter ego Rrose Sélavy, who, from then on, signed many of his personal letters and paintings and played a major role in his art-making. Asked by Calvin Tomkins why he felt the need to invent a new identity, Duchamp responded, 'It was not to change my identity, but to have two identities.'[25] His first thought, he said, had been to choose a Jewish name to offset his own Catholic background. 'But then the idea jumped at me, why not a female name? Much better than to change religion would be to change sex…Rose was the corniest name for a girl at that time, in French, anyway. And Sélavy was a pun on *c'est la vie*'.[26] Talking to Pierre Cabanne, Duchamp explains that he added the extra 'R' to 'Rose' because this gave him a further pun on 'arrose', 'arroser' meaning to water, to sprinkle, and hence also to make fertile, enrich. 'Sélavy', one should also note, contains the name 'Levy'—as common a Jewish name as Stein.

The iconic image of Duchamp's Rose is Man Ray's famous photograph of 1920–1, signed 'lovingly Rrose Sélavy alias Marcel Duchamp'. In this soft-focus photograph, Rose wears a cloche hat with a brim that comes down to her eyebrows; 'it is the lack of facial hair', Dalia Judovitz notes, 'that engenders sexual ambiguity. Duchamp's shaved face and discreet smile, generously framed by a fur collar (a punning displacement of facial hair), invokes the illusion of a feminine presence.'[27] Then again, this Rose hardly looks like a woman: Duchamp's own masculine features are unmistakable. But the ambiguity is intentional: the image is riddling, at once Marcel and Rose, masculine and feminine. Two further Man Ray photographs of Rrose Sélavy, this time in an even more elaborate headdress, sweeping velvet cape, and bead necklace, recalling Renaissance portraits of painters, are even more ambiguous.

Rose's first appearance in a Duchamp artwork was in the assisted readymade *Fresh Widow* in which a miniature French window, painted an ugly blue-green like that of beach furniture, contains eight glass panes covered with sheets of black leather. The French window stands on a wooden base bearing large capital letters 'FRESH WIDOW COPYRIGHT ROSE SELAVY 1920'. It is a brilliant pun, made simply by erasing the letter 'n' in both words. A fresh widow is a recent one (here perhaps a war widow) but also 'fresh' in the sense of bold, not easy to repress or squelch. What is this widow thinking? We don't know because the leather panes are impenetrable: we don't know what's behind them. The window is also closed but the little knobs suggest it could be opened.

Rrose next appears in *Belle Haleine, Eau de Voilette* (1921), whose punning title overtly plays on 'Belle Hélène' and violet water—extract of violet. But the perfume bottle itself is empty, and *eau de voilette* (veiled water) invokes the *eau de toilette* of Duchamp's *Fountain*. The bottle is labelled with one of Man Ray's photographs of Rose and signed 'Man Ray and Rrose Sélavy'. The same year, Duchamp put together a small wire birdcage, painted it white, and put inside some 152 sugar cubes (actually marble and very heavy), an ordinary fever thermometer, a cuttlebone, and a little porcelain dish. The construction was named *Why not Sneeze Rrose Sélavy?* The thermometer used to measure a girl's 'heat', the phallus-shaped cuttlebone and female dish, the sugar that is really cold marble: these objects placed in the empty cage create a complex and witty spectacle of unfulfilled desire. For unlike all those erotic eighteenth-century paintings of young girls who let the bird out of the cage and watch it fly about, this cage contains no bird and a good 'sneeze' is needed to change things, to *arroser la vie. Éros, c'est la vie.*

What I find especially interesting is that when Duchamp went back to France for a while in July 1921, he started signing his letters to friends Rrose Sélavy, sometimes with variants like 'Rose Mar-Cel' or 'Rrose Marcel', 'Marcel Rrose',

'Marcelavy' (in a letter to Man Ray), 'Selatz' or 'Mar-Sélavy' (in notes to Picabia).[28] After 1925 or so, the Rrose Sélavy signature disappears, replaced by Duchamp's nicknames 'Duche' and 'Totor', but most frequently simply 'Marcel'. The bisexual punning and wordplay, elaborate as it was in the early 1920s, gradually decreased in volume, although Duchamp's short book of puns, *Rrose Sélavy* was not published until 1939. Stein's own most playfully erotic verse ('Happy happy happy all the./Happy happy happy all the.') comes in the same period.

In *Alice B. Toklas*, Gertrude Stein recalls her first visit, soon after the war, to Man Ray's tiny studio on the Rue Delambre, where 'he showed us pictures of Marcel Duchamp'.[29] Man Ray was photographing Duchamp as early as 1916–17 and Rrose Sélavy had not yet been born, but it is hard to believe that Stein would not have been aware of Rrose's presence when she was composing her portrait in *Geography and Plays*. Conversely, although there is no proof that Duchamp based his pseudonym Sélavy on Stein or his sexy and 'feminine' 'Rrose' on her more equivocal Roses, it is, to say the least, an astonishing coincidence that Duchamp, who never seems to have expressed a particular interest in Jewish culture, would want to adopt a Jewish name and one that was the name of a lesbian writer whose name begins with an S, even as he chose as his first name the banal 'Rose' that Stein had made so prominent.

The two artists, in any case, seem to have understood one another's work perfectly. Consider Stein's portrait 'Next. Life and Letters of Marcel Duchamp':

> A family likeness pleases when there is a cessation of resemblances. This is to say that points of remarkable resemblance are those which make Henry leading. Henry leading actually smothers Emil. Emil is pointed. He does not overdo examples. He even hesitates.
>
> But am I sensible. Am I not rather efficient in sympathy or common feeling.
>
> I was looking to see if I could make Marcel out of it but I can't.
>
> Not a doctor to me not a debtor to me not a d to me but a c to me a credit to me. To interlace a story with glass and with rope with colour and roam.
>
> How many people roam.
>
> Dark people roam.
>
> Can dark people come from the north. Are they dark then. Do they begin to be dark when they have come from there.
>
> Any question leads away from me. Grave a boy grave.
>
> What I do recollect is this. I collect black and white. From the standpoint of white all colour is colour. From the standpoint of black. Black is white. White is black. Black is black. White is black. White and black is black and white. What I recollect when I am there is that words are not birds. How easily I feel thin. Birds do not. So I replace birds with tin-foil. Silver is thin.
>
> Life and letters of Marcel Duchamp.
>
> Quickly return the unabridged restraint and mention letters.
>
> My dear Fourth.
>
> Confess to me in a quick saying. The vote is taken.
>
> The lucky strike works well and difficultly. It rounds, it sounds round. I cannot conceal attrition. Let me think. I repeat the fullness of bread. In a way not bread. Delight me. I delight a lamb in birth.[30]

This is one of Stein's particularly opaque portraits, and readers seem to have avoided it as merely 'non-sensical'. Stein herself, after all, says in the third paragraph, 'I was looking to see if I could make Marcel out of it but I can't', thus presumably admitting her failure to portray her subject. Then again she published the piece and gave it a very specific name so that the reader is challenged to understand the portrait's meaning.

The title 'Next', for starters, can be understood either spatially or temporally. A can be *next* to B in a picture or A can be *next* in the queue at the grocer's; in either case, 'next' is always a relational term. One cannot be 'next' alone. Does this mean Stein is relating 'Next' to the previous piece in *Geography and Plays*, 'Tourty or Tourtebattre'? Or that this composition is 'next' on Stein's list? The question is left open: certainly the subtitle is parodic, for the 'Life and Letters' format hardly seems appropriate for the iconoclastic Duchamp. Still, the mock title does set the stage for Stein's opening sentence: 'A family likeness pleases when there is a cessation of resemblances.' If, it is implied, we can get rid of representational art or poetry, of the need to make a portrait or still life *look like* its subject, then its particular family likeness can become 'pleasing'. Take Duchamp's *In Advance of the Broken Arm*— that ordinary snow shovel hanging on a wire from the ceiling. This readymade doesn't *resemble* something else: like Stein's rose it is what it is. As for its family likeness, the shovel has a very particular family: the readymades that live with it in the Arensberg Collection in Philadelphia or elsewhere.

The Henry and Emil to whom Marcel is now compared are almost surely Henry James, whom Stein regarded as her model, and again Emil(e) Zola. Descriptive as Henry James is, he is never 'pointed' like Zola. Having made these analogies, the author hesitates. Can Marcel really be placed in such a literary context? 'But am I sensible. Am I not rather efficient in sympathy or common feeling.' When one reads this sentence aloud, one almost inevitably reads 'efficient' as 'deficient'—for it is standard phrasing to refer to someone as 'deficient in sympathy or common feeling'. Is efficient then perhaps a misprint? Or does Stein purposely take the cliché and invert it, calling herself not exactly overflowing with sympathy but at least 'efficient'—capable of the 'common feeling' that has made Zola such an icon. It is the character of Marcel that seems to escape her.

Still, Duchamp's place in the poet's life remains to be assessed. 'Not a doctor to me not a debtor to me not a d to me but a c to me a credit to me.' Duchamp is neither her mentor nor her disciple—indeed not a 'd' at all—but a 'c' for 'credit'— the 'C' phoneme perhaps of 'Sélavy', for whose existence Stein *can* take credit. And in the next sentence, she pays homage to the Duchamp's famous *Large Glass* (*The Bride Stripped Bare by her Bachelors, Even*), of 1923: 'To interlace a story with glass and with rope with colour and roam.' The portraitist wants to have control over her subject, but the fact is that Duchamp, the 'dark' Norman crusader is a 'roamer': he has, at the time of the portrait, gone back and forth between the US and France again and again and also spent time in Argentina the last year of the war. One could never be sure where he might be.

'Any question leads away from me.' Stein cannot 'collect' Marcel's art, which seems, at this moment in time, quite uncollectable, but she can 'recollect' his chess-playing: the black-and-white board to be mastered. 'Black is white. White is black. Black is black. White is black. White and black is black and white.'[31] But chess is also the paradigm for Marcel's art in which, like her own, 'words are not birds'; they don't fly away. And a few lines further down, 'The lucky strike works well and difficultly. It rounds it sounds round.' The sentence evokes not only the cigarette brand (already in use in 1917, and Duchamp was a big smoker) but also the 'difficulty' of rounding out sound. Duchamp, whose punning titles and anagrams came to be one of his chief signatures, is seen as a man of *letters* in both senses of the word.

Duchamp had by this time invented not only the word play of *Rrose Sélavy*, but also the elaborate verbal play of his readymade titles that begins as early as 1915 with *L'Égouttoir,* the Bottle Dryer or literally, a device that takes the taste out of something.

How closely allied is the composition of a portrait like 'Next' to Duchamp's own work? Negatively, the relationship is remarkably close: in both cases, we could say, the attack is on retinal art, in Stein's case on retinal poetry. In both cases, language is to be seen as well as heard, and one letter, or rather, phoneme, can make all the difference, as when 'deficient' becomes 'efficient' (Stein) or 'French window' becomes *Fresh Widow*. Again, both Stein and Duchamp eroticize the actual language as in the 'egg be takers' and 'parts of place nuts' of 'Sacred Emily' and in the family of Duchamp readymades from *L'Egouttoir* to the *Eau de voilette*, to the androgynous *Fountain* by R. Mutt and then Rrose Sélavy.

Indeed, Stein's poetics is surely much closer to Duchamp's than to Picasso's vigorous, masculinist and still essentially *painterly* aesthetic. Consider Duchamp's playful treatment of book art and page layout. In 1922, Henry McBride, who had been close to both Stein and Duchamp for years, commissioned Marcel, who was once again living in New York, to design a book for his art essays. The resulting pamphlet was composed of eighteen cardboard sheets, held together by three rings.[32] Its title, *Some French Moderns says McBride*, is spelled out in twenty-seven separate file tabs attached to the right edge of each page; when viewed from the verso, these same tabs spell out the name of the book's publisher: 'SOCIÉTÉ ANONYME INCORPORATED', and the copyright is designated as that of Rrose Sélavy. Rrose also provides her autograph, and underneath her name, we read 'for Joseph Solomon forty years later by Marcel Duchamp'. Rrose-Marcel's design also affected the typography: the first essay is set in standard type, but the print selected for each succeeding page gradually increases in size, until only a few words fit on the page and then drop back suddenly on the last page to standard type. McBride's essays could hardly be 'read'; rather, the 'unreadable' text forms a backdrop for the seven photographs by Charles Sheeler that grace its orange pages. 'It's a wonderful book,' Alfred Stieglitz wrote to McBride, who passed the sentiment on to Duchamp.[33] In Paris, the young Dada poet Pierre de Massot heard about the McBride project and in turn produced a book written in English called *The Wonderful Book: Réflections on Rrose Sélavy* (1924).

In her portrait, Stein presents Marcel as indefinable: she cannot produce a coherent identity from what she knows about the artist's work ('glass and with rope with colour and roam'), his chess-playing, his 'dark' Northern heritage. Then, too—although Stein doesn't say it—what to make of Rrose Sélavy, that 'woman of no importance' who *is* Marcel? Pierre de Massot, who again refers to Duchamp's preoccupation with chess—the 'black and move on the chequerboard of life'—here reinforces Stein's response to Duchamp, her perplexity mingled with 'delight', born of the conviction that 'The lucky strike works well and difficultly. It rounds, it sounds round'[34]—and takes it one step further as the pleasure of unreadability—the *illisible*. Wilde's dramatic treatment of the mystery of identity, becomes, for Stein, the recognition that human identity cannot be satisfactorily captured in words. 'I was looking to see if I could make Marcel out of it but I can't' looks ahead, not only to the blank calendar pages of Massot's *The Wonderful Book* but to such later responses to Duchamp as John Cage's Plexiglas box *Not Wanting to Say Anything about Marcel*. And the *illisible*, is, of course, central to our own aesthetic today.[35]

On the back cover of *The Wonderful Book*, Massot placed a series of Rrose Sélavy's choice puns, from 'Etrangler l'étranger', 'Ruiner, Uriner', to 'Orchidée fixe' and 'Poulet exaucé'—his pun on 'satisfied' chicken as one that has been 'de-sauced'. These puns, Massot evidently thought, could be related to Steinian wordplay, and indeed, in his incisive preface for *Dix Portraits*, Stein's important 1930 volume, which contained her second Picasso portrait (1923), 'Guillaume Apollinaire' (1913), and 'Erik Satie' (1922),[36] Massot gives this perceptive summary of her language art:

> Tout y est pesé, dosé, calculé, mesuré, déduit, ainsi que dans une mosaïque; chaque terme enclave le prochain, strictement, le compénètre, comme les plans et les volumes d'une nature morte; chaque élément est perçu avec une telle acuité que sa représentation équivaut à un element neuf; nous assistons à une re-creation abstraite, par le dedans, du monde extérieur que je nomme: miracle.[37]

> Everything here is weighed, released in doses, calculated, measured, deduced, just as in a mosaic; each term encloses the next, strictly, co-penetrating it, like the planes and volumes of a still life; each element is broken down with such acuity that its representation is equivalent to a new element; we are present at an abstract recreation, from the inside out, of the exterior world so that I can only call it a miracle.

> (My Translation)

One of the portraits Massot probably had in mind was 'Guillaume Apollinaire', which begins with the line, 'Give known or pin ware',[38] a homophonic translation of the poet's name of which the author of 'Orchidée fixe' and 'Des bas en soie...la chose aussi', would surely have approved.[39]

Throughout the 1920s, when Duchamp shuttled back and forth between Paris and New York, he and Stein kept in touch, especially through their mutual friend Picabia. In December 1932, when the latter was having an exhibition of his drawings at the Galerie Léonce Rosenberg in Paris, Stein was asked to contribute a preface to the catalogue. Her 'Preface' turned out to be Stanza LXXI of Part V of her long and difficult poetic sequence *Stanzas in Meditation*, and the stanza was translated by none other than Duchamp.[40] It was, we should note, the very first selection from *Stanzas* to be published anywhere. Indeed, except for a few extracts, *Stanzas* was not published during Stein's lifetime.

'These austere stanzas', wrote John Ashbery, reviewing the posthumous Yale edition (1956) 'are made up almost entirely of colourless connecting words such as "where," "which," these," "of," "not," "have," "about," and so on, though now and then Miss Stein throws in an orange, a lilac, or an Albert to remind us that it really is the world, our world, that she has been talking about.' And he calls *Stanzas* 'a hymn to possibility'.[41] No doubt, *Stanzas* is Stein's most abstract, her least 'retinal' work.

Stein's meditation begins with a fractured narrative, like a passage from a children's' book:

> There was once upon a time a place where they went from time to time.
> I think better of this than of that.
> They met just as they should.
> This is my could I be excited.
> And well he wished that she wished.
> All of which I know is this.
> Once often as I say yes all of it a day.
> This is not a day to be away.
> Oh dear no.[42]

Duchamp translates this as follows:

> Il y avait une fois un endroit où ils allaient de temps en temps
> Je pense mieux de ceci que de cela
> Ils se sont recontrés exactement comme ils devaient.
> Lui et moi puis-je être excité
> Et alors il a désiré qu'elle desire
> Tout ce que j'en sais c'est ceci
> Une fois souvent tout cela un jour quand je dis oui
> Ce n'est pas une journée à être loin
> Oh! mais non[43]

The translation is, if anything, even more prominently rhyming than the original, with 'fois' rhyming with 'endroit' and 'cela', 'ceci' rhyming with 'oui', and so on. Duchamp follows the original fairly closely but does make some subtle changes. For one thing, he eliminates the full stops which, in Stein's poem, terminate each line, emphasizing the separateness of each phrase. Then, too, in line 4, 'This is my could I be excited' gets an extra set of male/female pronouns so as to emphasize the union: 'Lui et moi puis-je être excité'. And in line 5, the choice of 'desiré' (rather than, say, 'voulu' or 'souhaité') for 'wished' and then the shift from the second 'wished' to the present tense—'qu'elle desire'—enhance the erotic element in the stanza: it's as if Rrose Sélavy could almost make an appearance.

With the introduction to Picabia in line 17, however, comes the admonition to 'forget men and women' ('oubliez hommes et femmes'), and the meditation culminates in the following passage:

> The thing I wish to say is this.
> It might have been.
> There are two things that are different.

One and one.
And two and two.
Three and three are not in winning.
Three and three if not in winning.
I see this.
I would have liked to be the only one.
One is one.
If I am would I have liked to be the only one.
Yes just this.
If I am one I would have liked to be the only one
Which I am.
But we know that I know.
That if this has come
To be one
Of this too
This one
Not only now but how
This I know now.[44]

In Duchamp's version:

La chose que je désire dire est ceci
Qu'aurait pu être
Il y a deux choses qui sont différentes
Un et un
Et deux et deux
Trois et trois ne sont pas en gagnant
Trois et trois si pas en gagnant
Je vois ceci
J'aurais voulu être la seule
Un et un
Si je suis aurais-je aimé être la seule
Oui rien que ceci ou exactement
Si je suis un j'aurais aimé être la seule
Que je suis
Mais nous savons que je sais
Que si ceci est venu ou celui-ci
Pour entre un
De ceci aussi
Celui-ci
Pas seulement maintenant mais comment
Ceci je sais maintenant

The French cannot quite reproduce Stein's clipped monosyllabic lines with their rhyme and paragram: 'not only now but how / This I know now'. But Duchamp captures the tone with 'maintenant', 'comment', and 'Ceci je sais'. The one subtle change he makes comes in the ninth line above: the revealing remark, 'I would have liked to be the only one', which in English has no gender designation, becomes 'J'aurais voulu être la seule'. And further, in translating line 13, 'If I am one I would have liked to be the only one', Duchamp creates an odd split, making 'one' masculine ('un') but the 'only one' ('la seule') feminine: 'Si je suis un j'aurais aimé être la seule'.

In her own writing, Stein never gave herself away so fully: her pronouns usually have a studied indeterminacy.[45] But Duchamp playfully implies that Stein is all too aware that to be 'the only one' is to be a male one—indeed, to be a man like Picabia—or, for that matter, Picasso. And she adds proudly, 'Which I am' ('que je suis'). Indeed, she *is* the one. It is what Stein has always wanted. 'Yes just this'. Here Duchamp embellishes the line slightly, making it 'Oui rien que ceci ou exactement'. Why, the extra emphasis? Perhaps because Duchamp sympathizes with Stein's need to be *exactly* that only one. It was a need not felt by Rrose Sélavy, for Rrose could always shift back to become Marcel: from his perspective, 'une' become 'un' any time. Stein, on the other hand, was who she was: she could not adopt another identity as readily as did Marcel; indeed, the ironic distance so central to Duchamp's *oeuvre* was not her métier. Serious (if also very funny) and single-minded, she understood that 'Three and three are not in winning'. Three—whether in the love triangle at the back of 'Stanzas in Meditations',[46] or in her relationship to Picabia and Picasso, was a crowd. Unlike Duchamp—and here she may have been more like Picasso, Stein had no desire to be a *translator* of someone else's work. No, she was 'the only one', 'This one'. 'Not only now but how,' she concludes, 'This I know now'.

Marcel, Marcelavy, le Marchand du Sel, Rrose Sélavy the Fresh Widow, the Rose of Eros, had no such ego. Certainly, he too wanted to be 'one', to have autonomy as creator, but for the sake of his close friend Picabia, who was getting a bad press in these years, he was quite willing to do a quick translation of a verbal composition, whose indeterminacy and wordplay he could obviously relish. Especially a composition by an author as *sympathique* as Gertrude Stein. 'This I know now'; 'Ceci je sais maintenant': in their dismantling of the painterly form and the dissolution of retinal identity, the Stein of 'a rose is a rose is a rose' and Marcel-Rrose were nothing if not natural allies. Indeed, from the vantage point of the twenty-first century, it is Duchamp rather than Picasso or the cubists, Duchamp rather, for that matter, than Apollinaire or Max Jacob, who stands 'Next' to Stein.

NOTES

1. Gertrude Stein, *Picasso* (Paris: Librairie Floury, 1938); English edition, translated by Gertrude Stein with Alice B. Toklas (London: B. T. Batsford, 1939); revised edition, *Gertrude Stein on Picasso*, edited by Edward Burns, afterword by Leon Katz and Edward Burns (New York: Liveright, 1970), pp. 3–76. This volume also contains Stein's two Picasso portraits, 'Picasso' (1909), pp. 79–81, and 'If I Told Him: A Completed Portrait of Picasso' (1923), pp. 83–91, as well as Stein's notebook entries on Picasso and extensive illustration.

2. Stein, *Picasso,* p. 67.

3. Gertrude Stein, *Everybody's Autobiography* (1937; New York: Vintage, 1973), p. 37.

4. Pablo Picasso, '21 december xxxv', in Jerome Rothenberg, *Writing Through: Translations and Variations* (Middletown, CT: Wesleyan University Press, 2004), p. 66. For a selection of Picasso's poems in French, see Picasso, *Poèmes,* edited by Androula Michaël (Paris: le cherche midi, 2005). In her Introduction, Michaël expresses great enthusiasm for Picasso's poetry:'Écrire n'est pas pour Picasso une occupation de circonstance, ni un violon d'Ingres mais une activité à laquelle il s'est adonné avec passion,' p. 14.

5. See, for example, my 'Poetry as Word-System: The Art of Gertrude Stein', in *The Poetics of Indeterminacy: Rimbaud to Cage* (1981; Evanston, IL: Northwestern University Press, 1999), pp. 67–108.

6. Stein, *Picasso,* p. 65.

7. Pierre Cabanne, *Dialogues with Marcel Duchamp,* translated by Ron Padgett (New York: Viking, 1971), pp. 42–3.

8. *The Steins Collect: Matisse, Picasso, and the Parisian Avant-Garde* (touring exhibition, San Francisco Museum of Modern Art, 21 May–6 September 2011, Grand Palais, Paris, 5 October 2011–13, January 2012, Metropolitan Museum of Art, New York, 1 February–3 June 2012), edited by Janet Bishop, Cécile Debray, and Rebecca Rabinow (New Haven, CT: Yale University Press, 2011).

9. Gertrude Stein, *The Autobiography of Alice B. Toklas* (1933; New York: Vintage Books, 1990), pp. 133–4.

10. As told by Calvin Tomkins in *Duchamp* (New York: Henry Holt, 1996), p. 130.

11. On Stein's mathematical interests, see Steven Meyer, *Irresistible Dictation: Gertrude Stein and the Correlations of Writing and Science* (Stanford, CA: Stanford University Press, 2001), especially Chapter 4, "At the Whiteheads": Science and the Modern World', pp. 165–206.

12. Stein, *The Autobiography of Alice B. Toklas, Bishop,* p. 26.

13. *The Letters of Gertrude Stein and Carl Van Vechten, 1913–46,* edited by Edward Burns (New York: Columbia University Press, 1986), pp. 58–9.

14. See my 'Of Objects and Readymades: Gertrude Stein and Marcel Duchamp', in *Forum for Modern Language Studies* 32:2 (1996): pp. 137–54; compare my *21st-Century Modernism: The 'New' Poetics* (Oxford: Blackwell, 2002), pp. 77–20.

15. 'Roche', is written in the style of the first Picasso portrait: it begins, 'Was one who certainly was one really being living, was this one a complete one, did that one complete have it to do very well something that that one certainly would be doing if that one could be doing something', Gertrude Stein, *Geography and Plays* (1922) (Madison; University of Wisconsin Press, 1993), p. 141.

16. See James Mellow, *Charmed Circle: Gertrude Stein & Company* (New York: Avon, 1974), p. 311.

17. Stein, *Geography and Plays,* p. 187.

18. Stein, *Geography and Plays,* p. 178.

19. The Zola reference was pointed out to me by Susan Barbour, who also alerted me to the image of Zola's tomb at the Cimitière Montmartre.

20. Stein, *Geography and Plays,* p. 187.

21. Cyrena Pondrom, 'Introduction', to Stein, *Geography and Plays,* pp. i–lv; xlv.

22. Stein, *Geography and Plays,* p. 178.

23. Stein, *Geography and Plays,* p. 415.

24. Stein, *Geography and Plays,* pp. 405–6.

25. Tomkins, *Duchamp,* p. 231.

26. Tomkins, *Duchamp,* p. 231.

27. Dalia Judovitz, *Unpacking Duchamp: Art in Transit* (Berkeley, CA: University of California Press, 1995), pp. 144–5. In her more recent book, *Drawing on Art: Duchamp & Company* (Minneapolis, MN: University of Minnesota Press, 2010), Judovitz writes, 'Not only did Duchamp borrow a stylish hat from Germaine Everling (Picabia's mistress), but, more importantly, he also borrowed her arms and delicate hands in order to enhance the illusion of femininity conveyed by the photograph...she stood right behind him in a sort of embrace', pp. 32–3.

28. See *Affect-Marcel: The Selected Correspondence of Marcel Duchamp*, French-English edition, edited by Francis M. Naumann and Hector Obalk (London: Thames & Hudson, 2000), pp. 87–160.

29. Stein, *The Autobiography of Alice B. Toklas*, p. 197.

30. Stein, *Geography and Plays*, pp. 405–6.

31. Stein, *Geography and Plays*, p. 405.

32. The pamphlet is reproduced in Francis M. Naumann's *Marcel Duchamp: The Art of Making Art in the Age of Mechanical Reproduction* (New York: Harry Abrams, 1999), pp. 89–91.

33. See Naumann, *Marcel Duchamp*, p. 98.

34. Stein, *Geography and Plays*, p. 406.

35. See, for example, Craig Dworkin, *Reading the Illegible* (Evanston, IL: Northwestern University Press, 2006).

36. Gertrude Stein, *Dix Portraits*, bilingual edition with French translations by Georges Hugnet and Virgil Thomson (Paris: Éditions de la Montagne, 1930). The other seven portraits are of Christian Bérard, Eugene Berman, Bernard Faÿ, Georges Hugnet, Pavel Tchelitchew, Virgil Thomson, Kristians Tonny.

37. Reproduced in Franklin, 'Portrait d'un poète', p. 13.

38. Gertrude Stein, *Dix Portraits*, pp. 1, 385.

39. For background, see Ulla E. Dydo, *Gertrude Stein: The Language That Rises 1923–1934* (Evanston, IL: Northwestern University Press, 2003), pp. 294–301. Dydo notes that Massot spoke excellent English and wanted to translate *Tender Buttons* and *Geography & Plays*, but this didn't come to pass. For discussion of the translations of the *Dix Portraits*, as rendered by Hugnet and Thompson, see Dydo, pp. 296–300. Dydo notes that word-for-word translation, as used in *Dix Portraits*, failed to reproduce any sense of the original world play. But, one might add, Duchamp, able to read Stein in English and now often producing English puns of his own, could appreciate the originals.

40. 'Préface', *Expositions de dessins* par Francis Picabia, Galerie Léonce Rosenberg, Paris, 1–24 December, 1932. English Preface by Gertrude Stein, pp. 1–2; French Preface by Marcel Duchamp, pp. 3–4. Reprinted in *Orbes*, 4 (Winter 1932–3): pp. 64–7 (where it is found in side by side with poems by Hans Arp and Picabia), and again in Olga Mohler, *Francis Picabia* (Turin: Ed. Notizie, 1975), p. 43. In the French translation, the stanza in question is numbered 'Stance 69 des *Stances de meditation*'. I produce both English and French versions from Mohler.

41. John Ashbery, 'The Impossible: Gertrude Stein' (1957); *Selected Prose*, edited by Eugene Richie (Ann Arbor, MI: University of Michigan Press, 2004), pp. 11–15; reprinted in Gertrude Stein, *Stanzas in Meditation, The Corrected Edition*, edited by Susannah Hollister and Emily Setina (New Haven, CT: Yale University Press, 2012), pp. 50–5. The editors explain Stein's misnumbering in successive manuscripts, pp. 264–7.

42. Stein, *Stanzas in Meditation*, Part V, Stanza 71, p. 241. For the variants, see *Stanzas*, pp. 372–3. In the *Orbes* version, for example, line 7, 'Once often as I say yes all of it a day', is misprinted, 'Once *of ten* as I say yes all of it a day'.

43. Mohler, *Francis Picabia*, p. 42.

44. Stein, *Stanzas in Meditation*, p. 242.
45. On the use of pronouns in *Stanzas*, see Retallack, 'On Not Not Reading *Stanzas in Meditation*', Introduction to *Stanzas in Meditation*, pp. 22–5.
46. On Alice's substitution of the word 'can' for every 'may' (a reference to May Bookstaver with whom Stein was once in love) in her transcript of the text, see Dydo, pp. 488–502; Joan Retallack, pp. 8–14. Appendix D to the Corrected Edition (pp. 268–379) tracks all the changes in the manuscript.

11

'A Cage Went in Search of a Bird'
How Do Kafka's and Joyce's Aphorisms Move Us?

Jean-Michel Rabaté

> I think we ought to read only the kind of books that wound and stab us. If the book we are reading doesn't wake us up with a blow on the head, what are we reading it for?...we need books that affect us like a disaster, that grieve us deeply, like the death of someone we loved more than ourselves, like being banished into forests far from everyone, like a suicide. A book must be the axe for the frozen sea inside us.
>
> (Franz Kafka to Oskar Pollak, 27 January 1904)[1]

After this well-known quote by Kafka, a quote in which we see the promise of a literary programme, I present a simpler epigraph by André Gide: 'Extremes move me.' This is the epigraph he chose for an anthology of his own texts, *Morceaux choisis,* a collection that he put together for Gallimard in 1921. The original is: '*Les extrêmes me touchent.*'[2] In this sentence, Gide distorts Pascal's famous phrase, '*Les extrêmes se touchent*' (Extremes meet). In his *Pensées,* Pascal had launched a powerful meditation on the two infinites, with a wink to God as adding another type of infinity. The two extremes of the very small and the very big meet as parallel or converging infinities—such a double infinity can frighten you at first, but then it can lead to another idea: a deeper consideration of its meaning should convert sinners and bring them closer to the divine. Pascal aims at generating epistemological shock, followed by moral contrition and religious conversion. Gide's sly variation provides an adequate development of Pascal's idea. If extremes meet, this very idea has to touch me, to move me. If I am moved by it, I may well start doing what it takes to gain salvation, as for instance by betting on eternity and relinquishing the 'world'...Pascal is not that far from Kafka's own concerns, since he read Pascal and Kierkegaard closely at the end of his life.

Moreover, by transforming a reciprocal pronoun (*se touchent* = touch each other) into a direct complement (*me touchent* = touch me), Gide introduces a post-Einsteinian variation that nevertheless remains true to Pascal's insight: human subjectivity is not the sole measure of the universe, since what has been demonstrated is that it cannot contain infinity, but cannot be eliminated from the equation, and, what is more, it may be the direct object of the equation. Gide's witty reworking of the phrase is sometimes translated as 'Extremes move me' (as in Jean Delay's biography of Gide[3]) but 'Extremes touch me' might be as relevant. It is safe to assume that '*Les extremes me touchent*' is impossible to translate into English without an explanation.

How touched are we when we are moved by the power of a text? What is it that moves us? A hidden force or a sudden flash of insight? When this happens, which is not so rare, one often speaks of having experienced an 'epiphany'. These we tend to keep private, though at times we can witness someone having an epiphany. I remember such a moment in a *Finnegans Wake* reading group meeting in Buffalo. I was explaining to students that I thought that a given passage contained an allusion to Augustine's *inter urinas et faeces nascimur*. Obligingly, I translated the Latin: we are born between urine and faeces. This was not clear for one male student. I had to be more graphic. The response was a loud: 'Oh my God!' This epiphanic confirmation shows how right Joyce was when he placed the 'meeting of the extremes' in a sexual context. This is in *Finnegans Wake* when Jaun gives tips about sexuality to his sister: 'Keep cool your fresh chastity which is far better far. Sooner than part with that vestalite emerald of the first importance, descended to me by far from our family, which you treasure up so closely where extremes meet nay, mozzed lesmended, rather let the whole ekumene universe belong to merry Hal and do whatever his Mary well likes.'[4]

Signs saying 'Metaphora' can be seen everywhere in Greece, and they advertise moving companies. This would be compounded by the amphibology of the gerund or present participle: 'The *Death of Harriet Frean* is a good example of how moving modernism can be.' Thus, following Richard Gray's hint about Kafka, I will try to present a system of 'meta-aphorisms' that will link Joyce and Kafka.[5] A point of convergence in their works (one among many) is their handling of the aphoristic fragment, a genre often classified as 'classical' or 'romantic' but which, as I hope to show, has serious claims to a modernist status.

Aphorisms should not be confused with 'sentences', the short philosophical maxims that I like to call 'philosophemes'. 'Philosophemes' are pithy little phrases full of meaning. Philosophemes are tags, mottos, and apophthegms that can be mentioned independently of their original context. They tend to be cryptic, dense, at times oxymoronic. They are arresting sentences that usually avoid mere sententiousness. Their brevity and notable structural parallels are additional features that make them come close to being maxims, lines of poetry that one can memorize easily. Here is a short and admittedly highly subjective list, in order to exemplify what I mean: '*Die Sprache spricht*' ('Language speaks', Heidegger), '*Tout autre est tout autre*' ('Every Other is wholly Other', Derrida), '*Le cœur a des raisons que la raison ne connaît pas*' ('The Heart has reasons that Reason does not know', Pascal), '*Die Welt ist alles, was der Fall ist*' ('The world is all this is the case', Wittgenstein), '*Je est un autre*' ('I is another', Rimbaud*)*, '*Les non-dupes errent*' ('It is the non-duped people who are erring', Lacan), '*Verum Ipsum Factum*' ('Truth is its very fact', Vico), '*Was wirklich ist, das ist vernünftig*' ('The Real is the Rational', Hegel), '*Rien n'aura eu lieu que le lieu*' ('Nothing will have taken place but place', Mallarmé), '*O my friends, there are no friends*' (Aristotle, translated by Derrida), '*D'ailleurs c'est toujours les autres qui meurent*' ('Besides, it's always the others who die', Duchamp's tombstone inscription), '*Ubi nihil vales, ibi nihil velis*' ('Where you are worth nothing, you will want nothing', Geulincx). I could multiply examples or bring in several of Oscar Wilde's famous paradoxes, yet the number of these sentences, great as it is, is not infinite. They share characteristics: a notable syntactic compression,[6] a high dependence on a given language's amphibologies, which is what renders literal translation almost impossible (often, they have to be memorized in their original languages). This is highlighted by Kafka's famous aphorism 46 from *Betrachtungen:* 'The word *sein* means two things in German: "being" and "belong-ing-to-him".'[7] We don't know where Kafka wanted to go with this, but I feel that this obvious semantic remark (*sein* as the possessive pronoun 'his' doubling as the noun or verb for 'to be' and 'being') can destabilize ontology as fundamentally as when Heidegger decided to oppose *Sein* as 'Being' capitalized to *seiendes* as the 'being' (lower case b) of a *Dasein* understood as existence. The tantalizing semantic ambiguity of these aphorisms will trigger a slew of proliferating commentaries, which will lead in several directions at once while feeding the sense of inexhausti-ble riches in the initial expression. We see Joyce hinting at a similar reworking of ontology via language in one dream epiphany (# 36):

> Yes, they are the two sisters. She who is churning with stout arms (their butter is famous) looks dark and unhappy: the other is happy because she had her way. Her name is R...Rina. I know the verb 'to be' in their language.
>
> —Are you Rina?—
>
> I knew she was.[8]

The dream concerns Ibsen, since Rina is the name of a character in *Hedda Gabler,* the old aunt who is terminally ill and dies at the end of the play. It is interesting to see Joyce remembering the verb '*å vaere*', which means 'to be' in Norwegian, perhaps because its signifier VÆRE calls up a Latin 'Truth', the truth hidden in dreams.

Are ontology and language pitted against each other at the extreme poles of a long conceptual arc, or are they like the two sides of a single coin? Are we moved by extremes when they are polarized, or startled to see that in spite of all they were so close? Does it help if, in my native French, I hallucinate the *vrai*, a 'true' or a *sein*, a breast, perhaps a Kleinian split object, divided between the good and the bad breast, on these quotes? Such questions can be answered more rigorously if we take a look at the two parallel corpuses I have already tapped into, Kafka's aphor-isms and Joyce's epiphanies. As most critics have noticed, the Joycean epiphany and the Kafkaian maxim have something in common. However, one might object that any attempt to put Kafka and Joyce into dialogue will look from the start glib or forced. Many readers have felt that the two authors are so fundamentally differ-ent that any attempt to align them will appear problematic. There are, neverthe-less, several points of entry into a comparative study of their aphoristic work. These would put into motion connections to Nietzsche, their common reverence for Flaubert's style, a similar awareness that clichés or 'received ideas' constitute the basis for popular wisdom, their reduction of myth to catchphrases, and their wish to condense culture in a synthetic and creative language.

In trying to compare the Kafkaian aphorism to the Joycean epiphany, one important difference has to be stated. Joyce began his career with these very short texts, which can be dated from 1902 to 1904, and then are seen to disseminate through *Stephen Hero, A Portrait of the Artist as a Young Man, Ulysses,* and even *Finnegans Wake.* On the other hand, Kafka almost ended his literary career with the two collections known as 'He' (dating from Autumn/Winter 1917 and 1918) and the Zürau aphorisms that were copied from notebooks and compiled in 1920 at a moment when he had renounced writing long novels. I will return to this fundamental difference while pointing out formal similarities. These short frag-ments, ranging in length from a single sentence to a paragraph have a content that is often cryptic, or so condensed that the meaning is not immediately apparent. The aphorisms and the epiphanies evince points of convergence in that they share a dialectical relationship between the particular and the universal, fragment and totality: 'Only fragments of a totality', Kafka writes in his third octavo notebook.[9] Above all, their tensions generate 'dialectical images' (to quote Walter Benjamin) that move you, in spite, at times, of the theories they contain or convey.

A study of the aphorism should begin by considering the cultural and literary tradition. This is what Richard T. Gray, whom I have already quoted, has done in his excellent *Constructive Destruction: Kafka's Aphorism, Literary Tradition and Literary Transformation.* Gray reminds us that the word aphorism derives from the Greek *aphorismos,* a term coined by Hippocrates to designate a set of symptoms (and the medical nuance is never very far from Joyce's epiphanies). Over time, the genre of the aphorism was expanded to address a wider range of scientific and artistic discourses. Aphoristic writing was practised by Pascal, Vauvenargues, La Rochefoucauld, Novalis, Lichtenberg, Kierkegaard, Nietzsche, and Wittgenstein, among others. The inveterate tendency of the aphorism to straddle literature and philosophy contributes to its complexity. Aphorisms can be defined as short, apo-dictic statements that attempt to embody abstract truths. Richard Gray emphasizes that the apodictic structure of the aphorisms is a disguise for much more malleable and proliferating meanings. Finally, Gray thinks that the aphorism is 'the ultimate expressive form of modernism', above all because it epitomizes modern scepticism facing universal reason. This perspective emphasizes the centrality of the mystery, as well a transcendental thrust beyond the limits of the written text. Fittingly, the aphorism's resistance to a single definition seems to parallel the form itself, present-ing a set of cryptic, fragmented hermeneutical puzzles to be unwound.

What makes an aphorism distinctly 'Kafkaian' or 'Joycean'? One of the most common characteristics of these short fragments is that they can be read as com-pressed fictions of a subjectivity struggling to balance their linguistic capabilities and the shock of the real, often aiming at the truth as directly and immediately as possible. A first approach might be that a Kafkaian or Joycean aphorism presents the shortest narrative form capable of capturing the dialectical intertwining of Self and Other. Can this definition, broad as it is, help understand the dynamism deployed by Joyce's epiphanies? Joyce's practice should be studied first, not only because it took place earlier, i.e. around 1903–4, but also because, despite its being invoked right and left by readers and critics, it has kept an enigmatic air.

I will survey Joyce's epiphanies briefly, summing up two main features: first, most of these short texts exhibit repeated ellipses, their many full stops dotting the texts, opening them up; then most of the vignettes stage some form of movement, even when it is just that of a person who reads a book and identifies with characters who are moving as in # 2. Thus # 21 depicts two female mourners hurrying through a crowd. # 23 presents a male dancer who moves noiselessly in an amphitheatre: 'He begins to dance far below in the amphitheatre with a slow and supple movement of the limbs, passing from movement to movement, in all the grace of youth and distance, until he seems to be a whirling body, a spider wheeling amid space, a star …'[10] Dancers, dream animals, passers-by all move with an oneiric precision. # 16 depicts 'an artic beast': 'Something is moving in the pool.'[11] The dreamer pushes it with a stick: 'He moves his paws heavily and mutters words of some language which I do not understand.'[12] # 6 presents bearded satyrs, half-men, half-goats, who 'move about me, enclosing me' threateningly.[13] # 31 has a more urging air: 'What moves upon me from the darkness subtle and murmurous as a flood…?'[14] # 32 begins with a crowd moving in a dream: 'The human crowd swarms in the enclosure, moving through the slush.'[15] # 33 evokes society ladies who 'pass in twos and threes amid the life of the boulevard'.[16] Many of these vignettes have an exhortatory function, shaking the speaker to some action or decision; in # 30, which is reused at the end of *A Portrait of the Artist as a Young Man*, we hear the voices of the roads beckon: '… they call to me their kinsman, making ready to go, shaking the wings of their exultant and terrible youth'.[17] Even the vignette that goes back to a time of pious devotion, showing the young man after communion in a church, begins with 'It is time to go away now…'[18] (# 7).

To grasp what Joyce does with his epiphanies, we need to go back to the introduction of the term in *Stephen Hero*. Close to the end, Stephen overhears a dialogue between a man and a woman. This takes place in Eccles Street one misty evening and resembles a scene written for the stage:

> The Young Lady—(drawling discreetly)…O, yes… I was… at the…cha…pel…
>
> The Young Gentleman—(inaudibly) …I… (again inaudibly)…I…
>
> The Young Lady—(softly)…O…but you're…ve…ry…wick…ed…[19]

This is admittedly a disappointing dialogue; dots and ellipses count more than what is said; judging from this, one may have the impression that an epiphany sends us to a quintessentially Pinterian mode of dialogue, in that silences are more significant than what is being said.

What is clear is that these three lines of broken dialogue have managed to touch or move the young poet's sensitivity. What is more, he is moved to completing a larger task, since he decides immediately to collect similar vignettes in a 'book of epiphanies'. The definition of the epiphany follows:

> The triviality made him think of collecting many such moments together in a book of epiphanies. By an epiphany he meant a sudden spiritual manifestation, whether in the vulgarity of speech or of gesture or in a memorable phase of the mind itself. He believed that it was for the man of letters to record these epiphanies with extreme care, seeing that they themselves are the most delicate and evanescent of moments.[20]

The lack of content in the actual words of the exchange is constitutive. Here, it condenses Irish paralysis and weird sexual innuendo: what was the young lady doing at the chapel such that this account is almost unspeakable? The suggestion forces the reader to become more 'wicked', even if the actual event was banal and harmless. Was a priest involved, was he in the dark when she was muttering her soft 'O... yes...'? What is she suggesting with her sensually drawling 'O's? Excited, seduced, a passer-by transformed into an involuntary voyeur, Stephen repeats this repetition. This is how he turns, almost all at once, albeit in a programmatic manner, into a 'man of letters'. Letters will have to be arranged in a series while pointing to a constitutive gap in language, whether hers or his. He will try to capture less a moment of plenitude or revelation than a void in speech, a loophole in a dialogue, the surprising emergence of truth understood as a hole in discourse. This sudden discovery moves Stephen when he decides to compose a book made up of cuts, swoons, and fade-outs.

There is even, one might say, a systematic attempt at voiding language of its meaning. This is apparent in an earlier passage that seems to describe the same experience and call up an identical literary practice:

> As he walked thus through the ways of the city he had his ears and eyes ever prompt to receive impressions. It was not only in Skeat that he found words for his treasure-house, he found them also at haphazard in the shops, on advertisements, in the mouths of the plodding public. He kept repeating them to himself till they lost all instantaneous meaning for him and became wonderful vocables....In class, in the hushed library, in the company of other students he would suddenly hear a command to begone, to be alone, a voice agitating the very tympanum of his ear, a flame leaping into divine cerebral life. He would obey the command and wander up and down the streets alone, the fervour of his hope sustained by ejaculations until he felt sure that it was useless to wander any more: and then he would return home with a deliberate, unflagging step piecing together meaningless words and phrases with deliberate unflagging seriousness.[21]

This passage is rarely linked with the famous account of the epiphany, yet it is obvious that both describe the same process. Here is the rationale for the striking lack of content we find in the initial words quoted. They have to lose all content and become meaningless, and only then will they be reshuffled and reworked in a patient creative process. The literary task is triggered by an order from outside, a commandment coming from an Other voice. There is even something psychotic in the idea of obeying the voice from above. This is because the task would be impossible otherwise—the aim being in fact the opening of the whole world to artistic recreation.

Joyce aims then first at emptying the Real of meaning and then at leaving the mark of the hole open, until it can be knotted with other 'holes'. We can see a good illustration of this process in epiphany number 19:

> '(Dublin: in the house in Glengariff Parade: evening)
> Mrs joyce—(*crimson, trembling, appears at the parlour door*)... Jim?
> Joyce—(*at the piano*)... Yes?
> Mrs joyce—Do you know anything about the body?...What ought I do?...There's
>   some matter coming away from the hole in Georgie's stomach....Did you ever hear
>   of that happening?

Joyce—(*surprised*)… I don't know.…
Mrs joyce—Ought I send for the doctor, do you think?
Joyce—I don't know.…… What hole?
Mrs joyce—(*impatient*)… The hole we all have …… here (*points*)
Joyce—(*stands up*)[22]

The vignette finds its way in *Stephen Hero* as the conclusion of Chapter XXII, where it becomes more dramatic, since the blank page that follows the last word ('—The hole… the whole we all have… here.') leaves us with an almost intolerable suspense.[23] The next chapter will jump ahead and tell us that Isobel (she has replaced George) has indeed died. The setting is also more theatrical. The scene is announced by a moment of despair in Stephen, who had been playing at the piano and suddenly stops to hear dusk coming, even before the bad news is brought to him. The characters are painted in dramatic shadows: 'A form which he knew for his mother's appeared far down in the room, standing in the doorway. In the gloom her excited face was crimson. A voice, which he remembered as his mother's, a voice of terrified human being, called his name. The form at the piano answered.'[24]

The fragment points to a nameless hole (belly button, or anus?) and leaves the reader as startled as both protagonists. Naming the impossible site of death, it allegorizes the presence of a void at the core of the Joycean epiphany. The epiphany is less 'full' than 'empty'; it is a verbal sieve pointing to the function of letters, in Lacanian terms, as the rim of the hole of *jouissance*. But its foundational role comes from its having testified to the emergence of Truth in the Real. What stands out is the difference between isolated snapshots like epiphany # 22:

[Dublin: in the National Library]
Skeffington – I was sorry to hear of the death of your brother.… sorry we didn't know in time.…. to have been at the funeral.….
Joyce – O, he was very young.… a boy.…
Skeffington – Still.…. it hurts.…[25]

and their novelistic framing. From the start, Joyce recognized that his epiphanies would become discrete parts of a greater whole—either a series of short texts, or as integrated into a novel. Joyce used many of his epiphanies as fragmentary sketches of scenes or conversations. These he inserted throughout his novels. Epiphany # 21:

'Two mourners push on through the crowd. The girl, one hand catching the woman's skirt, runs in advance. The girl's face is the face of a fish, discoloured and oblique-eyed; the woman's face is small and square, the face of a bargainer. The girl, her mouth distorted, looks up at the woman to see if it is time to cry; the woman, settling a flat bonnet, hurries on towards the mortuary chapel'[26]

was used in the 'Hades' episode of *Ulysses*:

'Mourners came out through the gates: a woman and a girl. Leanjawed harpy, had woman at a bargain, her bonnet awry. Girl's face stained with dirt and tears, holding the woman's arm, looking up at her for a sign to cry. Fish's face, bloodless and livid.'[27]

The preservation and the condensation of the language and imagery of the original passage are striking. This demonstrates how closely Joyce worked with his epiphanies, and how deeply he integrated them in his novels. From the opening scene of *A Portrait of the Artist as a Young Man* to Stephen's recurrent dreams of his mother in *Ulysses*, the epiphany plays a central role throughout Joyce's *oeuvre*. One can even say that it provides mainstays, pillars anchoring the rest.

Kafka's experience, starting as it does from a similar 'triviality', identical urban crossroads, leads to an aporia. The aporia, as with Plato's aporetic dialogues, requires a different passage, and often the dead end will only be overcome by an ascent, a groping for a revelation. This is allegorized by one of the shorter texts that echo with Joyce's urban epiphanies, 'Unmasking a Confidence Trickster' (*Entlarvung eines Bauernfängers*). This short story from 1913 presents a narrator who explains that he has come to a fine house where he has been invited for a party but has been followed for two hours by a man who has thrust himself upon him. Having decided to shake him off, he finally confronts him. The companion makes a mistake: trying to be seductive and pleasant, he stretches his arm along the wall, leans his cheek upon it and smiles, closing his eyes. The smile reveals to the narrator that the man is a confidence trickster (*Bauernfänger*). He says: 'Caught in the act!' He can then go up the stairs alone and give his coat to a servant. What is revealing in this tale is the suggestion of shame at the moment of the unmasking ('shame suddenly caught hold of me'[28]) and the idea of a doubling: the man of the city and the peasant are successive versions of the same person. But where are they planning to pay a visit?

Indeed, if we look more closely, the signs become more opaque. The story was triggered by a visit to a Parisian brothel with Max Brod during his 1911 trip. During these excursions, the two friends had to fend off seedy barkers, aggressive touts, and pleading middle-men trying to lure customers to their establishments. The final sense of ease at the end contrasts with the real-life embarrassment felt by Kafka, who fled at least once from a Parisian brothel in disgust. Yet despite all this ambivalence, this is one of the rare texts in which the narrator is able to reach his aim, that is, to move on without impediment to a company and enjoy a successful social life. The text ends with: 'With a deep breath of relief and straightening myself to my full height, I then entered the drawing room.'[29] But as we know from *The Trial*, one cannot shake off a confidence trickster so easily in Kafka's world.

Let us return to Joyce's own trivialities. We know from archival evidence and the testimony of friends that Joyce collected epiphanies in an album like so many snapshots caught at urban intersections. These Baudelairean flashes in the night of urban *spleen* are profane illuminations catching a flickering aura via chance encounters with strangers heard muttering troubling signifiers on street corners. Trivialities indeed. Like the crazy and magical signs 'invented' in the streets of Paris by Nadja in front of André Breton's wonderstruck eyes, epiphanies erupt as soon as one lets the Real intrude. What matters is to capture the evanescent sign when it flashes. Even though the truncated signs are displayed in corners so as send one on the path to writing, they appear on the spot of a missing corner, so are literally blind spots, like that darkened parallelogram in Euclid's 'gnomon', the geometrical figure evoked at the beginning of the first story in *Dubliners*.

In the epiphanies as we have them today, the forty vignettes that survived out of seventy-one numbered by Joyce, there is great variety. The short texts range between dream transcriptions, fragments of dialogues, first drafts of objective narratives and lyrical autobiographical confessions. Most of these passages reappear throughout the later fiction: *A Portrait of the Artist of a Young Man* is built upon twelve important epiphanies, spanning the trajectory from the first scene evoking castrating eagles (already the first epiphany) to the last page, where another epiphany, number thirty, is recycled. These texts seem to have played the function of the initialization of a file in a computer. They dot the disks or hard drive with recognizable patterns. The term 'epiphany' is not mentioned in *A Portrait of the Artist of a Young Man,* and it has become derogatory in *Ulysses:* Stephen muses ironically on his juvenile fantasy of sending copies of his 'epiphanies on green oval leaves' to 'all the great libraries of the world, including Alexandria'.[30] Is it that by the late 1910s, Joyce no longer believed in his theory of the epiphany? Has the term been swallowed by the movement of mimesis seen as the work of writing itself? If the epiphany does not define a particular style but a format, it is because epiphanies exhibit a pure writing, as Roland Barthes would argue, that is without any 'style'. Here, literature has been devoured by the encounter with the Real, implying the subsequent activity of writing. Writing is in a porous mode, invaded by an inner or outer stage.

While exhibiting the radiance of manifestation, the 'shine' of epiphanies does not conceal their blindness. This is why the term keeps the important connotation of 'betraying'. By revealing something that had been concealed, the epiphany condenses a process of *aletheia*, or truth as unconcealment. Joyce's epiphany is never far from a Freudian symptom but with a political twist—in the context of an Ireland endlessly abused and betrayed. In his brother Stanislaus's account, the 'manifestations or revelations' in which the epiphanies consist undo the very process of ideological concealment while exhibiting ironically the type of repression at work: '…these notes were in the beginning ironical observations of slips, and little errors and gestures—mere straws in the wind—by which people betrayed the very things they were most careful to conceal.'[31] In epiphany # 12, Hanna Sheehy, asked who her favourite German poet is, replies sententiously after a pause and a hush: 'I think… Goethe….'[32] A Proustian irony is created by the multiplication of dots; the pretensions of a provincial culture taking itself too seriously have been exposed in a conflation of personal, social, and cultural symptoms.

A similarly complex conflation can be observed in Kafka's aphorisms. They range from single sentences, such as 'A cage went in search of a bird', and 'No psychology ever again!', to long paragraphs that come closer to the parable. Most aphorisms tend to be serious, enigmatic, and even grotesque. There is often a weird sense of humour. Despite the range of format and tone, the aphorisms are bound together by a deconstructive dialectic. Within this structure, each new term, consisting of elements syntactically and conceptually parallel to those of a previous term, arises by means of an inversion of these elements. Patterns of 'chiastic recursion' construct parallel lines of inverted meaning within each aphorism, folding the text back on itself. Thanks to an inbuilt logic of paradox, each aphorism contains its own undoing. For instance, the first aphorism, 'The true way is along a tight-rope, which is stretched aloft but just above the ground. It seems designed more to trip one than to be walked along',[33] exemplifies the deconstructive energy of the Kafkaian aphorism. Here, Kafka sets forth the idea of a pure truth and then deconstructs it in three stages. He first imagines an ideal, lofty truth suspended in the air. Then he inverts the image of a rope suspended above, so that the rope is brought just over the ground. Finally, he transforms the tightrope into a tripwire, so as to juxtapose the image of a truth path with its inverted parallel, a tripwire. As Peter Sloterdijk has argued, the aphorism makes sense if we understand it as an ironical response to Nietzsche's axiom in *Thus Spake Zarathustra* that 'man is a rope over the abyss'.[34] In the 'Prologue' of the book, Zarathustra gives his first discourses and asserts: 'Man is a rope, fastened between animal and Superman—a rope over an abyss.'[35] Indeed, we meet a tightrope walker a little later. He walks between two towers in the village. When he has reached the middle, the devil appears, jumps over him, and the tightrope walker falls to his death. The dying man sees Zarathustra kneeling next to him, and confesses that he knew the devil would trip him, but Zarathustra refuses to pity him and mocks his belief in God or the Devil.[36] For Peter Sloterdijk, this marks a shift from asceticism to acrobatics in European thought.[37] The dying tightrope walker prefigures the dying 'Hunger artist' of the famous story with the same title. Kafka condenses a tension already present in Nietzsche by making it both move and immobilize us.

Although it is impossible to identify a common structure among the different epiphanic forms, some trends are worth noting. Fundamentally, arguing against Max Brod's thesis of a religious Kafka, Richard Gray suggests that Kafka's aphorisms tend to eschew any revelation. Kafka's aphorisms pose complex hermeneutical puzzles, shrouded in a 'willed obscurity' reached in the name of a blinding truth. 'In a certain sense you deny the existence of this world. You explain life as a state of rest, a state of rest in motion.'[38] Such a paradox leads us to the Way—but there are several ways at once, and how to organize the fragments in the same way as the logic and sequence of Pascal's *Pensées* is still a matter of dispute. Here is one of the 'ways' I would choose to negotiate the paradoxes of Kafka's 'Consideration on Sin, Pain, Hope and the true Way' by focusing on the paradigm of movement.

> # 14 If you were walking across a plain, had every intention of advancing and still went backwards, then it would be a desperate matter; but since you are clambering up a steep slope, about as steep as you yourself are when seen from below, your backward movement can only be caused by the nature of the ground, and you need not despair.[39]

> # 18 If it had been possible to build the Tower of Babel without climbing up, it would have been permitted.[40]

> # 21 As firmly as the hand grips the stone. But it grips it firmly only to fling it away the further. But the way leads into those distances too.[41]

> # 26 (second half) There is a goal, but no way; what we call a way is hesitation.[42]

> # 38 There was one who was astonished how easily he moved along the road of eternity; the fact is that he was racing along it downhill.[43]

> # 76 This feeling: 'Here I will not anchor', and instantly to feel the billowing uplifting swell around one.[44]

In the second half of the last aphorism (# 109), we are led back to the writing desk, in what seems to amount to an abolition of movement:

> It is not necessary that you leave the house. Remain at your table and listen. Do not even listen, only wait. Do not even wait, be wholly still and alone. The world will present itself to you for its unmasking, it can do no other, in ecstasy it will writhe at your feet.[45]

But when we have reached this point of stability, it is the world that moves by itself. We understand how for Kafka, writing has to go deep enough in order to 'move' a subjectless subject who can then remain still. It is the world that has to unmask itself; here is the promise of an absolute *jouissance* of the Other, of a subjectless affect similar to what Deleuze and Guattari speak of when they present their theory of 'affects' in *What is Philosophy?*[46]

The lack of narrative placement makes the aphorisms difficult to decipher. The technique evokes the abysmal aura of a Truth that will be withheld. If the aphorisms aim at some sort of truth, this truth is obscured and distorted beyond recognition. All that is visible is an occasional flicker of revelation. Furthermore, in light of Kafka's fixation with lies and deception, which runs throughout the Aphorisms, revelation is inaccessible, although not impossible in theory. Kafka's novels are marked by the absence of an expected revelation. In *The Castle* and *The Trial*, Kafka constructs an intricate labyrinth of relationships and possibilities, tracing the futile and seemingly endless journeys of the protagonists. *The Castle* concludes midsentence, lost in a tangle of narrative possibilities. *The Trial* ends with Josef K.'s humiliating death, which can be read as an anti-revelation, since it removes any possibility of illumination or final understanding. It simply serves to further obfuscate the plot. Against this tendency, the aphorisms correspond to a desire to reach the truth quickly and immediately—in other words, they echo what Hermann Broch called the 'impatience of knowledge'. Yet, even when they manifest this impatience, the aphorisms debunk it:

> There are two cardinal human sins from which all others derive: impatience and indolence. Because of impatience they were expelled from Paradise, because of indolence they do not return. But perhaps there is only one cardinal sin: impatience. Because of impatience they were expelled, because of impatience they do not return.[47]

Thus driven by 'impatience', Kafkaian aphorisms move constantly to explore the metaphorical division between the material world and a higher state of being while challenging this barrier in its impossibility. It does not matter that the ground is limited to where the subject can stand: (# 24) 'What it means to grasp the good fortune that the ground on which you stand cannot be greater than what is covered by your two feet.'[48] In the Kafkaian aphorisms the tension between the local and the eternal, the trivial and the universal, is central. Kafka's dialectical moves imply contrapuntal relationships in the flow from universal to trivial. The effect is one of deconstruction or demystification rather than revelation, yet the concept of Truth is not destroyed, on the contrary. In that sense, Truth plays a role similar to that which I have analysed in Joyce's epiphanies: a decentring tool, a hole in discourse.

But for Kafka, this Truth devours all the rest, and ends up destroying both the world and the subject.

We have seen that the porosity of Joyce's epiphanies led to a practice of writing buttressed on the letter. For Joyce the letter is the key because it contains and rims a hole. In a similar manner, the logical impossibilities in Kafka's aphorisms evoke a principle of verticality that is denied, lost, obfuscated. The hope that a vision of the vertical truth will bypass the obscure labyrinths of *The Trial* and *The Castle* is frustrated. The aphoristic style achieves a shortcut, but then it literally puts an end to the narrative, and thus also undercuts itself. This is how Kafka can generate a perpetual movement by using a very small textual surface. What moves Joyce, as we have seen, is what can be called the 'Style of the Real'. In discovering how the Real speaks on its own, the writer's language allows itself to be moved by an absolute singularity, in which one can detect the lineaments of an ethics: there is indeed immediately an imperative, and it is categorical: 'You must write!'

Conversely, what moves Kafka is the possibility of jumping from an ethics of language to a perception of the Law as such. This does not mean that singularity is abolished but that the writer tends to see himself from the outside. The writing becomes the writing of the Real once more, at least in so far as the divided subject is told to side with the world and not with subjectivity.

Here, three famous aphorisms are relevant:

> # 52 In the struggle between yourself and the world, second the world. # 53 One must not cheat anyone, not even the world of its triumph.

> # He has discovered the Archimedean principle, but he has turned it to account against himself; evidently it was only on this condition that he was permitted to discover it.[49]

We can distinguish three modernist attitudes facing what I have called the 'Style of the Real'. First, there is Proust's position: a writer has to come to terms with the signs written in him by reality and time—involuntary memory tells him that Time can be abolished. The operation of involuntary memory supposes that, in the end, all the particular places, names, or sensations can be brought together by the text. Time will be abolished once two sensations are superimposed. One could read this as a certain Platonism. Kafka would not allow such a way out. He is haunted by an ethics in which God, the Real, or the Unconscious still dominate. With Proust, in the end, the writer can learn to trust this Unconscious and find reassurance in the thought that the work of art continues being written, as it will in each of us. Thus, all of us should not only enjoy but make use of this writing process. What Proust calls a 'metaphor' depends upon the utopia of an abolition of time in exchange for the promise of a work of art to come. Moreover, Proust's promise of writerly bliss is granted without any personal God being present or even relevant, whereas Kafka needs the framework of messianic promise, or as a second-best theory, Kierkegaard's or Pascal's overcoming of the ethical by the religious. The Jewish Messiah embodies the principle of the 'to come'—he will come, as we know, not on the last day but on the day after the last day: 'The Messiah will come only when he is no longer necessary; he will come only on the day after his arrival; he will come, not on the last day, but on the very last day.'[50]

Joyce seems to be content with the promise as a law of seriality in the text to come. There will be other privileged moments to jot down; the task may be infinite but it remains possible. Yet, there is another version of the Unconscious at work here, the 'agenbite of inwit' that Stephen feels gnawing at his soul in *Ulysses*.[51] Thus, the fact that one can trust history does not liberate it from the taint of original sin, and *Finnegans Wake* becomes a universal history of original sin. Finally, while Joyce seems to gain always (loss was his gain, as Beckett would argue), Kafka prefers to lose always: gain is his loss. In this sense, he paved the way for Beckett's poetics of impotence and deprivation.

In order not to conclude on a disheartening note that there is nothing but the regressive endlessness of a Hegelian bad infinity, we can remember Kafka's very last writings, these slips of paper he would give to visitors in the hospital. This was when he could not speak any longer because of tuberculosis of the larynx. The first: 'A bird was in the room.'[52] This bird had not found yet its cage. After the penultimate entry, it is impossible to continue: 'It was all so boundless.'[53,54]

NOTES

1. Franz Kafka, *Letters to Friends, Family and Editors*, translated by Richard and Clara Winston (New York: Schocken, 1977), p. 16.
2. André Gide, *Morceaux choisis* (Paris : Gallimard, 1921), p. 1.
3. Jean Delay, *The Youth of André Gide*, translated and abridged by June Guicharnaud (Chicago: University of Chicago Press, 1963), p. 475.
4. James Joyce, *Finnegans Wake* (London: Faber, 1939,), 440:31–441:01.
5. Richard T. Gray, *Constructive Destruction: Kafka's Aphorisms: Literary Tradition and Literary Transformation* (Tübingen: Niemeyer, 1987). Title of chapter 6, p. 264.
6. See Virginia Tufte's *Artful Sentences, Syntax as Style* (Cheshire, CT: Graphics Press, 2006).
7. Kafka, *Great Wall of China*, p. 86.
8. James Joyce, *Poems and Shorter Writings* (London: Faber, 1991), p. 196.
9. Franz Kafka, *The Blue Octavo Notebooks*, translated by Ernst Kaiser and Eithne Wilkins (Cambridge: Exact Change, 1991), p. 14.
10. Joyce, *Poems*, p. 183.
11. Joyce, *Poems*, p. 176.
12. Joyce, *Poems*, p. 76.
13. Joyce, *Poems*, p. 166.
14. Joyce, *Poems,* p. 191.
15. Joyce, *Poems*, p. 192.
16. Joyce, *Poems*, p. 193.
17. Joyce, *Poems*, p. 190.
18. Joyce, *Poems*, p. 167.
19. James Joyce, *Stephen Hero* (London: Jonathan Cape, 1956), p. 216.
20. Joyce, *Stephen Hero*, pp. 210–11.
21. Joyce, *Stephen Hero*, pp. 30–1.
22. Joyce, *Poems*, p. 179.
23. Joyce, *Stephen Hero*, p. 163.

24. Joyce, *Stephen Hero*, pp. 162–3.
25. Joyce, *Poems*, p. 182.
26. Joyce, *Poems*, p. 181.
27. James Joyce, *Ulysses*, revised ed., edited by H. W. Gabler (New York: Garland, 1986), 6:517–6:520.
28. Franz Kafka, 'Unmasking a Confidence Trickster', translated by Willa and Edwin Muir, in *The Complete Stories* (New York: Schocken, 1971), p. 397.
29. Kafka, 'Unmasking a Confidence Trickster,' p. 397.
30. Joyce, *Ulysses*, 3:143.
31. Stanislaus Joyce, *My Brother's Keeper* (New York: Viking, 1958), pp. 134–5.
32. Joyce, *Poems*, p. 172.
33. Kafka, *Great Wall of China*, p. 79.
34. Peter Sloterdijk, 'The last hunger artist', in *You Must Change Your Life*, translated by Wieland Hoban (Cambridge: Polity Press, 2013), p. 64.
35. Friedrich Nietzsche, *Thus Spake Zarathustra*, translated by R. J. Hollingdale (Harmondsworth: Penguin, 1969), p. 43.
36. Nietzsche, *Thus Spake Zarathustra*, p. 48.
37. Sloterdijk, 'The last hunger artist', p. 64.
38. Kafka, *The Blue Octavo Notebooks*, p. 47.
39. Kafka, *Great Wall of China*, p. 81.
40. Kafka, *Great Wall of China*, p. 82.
41. Kafka, *Great Wall of China*, p. 82.
42. Kafka, *Great Wall of China*, p. 83.
43. Kafka, *Great Wall of China*, p. 85.
44. Kafka, *Great Wall of China*, p. 91.
45. Kafka, *Great Wall of China*, p. 98.
46. Gilles Deleuze and Felix Guattari, 'Percept, Affect, Concept', in *What Is Philosophy?*, translated by Hugh Tomlinson and Graham Burchell (New York: Columbia University Press, 1994), pp. 163–99.
47. Kafka, *Great Wall of China*, p. 79.
48. Kafka, *Great Wall of China*, p. 82.
49. Kafka, *Great Wall of China*, p. 105.
50. Erich Heller, ed., *The Basic Kafka* (New York: Simon & Schuster, 1979) p. 182.
51. Joyce, *Ulysses*, 1:481, 9:196, 9:809, 10:875, 10:879.
52. Kafka, *Letters to Friends*, p. 417.
53. Kafka, *Letters to Friends*, p. 423.
54. A portion of this text has been published in a chapter of my book, *Crimes of the Future* (New York: Bloomsbury, 2014), pp. 176–84.

DISCOURSES/VOICES

12

Literature Knows No Frontiers
Modernism and Free Speech

Rachel Potter

All my good wishes to the P.E.N. Even if I'm the black sheep amongst members yet I feel that wherever I go P.E.N. would accept me and be kind to me if I'd let them—all over the face of the earth—which is somehow comforting. (D. H. Lawrence, 1929)[1]

1. Literature, national though it may be in origin, knows no frontiers and should remain common currency between nations in spite of political and international upheavals. 2. In all circumstances, and particularly in time of war, works of art, the patrimony of humanity at large, should be left untouched by national or political passion.[2] (1927)

The two principles in the second of these quotations were agreed by members at the International PEN Congress held in Brussels in 1927 (PEN stands for Poets, Playwrights, Essayists and Novelists). They had been drafted that year by PEN president, John Galsworthy. They remain largely intact in the current PEN charter, attesting to their abiding significance—as well as the ongoing importance of the PEN organization itself. The claim that literature 'knows no frontiers' is similar to the reference to free speech overriding frontiers in Article 19 of the 1948 Universal Declaration of Human Rights (UDHR): 'Everyone has the right to freedom of opinion and expression; this right includes freedom to hold opinions without interference and to seek, receive and impart information and ideas through any media and regardless of frontiers'.[3] Both statements define free expression in relation to borders and rights, and do so by way of universal human claims: the 'humanity at large' of the PEN declaration and the 'Everyone' of the UDHR. The links, however, between a literary writers' organization and the UDHR, or in a wider sense between literary writers of the early twentieth century and the drafting of universal rights, have hitherto been little discussed.

Recent historians of human rights have analysed the political and cultural battles over what was 'universal' about rights in the lead-up to the UDHR, with Mark Mazower calling this universality a dream that 'never existed' and Samuel Moyn arguing that human rights did not become politically and diplomatically significant until the 1970s.[4] The special capacity of literary writers to tell stories about rights, either as a way of bearing witness to rights abuses or by imagining the subjectivity of the rights-bearing individual, has also been central to histories of human rights. Joseph Slaughter argues, for instance, that human rights are 'as much matters of literature as of law', and that there was a substantial connection between the *Bildungsroman*, particularly *Robinson Crusoe*, and the discussions that surrounded the drafting of the UDHR.[5] His book elaborates on 'the conceptual vocabulary, deep narrative grammar, and humanist social vision that human rights law shares with the *Bildungsroman* in the cooperative efforts to imagine, normalize, and realize what the Universal Declaration and early theorists of the novel call "the free and full development of the human personality".'[6]

Modernist writers have played no role in these accounts. In fact, the anti-humanism of much modernist writing has been seen as fundamentally at odds with the legalistic understandings of human 'personality' and human 'dignity' that were central to the UDHR.[7] Modernist techniques of fragmentation and interior monologue, as well as the writing of the unconscious, abjection, and exile, tend to expose and explore the barriers between self and community. It is partly for this reason that, while the global nature of literature in a geographical or comparative sense has been central to recent debates about modernist literature, the emergence of a rights agenda on the world stage has not figured in these debates.[8]

This essay reconsiders this relationship. By analyzing PEN as a cultural and non-governmental site of international literary exchange I argue that early twentieth-century writers were significantly engaged in the question of what an international right to free speech might mean. After the Second World War, PEN had a direct impact on UN debates about human rights. Both the UN and UNESCO sent representatives to the 1947 PEN Congress and in 1949 PEN acquired consultative status at the UN as 'representative of the writers of the world'. This essay analyses an earlier period in the history of PEN and argues that debates between PEN members reveal important insights into the changing meaning of free speech in the 1920s and 1930s.

Both the 1927 PEN resolution and the UDHR refer to frontiers—and to the transcendence of frontiers—in the areas of free speech and free expression, and identify nationalism and politics as barriers to free speech. The 'moving modernism' of this volume's title, then, will be read as a movement of books and words across borders. This is a motion which aims to create a speech and literature free of the demands of nationalism and politics. Galsworthy's protocols express such transnational literary rights as aspirations; the claims that literature '*should* remain common currency' and '*should* be left untouched by national or political passion' (my emphasis) do not pretend to have legislative force. In contrast, the 'right' in the UDHR 'Everyone has the right' does pretend to have legislative force, even if, as many historians have argued, in reality this force was limited by state sovereignty.

But towards what did such freedom from frontiers tend? Galsworthy looks to a community beyond the present and beyond national borders. Literature and art originate in nation states but they are also 'the patrimony of humanity at large', a phrase that describes literature as the world's past and future inheritance. Literature as a 'common currency', meanwhile, insists both on its present-tense transnational right to circulate and sees it as a kind of Esperanto—an international language through which a commonality could be expressed. The 'Everyone' in the UDHR phrase, meanwhile, also looks to a global population, even if there were all sorts of checks and balances to make sure that the statement would not be able to override the sovereignty of states.

Yet such claims were problematic for many. The so-called universal language of humanism—the 'humanity at large' or the 'everyone' free from politics—was seen as a new kind of Western imperialism by anti-colonial nationalists; an ideology of universalism that was tied to the interests of the Imperial powers. On this argument, the transcendence of politics was actually an assertion of particular Western and racial interests. As W. E. B. Du Bois pointed out, the proposed international Bill of Rights of 1945 omitted any mention of colonized peoples. When the American Jewish Committee's proposed declaration of human rights was sent him for signature, he protested that 'this is a very easily understood declaration of Jewish rights but it apparently has no thought of the rights of Negroes, Indians and South Sea islanders. Why then call it a Declaration of Human Rights?'[9]

Many novels and poems of this period expose the interests lying behind the language of universalism. George Orwell, in *Keep The Aspidistra Flying* (1936) ridiculed the English focus of PEN's universalist humanist language. The novel opens with a discussion between a Mrs Penn, an avid reader of Galsworthy's *The Forsyte Saga* and Mr Comstock. Mrs Penn declares that 'there's something so *big* about Galsworthy. He's so broad, so universal, and yet at the same time so thoroughly English in spirit, so *human*. His books are real *human* documents.' Orwell's satire on the English focus of Galsworthy's universal humanism and the class exclusivity of PEN—Mrs Penn's eye, we are told, 'signalled highbrow irony'—implies that there are other, less exclusionary ways of imagining humanism.[10]

In a number of novels H. G. Wells also ridiculed the English nationalism that stood opposed to internationalism. In his 1930 novel *The Autocracy of Mr Parham: His Remarkable Adventures in this Changing World*, Oxford don Parham confronts post-war pacifists who believe in the League of Nations and world government. Parham's self-assured promotion of 'the Empire and its Necessary Predominance in World Affairs, of the Historical Task and Destiny of the English, of the roles of Class and Law in the world' is greeted with stony scepticism by international financiers and United States political optimists.[11] After Mr Parham becomes inhabited by a militaristic spirit, through a bizarre seance, he mounts a fascist overthrow of the British government and then enters into military conflict with the United States. Washington issues a statement with the following words: 'no man on earth whatever owes more than a provisional allegiance to the rulers he may find above him . . . his profounder, his fundamental loyalty, is to no flag or nation, but to mankind'.[12]

Wells' transnational 'mankind' had a particular politics, as it was tied to his commitment to the creation of a world commonwealth. Other writers considered the difficulties of imagining a 'mankind' tied neither to flag nor nation. Wyndham Lewis, in his 1930s satire on English communist circles, *The Revenge for Love*, has communist Percy Hardcaster and his fascist Spanish prison warder Don Alvaro debate the rights and wrongs of Percy's imposition of English notions of equality and freedom on foreign states. In the terms of the novel it is nationalism, rather than the politics of international socialism, that is here exposed. Percy's reputation amongst Spanish socialists is based on his national identity: Britannia is a 'big stuffed British Lion whose roar rattles the Seven seas'. Despite such imperialist bellowing on the world stage, however, both Britain and Spain are

> going rotten at the bottom and at the top, where the nation ceased to be a nation—the inferior end abutting upon the animal kingdom, the upper end merging in the international abstractness of men—where there was no longer either Spanish men or English men, but a gathering of individuals who were *nothing*.[13]

Here, a class-based transcendence of nationalism—only those at the top are implicated in this process—involves the embrace of an international abstract 'nothing'. This vacuum, or 'false bottom', allows all sorts of sinister financial and sectional interests to assert themselves under the guise of transnational politics.

Virginia Woolf, in a very different novel, *The Years*, describes the conflicts of politics thus: 'Not black shirts, green shirts, red shirts—always posing in the public eye; that's all poppycock. Why not down barriers and simplify? But a world, he [North Pargiter] thought, that was all one jelly, one mass, would be a rice pudding world, a white counterpane world.'[14] North's fear of nationalist politics involves an equally sceptical response to the blank and wordless worldly universalism that might replace it. Both Lewis and Woolf reveal much through the texture of their language. Lewis' 'gathering of men' and Woolf's jelly-like 'mass' are threatening because they are images of a humanity undifferentiated by nation or class.

Out of such reflections Lewis and Woolf describe both the limitations and central importance of free thought or free expression. For Woolf, freedom of thought is a balancing act between private and public pressures. North concludes that 'silence and solitude...that's the only element in which the mind is free now'. This extreme form of negative freedom, however, creates new means with which to exert punishment: silence and solitude are also 'the worst torture...that human beings can inflict'.[15] Privacy is a tenuous kind of freedom; this last refuge of individual expression is redundant in its isolation.

In *The Revenge for Love* it is the freedom of literature or art, rather than thought, that is opposed to politics. When outsider Victor Stamp questions how Marx could possibly help him to understand Picasso, arch-politico Peter Wallace patronizingly counsels 'You *can't* regard painting as suspended in ether, attached to nothing in heaven or on earth. That's art for art's sake.'[16] The earlier reference to the 'nothing' of a gathering of men without nation is now used to describe the idea of an art separated from material reality. In the political atmosphere of Oxford and Cambridge pinks, 'the usual Marxist don', and a refugee, however, the act of writing isolates the individual from politics. The group of 'salon-Reds' are panicked by the idea that Percy Hardcaster is both a 'man-of-action' and a 'workman', but are reassured by the fact that he's written a few pamphlets: 'this made him much more human—almost a "Leftie" PEN man.'[17] Lewis caricatures PEN's humanism as a soft aestheticism divorced from political force. In terms of the novel as a whole, art and writing stand opposed to politics. In a description of Margot and Victor, love also escapes the political: it is based on a

> rugged unrevolutionary principle, founded on sentiment, not intellect...It was the pact of nature; but with the human factor it became more. Was it not the poetry of the social compact too? Here was one of the elemental things in life. Why, it was the psychological analogue of the 'great open spaces' upon the geographical plane.[18]

Here, the free relinquishment of individual rights in the service of something higher—in love as in the social contract—is akin psychologically to exploring an uncharted land.

It is my contention in this essay that such literary imaginings constitute important reflections on the evolving meaning of the human right to free expression in the 1930s and 1940s. On the one hand these descriptions suggest that there is something unimaginable about a world without frontiers, whether this worldliness is of a human or legal nature. This is partly to do with scale and partly a kind of illegibility. Woolf's 'rice pudding world', as well as being an image which captures the undifferentiated human chaos mentioned above, also suggests a world of substance without meaning. In order to give meaning to this 'white counterpane' world, or Lewis's 'nothing', it would be necessary to define some kind of new global community or new international language. Some texts, most obviously utopian or dystopian fictions of the period, created positivist descriptions of future communities. Wells in *Men Like Gods* (1923) imagines a global utopia without government but held together by a commitment to privacy, free movement, unlimited knowledge, truthfulness, and free discussion and criticism. Dystopian novels including Aldous Huxley's *Brave New World* (1932) and Orwell's *Nineteen Eighty-Four* (1948) picture the world as propelled into a more global politics in which the earth is divided into huge superstates in which free expression is both prohibited and fetishized as a significant route to freedom.

On the other hand, however, the descriptions detailed above also unveil a structure of thinking in which overriding nationalism and politics entails some kind of embrace of the international or universal. Out of this structure of thinking free speech is both defined and fought for. Alongside the defensive and negative definitions of free expression described above, there was also a more confident promotion of literature as a positivist embodiment of liberty and the embrace of new kinds of global communities. It is these latter ideas that were particularly important for many writers, whether this was expressed directly in essays or whether it fuelled the structural logic of novels or poems.

In order to bring to life the aspirations, complications, and shifting priorities attached to ideas of free speech, literature, and a new kind of global community I will focus on PEN's activities in the 1920s and 1930s. PEN was one amongst a number of non-governmental international writers' organizations founded after the First World War (in 1921). Debates at PEN congresses reveal the pragmatics of international dialogue and cooperation—extremely difficult at times—as well as evolving discussions concerning free speech and literature. While there were many new non-governmental international writers' organizations founded in the

post-war period, International PEN was unusual for its independence from gov-
ernmental control.[19] It was also singular in the successful creation of a global network of writers' centres, with the founding, amongst many others, of China PEN
in 1930, Argentina PEN in 1930, All India PEN in 1933, and Japan and Brazil
PEN in 1934. The organization, formed in the spirit of international cooperation
after the First World War, specifically aimed through its annual congresses to create
dialogues between writers. Many significant authors were either directly involved
in the organization—for example, John Galsworthy, Jules Romains, Rabindranath
Tagore, Sholem Asch, Ernst Toller, F. T. Marinetti—or were more loosely affiliated
or gave lectures at PEN events—for example, Thomas Mann, E. M. Forster, James
Joyce. The organization's global literary networks produced new authorial collaborations and literary works. The organization also became a significant forum for
debates (particularly after 1933) about whether literary writing should be seen as a
form of international property and whether exiled writers should have international rights. My contention is that these networks and debates constitute an
important and neglected episode in the history of free speech.

PEN AND WORLDLY FRONTIERS 1921–35

In the immediate aftermath of the First World War a number of new international
organizations were created with the aim of averting nationalist violence. The most
significant of these was the League of Nations, founded in 1919, whose principles
and values were linked to the imperialist aims of British democracy, the rights of
nations to self-determination and the rights of minority populations within nation
states. These priorities were opposed to other ways of understanding internationalism and rights: attempts by Japan to secure the rights of racial minorities, for
instance, were firmly dismissed by the most powerful League nations. Further,
these states made sure that discussions of minority rights did not extend, for
instance, to the rights of colonized peoples or black Americans. As Mazower puts
it, 'The League itself was an eminently Victorian institution, based on the notional
superiority of the great powers, an instrument for a global civilizing mission
through the use of international law and simultaneously a means of undergirding
British Imperial world leadership and cementing its partnership with the United
States.'[20]

This 'global civilising mission', as Mazower puts it, was centrally dependent on
the dissemination of British culture. From the late nineteenth century, British
intellectuals promoted the idea that the international dissemination of education
and learning from Britain to its colonies could and should produce the ethical
understanding of community which would produce civilized values. This brand of
civilizing internationalism had a significant impact on the principles of the League
of Nations.

While the global spread of 'civilized' British culture and education was a central
thread in the foundational aims of the League, and continued to inform a significant
section of British opinion, there were a series of oppositional views which questioned

this paternalistic approach to the world. These disputes became polarized in the 1920s, with some arguing that cultural internationalism involved the spread of a global civilized community grounded in British democratic values and others seeing a global community as something that would need to be created through international collaborations. Key figures in this debate in Britain were Gilbert Murray and H. G. Wells, both of whom were involved in the setting up of the League of Nations Union in 1918, but who stood on opposite sides of a debate about its role in the world. Murray believed in the civilizing force of education and literature—civility here was linked to citizenship modelled on Hellenic lines, in which change was seen as a progressive unfolding of man's capacity for self-realization.

Wells's commitment to an enlightened world government as a means with which to combat nationalism was partly a critique of the inadequacy of the League. In his 1920 work *The Outline of History: Being a Plain History of Life and Mankind* he argued that the catastrophe that was modern imperialism would only be averted through education and the creation of an international 'federal assembly'.[21] In his *Men Like Gods* Mr Barnstaple, the novel's liberal protagonist, bemoans the state of modern society: the 'League of Nations, of which Mr Barnstaple had hoped enormous things in the great days of President Wilson, was a melancholy and self-satisfied futility; everywhere there was conflict, everywhere unreason'.[22] The failure of the League to prevent nationalist aggression, described as a futile melancholia here, was a common complaint, as was its self-satisfaction.

By the late 1920s Murray and Wells were on opposite sides of a debate, with Wells critical of Murray's paternalistic commitment to Englishmen 'civilizing' Africa through education. Other British leftist thinkers in the late 1920s and 1930s had begun to question the idea that it was possible to support both the League and the Empire at the same time. The difference in perspective centred on a divergence of opinion on what constituted community and culture.

In the 1920s PEN sat somewhere between these different ways of understanding literature and community. It was founded in London 1921 by Catherine Amy Dawson Scott, with John Galsworthy as its first president and Herman Ould as secretary. It had a London-based focus until British and International PEN separated into two separate organizations in the 1930s, although as described above, centres began springing up around the world from the mid-1920s. Started as a dining club for London writers, the group's ideological focus can be characterized as broadly liberal, but with a particular interest in worldwide dialogue. So, while its main beliefs were a strong commitment to free speech and to friendliness between nations, Scott also advocated a feminist requirement that PEN centres should always allow equal rights to women writers, and a deliberate policy of education and promotion of young writers. Scott's international ambitions are clear in the following description: 'it occurred to me that out of social intercourse comes understanding; and that if the great writers of the world met in friendship and exchanged ideas, a nascent kindliness would deepen till it appeared in their books'.[23]

Many of the writers involved in PEN came at the issue of free speech from experiences of book or stage censorship. Galsworthy, Joseph Conrad, and W. B. Yeats, who were all early members, had protested against UK stage censorship in the early 1900s. This was no less significant for its continental members. The Polish-born Jewish writer Sholem Asch, for instance, joined International PEN in the late 1920s after having his play *God of Vengeance* (1907), which was set in a brothel and featured a lesbian relationship, banned from Broadway in 1923. Asch attended PEN congresses and became honorary president of the Yiddish PEN Club, the first Club allowed membership on a 'non-territorial basis' in 1932. Many of the novelists and poets involved in PEN had also experienced book censorship for political sedition or obscenity.

PEN's commitment to free speech meant that it was unusual in allowing writers of different political beliefs to be members. A number of socialists and communists were active members of International PEN, such as H. G. Wells, André Gide, and Ernst Toller, but there were also fascist members including F. T. Marinetti, who was Italian delegate to PEN in the mid-1930s, and Carlos Ibarguren Uriburu, who was an Argentinian PEN delegate in the 1930s.[24] This catholic approach to membership was the result of PEN's deliberate desire to steer clear of politics. As a result, there were some extremely fraught debates, particularly in 1933 and 1936, over whether free speech *could* override politics and nationalism.

When D. H. Lawrence was asked what PEN meant to him in 1929, he replied, as quoted at the beginning of this essay, by highlighting another kind of openness to difference: 'All my good wishes to the P.E.N. Even if I'm the black sheep amongst members yet I feel that wherever I go P.E.N. would accept me and be kind to me if I'd let them—all over the face of the earth—which is somehow comforting.'[25] Lawrence's self-deprecating description of PEN's comforting world presence and tolerance for nonconformists acts as a corrective to Orwell's construction of the organization as elitist and exclusive. It also, importantly, sketches a picture of a scattered global community—but a community nevertheless.

A reading of the PEN newsletters from the late 1920s through to the late 1930s reveals a shifting agenda. Significantly the 'humanity' that features in Galsworthy's protocols changed from being a futuristic aspiration that would override the localized interests of restrictive nationalism to being a basic universal substance that required protection from tyrannical governments. This, in turn, had a number of consequences in debates about the nature of free speech.

From early on, PEN members were keen to stress the importance of cultivating a global humanity dependent on openness—a friendliness as Scott had put it—to cultural difference. Arne Kildal, internationally prominent librarian and president of the Norwegian PEN Centre, introduced the Oslo Conference in September 1928 with a speech which insisted that internationalism was essential if one wanted to look to a more emancipated future:

> it must be significant that the writers of the one country learn to know and under-
> stand and respect and sympathize with the writers of other lands, their aims and ideals,
> their hopes and longing, and their humble efforts to contribute to the improvement
> of the world and of humanity.[26]

Kildal assumes that writers belong to a nation—writers are 'of' a country—an assumption that would prove horribly problematic in the 1930s. He also, by looking to the future, imagines a new community dependent on the knowledge and under-standing that emerges through open-ended international encounters. This fantasy of a free-thinking community is grounded in humanitarian ideals: empathy, sympathy and respect for cultural difference. Such ideas were central to PEN's aspirations, both intellectually, and practically—the creation of different PEN centres and the struc-ture of PEN congresses encouraged precisely such collaborations.

But the creation of this international community would have consequences. Felix Salten, best known now for his work *Bambi, A Life in the Woods* (1923), which was made into a Hollywood film in 1942, had taken over the presidency of the Vienna PEN club from Arthur Schnitzler in 1927. He is more concrete than Kildal in imagining a new kind of international person: the tendency of the PEN club, he states, is 'to let the adjectives [French, German, etc.] vanish before the substantive, finally to enforce among Frenchmen, Englishmen, Italians, Germans and other peoples the man as a substantive!' This 'man' is both European and 'other', a description which reveals the Eurocentric nature of Salten's view of internationalism. Nevertheless, Salten is historically acute in his claim that this cognate international man will, by definition, override nationalist identification. By escaping national roots he is, for Salten, the man of the future:

> We have the task of transmitting to our posterity a mental disposition, we have to implant into it a conception of history, a fair-minded attitude from people to people which makes possible a national feeling to flourish in these new men of the future, free from provocation and presumption, a state of mind which is not infected by resentment.

Salten's fair-minded, free-thinking new man is dependent on the creation of a new kind of global community. It is intellectuals who are particularly well-placed to create this new community: 'It is only the mentally, only the artistically and scientifically working men of all nations which are able to fulfil the task in co-operation.'[27]

Salten's claim that intellectuals have a particular role to play in transcending the proprietorial resentment of nationalism was a central plank of PEN discussions and its sense of itself as an organization in the late 1920s. But by the early 1930s, political events in Europe meant that PEN's orientation changed. At the ninth annual Congress of PEN, held in 1931 in Holland, humanity was again put centre stage, but it no longer signified an aspirational community or emancipated human. The following statement was submitted by the International Committee and passed unanimously:

> From time to time the conscience of the world is stirred and shocked by revelations of the ill treatment in this, that or the other country, of people imprisoned on political or religious grounds. We submit that, in such cases Governments are specially bound to see that humanity is not violated in the treatment of such prisoners.[28]

Here humanity is not a futuristic global aspiration dependent on subsuming nationalist identification, but a substance that needs to be sheltered from state violation. The statement insists that it is the 'conscience of the world' that must work to shield individual freedom, particularly freedom of religious and political thought. In isolation the idea of a worldly conscience is so broad as to be almost meaningless; it is a version of Woolf's 'white counterpane world'. But its rhetorical function in this statement is to demand that people think globally. The statement in effect creates and defines a shared morality opposed to torture and the prohibition of free thought. The impulse here is to use a written declaration to represent the rights of the persecuted; and to see the literary community as duty-bound to tell the story of persecution.

This commitment altered the remit of PEN considerably, shifting it from a position outside politics to one in which it was poised to protest against government policies: 'This protest is made by the PEN without regard to political considerations but entirely in the interest of literature and in loyalty to the principle that the thoughts of authors worthy of the name should be given complete freedom of expression.'[29] Not only do such statements reveal the extent to which freedom of expression was uncertain, they also pin PEN's aims firmly to its defence. Given the fact that PEN had found itself straying into political territory, Galsworthy felt called upon to clarify PEN's apolitical stance:

> Such words as nationalist, internationalist, democratic, aristocratic, imperialistic, anti-imperialistic, bourgeois, revolutionary, or any other words with definite political significance should not be used in connection with the P.E.N. for the P.E.N. has nothing whatever to do with State or Party politics, and cannot be used to serve State or Party interests or conflicts.[30]

Galsworthy's defensive and negative definition of freedom of expression withdraws language from political or nationalist allegiance.

PEN changed course more emphatically in 1933, partly because of events in Germany, but also because Galsworthy died and H. G. Wells, a more controversial figure, took over presidency of the organization. It now actively took on the role of speaking on behalf of this worldly 'conscience' and Wells immediately sought to redefine the organization's aims. Given the political situation in 1933, 'the time had come for the PEN Club to revise very carefully what it is and what it stands for, and to make its laws and projects more comprehensive and more precise'. Wells' vision reflected his long-standing interests in a world government in which the creation of a community with shared ideals was central: 'We (in PEN) are trying to evoke a mental community throughout the world.' He seeks to give substance to the psychological orientation of this 'mental community' by historicizing its evolution: 'A century and a half ago, in the beginning of this process, there was a tremendous dissolution in the binding ideas of communities. We were all for liberty, and liberty ran wild.' The unleashing of libertarian principles of equality, freedom of person, and freedom of speech is presented as a stage in the history of enlightenment whose end must be a new kind of global community held together by strong government. The choice, for Wells, is between different models of authority, either a 'world commonwealth' based on 'liberty of expression' or a tyranny grounded in the suppression of ideas.[31] In marked contrast to Galsworthy's negative definition of free speech, Wells argues that freedom is a positive attribute, guaranteed and produced through the community and the State.

Such intellectual debates about whether free speech was a freedom from constraint or a positive humanist philosophical and ethical ideal were soon to be tested in PEN's own congress halls. In 1933 Ould had been sent by the London centre to enquire into the position of the German PEN in relation to the Hitler regime, and in particular whether the Berlin centre had issued a notice to its members depriving those of communist or 'similar' views of their rights to membership. As Ould stated, this was a violation of 'the first rule of the PEN that it should stand aside from politics', but it was also an abuse of the PEN commitment to free speech.[32] The Belgian poet and essayist and delegate René Lyr wrote a resolution in response to the situation:

> 1. La défense des droits de l'esprit en toute circonstance 2. Le rapprochement des peuples par les voies intellectuelles et spécialement par la littérature 3. En conséquence, la condamnation de tout ce qui peut menacer les droits de l'esprit, soit le rapprochement des peuples; en particulier, les préjugés de race or de confession religieuse et les fanatismes nationaux.[33]

Once in the conference hall, however, the 'défense des droits de l'esprit' came to mean different things. The German delegates had agreed to support Lyr's resolution, on the condition that there was no discussion of the situation in Germany. In particular, German delegate Fritz Otto Busch tried to prevent Ernst Toller, one of the first German writers to be denied German nationality in 1933, from speaking. Wells refused to bargain. Summarizing his speech, *P.E.N. news* reported: 'P.E.N. existed very largely to advocate freedom of expression, and that if those who had come to Jugoslavia [the conference was being held in Dubrovnik] with the intention of discussing the extremely critical situation in Germany were prevented from doing so, the P.E.N. would be stultifying itself.'[34] German PEN stormed out of the building.

Not only was the organization forced to take a stand on free speech by expelling some of its own members, it also created the first of the PEN centres abroad. This exiled centre was consolidated through a library called the 'German Library of the Burned Books', a library that contained 'all those works which in the "Third Reich" have been burned, censored, and suppressed'. The library contained suppressed books 'from Gotthold Ephraim Lessing to Heinrich Mann, from Heinrich Heine to Jacob Wasserman, from Marx to Stalin, from Einstein to Freud, from Voltaire to André Gide'. It also comprised the 'libraries of the many German refugees who have placed their books at the disposal of the library', works that are 'indispensable for the study and analysis of Hitlerism'.[35] Dr Alfred Kantorowicz, a Jewish-German professor of dentistry at Bonn University, who had been interned in a concentration camp before being released and reaching Turkey, wrote of the library:

> It signified that for these works of advancement there is no longer a place officially under the rule of National Socialism in Germany. It is also significant that the Provisional Committee has chosen this very day for the inauguration of the library in order to demonstrate that these documents of historical value to humanity shall not

be lost; that the very fact of their outward destruction and suppression has made them all the more precious to all who are striving for liberty, progress and a new, better world order.

'Humanity' is here seen as a product of the Enlightenment. Human rights, Kantorowicz insists, are the product of history, philosophy, and literature, and the culture of free speech which allows these ideas to flourish. Kantorowicz, and others, were also part of a displaced community whose ties to the German homeland had been severed. In such circumstances this humanist inheritance had been transported successfully across frontiers: 'For the first time since the German emigration in 1933 a comprehensive cultural offensive is being launched in order to save and preserve all these cultural values which Germany has contributed to the evolution of humanity during the eighteenth, nineteenth and twentieth centuries.'[36] Kantorowicz claims a tradition and an inheritance and importantly also a future—a patrimony as Galsworthy would have put it. He insists on the indestructability of this history of free thought—despite current political realities.

The PEN aspiration that literature should know 'no frontiers' had taken on an unforeseen resonance. Not only was the library a housing of documents outside any particular nation state; its precarious sovereignty reflected the position of innumerable individuals cast out from national homelands. In September 1935 the organization made a declaration on freedom of expression that signalled this shift:

> this conference reaffirms its conviction that freedom of expression and publication is an inalienable right of all creative workers, that any censorship of literature hinders authors in their work, and is treason to the rights of conscience, and should be resisted by all authors, whatever the nature of censorship.[37]

There are two different kinds of rights in this sentence. There is the language of natural rights, which states that the right to free expression and publication is inalienable; it is part of what it means to be human and cannot be transferred or taken away from the individual. This takes the organization's commitment to the universal right to free expression and situates it firmly in the individual, irrespective of national belonging. The statement also makes a slightly different claim focused on the individual: that censorship is 'treason to the rights of conscience'. Not only do writers have the right to express themselves, and to publish what they like; self-policing is a betrayal of the author's duty to tell the truth about persecution. Such inalienable rights point towards the rhetoric of rights that emerged more profoundly during and after the Second World War.

LITERARY FRONTIERS

Novels, plays, and poems which tried to give expression to the contradictions in claims to universal human rights become clearer, I propose, when situated in relation to the shifting history described above. I have suggested that understandings of free expression without frontiers changed in the 1920s and 1930s; post-war expansionist ideas about international dialogue between writers from different

nations were replaced with the desire to protect the individual from state persecution by situating the inalienable right to free speech in the person. The global
community, in turn, changed from being seen as a futuristic international group of
freethinkers to being a community of individuals, many of whom were without a
homeland, held together by a history of literature, philosophy, and science.

I have already discussed a number of writers who grappled with the difficulties
of imagining a meaningful kind of internationalism, some of whom were involved
in PEN, some of whom were not. Writers also engaged with the idea that a last
humanist remnant resided in a language of universalism divorced from the nation
state. Some novels or poems were akin to testimony—when Arthur Koestler tells
the story of an individual Bolshevik being tortured by Stalin's Communists in
1940, he does so by pitting the rhetoric of universal human rights against the revolutionary transformation of mankind: 'I plead guilty', states Rubashov, 'to having
placed the idea of man above the idea of mankind.'[38] The content of this novel sees
truth-telling sacrificed for the good of the revolution; the form of this novel refuses
any such sacrifice and instead pits truth-telling against the Soviet State and
Communist apologists. Some texts position human rights against the inhumanity
of war or conflict. Robert Conquest, in 'For the Death of a Poet' written in 1944
has the lines: 'Our only hope must be the truly human/Unclearly visible through
poetry's mist and dazzle/But shining so brilliantly beneath the inhuman stars:/No
angel; no hero; but truth.'[39] Conquest's secular humanist 'truth' in the 'truly
human' is distinguished from religious or military deities. Other texts negate
humanist conventions and values and voice the abject position of the outlaw whose
exilic position exposes the illusory idea of self-realization through community.
Djuna Barnes concludes *Nightwood* with her protagonist Robin Vote, whose name
evokes democratic process and who is first described as being like a painting, crawl-
ing on all fours with a dog. Here narrative development involves a falling away
from democracy, culture, humanity, language, and dignity.

I want to conclude this essay, however, with some final thoughts on *The Years*, a
novel that seeks to capture a changing understanding of internationalism and pac-
ifism. In a conversation during and after a London bomb raid in 1917, Sara,
Nicholas, Renny, Maggie, and Eleanor discuss the psychology of great men and
what kinds of laws should govern civilized states. They drink to the 'New World'
and look to Nicholas, the gay Pole, to make a speech about the future. The future
is connected to a number of loosely conceived notions: humans are going to
improve, live 'more naturally', and be 'free'. There are two descriptions with more
texture. Nicholas declares that the soul will 'expand; to adventure; to form—new
combinations?' and Eleanor considers the future by looking within: 'she felt not
only a new space of time, but new powers, something unknown within her'.[40] The
outward-facing adventure is connected to the exploration of the unknown within,
as though the one should inform and define the other.

Years later, in the 'Present Day', roughly the mid-1930s, a rearranged group
discuss again the psychology of great men, freedom, law, and self-knowledge.[41]
Freedom is now connected to the mind rather than the future, and the international political context is one of bullying tyrants—'at every street corner was

Death; or worse—tyranny; brutality; torture; the fall of civilization; the end of freedom'.[42] Eleanor's 'unknown within her', far from being something that might evolve through an adventure abroad, has become something that bullying tyrants seek to control. Nicholas's 1917 argument that people should stop living as a 'tight little knot' is rethought in relation to this political context.[43] Now the knot is a barrier against the invasive external world—'how did they compose what people call a life?... Perhaps there's "I" at the middle of it, she thought; a knot; a centre.'[44] This new world is one in which individuals must struggle to create the freedoms with which to be happy: Eleanor 'saw, not a place, but a state of being, in which there was real laughter, real happiness, and this fractured world was whole; whole and free'.[45]

What is important about these descriptions is the way that the self as a knot—a kind of inalienable self—is partly dependent on the ability to write a life. The ability to 'compose what people call a life' is as much a matter of language as of community. It is this struggle with a language of self-realization that is expressed so powerfully in this novel. North suggests he has only 'broken sentences, single words, with which to break through the briar-bush of human bodies, human wills and voices, that bent over him, binding him, blinding him'.[46] Woolf had long been sceptical of writers, such as Bennett and Galsworthy, who presumed they already knew how to plot a life irrespective of the nature of the life being described. Here, the question of how to compose a story of selfhood is given political force. The novel expresses a predicament about trying to write about the political world of the 1930s. It signals the importance of freedom of thought and freedom of expression but suggests that the narrative form of such freedoms is uncertain. The novel suggests that narratives, like people, are fractured and single. Given the external squeeze on freedom of thought and the absence of community, the narrative form that might 'compose a life' might well need to be a fragmentary one. Woolf suggests that the mind is the place where the outcast is both controlled and set free.

Literature knows no frontiers? Modernism and free speech? This essay has suggested that a wide variety of writers considered the right to free expression in its relationship to nationalism and internationalism in the 1920s and 1930s. There was a significant engagement with both the historical necessity and the difficulties of imagining the right to free expression without frontiers. Such imaginings are important to the history of the universal right to free speech—a right that has carried these aspirations and complications within it into today's world.

NOTES

1. D. H. Lawrence, *P.E.N. News*, 20 (April 1929), p. 5.
2. *P.E.N. News*, 6 (November 1927), p. 2.
3. United Nations, *Universal Declaration of Human Rights*, 1948, Article 19, www.un.org/en/documents/udhr accessed 1 Feb. 2016.
4. Mark Mazower, *No Enchanted Palace: The End of Empire and the Ideological Origins of the United Nations* (Princeton, NJ: Princeton University Press, 2009), p. 189; Samuel Moyn, *The Last Utopia: Human Rights in History* (Cambridge, MA: The Belknap Press,

2010). Mark Mazower's book *Governing the World: The Rise and Fall of an Idea* (London: Allen Lane, 2012) is also a significant contribution to this field.

5. Joseph Slaughter, *Human Rights, Inc.: The World Novel, Narrative Form, and International Law* (New York: Fordham University Press, 2007), p. 3.

6. Slaughter, *Human Rights*, p. 4.

7. Simon During, 'Modernism in the Era of Human Rights', *Affirmations: of the Modern*, 1.1 (Autumn 2013), pp. 139–59.

8. Wai Chee Dimock, *Through Other Continents: American Literature Across Deep Time* (Princeton, NJ: Princeton University Press, 2006); Susan Stanford Friedman, 'World Modernisms, World Literature, and Comparativity', in *The Oxford Handbook of Global Modernisms*, edited by Mark Wollaeger (Oxford: Oxford University Press, 2012); Paul Giles, *The Global Remapping of American Literature* (Princeton, NJ: Princeton University Press, 2011); Mark Wollaeger, ed., *The Oxford Handbook of Global Modernisms* (Oxford: Oxford University Press, 2012).

9. *Correspondence of W. E. B. Du Bois: Selections, 1944–1963*, edited by H. Aptheker (Amherst, MA: Massachusetts University Press, 1997), p. 39.

10. George Orwell, *Keep the Aspidistra Flying* (Harmondsworth: Penguin Books, 1975), p. 15, 16.

11. H. G. Wells, *The Autocracy of Mr Parham: His Remarkable Adventures in this Changing World* (London: William Heinemann, 1930), p. 76.

12. Wells, *The Autocracy of Mr Parham*, pp. 306–7.

13. Wyndham Lewis, *The Revenge for Love* (Harmondsworth: Penguin Books, 1982), pp. 25, 12.

14. Virginia Woolf, *The Years*, edited by Hermione Lee (Oxford: Oxford University Press, 1992), p. 389.

15. Woolf, *The Years*, pp. 402, 403.

16. Lewis, *Revenge for Love*, p. 158.

17. Lewis, *Revenge for Love*, p. 149.

18. Lewis, *Revenge for Love*, p. 81.

19. See Akira Iriye, *Global Community: The Role of International Organizations in the Making of the Contemporary World* (Berkeley, CA: University of California Press, 2002) for a discussion of the many organizations formed in the post-war period.

20. Mark Mazower, *No Enchanted Palace*, p. 21.

21. H. G. Wells, *The Outline of History: Being a Plain History of Life and Mankind* (New York: Doubleday and Co., 1971), p. 890.

22. Wells, *Men Like Gods*, p. 194.

23. C. A. D. Scott, 'The First International Club of Writers', *Literary Digest International Book Review*, 1 (November 1923), p. 47.

24. For a discussion of Marinetti's involvement in PEN see my essay 'Modernist Rights: International P.E.N.1921–1936', *Critical Quarterly*, 55.2 (July 2013), pp. 66–80.

25. D. H. Lawrence, *P.E.N. News*, 20 (April, 1929), p. 5.

26. Arne Kildal, 'Speech: Welcome at the Oslo Conference', *P.E.N. News*, 13 (September, 1928), p. 2.

27. Dr Felix Salten, 'Spoken by Felix Salten', *P.E.N. News*, 16 (December 1928), p. 7.

28. 'Appeal to All Governments', *P.E.N. News*, 44 (January 1932), p. 3.

29. 'The Suppression of Literature', *P.E.N. News*, 48 (June 1932), p. 3.

30. John Galsworthy, 'What the PEN Is', *P.E.N. News*, 48 (June 1932), p. 4.

31. H. G. Wells, 'Republic of the Human Mind', *P.E.N. News*, 56 (June 1933), pp. 2, 3.

32. Herman Ould, *P.E.N. News*, 56 (June 1933), p. 5.

33. René Lyr, 'Resolution', *P.E.N. News*, 56 (June 1933), p. 5.
34. 'The Situation in Germany', *P.E.N. News*, 56 (June 1933), p. 4.
35. *P.E.N. News*, 62 (March 1934), pp. 3, 4.
36. Dr Alfred Kantorowicz, *P.E.N. News*, 62 (March 1934), p. 4.
37. *P.E.N. News*, 73 (September, 1935), p. 4.
38. Arthur Koestler, *Darkness at Noon*, translated by Daphne Hardy (Harmondsworth: Penguin Books, 1972), p. 153.
39. Robert Conquest, 'For the Death of a Poet', in *The Book of the P.E.N.*, edited by Hermon Ould (London: Arthur Barker, 1950), pp. 131–7; 137. Brazilian novelist and playwright Paschoal Carlos Magno, who was living in England, had set up a PEN poetry competition open to any poet aged thirty or under. Entrants were anonymous and the judges were Richard Church, Cecil Day Lewis, and Herbert Read. Many poems were submitted from all over the world. Conquest's was the winning poem.
40. Woolf, *The Years*, pp. 281, 282–3.
41. Woolf, *The Years*, p. 299.
42. Woolf, *The Years*, p. 369.
43. Woolf, *The Years*, p. 282.
44. Woolf, *The Years*, p. 348.
45. Woolf, *The Years*, p. 370.
46. Woolf, *The Years*, p. 391.

13

Moved by Language in Motion
Discourse, Myth, and Public Opinion in the Early Twentieth Century

Ken Hirschkop

In an 1898 article entitled 'Opinion and Conversation', the French sociologist Gabriel Tarde noted a new force in French public life, the power of public opinion, which, although its medium was language, did not depend on the slow labour of argument. Public opinion moved quickly and unreasonably: Tarde had seen it move with fearsome rapidity during the Dreyfus affair, when the press and the discourse it inspired tossed the public to and fro like a sailing boat in a storm. Nor was Tarde alone: at the *fin de siècle* and in the decades following, many European intellectuals noted the speed with which appealing phrases flowed through the public, and they thought long and hard about whether this velocity could be harnessed for the public good or should be restrained in the interests of social order.

Was this really something new? Hadn't people always had opinions? Tarde conceded they had: what was new was their shape and mode of transmission. In the pre- and early modern era opinion had had a local and isolated flavour; there were strongly held views, but they pertained either to local matters or to transcendental affairs, and there was no medium in which they could be 'nationalized'. Even the parliaments of the early modern era were heterogeneous assemblages of local mandates (based on professions or institutions as well as geography). It was the press that made opinion public, or—what amounts to the same thing for Tarde—national: 'The work of journalism has been to nationalize more and more, and even to internationalize, the public mind.'[1] Nations come into being by virtue of an opinionated citizenry, who do not, however, storm the Bastille or assemble in Frankfurt. In fact, they 'do not come in contact, do not meet or hear each other; they are all sitting in their own homes scattered over a vast territory, reading the same newspaper'.[2]

They read the newspaper—and then they talk about it. Without conversation, newspapers 'would be like a string vibrating without a sounding board'.[3] 'The press', Tarde argues, 'unifies and invigorates conversations, makes them uniform in space and diversified in time. Every morning the papers give their publics the conversations for the day.'[4] These conversations spread and unify public opinion, so that in the end citizens not only share a common view, but are aware that they do so. The result is a new, symbolic bond:

> It is also essential that each of these individuals be more or less aware of the similarity of his judgments with those of others; for if each one thought himself isolated in his evaluation, none of them would feel himself to be (and hence would not be) bound in close association with others like himself (unconsciously like himself).[5]

Public opinion is a force: a 'storm', 'wind', or 'social river' that can protect our liberties and bend elected parliaments to its will. But it's a neutral force, which, with equal ease, can protect our liberties or raise the alarm against unpatriotic Jews. Tarde, we can safely assume, had read Zola's 'J'accuse', but also Drumont's tirades against the cancer within French society.[6] Opinion is different, therefore, from the 'public sphere' Habermas described, because public spheres exist not whenever private citizens gather to discuss public matters, but only when they also adopt certain 'rational-critical' aims and assumptions. The question is whether public opinion was the public sphere's cousin or grandchild.

For Habermas, it was clearly the latter, the consequence of the public sphere's structural transformation. When the nineteenth-century public was 'subverted by the propertyless and uneducated masses', the ideal of critical debate gave way to the ideal of tolerance, and the middle classes sought protection from opinion in 'an esoteric public of representatives' whose critical debates would be separate from those circling through the now much wider public.[7] Tarde takes the other tack, by making opinion the modern centrepiece in a triptych of discursive forms. On its right stands 'tradition', the customary repetition of inherited formulas and forms of speech; on its left, 'reason', characterized by argument, but restricted to the elite institutions—universities, law courts, and so on—of French society. The political fate of French society rested on the relationships between these forms. 'All would be best', Tarde sighs, 'if opinion limited itself to popularizing reason in order to consecrate it in tradition.'[8] Of course, all was not best: public opinion was encroaching on reason rather than serving as its ambassador. Nevertheless, Tarde did not think of public opinion as simply reason gone awry: it was a different kind of discourse, with a distinct but crucial role to play in a democratic society.

Conversation did not simply mimic the procedures of reason. Like the latter, it secured convictions through discussion, but the discussion was necessarily of a different sort, relying less on the cold rigour of strict argument and more on the spontaneous need for human sociability. Conversation was defined as inessential dialogue, dialogue without any practical or immediate purpose, 'in which one talks primarily to talk, for pleasure, as a game, out of politeness'. Such dialogue was 'the apogee of the *spontaneous* attention that men lend each other' and 'consequently, the strongest agent of imitation, of the propagation of sentiments, of ideas, of modes of action'.[9] It was a discourse speakers made effective by 'the tone of their voices, glances, physiognomy, magnetic gestures'.[10] Democracy required a bit of magic: it was the charm speakers exercised over one another that drew them into agreement.

Tarde's contemporaries were more sceptical. For Simmel, relying on imitation was tantamount to making public opinion a matter of mere fashion. It is the field of 'externals'—amusement, clothes, and so on—'which we can most easily relinquish to the bent for imitation, which it would be a sin to follow in important questions'.[11] No doubt this was to avoid the 'polar oscillations', the 'element of feverish change' that characterized the sphere of fashion.[12] Yet even Simmel distinguished the logic of imitation from mindless copying. Imitation, he argued, could be understood as 'the child of thought and thoughtlessness. It affords the pregnant possibility of continually extending the greatest creations of the human spirit, without the aid of the forces which were originally the very condition of their birth.'[13] To recognize the value of an innovation itself required an element of cognition: being persuaded to a position wasn't the same as arriving at it in the first place, but it required serious thought nonetheless.

One road not taken here would have been to recall the situation of an earlier democracy, the Athenian example, and think through these questions under the rubric of rhetoric. Wasn't rhetoric the practice of persuading a democratic citizenry through argument, of leading them to adopt a position they didn't have to arrive at independently? But rhetoric had fallen on hard times, and it seemed to require a homogeneous political mass, a citizenry who knew neither the social differentiation nor the individualism of the modern, to do its work. Its politics seemed to flow directly from the social whole, whereas now establishing that social whole was the task of politics itself.

Could one reconcile that task with the feverish change that imitation encouraged, or at least made likely? Tarde had thought conversation was up to the task, and up to the task precisely because its persuasiveness included elements beyond reason alone. This was—to borrow the most unfortunate of phrases—a kind of 'third way' in discourse, not quite reason, but reasonable, a way to attract the populace to positions that made sense, but by relying on something other than sense.

But like the more recent 'third way', this earlier one was the subject of disagreement. The shared starting point was the conviction that the reasoning of parliaments, the model for a rational, society-unifying political debate, could not simply be extended outwards into the newly enfranchised, working-class male populations of Europe. But the issue was not only how to produce the requisite *quantity* and range of agreement on social matters amongst the citizenry—it was also how to produce the right *kind* of agreement. The genius of conversation lay in the way it exploited the 'spontaneous' attraction citizens had for each other to create not only consensus, but a reflective consensus, in which each man felt 'bound in close association with others like himself'. Opinion didn't simply spread through the public—it created the public. A good conversationalist, Tarde noted, can be called 'a *charmer* in the magical sense of the word'.[14] He located that charm in what we would today call 'paralinguistic' features of discourse: the tone, bodily expression, and so on that accompany our words. But the more typical line was to appeal to a magic or charm that was located within language itself, a magic or charm that usually went under the name 'myth'.

This was not myth in Eliot's sense, 'a way of controlling, of ordering, of giving a shape and a significance to the immense panorama of futility and anarchy which is contemporary history'.[15] This was myth in the sense that Kenneth Burke used it in

1935, in a discussion of 'Revolutionary Symbolism in America', when he controversially recommended that the Communist movement ditch the myth of the worker and replace it with the myth of the people. In this context, myths were words or images that could mobilize a people, 'psychological tools for working together' that not only established opinions but also moved people to act on them.[16] If anything, the myths that interest us were images likely to create the very anarchy Eliot feared. Such, for example, was Sorel's myth of the General Strike, which would inspire the working-class masses to rise up and reject not only their parliamentary representatives, but parliamentary representation itself. These were words or collections of words that would organize and move opinion without the rational-critical testing of claims.

In recent parlance, we would call such myths 'metonyms': they were images of particular, concrete elements that signified a larger movement or ideology with which they were associated. But tropology was not the frame within which myth was understood in the early twentieth century. Alternately praised and feared as a weapon in the arsenal of democratic politics, myth was language's wild card, a collection of signs that suddenly acquired a force and density beyond their face value. It could, and had been used to create that public opinion, that sense of association, that national democracies needed. But, like Tarde, theorists of myth were unsure how to harness its power, and some were fairly sure one should not even try. That ambiguity, that unsureness, was reflected in how one conceived of myth. As a 'third way' in actual discourse it could be interpreted either as a flaw or defect in the ordinary functioning of language or as the blossoming of a linguistic bud that usually lay dormant.

For adherents of the former view, mythic language was a problem, a discourse leading the masses to confusion and to reckless enthusiasms. As I'll detail below, the problem was usually cast in quite interesting terms, myth being understood as a kind of short-circuiting of discourse, in which the usual route for a series of associations was bypassed and disparate meanings packed into a single signifier. Myth was language in which the network that mediated the linkage of sound and meaning was reduced to an immediate connection, and the solution to myth—it needed, in this view, a solution—was to prevent the short-circuiting by restoring the original network. For adherents of the latter view, however, myth was an ineliminable element of discourse, not so much a short-circuiting of linguistic energy as the very source of it. The modern age had repressed this energy, or dissipated it, and the task was therefore to recognize its power and harness it to the democratic cause.

For the classic formulation of the first, sceptical position, we couldn't do better than look to the description of 'word magic' offered by C. K. Ogden and I. A. Richards in *The Meaning of Meaning* (1923). Ogden was well-nigh obsessed with modernity's inability to shake off the primitive word magic of the past: the first edition of *The Meaning of Meaning* devoted sixty-eight pages to cataloguing instances of the magical powers attributed to words; a brief note to the edition announced that in that very year Ogden would publish a separate text, *Word Magic*, which would expand on the extant book chapter (the announced text never appeared); and when understandable editorial pressure gradually reduced the discussion of word magic to a mere twenty-four pages by the sixth edition in 1944, Ogden responded by publishing a 105-page article on the topic in his own journal *Psyche*.[17] Having noted that '[i]n some ways the twentieth century suffers more grievously than any previous age from the ravages of such verbal superstitions', Ogden and Richards set out to the put the century on the right path by making a sketch of the proper circuitry of meaning.[18] Their account of how symbols are created would

> throw light on the primitive idea that Words and Things are related by some magic bond; for it is actually through their occurrence together with things, their linkage with them in a 'context' that Symbols come to play that important part in our life that has rendered them not only a legitimate object of wonder but the source of all our power over the external world.[19]

That context was what Ogden and Richards called a 'sign-situation', wherein things were correlated with thoughts and thoughts then with symbols. It's represented in their notorious triangular account of meaning, which purports to show that while symbols are directly related to thoughts and thoughts are directly related to things, what philosophers call reference—the relationship between symbol and thing—is merely an 'imputed', indirect relationship, depending on the other two. When this indirect relation is understood as direct, when the charge of meaning seems to leap immediately from symbol to thing, we get the metonymic confusion that typifies myth:

> The greater part of mankind must once have believed the name to be that integral part of a man identified with the soul, or to be so important a portion of him that it might be substituted for the whole, as employers speak of factory 'hands'.[20]

But what kept Ogden and Richards awake at night wasn't religious superstition, but the modern, secular version. The two had become friends outside Ogden's office on the night of the Armistice, while students destroyed the bookshop where he had produced the *Cambridge Magazine*, a forum for alternative and pacifist views on the First World War.[21] The war had demonstrated the power of 'militant nationalism', and the extension of the suffrage that followed it in 1918 had made propaganda even more central to that nationalism.[22] When Ogden reprinted most of 'The Power of Words' in the *Cambridge Magazine* in 1923, the photograph that accompanied it was of Horace Bottomley, a rabble-rousing patriot addressing a mass meeting.[23] 'New millions of participants in the control of general affairs', Ogden and Richards remarked, 'must now attempt to form personal opinions upon matters which were once left to a few'.[24] With an enlarged field of action, word magic was deadlier than ever.

Hostility to myth wasn't limited, however, to the likes of English pacifists. In an entirely different political context, an entirely different kind of intellectual, M. M. Bakhtin, also attacked myth as a kind of short circuit, as a mystifying elision of discourse's situation. Bakhtin is best known for opposing the dialogical language of the novel to the monological language of the traditional poetic genres. But in fact monologism tends to fade from view in Bakhtin's most impressive work, the literary-philosophical essays of the 1930s, where he finds alternative ways to describe the oppressive language that novels undermine. In 'Discourse in the Novel' (1930–6), Bakhtin describes the moment when the novel blossoms, when modernity enforces itself on language, in the following terms:

> What is at stake is a very important, in essence, radical revolution in the fate of human discourse: the essential liberation of cultural-semantic and expressive intentions from the power of a single and unified language and, consequently, the loss of a feeling for language as myth, as an absolute form of thought.[25]

Language is mythic when it makes the bond between word and meaning immediate, when it ignores the social context that shapes and styles every utterance. On the next page Bakhtin will argue that one of the 'essential and constitutive features of myth' is an 'absolute fusion between the word and the concrete ideological meaning', such that the mythical world substitutes itself for the 'connections and interrelations of the moments of actuality itself'.[26]

Myth rears its head in the second half of this rather long essay, where Bakhtin makes clear that the novel and its distinctively 'dialogical' language are at one with modernity itself. According to the historical trajectory he sketches, myth is an outdated form of language and thought, which survives only as flotsam washed up in the wake of the modern. But the tone, structure, and timing of the essay imply it exists as a strong undercurrent as well. That Bakhtin expends so much effort making the case against a kind of language that supposedly belongs to the distant past is, on its own, revealing. More telling, however, is the fact that myth is effectively monologism with a human face.

Bakhtin's project was, from its very beginnings in the 1920s, polemical: he wanted to provide an alternative to the monological, 'theoreticist' view of culture he saw all around him. But for roughly the first ten years, monologism was presented as a species of positivism, an invasion of bloodless, objectivistic science into ethical matters. The monological habit was 'not a theory, created by this or that thinker, but a profound structural feature of the ideological work of modernity'— it was 'the modern', crushing an older dialogical tradition under its feet.[27] But when the novel takes centre stage in the 1930s, there is a subtle but distinct recasting of the linguistic villain, which is no longer science, but something human and social, no longer the modern, but something distinctly old-fashioned. Mythic discourse, epic discourse, the declamatory genres, authoritarian discourse (there are many different names for this newly reconceived foe): these are forms of linguistically embodied 'authority' rather than forms of linguistically embodied 'objectivity'. They don't pretend to be the objective, speakerless utterances of science, remote from human interaction; they are the utterances of certain kinds of speakers (political leaders, priests, judges, etc.), encouraging certain kinds of human interaction.

As is so often the case with Bakhtin—so often as to be, really, the rule—there is a conflict, an interference between the theoretical claim and the language and tone of the argument. In theory, myth is a form of discourse in which the speaker ignores or represses the 'heteroglot social opinion' that surrounds every possible topic of discourse, the threads of what has been said and must be reacted to that are woven around every object.[28] In the details of description, though, myth is an aggressively social and modern form, which depends not on ignorance but on a tactic to dominate the social, to organize and mobilize public opinion around authoritative figures and doctrines. It isn't an historic relic: it's Stalinism.

There are others who will pursue a similar line. When Saussure briefly mentions myth in his notes, he claims that the power of mythical names increases to the extent that those names separate themselves—as *names*—from the common names that depend on the language system for their signifying force.[29] When Roland Barthes, some forty-odd years later, decides to employ Saussure's theory to explain the mythologies of petit-bourgeois France, his explanation of myth describes it precisely as a kind of short-circuiting between two levels of significa-tion, 'a sort of constantly moving turnstile' that disguises the chain of associations that make it work.[30]

Ogden and Richards, Bakhtin, Saussure: very different writers, who often spend a good deal of time criticizing one another's doctrines. But their arguments share a common concern, a common diagnosis, and a common prescription. For each, there is a form of discourse, mythical and magical, that draws public opinion astray, draws it astray in such a backwards manner that they will not even admit this ideological suasion deserves to be called 'public opinion' (it seems like an unreasoning retreat to the past). For each, this magic power stems from a flaw in the ordinary functioning of language, a short circuit or shortcut which skips an element of the linguistic structure, whether it is the two sides of the referring tri-angle, the language system, or the complexities of heteroglossia. For each, finally, myth has no rightful or justified place in a modern society: it's a form of magical, premodern ignorance, which belongs in the dustbin of history.

No one doubted the antiquity of myth. But the belief that myth was 'the prod-uct of a basic shortcoming, an inherent weakness of language' had broader impli-cations, which led the philosopher Ernst Cassirer to become its most articulate and sophisticated modern defender.[31] It implied that there was really only one possible relationship between language and the world, that of strict imitation, and that any contribution language or image made to reality was no more than 'mere fraud and illusion'.[32] Cassirer realized that mythical belief in the 'power of words', in the 'objective character and objective force of the sign' was not mere delusion, but acknowledgement of the role symbolic form played in the constitution of the world around us, even in science.[33] Dismissing myth as malfunction and illusion therefore led not only to the misunderstanding of myth itself, but to the misunder-standing of discourse in general, science included.

When Cassirer embarked on his three-volume study of the philosophy of sym-bolic form, myth was accordingly given a seat at the top table. Volume I was devoted to language, Volume III to scientific knowledge, and Volume II to mythi-cal thought, which was thereby honoured as 'an independent mode of spiritual formation' with its own logic, which we would never abandon once and for all.[34] Myth would continue to haunt science (in the form of an incessant urge to 'sub-stantialize' what should be expressed as mathematical functions), it would con-tinue to play a role in religious consciousness, and it would eventually find itself partially transformed into art.

The logic of myth could be summarized as the tendency to confuse and conflate the ideal and the substantial, to treat all properties, qualities, concepts, and names as substances and real parts of the things to which they were attributed. Thus in alchemy, for example, every similarity between things, every common property or attribute of empirical objects, 'is ultimately explained by the supposition that one and the same material cause is in some way "contained" in them'.[35] Likewise, spiritual and even moral attributes were 'in this sense regarded as transferable substances'.[36] But the most important aspect of this logic for our purposes was that it meant that names and signs were deemed part of the objects they signified. In the universe of myth, Cassirer noted, 'the basic presupposition is that word and name do not merely have a function of describing or portraying but contain within them the object and its real powers'.[37] Hence in the religious rite, what takes place 'is no mere imitative portrayal of an event but is the event itself': words and action don't serve to represent something else, but are woven into the reality they seem to represent.[38]

That language, myth, and scientific knowledge were each considered an independent symbolic form, deserving of its own volume, was revealing. It made clear that not only was language more than simple representation, but also that it was not in control of its own fate: it could fall under the sway of, be combined with, either the impulses that led to myth or those that led to theoretical science. But in a long essay, 'Language and Myth', published while the second, 'mythic' book of the three volumes was nearing publication, Cassirer made the link between the two even closer. For language, Cassirer argued, depended for its initial creation on the mythical, not the scientific impulse. In language and myth, 'thought does not dispose freely over the data of intuition, in order to relate and compare them to one another', as in science, 'but is captivated and enthralled by the intuition which suddenly confronts it'.[39] This captivation, this sudden focusing, leads to a moment Cassirer describes as 'condensation' or—shades of poststructuralism!—'radical metaphor', in which the mythic image or the verbal structure is suddenly used to separate this impression out from the context surrounding it.[40] The sacred and the significant are, according to Cassirer, two sides of the same coin, and it turns out that short-circuiting is not a defect in speech, but its precondition:

> As soon as the spark has jumped across, as soon as the tension and emotion of the moment has found its discharge in the word or the mythical image, a sort of turning point has occurred in human mentality: the inner excitement which was a mere subjective state has vanished, and has been resolved into the objective form of myth or of speech.[41]

Acknowledgement of this common origin could be found in the tales of religion itself, where it was often the Word, the divine utterance, that created the world and where 'it is the *name* of the deity, rather than the god himself, that seems to be the real source of efficacy'.[42]

In these texts, composed in the 1920s, myth was a primitive, original form that survived into modernity thanks to the role it played in religion and art; it had no part to play in politics. Twenty years later, when Cassirer wrote *The Myth of the*

State, myth finally made it onto the political stage, but cast as the most maleficent of villains, nothing but a primitive intrusion into the sphere of liberal reason.[43] One can hardly be surprised, given what had happened in the interim, but it's hard not to think that the gravitational pull of extraordinary political events drew the theory of myth off course. For in the earlier writings Cassirer had implied that myth was an enduring symbolic form, which could no more be dispensed with than science or art. As for the formation of political will and the exercise of practical reason, these were matters of symbolic form left to one side, so that one could only guess at the contribution myth might make to them.

In theory, then, both myth and theoretical science would be able to audition for a role in the drama of political argument. And if, at first glance, it would seem Cassirer (a staunch defender of the Weimar Republic) was likely to have hoped science would win the part, the association of myth with particular forms of practice implies other possibilities. Myth is dominated by forces and power, which may be localized in gods, daemons, or magic words, or which can take the form of an undifferentiated and pervasive *mana* or orenda. But this is simply the way in which myth takes its cue from action, not Being. For the features articulated by myth 'are guided, not by any "objective" similarity among things, but by their appearance through the medium of practice, which relates them within a purposive nexus'.[44] Its vocabulary, therefore, is organized around functional considerations and shared practices, and its words do not designate from afar but participate in the force of whatever thing they name. To the extent that politics was an activity rather than an exercise in discovery, myth had a logical role to play.

In fact, by Cassirer's time myth had already stridden onto the public stage, in theory as well as practice, and it had entered from the left, not the right wing. The rise of syndicalism at the turn of the century and the emergence of the general strike as a political tactic led Georges Sorel to pen the articles that would be published in 1908 as his *Reflections on Violence*, a sustained justification not so much of the General Strike itself as of the mythification of it. Revolutionary activity requires something beyond both everyday language and the scientific babble of social reformers:

> Ordinary language could not produce these results in any very certain manner; appeal must be made to collections of images which, *taken together and through intuition alone*, before any considered analyses are made, are capable of evoking the mass of sentiments which correspond to the different manifestations of the war undertaken by socialism against modern society. The syndicalists solve this problem by concentrating the whole of socialism in the drama of the general strike.[45]

The General Strike is an image of the great battle for socialism, and like every myth the image itself seems to contain and evoke the forces it also designates. It is, in that sense, not just an image, but that which gives 'an aspect of complete reality to the hopes of immediate action upon which the reform of the will is founded'.[46] While the image acquires the forcefulness of events, events themselves acquire the significance of images, so that syndicalists are led to 'see in each strike a model, a test, a preparation for the great upheaval'.[47] It therefore 'matters little whether the general strike is a partial reality or simply a product of the popular imagination'.[48]

Sorel's theoretical inspiration for the adoption of myth was Vico, not, as with Cassirer, the Abby Warburg library and contemporary anthropology; yet it's clear he refunctioned the idea so it could serve as an instrument of modern public opinion. Sorel is not talking of an image constructed in a society organized around cultic practice, but about myth superimposed on a political discourse already traversed by rational argument. At issue is not the revival of an ancient practice, but the conversion of ordinary political language into a new kind of image, one *more* suited, not less, to the modern era and the political tasks of working-class radicalism. Myth is thus not a tactic according to Sorel, but the only form proletarian opinion can take while remaining true to itself.

Proletarian, not public opinion: because the proletariat's distinctive voice will only emerge by virtue of myths which produce a profound cleavage in society, and that voice will be distinctive not only in content but also in its mythic form. Sorel encourages the proletariat to reject the bourgeois reason of social reformers and bureaucrats not only because it propagates a false image of social progress, but also because it is a discourse lacking in energy and sublimity. The proletarian violence embodied in the strike should 're-establish the division into classes and so restore to the bourgeoisie something of its energy': the point of putting the proletariat on a war footing is as much about creating the necessary heroic virtues as anything else.[49] The moral convictions of the working-class socialist 'never depend on reasoning or on any education of the individual will; they depend upon a state of war in which men voluntarily participate and which finds expression in well-defined myths'.[50] Myth, which Cassirer described as an objectification of passions, is tasked with creating a heroic ethico-political attitude, an 'entirely epic state of mind' that lives in these passions.[51] It's as if the very charm, the magic, which Tarde ascribes to public conversation becomes not the necessary vehicle of public opinion, but its goal.

One could argue, however, that Sorel's myth solves the problem of an enlarged political constituency by abolishing politics together. The syndicalist vision of an instantaneous displacement, whereby the power of the bourgeois state is replaced by the forms of the labour movement, implies that there need be no separate institutional sphere of political life. As Pierre Rosanvallon has argued, the transformation of modern societies in the nineteenth century provoked in many the wish that society could be rendered immediately legible, without the need for a political deliberation and decision about its form. 'Politics', he claims, 'often seems simultaneously like an irritating residue, to be eliminated if possible, and like a tragically lacking dimension of life, a cruelly absent grandeur.'[52] Both tendencies are evident in Sorel: impatience with the wrangling and messy compromises of the parliamentary state, and desire for an epic, sublime politics.

Tarde had argued that the new democracies gave conversation and the press a newly important task; Sorel had claimed the essential ingredient was political myth, which required no special institutions of its own but a moment of social cleavage. When Antonio Gramsci came to formulate the myth of the modern Prince in his *Prison Notebooks*, he took on board Sorel's devotion both to mythic discourse and to 'the spirit of cleavage' he had championed, but with a signal and revealing difference.[53] For Gramsci was possibly even more interested in the press and conversation, more convinced of their essential mediating role than Tarde had been. The spirit of cleavage required not a single myth, according to Gramsci, but 'complex ideological work', and that work was embodied in the countless articles from journals, magazines, and newspapers on which the *Prison Notebooks* are something like a running commentary.[54]

In the first note, from 1932, where Gramsci proposes the plan for a text entitled 'The Modern Prince', he says the following of the book that serves as his exemplar:

> Machiavelli's *Prince* could be studied as a historical example of the Sorelian 'myth', that is, of a political ideology that is not presented as a cold utopia or as a rationalized doctrine but as a concrete 'fantasy' that works on a dispersed and shattered people to arouse and organize its collective will.[55]

The modern Prince—the thing—will be the Communist Party; 'The Modern Prince'—the text—will establish the party as myth, that is, as the local god or daemon of political action.

This magical, mythical element of politics cannot, however, do its work in the instantaneous, immediate fashion Sorel imagines. In a note on Croce and Sorel, Gramsci observes that '[p]olitical will must have some other mainspring besides passion';[56] myth only works immediately, is only a directly effective catalyst for immediate political action, when that action 'is a "defensive" rather than creative type of action... based on the assumption that an already existing "collective will" has dispersed, lost its nerve, and needs to be regrouped and reinforced'.[57] For the kind of political innovation Sorel has in mind, there is no royal road, no bypass around the 'complex of trenches and fortifications' Gramsci famously identified with the long-term ideological war of position.[58]

The 'most notable and dynamic part' of this complex 'is the press in general: publishing houses (which have an implicit and explicit program and support a particular current; political newspapers; reviews of every kind—scientific, literary, philological, popular, etc.; various periodicals, including even parish bulletins'.[59] The claim is borne out by Gramsci's relentless focus, while in prison, on the contents of a striking variety of periodical publications (scientific, literary, philological, etc., although no parish bulletins, so far as I know). The relationship between press and public, however, has been made problematic in Gramsci. Tarde described the journalist as someone who makes a collective, national force out of individually held sentiments. Hence the anti-Semite Drumont, enemy of Dreyfus, takes as his raw material anti-Semitism as a state of mind that was 'purely individual, with little intensity and even less contagion, unaware of itself' and creates from it 'a collective force, artificial perhaps, but nonetheless real'.[60]

But things were not so simple in Italy, where, Gramsci complained, writers lacked a '"national educative" function: they have not and do not set themselves the problem of elaborating popular feelings after having relived them and made them their own'.[61] As a result, the Italian people 'feel more closely related to foreign intellectuals than to "domestic" ones' and their preferred reading is the secular, thoroughly nationalized literature that comes to them in translation from republican France.[62] For it is republican ideology and practice, not conversation as such, which gives discourse the power of spontaneous attraction in France; Tarde's public is, in its form, already unified and nationalized. In Italy, by contrast, the public lacks the very medium in which it could become aware of itself. The Italian people are divided linguistically by dialect, Italian intellectuals are distant and cosmopolitan, and when the people attempt to articulate higher feelings, their only medium is an inflated 'operatic' style of expression, 'a theatrical rendering coupled with a baroque vocabulary'.[63] On this rocky and uneven terrain the cultivation of a collective will is difficult, if not impossible.

What France had in spades and Italy lacked, what Sorel detested and Gramsci thought essential, was Jacobinism. Italy needed 'an effective "Jacobin" force—precisely the force that creates the national-popular collective will, the foundation of all modern states'.[64] But Jacobinism was more than the Communist's devotion to the hard and tedious slog of political organization: it was also 'intellectual and moral reform',[65] which meant, among other things, the 'formation of a lively, expressive and at the same time sober and measured prose'.[66] To make the terrain of Italian public opinion arable, one had to establish a suitable linguistic medium in which the nation could converse.

In fact, no one disagreed about the need for a national language in Italy: the issue was how to bring it about and what the character of that language would be. What's distinctive about Gramsci's suggestions, and interesting from our point of view, is the degree to which they identify the national-popular character of the desired form of Italian with the mythical and figurative side of language. Just as Sorel identified parliamentary reason with reformist treachery, so Gramsci sees the authoritarian side of liberalism in proposals to unify Italian from above, by means of models and prescriptions. In a prison notebook dedicated to grammar, Gramsci remarks that while it makes sense to take steps to establish a unified national language, one mustn't 'imagine that the ends proposed will all be reached in detail, i.e., that one will obtain a *specific* unified language. . . . What this language will be, one cannot foresee or establish.' Planned interventions in a language can be more or less well thought out, rational in a tactical sense, but the actual path to a unified Italian depends upon establishing national channels of discourse—the press, education, conversation, and so on—that will, by means of 'a whole complex of molecular processes', nationalize the language in their own way.[67]

Gramsci was not original on this question and did not pretend to be. He drew heavily on the polemic Graziadio Ascoli had conducted with Alessandro Manzoni—who had proposed that the national language be modelled on the Tuscan dialect—and his general approach to the 'diffusion of linguistic innovations' reflected the neolinguistics of his teacher and mentor at Turin, Matteo Bartoli (Gramsci's university studies had focused on linguistics, not politics).[68] His originality lay in the conviction that a national-popular language would necessarily be an energetic language, and that an energetic language would necessarily be one in which myth played a central role. When Gramsci insisted that arguments addressed to the Italian people should be presented 'dramatically', avoiding 'cold ratiocination', he was not making a tactical point—as if the Italian people were incapable of abstract thought—but a point about the nature of political opinion.[69]

This might explain the kind and degree of attention Gramsci pays to Bukharin's *The Theory of Historical Materialism* (called the *Popular Manual* in the *Prison Notebooks*), a text to which Gramsci returns repeatedly in the *Notebooks*. For the *Popular Manual* is not merely an abbreviated exposition of one kind of Soviet Marxism, but also a work of propaganda or popularization, and Gramsci appraises it as such, claiming that Bukharin aims at the wrong target and uses the wrong ammunition. So, Gramsci observes, Bukharin contrasts Marxism to other systematic philosophies, as if these were what stood in the way of popular acceptance of Marxism, whereas his starting point should have been the 'critical analysis of the philosophy of common sense', that is, a critical approach to the existing, unsystematized ideas of his popular audience.[70] More striking, however, is an entry on the *Popular Manual* subtitled 'Metaphor and language', where Gramsci takes Bukharin to task for calling attention to Marx's use of metaphor, as if such figures were poetic departures from rational argument. But, Gramsci insists:

> All language is metaphor, and it is metaphorical in two senses: it is a metaphor of the 'thing' or 'material and sensible object' and it is a metaphor of the ideological meanings attached to words in the preceding periods of civilization.... Language is transformed with the transformation of the whole of civilization and it absorbs the words of previous civilizations and cultures as, precisely, metaphors. Nobody today thinks that 'dis-aster' is related to astrology or claims to be misled about the views of those who use the word. The new metaphorical meaning spreads with the spread of the new culture, which moreover coins new words and gives a precise meaning to words acquired from other languages.[71]

It is precisely as mythic substitution and concentration that words arise, and they arise, and are remade, according to ideological needs, which means, for Gramsci, in accordance with the requirements and situations of a new kind of practice. There's a linguistic reference here, but it isn't, tellingly, to the usual suspects, Bartoli or Croce: instead, Gramsci mentions the work of Michel Bréal, the linguist and, incidentally, prominent Dreyfusard, whose *Essai de sémantique* made speakers the engine of linguistic change and innovation. To place semantics at the heart of linguistic change, was, in Bréal's view, to reveal its 'only true causes, which are human intelligence and will'.[72]

Bréal was proposing a thesis about language in general—Gramsci was thinking of what language would be like once it had become the medium for national-popular collective will. Myth, in this context, itself stood for (was the myth of?) a practical, active moment in language, the moment when practical effort or energy produced a useful verbal instrument, so that the more engaged the public became, the more mythical its language would be. But this was a slow magic: not the lightning flash of the General Strike or the sudden *J'accuse!*, but the gradual construction of a style—lively, expressive, and at the same time sober and measured.

The charm of conversation therefore returned, but with something of a political edge. The spontaneous attraction citizens felt for one another could be frustrated if no national-popular idiom was available for public dialogue; the public sphere would remain arid without the energy embodied in mythic language and metaphor. Of course, even at this time, there were voices—largely female—telling whoever cared to listen that publicness, or at least a certain conception of it, was part of the problem, and that an adequate language would have to draw on more intimate resources than Cassirer or Gramsci cared to think about. There was, however, magic in the air, and politics on the ground, and a feeling that the mixture of the two was sure to be combustible.

NOTES

1. Gabriel Tarde, 'Opinion and Conversation', in *On Communication and Social Influence: Selected Papers*, edited by Terry N. Clark (Chicago: University of Chicago Press, 1969), pp. 297–318; 304.
2. Tarde, 'The Public and the Crowd', in *On Communication and Social Influence*, pp. 277–94; 278.
3. Tarde, 'Opinion and Conversation', p. 307.
4. Tarde, 'Opinion and Conversation', p. 312.
5. Tarde, 'Opinion and Conversation', p. 300.
6. On Tarde's reaction to the Dreyfus Affair and the effect of it on his sociology, see Jaap van Ginneken, *Crowds, Psychology, and Politics, 1871–1899* (Cambridge: Cambridge University Press, 1992), pp. 203–22, and Louis Salmon, 'Gabriel Tarde and the Dreyfus Affair: Reflections on the engagement of an intellectual', *Champ Pénal/Penal Field* 2 (2005), http://champpenal.revues.org/7185 accessed 6 Feb. 2016.
7. Jürgen Habermas, *The Structural Transformation of the Bourgeois Public Sphere*, translated by Thomas McCarthy (Oxford: Polity Press, 1989), pp. 136, 137.
8. Tarde, 'Opinion and Conversation', pp. 298–9.
9. Tarde, 'Opinion and Conversation', p. 308.
10. Tarde, 'Opinion and Conversation', p. 309.
11. Georg Simmel, 'Fashion', in *On Individuality and Social Forms*, edited by Donald N. Levine (Chicago: University of Chicago Press, 1971), pp. 294–323; 298.
12. Simmel, 'Fashion', p. 319.
13. Simmel, 'Fashion', p. 295.
14. Tarde, 'Opinion and Conversation', p. 300.
15. T. S. Eliot, '*Ulysses*, Order and Myth', in *Selected Prose of T. S. Eliot* (London: Faber, 1975), pp. 175–8; 177.
16. Kenneth Burke, 'Appendix: Revolutionary Symbolism in America. Speech By Kenneth Burke to American Writers' Congress, April 26, 1935', in *The Legacy of Kenneth Burke*, edited by Herbert W. Simons and Trevor Melia (Madison, WI: University of Wisconsin Press, 1989), pp. 267–73; 267.
17. C. K. Ogden and I. A. Richards, 'Words of Power', in *The Meaning of Meaning: A Study of the Influence of Language on Thought and of The Science of Symbolism* (London: Kegan Paul, Trench, Trubner & Co.: 1923), pp. 32–100. See also Ogden and Richards, *The Meaning of Meaning*, 6th ed. (London: Kegan Paul, Trench, Trubner & Co., 1944), 'The Power of Words', pp. 24–47 and C. K. Ogden, 'Word Magic', *Psyche* 18 (1938–52): pp. 9–126. Further references to *The Meaning of Meaning* are to the 1st edition (1923).
18. Ogden and Richards, *The Meaning of Meaning*, p. 38.
19. Ogden and Richards, *The Meaning of Meaning*, p. 132.
20. Ogden and Richards, *The Meaning of Meaning*, p. 36.

21. The details of the events vary somewhat from account to account. Ogden's biographer, W. Terence Gordon, claims the shop was wrecked by 'angry rioters'; see *C. K. Ogden: A Bio-bibliographical Essay* (Metuchen, NJ: Scarecrow Press, 1990), pp. 18–19. I. A. Richards, on the other hand, describes the offenders as '[m]edical students, flown with the spirits of the occasion' (i.e., the signing of the Armistice); see 'Some Recollections of C. K. Ogden', in *C. K. Ogden: A Collective Memoir*, edited by P. Sargent Florence and J. R. L. Anderson (London: Elek Pemberton, 1977), pp. 96–109; 97.

22. Ogden and Richards, *The Meaning of Meaning*, p. 23.

23. Ogden, 'The Power of Words', *Cambridge Magazine* 11:2 (1923), p. 50. The photograph carries the caption 'Words of Power'.

24. Ogden and Richards, *The Meaning of Meaning*, p. 23.

25. M. M. Bakhtin, 'Slovo v romane', in *Sobranie sochinenii. Tom 3, teoriia romana (1930–1961)* (Moscow: Iazyk slavianskikh kul'tur, 2012), pp. 9–179; 122. Translations from Bakhtin's Russian are my own.

26. Bakhtin, 'Slovo v romane', pp. 123–4.

27. M. M. Bakhtin, *Problemy tvorchestva Dostoievskogo* (1929), in *Sobranie sochinenii. Tom 2* (Moscow: Russkie slovari, 2000), pp. 5–175; 61.

28. Bakhtin, 'Slovo v romane', p. 31.

29. 'As long as the word *agni* refers to both—hence confusion—everyday fire and the god *Agni*...we can never make *Agni* or *Djeus* a figure comparable with *Varuna* or Ἀπόλλων [*Apollon*], whose names characteristically do not refer simultaneously to any other earthly thing.' Ferdinand de Saussure, 'Notes on Whitney', in *Writings in General Linguistics*, edited by Simon Bouquet and Rudolf Engler, translated by Carol Sanders and Matthew Pires (Oxford: Oxford University Press, 2006), pp. 140–56; 154.

30. Roland Barthes, 'Myth Today', in *Mythologies*, translated by Annette Lavers (London: Vintage, 1993), pp. 109–59; 123.

31. Ernst Cassirer, *Language and Myth*, translated by Susan K. Langer (New York: Dover, 1946), p. 4.

32. Cassirer, *Language and Myth*, p. 6.

33. Ernst Cassirer, *The Philosophy of Symbolic Forms, Volume Two: Mythical Thought*, translated by Ralph Manheim (New Haven, CT: Yale University Press, 1955), p. 24.

34. Cassirer, *The Philosophy of Symbolic Forms*, p. xv.

35. Cassirer, *The Philosophy of Symbolic Forms*, p. 66.

36. Cassirer, *The Philosophy of Symbolic Forms*, p. 56.

37. Cassirer, *The Philosophy of Symbolic Forms*, p. 40.

38. Cassirer, *The Philosophy of Symbolic Forms*, p. 39.

39. Cassirer, *Language and Myth*, p. 32.

40. Cassirer, *Language and Myth*, pp. 34, 87.

41. Cassirer, *Language and Myth*, p. 36.

42. Cassirer, *Language and Myth*, p. 50.

43. Ernst Cassirer, *The Myth of the State* (New Haven: Yale University Press, 1946).

44. Cassirer, *Language and Myth*, p. 39.

45. Georges Sorel, *Reflections on Violence*, translated by T. E. Hulme (Cambridge: Cambridge University Press, 1999), p. 113.

46. Sorel, *Reflections on Violence*, p. 115.

47. Sorel, *Reflections on Violence*, p. 110.

48. Sorel, *Reflections on Violence*, p. 117.

49. Sorel, *Reflections on Violence*, p. 85.

50. Sorel, *Reflections on Violence*, pp. 207–8.

51. Sorel, *Reflections on Violence,* p. 250.

52. Pierre Rosanvallon, 'Inaugural Lecture, Collège de France', in *Democracy Past and Future,* edited by Samuel Moyne (New York: Columbia University Press, 2006), pp. 31–58; 55.

53. The phrase 'spirit of cleavage' is found in Antonio Gramsci, *Prison Notebooks,* Volume II, edited and translated by Joseph A. Buttigieg (New York: Columbia University Press, 1996), Notebook 3, § 49, p. 53. There is, naturally, lively debate over Gramsci's debt to his syndicalist predecessor. On his evaluation of Sorel before his imprisonment, see Darrow Schechter, 'Two Views of the Revolution: Gramsci and Sorel, 1916–1920', *History of European Ideas,* 12 (1990): pp. 637–53. I think Gramsci's ambiguous feelings about Sorel in his prison years are neatly summarized in the following: 'he [Sorel] is tortuous, rambling, incoherent, superficial, profound, etc., but he provides or suggests original viewpoints, he discovers unthought-of connections, he compels one to think and to probe', Notebook 4, § 31, p. 168.

54. Gramsci, *Prison Notebooks,* II, Notebook 3, § 49, p. 53.

55. Antonio Gramsci, *Prison Notebooks,* Volume III, edited and translated by Joseph A. Buttigieg (New York: Columbia University Press, 2007), Notebook 8, § 21, pp. 246–7.

56. Gramsci, *Prison Notebooks,* III, Notebook 7, § 39, p. 190.

57. Gramsci, *Prison Notebooks,* III, Notebook 8, § 21, p. 247.

58. Gramsci, *Prison Notebooks,* II, Notebook 3, § 49, p. 53.

59. Gramsci, *Prison Notebooks,* II, Notebook 3, § 49, pp. 52–3.

60. Tarde, 'The Public and the Crowd', p. 282.

61. Antonio Gramsci, *Selections from Cultural Writings,* edited by David Forgacs and Geoffrey Nowell-Smith, translated by William Boelhower (London: Lawrence & Wishart, 1985), Notebook 21, § 5, p. 207.

62. Gramsci, *Cultural Writings,* p. 209.

63. Gramsci, *Cultural Writings,* Notebook 14, § 19, p. 380.

64. Gramsci, *Prison Notebooks* III, Notebook 8, § 21, p. 248.

65. Gramsci, *Prison Notebooks* III, Notebook 8, § 21, p. 249.

66. Gramsci, *Cultural Writings,* Notebook 14, § 72, p. 204.

67. Gramsci, *Cultural Writings,* Notebook 29, § 3, p. 183.

68. Gramsci, *Cultural Writings,* Notebook 29, § 3, p. 183. Gramsci's uncompleted thesis at Turin would have examined the Ascoli-Manzoni debate and was to have been supervised by Bartoli. On Gramsci's training in linguistics, see *Gramsci, Language, and Translation,* edited by Peter Ives and Rocco Lacorte (Lanham, MD: Lexington Books, 2010); Alessandro Carlucci, *Gramsci and Languages: Unification, Diversity, Hegemony* (Leiden: Brill, 2013); Derek Boothman, 'Gramsci's Interest in Language: The Influence of Matteo Bartoli's *Dispense di Glottologia* (1912–13) on the *Prison Notebooks*', *Journal of Romance Studies* 12 (2012): pp. 10–23. On his use of Ascoli in particular, see Luigi Rosiello, 'Linguistics and Marxism in the Thought of Antonio Gramsci', pp. 29–49; 32–4, and Tullio De Mauro, 'Language from Nature to History: More on Gramsci the Linguist', pp. 51–62; 54–7, both in Ives and Lacorte.

69. Gramsci, *Prison Notebooks* III, Notebook 8, § 21, p. 249.

70. Antonio Gramsci, *Selections from Prison Notebooks,* edited and translated by Quintin Hoare and Geoffrey Nowell-Smith (London: Lawrence & Wishart, 1971), 'Critical Notes on an Attempt at Popular Sociology', p. 419.

71. Gramsci, *Prison Notebooks* III, Notebook 7, § 36, pp. 187–8.

72. Michel Bréal, *Semantics: Studies in the Science of Meaning,* translated by Nina Cust (New York: Dover, 1964), p. 6.

14

Precarious Voices
Moderns, Moods, and Moving Epochs

Patricia Waugh

NO PERIOD SENSE AT ALL

Any attempt to name where fiction moved, After Modernism—or at least after the modernisms of 1900–30—seems to produce the kind of nomenclatural confusion of Beckett's Watt, feeling as he does, thrown into 'the midst of things which, if they consented at all to be named, did so as it were with reluctance'.[1] But *why* has British fiction of the middle years of the twentieth century seemed so immovable, so implacable, so resistant to the naming and identifying of distinctively new movements? Historians seem to set about their cartographic operations with much less uncertainty. From their perspective, a secure epochal narrative has long been in the making whose details are orchestrated to capture a structure of feeling or mood, a prevailing atmosphere, the encapsulation of an epoch through a history of its distinctive modes of feeling. As one recent historian has explained, for example: 'the thesis of civilisation in danger won a broadly popular audience in inter-war Britain receptive to anxiety as one of the defining features of contemporary culture...The language used for much of this discourse was explicitly morbid.'[2] Literary critics have sometimes paid lip service to this judgement on the middle years after high modernism, yet, despite their recent more historicist turn, have barely attempted to investigate what mood or affect or structure of feeling might mean, in all their complex detail, as factors shaping appropriate descriptors of a movement or an epoch as articulated through literary artefacts. The argument of this essay is that a profound awareness of the true fragility of things and of humans and of their worlds produced a characteristic mood of the mid-century that has become, suddenly, in our own era of the so-called post-postmodern, all too recognizable, only now fully identifiable as a way of grasping the forms and imports of its literary products. Judith Butler has recently argued that 'if the humanities has a future as cultural criticism, and cultural criticism has a task at the present moment, it is no doubt to return us to the human where we do not expect to find it, in its frailty and at the limits of its capacity to make sense'.[3] Endorsing Butler's view of the task of the humanities, this chapter explores how, in returning us to the human where we might not expect to find it, the novel of the mid-century found the formal and stylistic means to encapsulate and shape an epoch that was singularly its own but speaks especially to ours.

In Muriel Spark's *Memento Mori* (1959), the waspish septuagenarian Guy Leet entertains the once popular, but now largely forgotten, octogenarian novelist Charmian Piper to a soothing disquisition on the fortunes of the British novel in the middle years of the twentieth century: 'If a valuable work of art is rediscovered after it has gone out of fashion, that is due to some charity in the discoverer, I believe. But I say, without a period sense as well, no one can appreciate your books.' With a marked 'period sense' that is all his own, Guy plays gallant, unaware that Charmian sees through the performance to his actual complicity with the niggardly professional envy of her son Eric. 'Eric is a realist. He has no period sense': Guy ingratiatingly dismisses the writing of both Charmian and her novelist manqué son, in a single barb.[4] But his assumption that Charmian's fondness for dwelling on the past is simply a reflection of her writerly narcissism is far wide of the mark, a further measure of Guy's own self-delusion. For Charmian's preoccupation with reviewing and putting her life in order is an intentionally ethical response to a now unavoidable reflection on mortality; from Guy's perspective, it is simply a flight into vanity. She is one of the few characters in the novel who has listened to and is able to acknowledge the reality and true import of the anonymous and disembodied voice calling to each one of them, heard in a different guise, reminding them they will die. Charmian knows that in the context of a properly good life, the fading of professional reputation is but a minor cross to bear in that slow journey towards nothingness, the gradual fading out of self-awareness, that is the imminent fate of all her circle, the aged and variously demented, the mildly and more floridly amnesiac. In this scene with Guy, a complex play of small ironies, defensive blindnesses, in-spite-of-oneself spite, the scuppering of empathy, and the comic pathos of miscommunication, is signature Spark, a glimpse in miniature into her novelistic *Weltanschauung*. Charmian sees through Guy's fawning insincerity with perspicacious ease; but her almost-still-intact novelist's mind is far more fascinated, like her maker's, with the ways in which 'the art of fiction is very like the practice of deception'.[5] For Spark's interest lies in how those externalized voices that seem delusional or the products of a degenerating brain may, like the strange reality of fictional illusion, convey truths that would otherwise remain invisible to the hearer locked in the silent space of thought before thinking.

In this scene, Spark shows her growing prowess as the satirizing anatomist of the variegated tribal archipelagos of post-war British culture, a demographic that is worked into a cosmogony that involves the self- referential laying bare of fictionality itself as a kind of controlled delusional condition for writer and reader. But Spark is reflecting also on the logistics and vagaries of writerly fortune and reputation as these impinge on her own historical moment. For Guy's double-edged comment reveals two resonances of the term 'period sense'. The first, a pronouncement of death for the still breathing but abandoned writer: to be something of value but only with reference to a context of evaluation no longer valid. The second connotes the possibilities of the future anterior, the judgement of posterity as the guarantee of a continuing and vital life as that material spirit which is the ongoing life of words after the mortal death of the body. In a characteristic meditation on death and writing, Spark also raises the legitimate anxiety of her generation of writers concerning their own imaginary afterlives. For the writers who began their careers or rose to prominence in the middle years of the twentieth century, roughly between the late thirties and the late fifties, were already under threat of being beige-washed by literary history into invisibility, sunk in the blank space of an uneventful interregnum, an age of no style, of the novel no longer novel, of the return to realism and the reaction against experiment after modernism.[6] The critical legacy of such assumptions has, ever since, shaped the periodization of British fiction after modernism, its collateral damage an overpopulated school of exceptionalizing apologia representing all those one-off but essentially eccentric geniuses, like Spark, who somehow managed to keep swimming, alone, but upstream. The assumption that there was only stasis—no collective movement or distinctive style—after modernism, until the fanfared return to experiment (in the key postmodern manifestos of the late 1960s), has been entrenched in histories of modern British fiction ever since.[7] That the only movement of the mid-century that self-consciously saw itself moving, The Movement, was mainly intended to be a rallying post for avowedly backward-looking anti-modernists and anti-experimentalists such as C. P. Snow, Pamela Hansford Johnson, and William Cooper seems to confirm the absence of a compelling 'period' nomenclature as ushering in the 'new'.[8] The canny demon of literary history has since sorted those writers it deemed innovative and therefore worthy of distinction into the camps of the modern or postmodern. To be a middle-born seems fated to be overlooked; to be in the middle is not to be 'hot', but neither is it to be 'cool'.

No wonder that Frank Kermode referred to period as a kind of fiery particle, a 'fiery ism';[9] Ihab Hassan lamented the violence of nomenclature, its power to exclude, select, elevate, and destroy;[10] T. S. Eliot knew better than most how far the literary monument that is the individual great work is only as solid as the ground of tradition on which it stands, and which must provide insurance against a risky future.[11] Poet, rather than novelist, Eliot nevertheless recognized the imperatives of narrative and saw how far the plot of literary history too requires and exerts the robust anticipation of a retrospection. But although Raymond Williams later presented a more malleable sense of period as a shifting play of the dominant, residual, and emergent across a complex historical process of evaluation, the major period outlines of twentieth-century fiction now seem set more in marble than in stone.[12] The literary historical timeline swung out in the late 1950s was hitched for fifty years to the immovable monoliths of postmodernism and modernism, flanking a still precariously swaying middle. But once postmodernism went native and fully late-capitalist, dissipating its avant-garde edge (so the story goes), by the early 2000s, an expanded Modernist Studies, revivified by the very array of cultural and theoretical 'differences' spawned in the postmodern years, flowed in to fill the legitimation vacuum. Everything, since, has gone modern, or suffered further neglect. In spite of the recent renewal of interest in aspects of mid-century fiction, therefore, the shadow of modernism grows, if anything, longer.

But what makes an epoch? What might confer on the fiction of the middle years something of epochal status? If it is style, is there a perspective on the range of writing of the period that might suggest an at least lurking commonality, something distinctively different from what came before and after? The writers who rose to prominence or began writing between the late thirties and the late fifties include Henry Green, Elizabeth Bowen, Evelyn Waugh, Ivy Compton-Burnett, Edward Upward, Rex Warner, John Wyndham, Samuel Beckett, Alexander Trocchi, Al Barker, William Golding, L. P. Hartley, Dodie Smith, Iris Murdoch, J. G. Ballard, Doris Lessing, Alan Sillitoe, Keith Waterhouse, C. P. Snow, Elizabeth Taylor, to name just a few. On the surface this seems as heterogeneous a list as one could imagine. A growing body of critical work has steadily refined and extended and pluralized the original holy trinity of modernism, realism, and postmodernism, but they remain the convenient reach-me-downs. Given the variety of writing reflected in this list, the periodizing terms have served it badly, leaving many capsized in a dead sea of default realism. In 1997, Brian Richardson called for a more complex picture of twentieth-century literary history, one that recognized a network of more variegated currents—the fantastic, the romance, the varieties of European avant-gardes, utopias, allegories, and older genres such as satire—that might be seen mixing and meshing, running underground, to re-emerge from time to time and come together as new formations.[13] But Richardson's challenge has been mostly ignored. Modernists are even more 'cats which have licked the plate clean'.[14] And studies that claim to take a more capacious view continue to offer variations on the modern (late modernism, inter-modernism, counter-modernism, alter-modernism, limit modernism) or on realism (hysterical, neo-, paranoid) or ring the changes on pre- or post- or avant- postmodernism.

Tyrus Miller's is the most influential account, reading the 'late' modernism of the mid-century as a belated allegorization of the ruination of the modernist myth and the collapse of the ethos of formal autonomy.[15] Here fiction irrupts into a strident counter-modernism of the satiric, the comic, and the grotesque. Miller presses hard on the usual arguments for the formalist integrity of modernism, and yet clings to the myth of autonomy, reading his counter-modern carnivalesque as an already internalized avant-garde 'other' that simply erupts out of modernism's own dying entrails. But Miller says little about any external historical forces driving the literary system, preferring a kind of internalized autopoeisis of autonomic self-(re)generation. Jed Esty, on the other hand, errs in the opposite direction. His counter-modernism is more of a gentle cooling-off after a strenuous performance, a wind-down rather than wind-up.[16] But he shares the predilection for allegory as his main hermeneutic tool. Esty reads the avowed retreat from a modernism entangled with the triumphal moment of the British Empire, into a gentle and genteel anthropological Englishness, as a strategic and pre-emptive strike against historical decline. National identity is hereby reinvented after the loss of Empire as an always and already pastoralized Englishness. In Esty's reading, the middle years become the literary period of an uneasy coalition, devoted to saving national face and containing the crisis: they begin to sound remarkably like the British Government circa 2010. Like Miller, Esty presents a strong revisionist thesis. Like Miller's, too, this one is somewhat underdetermined by data: a very small selection of texts to illustrate a very large thesis. For Miller, these are mostly the carnivalesque of Wyndham Lewis, Djuna Barnes, and Samuel Beckett; for Esty, it is the mellow fruitfulness of late Woolf, E. M. Forster, John Cowper Powys, and the Eliot of *Four Quartets*. Neither offers much reflection on how the restricted set of variables comprising the theory might only ever produce a very partial model of such a complex and dynamic open system as a 'period', with its many possible avenues of entry, exit, and emergence. Exemplarity is not even raised as an issue. As in most other accounts of 1930–60, when it comes to the question of constructing a substantive as opposed to a relational identity for the middle years, they remain, well, suspended as *the middle years*, Bowen's 'looking at everything down a darkening telescope'.[17]

The very proliferation of terms shows the failure of any nomenclature to 'stick' unless it reiterates the tag of the modern, as in the (post)modern. And so the mid-century (like the excluded middle that guarantees the stability of classical bivalent systems of logic) remains stuck, elusive, slippery, and apparently unnameable. After Beckett, Wyndham Lewis, and Djuna Barnes, the fog that brings in the invisibility of namelessness begins to roll in; indeed literally (or literarily) so in Henry Green's magisterial *Party Going* of 1939 (a novel held up by Frank Kermode as the example, par excellence, of a literary work that portentously flaunts its bristling hermeneutic possibilities but knowingly refuses to ground them in any finally authoritative hermeneutic frame).[18] But Green, Golding, Beckett, Bowen, and, at a pinch, Waugh, are often allowed to lie, if sometimes uncomfortably, on the Procrustean bed of experimental modernism; L. P. Hartley, Dodie Smith, Keith Waterhouse, the Larkin of *Jill*, C. P. Snow, William Gerhardie, William Cooper, and even much of Kingsley Amis suffer relegation to 'period sense' as faded 'realists' (like Muriel Spark's Eric), ripe only for the cultural materialist assemblage; Spark, despite her own sparkiness on the matter, continues to be dangled on the Moebius strip of the postmodern. Rex Warner, George Orwell, John Wyndham are sniffily relegated to the outer regions of the 'minor genre', to science fiction, the dystopian, or the fantastic, while a few, ripening later, like J. G. Ballard, regain status as popular redeemers renewing the aged and inbred stock of high modernism. Then there are the English eccentrics, the purveyors of bizarrerie, the *sui generis*, such as Ivy Compton Burnett, A. L. Barker, Stevie Smith, Dodie Smith, or William Sansom, or those that are simply 'foreign' (and drug-addicted or regarded as psychotic) such as Alexander Trocchi or Leonora Carrington, or simply 'foreign' like Sam Selvon and George Lamming. The oxymoronic hybrid sweeps up the remainder: the domesticated modernism of Sillitoe, the fantastical social realism of Edward Upward; or new categories are invented such as 'talk fiction' into which Patrick Hamilton, Ivy Compton-Burnett, and any number of others can be placed (as against modernist 'thought' fiction). Many, like Iris Murdoch and Doris Lessing, turn up in almost every category. Richardson's variegated pluralism seems wholly exemplified by this list but, without the kind of prior nomological security that has allowed modernism to withstand the potentially fragmenting effects of Modernist Studies, such an argument for pluralization simply consolidates assumptions of the non-identity of an 'An Age of No Style'. Etymologically, epochality signals newness: the era that is ushered in by the eruption of an 'event'; in literary history, it is usually the Style that names the Moment. The mid-century appears to be definitively non-epochal.

Literary periodization, at its simplest, like form and content, is an entanglement of style and history, driven by what René Wellek first referred to as internalist and externalist imperatives, the pressures of a medium and its formal potential and history, and the pressure of institutions, politics, economics, technologies, science, and philosophical thinking.[19] But the middle years of the twentieth century have attracted polarizing rather than dialectical or complex accounts, tending to point towards external crisis, conflict, and declinist theses or the kinds of internalist accounts grounded in the elevation of modernism as the magic touchstone for experiment, on the other. But in refusing to treat the literary as a complex dynamic system, this kind of polarization militates against the establishment of a distinctive stylistic affiliation that is also closely interwoven with wider historical narratives.[20] Modernism has been safely pluralized, heterogenized, and expanded with no loss of identity; postmodernism was, from the start, understood and configured in a complex relation with the variety of analyses—cultural, economic, technological, political—of the condition of postmodernity, and in its articulation of itself as a dynamic and transformative outgrowth of modernism. The mid-century has either been absorbed into modernism as its eruptive and satiric other or its temporary falling away into a parochial Englishness; rarely is it confirmed as dynamic, outward looking, and experimental in its own right, and on its own terms.

THE MOODS OF MODERN WRITING: A NEW AGE OF ANXIETY?

That there might be something sufficiently distinctive and powerfully shared in the fiction of this period that has not received sufficient attention and might facilitate epochal reconsideration is the argument of the remainder of this essay. One place to begin this process might be with that version of the idea of the 'Spirit of the Age' that tends to be thought of now, in more secular terms, as 'mood'. Auden's long poem of 1947 announced the era as 'The Age of Anxiety'.[21] In 1939, Orwell had expressed something similar in his somewhat less portentous phrase: 'the world gone wrong'; 'Ordinary chaps I meet everywhere, chaps I run into in pubs, bus drivers, and travelling salesmen for hardware firms, have got a feeling that the world's gone wrong. They can feel things cracked, and collapsing under their feet.'[22] But 'anxiety' also dominated the 'official' medical literature of the period that engaged with mood and its disordering. In the first major diagnostic manual of psychiatry, published in 1952, anxiety is everywhere—underpinning phobias, obsessions, dissociative and many other conditions—where the 'chief characteristic of these disorders is anxiety, which may be directly felt and expressed or which may be unconscious and automatically controlled by the utilization of various psychic defence mechanisms (depression, conversion, displacement).[23]

Richard Overy's recent history suggests there was already, before anxiety, a pervasive culture of morbidity in the era between the wars, where the preoccupation with individual 'sickness' was reinforced by biomedical, economic, political, and cultural discourses, to create a new diagnostics for a perceived condition of generalized malaise. Yet, although exhaustively documented, Overy's book makes surprisingly scant reference to imaginative literature, the visual arts, or film, nor does he develop the kind of theoretical reflection on the metaphor of morbidity evident, for example, in Susan Sontag's analysis of 'illness as metaphor'.[24] Overy gives exhaustive substance to zeitgeist through the evidence of official—government, political, medical—documentation that indeed appears to deliver a persuasive historical consensus around 'morbidity' as definitive of the era. Yet his chosen material sets limits to what might be captured, especially those more intangible and ineffable properties of mood, for example, that shape a cultural imaginary or atmosphere and are the distinctive feature of the more tropic languages of art and literature. Virginia Woolf had seemingly—and artfully—demolished the presumption of *Geist* to designate an epoch, in the playfully parodic *Orlando*, of 1928, where *Geist*'s colonizing pretensions are comically extended to language, the weather—especially the weather—goods and chattels, sexuality, gender, and the shape of desire: from the crystalline austerity and clear skies of the Age of Reason, to the murky fogs of the ponderously, verbosely, and prudishly Victorian.[25] Despite Woolf's comic subversion, however, it was *Geist* that was translated into its modern equivalent of 'mood' in Auden's *Age of Anxiety*. Two years later, it reappeared implicitly in such terms in that most unlikely of places, in the analytical British philosopher of mind, Gilbert Ryle's *The Concept of Mind* (1949), with his explanation for why moods 'monopolise'. For, as Ryle goes on to explain,

> somewhat as this morning's weather in a given locality made for the same sort of difference to every section of that neighbourhood, so a person's mood during a given period colours all or most of his actions and reactions during that period. His work and his play, his talk and his grimaces.... His own corresponding inclination will be to describe the whole world as menacing, congenial, or grey.[26]

INTRODUCING BRITISH NEO-EXPRESSIONISM

A renewed interest in Kafka's writing and in early silent and German expressionist cinema was a marked feature of the late thirties and forties. Writing on Kafka between 1952 and 1954, Theodor Adorno first observed this kind of externalizing feature of his writing that seemed to link his work to an expressionist aesthetic:

> again and again, the space-time continuum of empirical realism is exploded through small acts of sabotage.... The self lives solely through transformation into otherness... The more the I of expressionism is thrown back upon itself, the more like the excluded world of things it becomes... [an] objectivity which expresses itself through its own estrangement. The boundary between what is human and the world of things becomes blurred'.[27]

Adorno is observing how, in Kafka's writing, and in expressionism more generally, psychic life continuously externalizes itself as perception, mood, object, image, action, gesture, talk, and movement, to the extent that without constant self-referential reassurance, the centre of self is entirely diffused across its environments. 'I', Adorno argues, 'becomes a 'magnetic field.''[28] One might immediately recognize in this description the broad stylistic qualities and effects of much mid-twentieth British fiction. Like earlier expressionist writing, all or most of these novels, in some way, employ the grotesque, farcical, blackly comic, melodramatic, tragic, fractured, and semi-allegorical, in other words, the carnivalesque; their narratives often feature dissociated or complicatedly submerged or split-off voices, fractured consciousnesses, or roaming and multi-perspectival focalization, where dramatic shifts of scale may suddenly occur to produce a sense of the world looming into alarmingly close focus one minute and then fading away to nothing in the next; time may randomly slow down or speed up, and distinctions blur between memory and perception; déjà vu and *jamais vu* effects are common; borders, frontiers, thresholds, limit experiences of madness, death, extinction, and rites of passage occur frequently, mostly but not always outside of domestic contexts, in crowds, sets, sects and groups with their processes of inclusion and exclusion laid bare. A recurring tropic opposition is of the solipsistic, the enclosed or bubble-like—domes, vaults, cars, cabins, booths, stations, telephone booths, glass screens—entangled with the distributed or the net—networks of thought and talk, telephone lines, typewriters, wirelesses, thought broadcasting, and mind-reading. Minds become separated from bodies: a disappearing homology between embodiment and voice appears so that multiple voices may occupy one body or voices may be entirely disembodied; this is a feature across the many 'styles' from the modernist-oriented such as Green, Bowen, Beckett, and Waugh to the so-called realists such as Upward, Waterhouse, and Amis, and the evidently 'postmodern' such as Spark. Everywhere you look boundaries blur; inner and outer worlds become impossibly entangled.

So the most powerful effect that is shared across these texts is one of disorientation: a disorientation within the storyworld and the narrator's and characters' relations to it, but also the inducement of a mood of perplexity and puzzlement in the reader, who may struggle to locate the intended primary ontology of the text or storyworld or to infer from the narrative a final level of 'meaning'. Anxiety is evidently everywhere, as Auden noted, but these texts might be said to generate a powerful sense of 'mood' that goes beyond the normal understanding of anxiety as a feeling of pervasive threat or the dislocating unpredictability of a world or situation. There is a sense of being enveloped in something that might be described as a delusional *atmosphere*, a 'mood' in the most expanded sense, that disturbs the normally tacit assumption of being safely anchored in a primary reality. This produces a perplexing feeling of provisionality; of a world and selves that might, simply, disappear at any moment. The slippage from what appears initially as an oddly awry but just plausibly mimetic representation of an historical world, to a full-blown experience of what might be a mode of the fantastical, or a psychotic delusion, or an end of world event, is sometimes evoked through what at first might seem recognizably realist, modernist, or even postmodernist conventions, but all share marked features and effects of the writings of the earlier twentieth-century European avant-gardes, especially those of expressionism.

Although I can't hope to do justice to the numerous texts available, some more specific reference seems in order. Before developing a more theorized account of what I am calling the neo-expressionist, therefore, I propose to pause and offer, at this stage, a few somewhat discursive examples of the type of thing I have in mind. The years 1938–9 are a good place to start, for a spate of novels of this kind began to emerge. We might begin with Rex Warner's *The Aerodrome*, published in 1941 and Edward Upward's *Journey to the Border* (published in 1938, the year of Beckett's first extensive plunge into the territory of the delusional, in *Murphy*).[29] *The Aerodrome* bears a marked resemblance to Fritz Lang's 1927 *Metropolis*, one of the best-known, if relatively late, German expressionist films, which shares with Warner's novel a strangely alienated and dislocated atmosphere created in the juxtaposition of two worlds: one, the pastoral, the village life, of the *Volk*, the second, the chilling but sublime technopolis of an aerodrome with its Spenglerian fantasies of a technopolitical power that might defeat the forces of degeneration: for

> the intoxicated soul wills to fly above space and time...Man would free himself from the earth, rise into the infinite...hence comes the ambition to build giant halls for machines...works of steel and glass in which tiny man moves.[30]

Warner's novel darkens the urban pastoral of Lang with its nostalgia for the organic community, for the aerodromic is not simply a techno-fascistic projection out of (the now degenerate) heart of England: it reveals those safe shires already rife with unacknowledged, proto-fascistic, desire. The delusional atmosphere—as in Kafka's writing—is created through techniques of distancing, telescoping, and externalization that drain substance out of both worlds and yet suggest, as in the delusory condition, that even though neither appears to embody a sense of material substance, they both seem more than a gleam in the visionary eye. Neither quite allegory nor dystopic vision, the effect of Warner's novel is to create the feeling that these worlds exist in a strange territory somewhere between an inside and an outside that is also the experience of living and writing at this moment in history.

Upward's *Journey to the Border* creates a similar delusional atmosphere. The narrative begins with a portrait of the tutor, a hired servant in the squirearchical household of the proto-fascist Mr Parkins. The tutor is never named, and though at times represented in the third person, he narrates most of the novel in the second person, an extended address to himself (or the reader?) that immediately establishes a sense of voice which in its dialogic formulation confusingly merges inner with outer speech. Crisis over assimilation and distinction is the abiding motif of the novel. For the tutor, increasingly conscious of adopting a kind of elaborate mimicry as defence against his 'horror of being subdued to what he worked in, like the dyer's hand', gradually becomes more and more dissociated from his environment.[31] Things deteriorate as he rides in his employer's Daimler to a race meeting, where a loud ringing begins in his ears and the sounds around him begin to grow distant and unreal. The inner voice of the second person now whirs into hyperactivity, with bizarre parallel commentary questioning everything that comes into his perceptual field: his

> brain wove its neat private opinions and theories in an immense unconsidered wilderness. The ringing in the tutor's ears grew louder.... Thinking was only an exercise, a weaving of decorations. You looked through the windscreen and saw something and thought 'beech hedges' and imagined they were brown, but you might just as well think 'parrots' and imagine they were black.[32]

Language begins to unweave from referential attachment as if to release the thinker from a life of performative sham. Convinced that his feeling of dissociation is still strategic, however, the tutor falls into a psychotic episode when, arriving at the races, he stumbles—amidst the jodhpurs, pearls, and polite chatter of the county set—on a blackshirt uprising that erupts into a violent but passionate display of power, hate, and aggression. In a kind of mesmerized trance, the incantatory assault on feeling meshing with his own oddly somnambulist state of mind, the tutor begins to hear the handful of chanting voices as 'thousands, tens of thousands'; he becomes temporarily immobilized, caught up in the strange delusory atmosphere. His former dialogic and reflective style of thinking is suspended as he becomes immersed in crowd ecstasy; but this is where Upward reverses ideas of the 'real' and the 'delusional', sane and insane, to political effect. The tutor's psychosis takes the form of a disembodied voice that, although arriving in the midst of his delusional state, serves to release him from the mesmeric atmosphere that had willed him into the incantatory arms of the British Union of Fascists, a condition of assimilation floated on a powerful impulse of mimetic feeling, the suspension of reflective thought. Through its externalization of his suspended inner dialogic speech, the voice restores his capacity to reflect, breaking in on the political madness. Now the inner voice that had addressed him as 'you' and seemed at the beginning of the narrative simply the mark of the hyper-reflexive, becomes a commanding but disembodied interlocutor that eventually even reassures him that he is not mad:

> You don't hear the words. They are not audible to you physically as the ringing is. They are part of an internal dialogue that you are carrying on with yourself. This could be a perfectly sane and effective way of discovering the truth about yourself, if you want to discover the truth and not merely to find plausible arguments in favour of your delusory preconceptions.[33]

Like Robert Weine's silent film, *The Cabinet of Dr Caligari* (1920), which also features a bizarre episode of 'hearing' voices—as letters superimposed on the set dance around Caligari's head, announcing 'Du bist Caligari'—Upward recreates the atmosphere of Weine's film, with its merging of boundaries between inner and outer, and its critique of official notions of madness and sanity (Caligari bearing a marked resemblance to Jean-Martin Charcot, the neurologist, psychiatrist, and mesmerist, infamous for parading his patients like a showman huckster). They share, too, the blurring of objective space and subjective perception and the sudden obtruding of impossible or illuminated objects that bristle with a kind of auratic possibility of meaning, yet seem to occupy actual space (the bizarre and hallucinatory paean to the steamroller is one of the strangest effects in Upward's novel). This is a feature of much of this fiction, a kind of sublimation of the realist preference for the metonymic taking on a symbolic resonance, but where the metonymic object seems filled in miniature with the condensed atmospheric energies of the entire fiction, a kind of expressive black hole of compressed and explosive energy.

Patrick Hamilton's *Hangover Square*, with its metropolitan demi-monde, seedy bars, and constant streams of traffic seems a world away from the pastoral setting of Upward and Warner, but its louche milieu is similarly striated with fascistic violence. Harvey Bone is another character taken over by dissociated or 'dead moods', arriving with a click, like a camera shutter, and transforming experience into the screening of 'a silent film without music'.[34] Even outside his dead moods, Bone's life is one of passivity, a round of petty humiliations prompted by his masochistic desire for the vapid Netta, which he experiences as a dangerous magnetic field that 'pervaded the whole, trembling atmosphere amidst the roar of passing traffic, and cast its enthralling, uncanny influence upon every fixed object or passing person in the neighbourhood'.[35] In this novel, everything feels mediated; technology is the vehicle for the distribution of mood thought of as 'wired'. Lives are lived through wires, phones, reproduction of talk. Images of the 'net' and the mediated and distributed network of modern communications, wireless waves, magnetic resonances, phone lines, string themselves across the locked-in, the screened, distant and celluloid, the cinematic performance; it is as if to be in this world is to have the experience of an experience, to live in a condition of 'as if', the world a set of images running on a screen. Again at its centre is the self-referring object, the auratic metonymy standing in for a whole that is inarticulable except as a kind of mood:

> In the line of telephone booths there were a few other people locked up and lit up in glass, like waxed fruit, or Crown jewels, or footballers in a slot machine on a pier, and he went in and became like them—a muffled, urgent, anxious, private, ghostly world, composed not of human beings but of voices, disembodied communications'.[36]

The booth, a kind of centre of abstraction, encapsulates and reflects back the networked and the solipsistic, even as it takes up a 'realistic' or metonymic space in the storyworld of the novel.

In his preface to the 1990 edition of William Sansom's *The Body* (1949), Anthony Burgess notes its 'realism and not realism' and suggests how its 'external world is the composite symbol of an emotion', recorded with a kind of hallucinatory exactness.[37] This is another delusory world realized through something more akin to Breton's notion of 'compulsive beauty' or 'the veiled-erotic' announced in 1937 in *L'Amour fou* (a concept also satirized and enjoyed in Iris Murdoch's exuberant debut *Under the Net*, published some five years later), but where the auratic object in the everyday world has now become the over-interpreted or anxious sign of the more paranoid surrealism of the enigma, of Max Ernst and De Chirico.[38] Sansom's Britain is another transfiguration of the commonplace, of the new post-war suburbia, reconfigured as a kind of exotic and inverted pleasure dome of erotic energy that will find expression shortly in the novels of Spark, Murdoch, Ballard, Angus Wilson. Here the aquarium is the auratic object that also constitutes the text's self-reference: that takes on the auratic: the strange exotic fish swimming round and round behind glass—that familiar motif of solipsistic derealization—looking out on a world no longer their own. Its tubes of bubbling water connect to the bizarre extrusions of pipes and plumbing, and the inversion of organic and inorganic that characterizes the entire novel, reiterated even in the description of Diver's face turned upside down, a 'deep red bladder, the pendulous sac heavy as bad blood'.[39] But it is the final image that, in its surreal merging of the organic and the inorganic, the eruption of the sublime out of the depths, that the reader begins to suspect that Bishop's delusional obsession with his wife's imagined adultery and his disgusted fascination with the body of Charlie Diver is a way of displacing desires in himself so complex and so inarticulable in this suburban space of the coyly licit illicit that the encounter with the final object of compulsive beauty comes as something of a revelation to the reader too:

> The sun immobilised each high window. I saw a public lavatory, tiled and sunless—I went in and down....Other men were there, but they stood independently—the sense of crowd was gone. There was a bubbling of irrigation water—and suddenly, very suddenly, almost as a revelation to my aching head, I realised the presence of the pipes. Pipes I saw. They ran everywhere—white-painted pipes, gleaming copper pipes, old dust-laden pipes, all of them curling and branching and forking like things alive and waiting; some suddenly bulged like snakes digesting a swallowed prey'.[40]

The later novels of the fifties continue to work with expressionist effects – think of Golding's *Pincher Martin*, where the language of psychosis is used to imagine beyond any limit experience of the human, the ultimate Cartesian fantasy of the creation of a world through thought that is a consciousness creating and peopling an entire world after the death of the body.[41] Christopher Martin, thrashing around like Wittgenstein's fly in the fly-bottle, manufactures out of his gargantuan and Fichtean solipsism, not only a refusal of acknowledgement of his death by drowning, but the externalization of an entire world—voices, people, rocks, bodily existence, crowds—out of the phantom concreteness of his own thoughts.[42] Mind is entirely reified as place; what Freud analysed in his study of the paranoid schizophrenic judge Daniel Schreber as the projection outward of an internal catastrophe as the end of the world is given full substance.[43] And as in *Dr Caligari*, Golding again uses the device of ambiguous framing leaving the reader in final doubt as to the ontological status of the text, and whether Christopher Martin is simply a study in the grandiloquent paradoxes of full-blown solipsism, or a hero fighting against death and inducing as defence against ultimate trauma a delusion that he is mad or a vision of the purgatorial soul in a world beyond the living and the dead.

Again, in this novel, as in those examined earlier, rather than presenting cognition as *internalized* dialogue or thinking and mentalization (the representation or modelling within a mind of other minds), through interiorized monologue, internal thought reporting, or extensive free indirect discourse (as in modernism and realism), mind is here primarily represented as an externalized phenomenon—Christopher's mind becomes the place of a rock in the middle of an ocean—the inner percept is objectified so that it becomes impossibly entangled with the picturing of an external world. There is a kind of metafictional edge to this, as in all these novels, a knowing nod to the reader's own flirtation with delusion in the assimilation to and co-construction of an imaginary world. The multiple voices that variously accuse, assail, and jibe at Christopher Martin, re-enacting his past, calling him to account, are similarly externalizations of the inner voices of memory and fantastical inventions as his language breaks deeper into the psychotic. Though inner speech and internal dialogue occur, they are either diminished in frequency compared to the modernism of Woolf or Joyce or so positioned that as readers we are simply not given the narrative grounding that would allow us to distinguish an inner from an externalized voice. In this delusional world the voices eventually lose all spatial localization.

MOVING MODERNISM: FROM THE MELANCHOLIC TO THE DELUSIONAL MOOD

As Woolf recognized through her parodic subversion of 'Spirit of the Age' thinking in *Orlando*, epochs do not suddenly begin and end with a change in mood, as if mood were indeed interchangeable with the British weather. And though modernism, in its broad and varied concern with dissociation of sensibility, seems more concerned with the role of affect in thinking, there is no absolute shift from object-focused emotion (as in fear) to the more non-cathected idea of mood (as in anxiety). In any case, the effect of mood is to shape cathected emotions: the anxiety of the delusory mood may be resolved through its anchoring to a fetishized or phobic object. If modernism is 'mooded' at all it is almost always as melancholic, but moods outside the diagnostic formulary rarely fit the diagnostic category. In the melancholic experience of grief, for example, the lost object is often unfathomable; in losing you, I become inscrutable to myself; that in itself provokes both anxiety and a delusory feeling of unreality, for, in losing you, I have lost part of what I am. So if we take the dominant atmosphere of modernism to be the melancholic, this mood is not 'pure', but also complicated by anxiety and perplexity.

Two modernist texts that seem closer to the mid-century sense of mood that I am suggesting here are *Mrs Dalloway* (1925) and Elizabeth Bowen's *The Last September* (1929). *Mrs Dalloway*—the only one of Woolf's novels to reflect directly the experience of psychosis—uses mood or atmosphere to undermine the Cartesian distinction between the objective and subjective, or inside and outside, in the manner that is moving towards what I am calling neo-expressionist. In *Mrs Dalloway*, everything, including the composite self that emerges out of the connection between Clarissa and Septimus, is distributed and non-localizable; it becomes impossible to say whether thoughts, sounds, feelings, exist within or outside the mind (for even the chimes of Big Ben are carried on the atmosphere as vibrations into the very core of the body). Even the narrative voice takes on the shifting quality of a variegated group, picking up, echoing, and mimicking tones, restless and moving, built out of the minute trails, the skeins, habits, rhythms of custom that enter the body, echo in the mind as leaden circles dissolving into air, circulating rumours that in a kind of choric incantation reveal a world poised on the edge of terror: the dawn of an age that will be fully explored in the next two or three decades and that will marry the crowd with the machine, impose statistically calculated 'norms' and measurements, and construct, through scientific calibration, the deviant and the abnormal. The new 'border cases', the marginal and vulnerable, already circle like ghosts amongst the powerful and wealthy: the lower middle-class clerks, the mothers of Pimlico, the war veterans who have seen too much horror, the vulnerable old and poor, the refugees and returning exiles. Woolf wrote how 'I want to give life and death, sanity and insanity; I want to criticise the social system, and to show it at work, at its most intense.'[44] In this novel too, everyone 'hears voices'. Unexpressed thoughts magically take on the properties of speech, while speech enters the mind, echoes, and spills out, to slip in elsewhere. Characters 'went in and out of each other's minds': the mind is a whispering gallery.[45] Thoughts are voices heard outside as well as inside: 'I am alone! I am alone!', 'Horror! Horror!' 'Richard! Richard!', 'No! No!', He cried! 'She is not dead! I am not old!';[46] objects strangely transmogrify in new contexts, 'knobs' begin as railings and end as knees, boundaries between inside and outside, thoughts and things, merge.[47]

Woolf articulates a pervasive anxiousness that shows Septimus's madness to be part of Clarissa's fragility and both expressive of a moment of extreme historical precariousness, a world on the edge, fearful of another world war, economic depression, and the break-up of Europe. Bowen's *The Last September*, set in the last year of the Troubles before the Irish Independence of 1922, also creates a powerful and pervasive mood of hidden threat, that borders on the delusional, again mostly through techniques of expressionist externalization. The text is built out of a shifting kaleidoscope of perspectives that never quite coalesce; everything seems on the edge of deliquescence and dispersal: 'seen from above, the house in its pit of trees seemed a very reservoir of obscurity; from the doors, one must come out stained with it'.[48] Threatened erasure articulates another world on the edge, another politically charged historical moment presented through a strangely delusional atmosphere of suspended terror that is created, as in Woolf, through the development of formal and technical equivalents to what Karl Jaspers described in the first formal and medical account of that terrifying slipping away of the real into the full-blown experience of the delusional in the terms of 'mood' or atmosphere, in his definitive study of 1913, *The General Psychopathology*. For Jaspers, *Wahnstimmung*, or the delusional atmosphere, referred to the peculiar mood that defines the prodromal phase of psychotic breakdown, perhaps the most intense experience of precariousness and fragility within the range of human possibilities and yet, from the perspective of the lens of sanity, seemingly unreachable and not understandable. Bowen reflects the perceptual changes that accompany this experience but uses their effect to illuminate an historical situation: the symptomatology of a world stretching, fading, locking in, floating, shifting, speeding up, slowing down, kaleidoscopically slipping away. And here too this atmosphere is conveyed without inner views of the characters, but through the way in which the house, its furnishings, and grounds, the landscape around it, are described and modelled as if more alive than the characters. Marda tells Told 'she could not conceive of her country emotionally: it was a way of living'.[49] The Great House is already a mausoleum, where the characters creep, ghosts of themselves, amidst the skins of dead animals, fraying and decaying brocades, giant mirrors that absorb their bodies leaving ghastly reflection, but it is possessed with a dark energy that feeds off the vitality of the living. Inside and outside blur, transferences across animate and inanimate realms are stitched into the language and syntax. This is a house with eyes, mouths, 'doorway yearned up the pathway like an eye socket';[50] in its rooms, mouldering cushions smother but do not comfort; everything is absorbed into dark space: 'the distant ceiling imposed on consciousness its blank white oblong, and a pellucid silence...In to this silence, voices went up in stately attenuation. Now there were no voices.'[51] Everything is presented perplexingly on the edge of non-existence: 'as they mounted they seemed to be striking deeper into the large mild crystal of an inverted sea. Out of the distance everywhere, pointless and unrelated, space came like water between them, slipping and widening. They receded from each other into the vacancy.'[52]

This complex concatenation of a sense of historical crisis as the precariousness of things with a sense of the fragility of the minds that live in and through the particularized moment becomes the dominant of fiction by the late thirties. But in ranging across the fiction of the mid-century years, three phases are evident, shifting dominants, rather than exclusive properties with well-defined edges. Novels such as *Party Going*, *The Aerodrome*, *Journey to the Border*, *Heat of the Day*, *Hangover Square*, *Watt*, written between the late thirties and late forties, seem committed to the creation of the delusional atmosphere as a way of examining and bringing forth a feeling of the threat to distinction, of the confusion of boundaries and of dark space as the threat of annihilation by absorption that begins in *Mrs Dalloway* as the sense of a new age of crowds. Elias Canetti would describe in 1960, the disturbing effect of the crowd, for there is 'nothing that man fears more than the touch of the unknown. He wants to see what is reaching towards him, and to be able to recognise or at least clarify it.'[53] But although this effect continues in the writing of Golding, in particular, in *The Inheritors* and *Pincher Martin*, as the fifties begin to roll in, with Sansom's *The Body*, Amis's *Lucky Jim*, Iris Murdoch's *Under the Net*, the writing of Angus Wilson, a new ethnography of the everyday turns its light on the suburban and the threat to distinction not so much now of the limit experiences of war, death and extinction, but more the new threat of absorption by the market and the institution, the new corporatism, and consumerism that now inculcates the conformist and mimetic through market persuasion, mores, and manners. Though the objects of analysis shift, the delusional is perhaps surprisingly still the vehicle or medium for exploration, and, if anything, actual delusion and madness as an individual condition becomes more apparent in the writing of the 1950s (in the work for example of Spark, Beckett, Hartley, Murdoch, Amis, Lessing, Waterhouse, Selvon, Ableman, Waugh, and many more).

These novels explore the delusional as the impossibility of any longer distinguishing between the authentic and the fake, the copy and the real and, as in Amis, Murdoch, Wilson, Spark, their tone is most often comic. Whereas mimicry in fiction circa 1938–49 provided a defence that always risked incorporation into the threatening emanations of dark space that it sought to resist, from around the end of the forties, it begins to take a more offensive mode of operation, mimicry used as a weapon against the threat of absorption and the dissolution of self into a generalized other of social conformism, perhaps to greatest comic effect in three debut novels, Amis's Tourettish tour de force, *Lucky Jim* and at its most metaphysical in novels such as *The Comforters* (1957) by Muriel Spark and *Under the Net* of Iris Murdoch. But there is a further shared tendency in many of these texts that also grows more marked in the 1950s. As Jaspers noted, as the feeling of perplexity intensifies, this loss of the tacit and the normally assumed may give rise to a kind of numbed detachment characteristic of that mental dissociation that is often employed to manage situations of crisis, but at some point, the diminution of the sense of a primary real gives rise to a compulsive, anxious, and hyper-reflexive questioning that, far from assuaging doubt, creates an even more profound sense of disembodiment and disorientation. This is the source of the dark comedy of Beckett. In *Watt* (1948), for example, all distinction between phenomenological states of mind—perception, imagining, remembering, and recalling—is eventually lost, and as the sense grows that no system of meaning might fathom or represent the complexity of the real, so the idea that language in any way hooks on to the world is also lost entirely:

> For it was not a pot the more he looked, the more he reflected, the more he felt sure of that, that it was not a pot at all. It resembled a pot, it was almost a pot, but it was not a pot of which one could say, Pot, pot and be comforted...And Watt's need of semantic succour was at times so great that he would set to trying on names on things, and on himself, almost as a woman, hats. Thus of the pseudo-pot he would say, after reflexion, It is a shield, or, growing bolder, It is a raven, and so on.[54]

But it is in the 1950s, that this hermeneutics of suspicion that produces such play with the self-referentiality of language is turned on to the macro-level of narrative discourse. This introduces into the novel genre an early metafictional turn. But with a difference. In later postmodernism, metafiction arises mostly out of epistemological foregrounding that leads to ontological instability through formalist and textualist play with transgression of levels of representation. Here realism's sleight of hand is laid bare: that what is described as already existing is brought into existence through its description. Novels such as *Pincher Martin* or Spark's *The Comforters*, however, present characters that hear voices discussing their activities, making accusations; the conceit in the fiction is that they start to believe they are characters being written into someone else's book, an idea that occurs in a number of earlier fictions, such as Bowen's *Heat of the Day* (1949), but in these novels is developed into a metafictional structuring principle that provides the ground for a new metaphysics of morals, opening up a way of addressing in a secular world, questions concerning the nature of free will, the possibility of ontological pluralism, of the complexities of intentionality. These texts also foreground the reminder that what is a hermeneutic norm in the teleological worlds of fiction, that every sign is potentially motivated and overdetermined with significance, becomes axiomatic evidence of what is 'normally' taken to be the abnormality of the paranoid and the pathologically delusional, outside the text. Fiction is *like* the art of deception; it bears some similarities with the delusional; but we are reminded that art is not life and that the most delusional of all is to believe that such is not the case.

Periodization is fraught with problems. Not the least is the choice between greater inclusivity, as in the practice of making one's argument through the herme-neutic equivalent of statistical preponderance, or the route of close reading and textual distinction that enables the detailed revelation of a singularity that might subsequently be tested against a wider range and volume of material. But one test of a new frame is its generativity and fruitfulness. Might an argument around mood reframe a text that has defeated or perplexed interpreters? One such text is Henry Green's *Party Going* (1938) with its roots in an earlier, Woolfian sketch entitled 'Mood',[55] whose technique of roving focalization and fugue-like repeti-tion of voice is extended to the larger canvas which switches vertiginously between actual multiple focalization, apparently 'objective' but in reality aspectically charged representation, and the elaborated views of anonymously invoked hypo-thetical observers in parallel worlds who may even be posited as existing 'seven thousand feet up' and yet still under the great dome of the metropolitan railway terminus where the action (or rather inaction) of the novel takes place.[56] We seem inside Madame Sosostris's vision of hell, with crowds walking round in circles in the hallucinatory obscurity of fog and smoke that hangs like a carapace below the huge green glass vault of the station. As the dead bird falls past the Departures sign, a classic expressionist-style conjuring of the purgatorial begins, even presided over by a top-hatted station master who seems straight out of *Dr Caligari*. Like Wiene's retrospective on the Great War, this too seems Green's vision of the coming Apocalypse, the dead already gathering in the 'exaggerated graveyard' of luggage, the 'pall' of smoke and fog shrouding everything, like the fog of *Bleak House*, as Europe lurches inevitably towards a second world war.[57]

But Green seems to be doing more than this. He is surely also invoking another Terminus: the Roman God of Distinction. For this is a novel, like those discussed earlier and like Bowen's and Woolf's, that is about distinction and the group, espe-cially class; Le Bon's massified crowd has now been refined into two broad social groups: those who can't afford not to work and those who wouldn't even dream of it.[58] The members of the leisure class, the Mayfair Set, are setting off to the South of France, *en vacances*, with their retinues of drivers, porters, nannies, waiters, maids, and manservants to see them off, but they ascend to the higher level of the hotel and are barricaded in as the crowd and fog swell below; the mostly office and service workers, the weary commuters, returning home after the daily stint, stream in and remain at ground level. However, as hundreds of thousands swarm in and space stretches up to the green glass of the vault or disappears into the rolling pall of the fog (or so we are informed), it becomes more evident that what is being presented again is the aspectical in the guise of the 'objective'. From the beginning, the language hints at this, the odd deictics, 'those two nannies' that pick them out from the mass but never give them a name; the view from above so people, faces become blank 'lozenges' or 'smudges' in the indistinct light.[59] For the crowd is both a 'real' crowd in the storyworld and the externalization of an emotion—that of class fear—that is intensified by the delusional atmosphere generated by the failure of the trains. Crucially, however, these are the workers presented through the world-revealing mood of a soon-to-be-extinct leisure class, but through an objectification that renders their aspectival involvement in the perspective, like so much else, befogged, obscure, and invisible. They remain apart, like Homeric or Hollywood gods, squabbling chattering, parading, concerning themselves with the preservation of the minutiae of distinction through the contents of their luggage, their fashion style, dress, or whatever else money can buy, demand, or supply.

And here, surely, we encounter another meaning of 'Terminus'. For a curiosity of the novel is its constant recourse to insect imagery: swarms, tunnels, capillaries, beetles, scuttling, indistinct creatures streaming down conduits, Miss Crevy and her partner as lilies in a pond coveted by the indistinct water beetles that swim all around. What is being presented in this mode of 'abstraction' is another aspect of the externalization of the upper class's hidden terror, its threatened loss of distinction: 'she had seen those doors bolted, and though being above them by reason of Max having bought their room and by having money, she saw in what lay below her an example of her own way of living because they were underneath and kept there'.[60] What Julia is peering down on, along with her 'set', is the swarming energy of the world conceived as an insect colony. Curiously, 1935 saw the publication of an essay that, like Green's novel, also brought together insects, the fear of losing distinction, mimicry, and dark space. This was Roger Caillois's 'Mimicry and Legendary Psychasthenia', published in the key surrealist journal *Minotaure*, which begins: 'Beware: whoever pretends to be a ghost will turn into one. Ultimately, from whatever angle one may approach things, the fundamental question proves to be that of *distinction*.'[61] Caillois then analyses and likens the morphological blurring involved in insect mimicry to the idea of a spatial derealization that risks the assimilation of the individual into the indistinctness of the mass. Referring to the work of Pierre Janet and Eugène Minkowski, he continues with a passage that seems to sum up the delusional atmosphere observed in the novels discussed here:

> when asked where they are, schizophrenics invariably reply, I know where I am but I don't feel where I am. For dispossessed minds such as these, space seems to constitute a will to devour. Space chases, entraps, and digests them like a huge phagocytosis. Then it ultimately takes their place. The body and mind thereupon become dissociated; the subject crosses the boundary of his own skin and stands outside his senses. He tries to see himself from some point in space. He feels that he is turning into space himself—dark space into which things cannot be put. He is similar; not similar to anything in particular, but simply similar.[62]

Caillois likens this effect to the collapse of ontological distinctions between planes and levels in space that is also the discovery of the new geometries and physics, and to the potential erosion of categories of the vegetable, animal, and human that is also a feature of surrealism (in many of these texts too) In Green's text, however, the fear of mimicry and the obsession with fashion and distinction is the preserve of the leisure class who look out and see the workers as ants, beetles, scuttling creatures, feared as a swarm, but also required to be swarm-like, for, without the persistence of an homogenized mass, the leisure class will lose that final guarantee of its own distinctiveness that the winds of change are bringing in. For those behind the glass, existence is style; on the ground, the workers gather in gestures of solidarity; good heartedness prevails and from the perspective along the ground there is not an insect in sight. The human as insect, as in Kafka, is an aspectival effect of skewed vision. But the model of the insect colony as the ideally altruistic society prevails as a ghostly abstraction as the novel closes and the workers cheerfully disperse.

FICTION AND THE POLITICS OF THE PRECARIOUS AND THE FRAGILE

These novels raise questions about the nature and relations between individual and collective agency that transcend the limits of liberal psychology—including its theories of affect—as the foundation for 'character' in the fiction of the future. In refusing to situate subjectivity as anything other than a distributed entity, in invoking 'mood' as something neither simply inside or outside, they also raise difficult political questions about responsibility and agency: for if subjectivity is distributed, where does individual responsibility begin and end? When does solidarity become mindless or exclusive 'groupthink', a way of not thinking or refusing responsibility? This question of the relation between the individual and the group is a common thread that runs through them. Most examine the sources of political ideologies such as fascism and the creation of a passivized subject that is both a 'normal' political and an 'abnormal' or psychotic experience. Whatever it is in moods that gets inside us, like crowds, we are also in it and mostly unaware of its workings: these novels further reveal that ideology critique needs to be more than the epistemological or rational choice between true and false consciousness. The anxiety that floats freely and disturbingly around my group might be resolved into a localization that converts it to fear through the victimization or scapegoating of another; even the metamorphosis into an insect forced to creep shamefully.

However, if 'I' is revealed as a reflexive composite of moods and voices, neither inside nor outside, in dividing the self from its normative assumptions about its own integrity the possibility opens up, as in this fiction, of a more radical empathy with those experiences, worlds, and others, that may appear most unlike our own. Part of me is the enigmatic traces of others, but it may take an intense kind of disorientation for me to realize this and to accept that what I hear as most alien to myself may be a voice that I need to attempt to incorporate consciously into my own. So it seems no coincidence that this idea was articulated in the political thinking on thinking of this period, in Hannah Arendt's writing (incidentally a close associate of Jaspers and a direct influence on many of the writers discussed here such as Spark and Murdoch). Arendt wrote of Eichmann: 'his inability to speak was closely related to his inability to think, namely to think from the stand-point of someone else'.[63] She too intimates that representation is a matter of the adequacy of *voice*, talking to myself when I think in inner dialogue, but hearing, therefore, and listening to the voice of the other in my own: she argues:

> being and thinking in my own identity where I am not. The more people's standpoints I have present in my mind while I am pondering a given issue, and the better I can imagine how I would feel and think if I were in their place, the stronger will be my capacity for representational thinking and the more valid my final conclusions, my opinion.[64]

For the writing examined here is neither experimental nor preoccupied with mad-ness for the sake of it, nor is it simply taken up with formalistic navel-gazing about living in the shadow of modernism. It is, however, fascinated with how a cultural imaginary is generated and might be resisted, how doxa as collective thinking and 'atmosphere' might enter the individual mind and colonize it, but equally how that sense of myself as other and multiple might threaten madness, but also serve to split apart liberal assumptions and to begin to rethink the relation between 'I' and 'we'. Similarly for Jaspers: 'extreme psychotic states offer us a human parable, con-taining inverted and distorted attempts to realise and elaborate marginal situa-tions, which are common to us all'.[65]

There may be good reason, perhaps, why it becomes possible only now to begin to articulate this distinctive 'mood' of the mid-twentieth century in the terms I am suggesting. For this sense of precariousness—that things are balanced on a knife edge—and the feeling of fragility—that something will break—work together to underpin the 'mood' of contemporary culture too (hence the way in which the metaphor of the 'tipping point' is a pervasive feature of our own time). Period is always, to some extent, hermeneutically fashioned after the fact and, like memory, inevitably driven by the emotional imperatives of the moment of recollection. A sense of the precariousness of things—now on a truly global scale—and the fragil-ity of mind—alarming statistics on the increase of anxiety, depression and addict-ive disorders—has returned to haunt and envelop the atmosphere of our own historical moment. The profound threats to the planet's ecosystems, the precari-ousness of the global (especially the Western) economy, rising levels of chronic illness and malaise, terrorism and fears about security, failures of probabilistic cal-culation to forecast futures. 'Precarity' and 'fragility' name our condition in the vocabularies of tipping points, risk, resilience terror, security, interconnectedness, but they resonate with and echo the mid-century's preoccupations with war, nuclear threat, disease, madness, and the unpredictable, reflected in their vocabu-laries of menace, apocalypse, morbidity, dark space, delusion, and barbarism. Even the term 'precarity'—deemed to have been invented in the post-2008 context of global economic crisis and instability, to describe the normalization of expectations of occupational insecurity, exploitation, and an uncertain future in the context of the growing disparity between rich and poor—was first used (and then rapidly disappeared) in an article of 1952, written by Dorothy Day, for the Catholic worker movement. Under the banner of social justice, Day called for a greater awareness of the condition of what she called 'precarity' as the lived experience of ambient insecurity and threat peculiar to the impoverished that, by the 1950s, was coming to be largely ignored by an affluent elite, blind to the effects of its own greed. Her short article further described the rise in this context of a newly passivized subjectivity that struggles to articulate any sense of integrity, agency, or interiority that can be felt as or called its own.[66] Judith Butler has recently drawn attention to the way in which precariousness is felt as a 'mood', but how the existence of mood as 'world-revealing', neither within nor without, opens up a space for ethical and political reflection on vulnerability. As we have seen from the fiction examined above, moods infiltrate: one is overwhelmed by grief, beside oneself with anxiety, or transported by ecstasy: mood is more the incorrigible experience of a world than the feeling of an emotion. Precariousness for Butler is 'I' in the mode of unknowingness, like mood, for, as in mood, the 'I' is axiomatically discovered in the 'we'.[67] But these novels reveal how 'we' is also a construct that operates mostly sub-politically, often outside of official discourses, to set limits and possibilities to what is recognized as fully human or what is allowed full human representation. To hear a voice when no one is speaking might be to listen to the 'we' that has not yet been represented; that has not been allowed to be represented.[68]

NOTES

1. Samuel Beckett, *Watt* (London: Calder, 1948), p. 78.
2. Richard Overy, *The Morbid Age: Britain and the Crisis of Civilisation, 1919–1939* (London: Penguin, 2010), p. 2.
3. Judith Butler, *Precarious Life: the Powers of Mourning and Violence* (London and New York: Verso, 2006), p. 151.
4. Muriel Spark, *Memento Mori* (Harmondsworth: Penguin, 1961), p. 186.
5. Spark, *Memento Mori*, p. 187.
6. There is a huge literature here, but the following give a representative view from within the period and after: see Kenneth Allsop, *The Angry Decade* (Peter Owen: London, 1958); Malcolm Bradbury, *No, Not Bloomsbury* (Arrow Books: London, 1989); Hugh Kenner, *A Sinking Island: The Modern English Writers* (Barrie and Jenkins: London, 1988); Doris Lessing, 'The Small Personal Voice', in *Declaration*, edited by Tom Maschler (London: MacGibbon and Kee, 1959), pp. 11–29; Rubin Rabinowitz, *The Reaction against Experiment in the English Novel 1950–60* (New York: Columbia University Press, 1967); Angus Wilson, *Diversity and Depth in Fiction: Selected Critical Essays*, edited by Kerry McSweeney (London: Secker and Warburg, 1983).
7. John Barth, 'The Literature of Exhaustion', *Atlantic*, 220:2 (1967): pp. 29–34; Ihab Hassan, *The Dismemberment of Orpheus: Towards a Postmodern Literature* (New York: Oxford University Press, 1977); Frank Kermode, *Continuities* (London: Routledge, Kegan, and Paul, 1968).
8. For a useful discussion of the history of Snow's campaigns against literary modernism, see Guy Ortolano, *The Two Cultures Controversy: Science, Literature and Cultural Politics in Post-War Britain* (London and New York: Cambridge University Press, 2011).

9. Frank Kermode, *History and Value: the Clarendon and Northcliffe Lectures* (London and New York: Oxford University Press, 1989).

10. Ihab Hassan, *The Postmodern Turn: Essays in Postmodern Theory and Culture* (Columbus, OH: Ohio State University Press, 1988).

11. T. S. Eliot, 'Tradition and the Individual Talent', in *The Sacred Wood*, 2nd ed. (London: Methuen, 1920), pp. 47–59.

12. Raymond Williams, *Marxism and Literature* (Oxford: Oxford University Press, 1977).

13. Brian Richardson, 'Remapping the Present: The Master Narrative of Modern Literary History and the Lost Forms of Twentieth Century Fiction', *Twentieth Century*, 43: 3 (Autumn 1997): pp. 291–309.

14. Henry Green, *Surviving: The Uncollected Prose Writings of Henry Green*, ed. Matthew Yorke (London: Chatto and Windus, 1992), p. 247.

15. Tyrus Miller, *Late Modernism: Politics, Fiction and the Arts between the Wars* (Berkeley, CA, and London: University of California Press, 1999).

16. Jed Esty, *A Shrinking Island: Modernism and National Culture in England* (Princeton, NJ, and Oxford: Princeton University Press, 2003).

17. Elizabeth Bowen, *The Heat of the Day* (1948) (Harmondsworth: Penguin, 1962), p. 114.

18. Frank Kermode, *The Genesis of Secrecy: On the Interpretation of Narrative* (Cambridge, MA: Harvard University Press, 1979), pp. 5–15.

19. René Wellek, *Concepts of Criticism*, edited by Stephen G. Nichols (Newhaven, CT: Yale University Press, 1963).

20. Edgar Morin, *On Complexity*, translated by Robin Postel (Cresskill, NJ: Hampton Press, 2008).

21. W. H. Auden, *The Age of Anxiety: A Baroque Eclogue* (Princeton, NJ, and Oxford: Princeton University Press, 2011).

22. George Orwell, *Coming Up for Air* (London: Victor Gollancz, 1939), p. 158.

23. American Psychiatric Association, *Diagnostic and Statistical Manual of Mental Disorders 1* (Washington, DC: American Psychiatric Association Mental Hospital Service, 1952) p. 31.

24. Susan Sontag, *Illness as Metaphor* (New York: Farrar, Straus and Giroux, 1978).

25. Virginia Woolf, *Orlando* (London: Hogarth Press, 1928).

26. Gilbert Ryle, *The Concept of Mind* (London: Hutchinson, 1949), pp. 99–100.

27. Theodor Adorno, 'Notes on Kafka', in *Prisms*, translated by Samuel and Sherry Weber (Cambridge, MA: MIT Press, 1981), pp. 260–1.

28. Adorno, 'Notes on Kafka', p. 261.

29. Samuel Beckett, *Murphy* (1938), edited by J. C. C. Mays (London: Faber and Faber, 2009).

30. Herbert Spengler, *The Decline of the West, vol. 2*, translated by Charles Francis Atkinson (New York: Knopf, 1926), p. 503.

31. Edward Upward, *Journey to the Border*, introduced by Stephen Spender (London: Enitharmon Press, 1994), p. 20.

32. Upward, *Journey to the Border*, p. 28.

33. Upward, *Journey to the Border*, p. 112.

34. Patrick Hamilton, *Hangover Square* (1941), introduced by J. B. Priestley (London: Penguin, 2001), p. 17.

35. Hamilton, *Hangover Square*, p. 57.

36. Hamilton, *Hangover Square*, p. 60.

37. William Sansom, *The Body* (1949), introduced by Anthony Burgess (London: Robin Clark, 1990), p. vii.

38. André Breton, *L'Amour fou* (1937), translated as *Mad Love* by Mary Ann Caws (Lincoln, NE: Bison Books, 1987); The key phrase is 'interpretive delirium begins only when man, ill-prepared, is taken by a sudden fear in the *forest of symbols*', p. 15.

39. Sansom, *The Body*, p. 131.

40. Sansom, *The Body*, pp. 207–8.

41. William Golding, *Pincher Martin* (London: Faber and Faber, 1956).

42. Ludwig Wittgenstein's description of the mental activity of the solipsist, in 'Notes for Lectures on Private Experience and Sense Data', *Philosophical Review*, 77: 3 (1968): pp. 275–320; 300.

43. Sigmund Freud, 'Psychoanalytic Notes on an Account of a Case of Paranoia' (1911), republished as *The Schreber Case*, translated by Andrew Webber, introduced by Colin MacCabe (London: Penguin: 2003).

44. *The Diary of Virginia Woolf*, vol. 2, 1920–1924, edited by Anne Olivier Bell (Harmondsworth: Penguin, 1981), p. 248.

45. Virgina Woolf, *Mrs Dalloway*, edited by Claire Tomalin (Oxford: Oxford University Press, 1992), p. 53.

46. Woolf, *Mrs Dalloway*, p. 43.

47. Woolf, *Mrs Dalloway*, p. 35.

48. Elizabeth Bowen, *The Last September*, introduced by Victoria Glendenning (London: Vintage, 1998), pp. 66–7.

49. Bowen, *The Last September*, p. 34.

50. Bowen, *The Last September*, p. 68.

51. Bowen, *The Last September*, p. 20.

52. Bowen, *The Last September*, p. 62.

53. Elias Canetti, *Crowds and Power* (1960), translated by Carol Stewart (London: Victor Gollancz, 1962), p. 73.

54. Samuel Beckett, *Watt* (1953) (London: Calder, 1970), pp. 80–1.

55. Green, *Surviving*, pp. 28–48.

56. Henry Green, *Party Going*, in *Loving Living Party Going*, introduced by John Updike (London: Picador, 1978), p. 388.

57. Green, *Party Going*, p. 403.

58. Gustav Le Bon, *The Crowd: A Study of the Popular Mind* (New York: Macmillan, 1896).

59. Green, *Party Going*, pp. 385, 438, 467.

60. Green, *Party Going*, p. 469.

61. Roger Caillois, 'Mimicry and Legendary Psychasthenia', in *The Edge of Surrealism: A Roger Caillois Reader*, edited by Claudine Frank, translated by Claudine Frank and Camille Naish (Durham, NC, and London: Duke University Press, 2003), pp. 89–107; 91.

62. Caillois, 'Mimicry and Legendary Psychasthenia', p. 100.

63. Hannah Arendt, *Eichmann in Jerusalem: A Report on the Banality of Evil* (1963) (Harmondsworth: Penguin, 1994), p. 49.

64. Hannah Arendt, 'Truth and Politics', in *Between Past and Future: Eight Exercises in Political Thought* (London: Penguin, 2006), pp. 223–60; 241.

65. *General Psychopathology*, p. 309.

66. Dorothy Day, 'Poverty and Precarity', *The Catholic Worker* (May 1952), pp. 2, 6, http//www.catholicworker.org/dorothy day/articles/633.pdf accessed 6 Feb. 2016.

67. Butler, *Precarious Life*, p. 22.

68. The research for this essay was supported by a Wellcome Trust strategic award (WT098455MA) and a Leverhulme award (F/DO128BF).

MOTION STUDIES

15

Stillness and Altitude
René Clair's *Paris qui dort*

Paul K. Saint-Amour

Glorious or deplorable crashes. The adrenaline aesthetic. Accelerandos of the body, the datum, the product; of urban life, markets, and modern war. More and more, the question of movement in late modernity leads to the answer of *speed*, in turn revising our stories about modernism—its aesthetics, its hedonics, its politics—to accord with modernity's quickening tempos.[1] Without abandoning the analytic of speed, we're now in a position to complicate it by revisiting an enigma Roland Barthes identified in his essay 'The Jet-man', written in the mid-1950s and published in *Mythologies*. The enigma is the stillness that lies on the other side of speed—not the stasis speed negates but the poise in which it culminates. For Barthes, it was this apparent oxymoron of stillness-in-speed, rather than raw velocity, that had become a common 'proof of modernity':

> We must here accept a paradox, which is in fact admitted by everyone with the greatest of ease, and even consumed as a proof of modernity. This paradox is that an excess of speed turns into repose. The pilot-hero was made unique by a whole mythology of speed as an experience, of space devoured, of intoxicating motion; the *jet-man*, on the other hand, is defined by a coenaesthesis of motionlessness...as if the extravagance of his vocation precisely consisted in overtaking motion, in going faster than speed.[2]

The remainder of Barthes's short essay extends the distinction between the pilot-hero and the jet-man, the former a gentleman amateur intoxicated by the adventure and fitfulness of 'classical speed', the latter a professional marked by a monastic discipline so austere as to result in his speciation—what Barthes refers to, variously, as a 'metamorphosis of species', the emergence of 'a new race in aviation', and 'a sudden mutation between the earlier creatures of propeller-mankind and the later ones of jet-mankind.'[3] The propeller-using race were addicted to speed as an *event*; the jet-man, by contrast, has attained a *condition* in which repose, stillness, even stoppage are neither the obverse nor the absence of speed, but its apotheosis, the asymptote approached by speed.

The word *coenaesthesis* (in French, *cénesthésie*), which Barthes uses to describe this condition—'a coenaesthesis of motionlessness'—is not his coinage but a term from mid-nineteenth-century physiology and psychology. Grafting the Ancient Greek preface *koinos*, or 'common' onto the root *aisthesis*, 'sensation or perception', the term denotes the common or vital feeling that is the sum of the body's internal sense of itself, as distinct from more particularized sense data about the external world's stimulation of the body. Barthes writes in *S/Z* of the 'coenaesthetic' dimension of human song on the listener (there, Balzac's Sarrasine) as 'linked less to an "impression" than to an internal sensualism, one that is muscular and humoral'.[4] And he uses the term a second time in 'The Jet-man' to describe the movement from propeller-humankind to jet-humankind as a succession of the buffet by the swoon. He writes:

> Mythology abandons here a whole imagery of exterior friction and enters pure coen-
> aesthesis: motion is no longer the optical perception of points and surfaces; it has
> become a kind of vertical disorder, made of contractions, black-outs, terrors and
> faints; it is no longer a gliding but an inner devastation, an unnatural perturbation, a
> motionless crisis of bodily consciousness.[5]

Note that what Barthes earlier called the 'repose' achieved by excess speed is anything but restful: bottled in a cockpit, the jet pilot retains an external composure but goes internally haywire, experiencing nothing less than an inner devastation. Speed used to happen *to* the body. Now it happens *in* the body.

Barthes's term 'coenaesthesis' invites us to think about bodily movement not just as affective; not just as *exteroceptive* (or involving exterior sense data); not just as *proprioceptive* (or involving a sense of the body's physical disposal in space); but also as *interoceptive*—as involving an internal, humoral sensualism, to use his phrase. For Barthes, the jet-man's Mach-3 interoception belonged to the space age alone: to the moment when an ascetic order of intubated cyborgs gained the world-picture but lost their aviator-souls. Were we to look for companion works to 'The Jet-man', one obvious choice would be Don DeLillo's 1983 short story 'Human Moments in World War III', whose orbiting metaphysicians, serene among their firing codes and monkishly severe routines, have so few 'human moments' that they must dub them human.[6] Instead, I offer a more counter-intuitive choice in the French director René Clair's debut feature, *Paris qui dort* (1924), known to English-speaking audiences as *The Crazy Ray*.[7] Written in 1922 and filmed the following year on location in Paris, Clair's urban castaway narrative clearly belongs to the epoch of the propeller, the wing-walker, the barn-stormer or aerial stunt man. Yet in the film's play with vertiginous altitudes, in its science-fiction conceit of a ray that can alter and even halt the pace of time, and in the attention it draws to the rapid frame rate at which even static images travel in cinema, we find some premonition of G-suit, blackout, and power dive—some leading edge of the coenaesthesis of motionlessness at speed's apogee. What's more, *Paris qui dort* insists on at least one thing about high-speed coenaesthesis that 'The Jet-man' only hints at: the reliance of that unquiet repose on the velocity of capital.

Annette Michelson draws near to such a claim when, in her classic article on *Paris qui dort*, she describes Clair's film as a comic reading of Marx's *Third Manuscript* and as 'the conjunction of a metacinematic discourse and a cine-matic critique of capital'.[8] In staging its hero's '"awakening" to his implication in the cash nexus' through its games with time, says Michelson, the film allegorizes cinema's power to awaken the masses to money's function as general equivalent, and to its role in producing alienated selves.[9] Since Michelson's piece appeared, however, commentaries on *Paris qui dort* have emphasized its metacinematic discourse to the near exclusion of its critique of capital via questions of speed and temporality. This formalist emphasis results partly from Clair's own remarks on the film, which stress his technical interest in 'the movement produced by the cinematographic machine', and partly from the disparity between *Paris qui dort*'s conventional fabular premise and the innovative technical means of its execution.[10] Thus scholars who address the film's science-fiction plot tend to treat it either as a distraction from Clair's purely aesthetic aims[11] or as a means of importing cinema's technical innovations and temporal conditions into the film's diegetic world.[12] Without contesting the latter reading, I'll argue that it tells only half the story. Clair's film opens a wide passage between technique and diegesis not just to restage the invention of cinema through a sci-fi device but also in order to think cinema and capital together under the sign of their velocities, which it makes us feel accelerate toward the swoon of coenaesthesis.

Paris qui dort begins with a high-altitude shot of either the Arc de Triomphe or the Île aux Cygnes (**Fig. 15.1**), depending on which of the two most readily available prints you consult. (Neither of them is the hour-plus print originally shown to French audiences: one is the re-edited, hour-long version with English intertitles;

Figure 15.1. Île aux Cygnes, opening. *Paris qui dort*, directed by René Clair (Kastor and Lallement, 1924).

the other a thirty-six-minute version Clair recut in 1970 for TV broadcast.)[13] This is the first of many panoramic shots of Paris taken from the Eiffel Tower itself, and although it shows us some limited motion, it also establishes two facts of high-altitude optics that the film will exhibit repeatedly. First, that from an aerial remove even the City of Speed slows to a crawl, if not a standstill. And second, that the seeming motionlessness of the vista is correlated with the viewer's sense of being endangered by the physical vantage that permits it—of being hundreds of feet above the city with no guard rail, mesh, or safety cable; of a certain humoral sensualism gone awry in a nausea that has less to do with specific incoming sense data than with a spreading sense of emergency in the viscera. Even in those ground-based scenes where it lets our internal organs resolidify, *Paris qui dort* will be sponsored by this effect of optical distance, the conceit of a frozen city sustained in the film's many tower-top panoramas by street-level motion's approach to the vanishing point. For we soon learn that we are seeing the city from the vantage of the film's protagonist, Albert, who, as night watchman at the Eiffel Tower lives, a little improbably, in a shack near its summit. There he wakes and, while smoking his first cigarette of the morning, finds the tower's observation deck strangely unvisited by the usual tourists. And when he looks out over the city, Paris seems still to be asleep in daylight (**Fig. 15.2**). After waiting a lonely hour, he descends from his perch down helical stairways through a lacework of girders, in one of several visual tributes to the tower so loving, and so protracted, that it threatens to bring the plot

Figure 15.2. Albert, looking down, sees the city motionless. *Paris qui dort,* directed by René Clair (Kastor and Lallement, 1924).

Figure 15.3. Albert descending the Eiffel Tower. *Paris qui dort*, directed by René Clair (Kastor and Lallement, 1924).

of the film to a halt (**Fig. 15.3**). In this way, too, the tower gets affiliated with stoppage: its visual magnetism is so powerful that it threatens to snake-charm the camera into bringing about the annulment of narrative.

But Albert *does* emerge from the tower and finds that clock time, not narrative, has ground to a halt: the streets are nearly empty, the timepieces all read 3.25, and the few people who were still out at that late hour—ragpickers, revellers, and cabbies—are frozen in mid-action, crook and cop locked in their chase (**Fig. 15.4**). Initially bemused, Albert soon grows lonely, though less for human company than for the city's kinetic pulse, and we see him fall into a flashback reverie on the high-speed circulation of motor cars and pedestrians through teeming streets. But this tribute to traffic is broken by the arrival of a lone car containing five other animate people—the pilot and passengers of a plane recently arrived from Marseilles. These antecedents of the millionaire and his wife, the professor and Mary Anne, fulfil the central casting typology of castaways: the dashing aviator, the purse-proud merchant, the debonair kleptomaniac with the decent but priggish detective who is escorting him to jail, and lastly Hesta, a wealthy, languid woman of the world. Like the tower watchman, they have been spared from stasis by altitude, their plane having been high over the city at the moment of paralysis. Joining forces with Albert, they decide, as a title in the English version puts it, to 'rule the world, using the Tower as their General Headquarters'. During the day, they descend from their high-altitude safe house to forage in the city's four-star restaurants for free champagne

Figure 15.4. Burglar and policeman frozen in place. *Paris qui dort*, directed by René Clair (Kastor and Lallement, 1924).

and pâté, bathing in the Trocadero fountains, amassing a fortune in banknotes picked from the pockets of waxwork Parisians, stockpiling stolen luxuries, even making off with the Mona Lisa, which we see at one point jammed unceremoniously in the back seat of their car (**Fig. 15.5**). But soon, as Albert did earlier, they become bored and lonely for motion; in another sequence of near-plotlessness we see them turning 100-franc notes into paper aeroplanes and lofting them with a shrug out over the sleeping city (**Fig. 15.6**); dropping pearls one by one off the tower summit; indulging in dangerous pranks and stunts that suggest how little survival has come to matter; losing their pleasure in gambling because money is meaninglessly plentiful. Finally the men begin to fight for the attentions of Hesta, the sole woman, who looks bored even as she eggs on her brawling suitors. Clair has afflicted a society of six with decadence.

But the castaways' ennui is suddenly broken by the sound of a voice over the wireless: the sender, a woman, is being held captive by her mad-scientist uncle and broadcasts her address to any would-be rescuers. 'At last: someone else to live for!', the title tells us, and the castaways troop to her aid. After they have freed her, she explains that her uncle imprisoned her when she protested against his latest invention: a ray with which he planned to immobilize the world. She has been shut up in a shielded room containing nothing but a wireless transmitter; thus the wireless joins the tower and the aeroplane as super-modern sites of exemption from motionlessness (**Fig. 15.7**). The band confront the scientist and force him to reverse the

Figure 15.5. Castaways in car filled with loot. *Paris qui dort*, directed by René Clair (Kastor and Lallement, 1924).

Figure 15.6. The pilot throwing a banknote aeroplane from the tower. *Paris qui dort*, directed by René Clair (Kastor and Lallement, 1924).

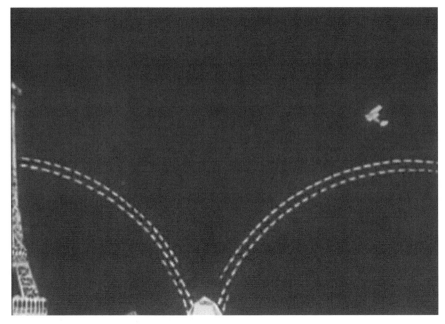

Figure 15.7. Still from animated sequence showing the tower's and plane's exemption from the ray. *Paris qui dort*, directed by René Clair (Kastor and Lallement, 1924).

effects of the ray, an action rendered through the reanimation of freeze-frames: human statues lurching back to life, cars jerking into motion. With the longed-for rush and roar of the city restored, the castaways disperse to resume their lives, Albert taking up with the scientist's niece. Only now does he realize that in an earlier fit of boredom he threw his new wealth to the winds. 'Yesterday he could've given her a Rolls Royce but today—nothing!', the title reads. Albert and the niece decide they need to raise some funds, so head back to the scientist's lair to stop time again (**Fig. 15.8**). There, a struggle between the scientist and a sceptical colleague ensues in which the ray's lever is wrenched back and forth, with the city stopping, starting, speeding up, slowing down accordingly. Finally the device explodes and motion is restored to its proper pace. But Albert and the niece have been caught red-handed while picking a pocket and taken to a psychiatric ward, where they find the rest of their band have been incarcerated for their seemingly delusional claims about having lived in a frozen city. The gang are released after making a false confession that they were merely pranksters, and again they disperse. Albert and the niece ascend the tower, wondering 'Was it really a dream?' But a diamond ring perched on a girder—'The last souvenir'—confirms that it was not, and after Albert places it on the young woman's finger the couple look out over Paris, stretched below them, and the film ends with their silhouettes fading into a panoramic shot that echoes the first (**Fig. 15.9**).

   In a contemporary review of the film, René Bizet referred to *Paris qui dort* as a 'study of movement', praising the fact that 'Everything is images and nothing but

Figure 15.8. The mad scientist's niece activates the ray again. *Paris qui dort*, directed by René Clair (Kastor and Lallement, 1924).

Figure 15.9. Albert and the mad scientist's niece kiss; fade to panorama. *Paris qui dort*, directed by René Clair (Kastor and Lallement, 1924).

images, without useless intellectualism. Its psychology isn't born before the image, it's born from it.... Now, that's cinema.'[14] As we've seen, Clair's study of movement is equally a study of stasis, both in the film's unusual proportion of still images and depopulated scenes and in its narrative lulls. But *Paris qui dort* does not offer a generalized study of movement and stillness in themselves; motion and its negation are referred implicitly but unrelentingly to the medium of film. Both the static aerial panoramas and the street-level *tableaux dormants* depicting the effects of the paralysis ray insist, yet more specifically, on the still photograph's constitutive role in cinematic experience. In the sequences where the city comes to life or returns to stasis, Clair's freeze-frames offer a study of motion-in-repose. These shots were probably achieved by filming a screen on which first-order footage was being projected and halted through the stilling of the projector (or possibly through the insertion of multiple duplicates of a frame). The resulting second-order footage, then, asks the film's viewers to tarry with the imperfections of a particular stilled frame of a particular print of the shot. To these imperfections are added the flaws in the print of the second-order footage, which cause the image to flicker and sizzle (see **Figs. 15.10–12**). Although the mimetic content of the image is static, as a visual field it pulses and coruscates with motion. Standard kinetic shots create the impression of velocity through the use of a series of stills. Clair's freeze-frames appear to invert this instrumentality, demonstrating that what we experience as the phenomenon of cinematic stillness is really the epiphenomenon of a nonstop cinematic velocity. Speed in the innards of stillness: this is *Paris qui dort* at its most

Figure 15.10. Champs-Élysées freeze-frame, still 1. *Paris qui dort*, directed by René Clair (Kastor and Lallement, 1924).

Figure 15.11. Champs-Élysées freeze-frame, still 2. *Paris qui dort*, directed by René Clair (Kastor and Lallement, 1924).

Figure 15.12. Champs-Élysées freeze-frame, still 3. *Paris qui dort*, directed by René Clair (Kastor and Lallement, 1924).

coenaesthetic, repeatedly shifting the viewer's attention from images of hurtling bodies to a perpetual hurtling in the body of the image.

Yet even as cinema operates in *Paris qui dort* as the chief incarnation of modern life's dangerously hectic pace, it is also allegorized as the thing most in peril. The film's unpeopled plazas and vistas recall the empty cities of early urban photography, whose forcibly long exposure times preferred either stock-still human subjects or none at all.[15] It's as if the resurgent role of the still in Clair's film threatened the uninvention of cinema. The medium is menaced, too, by the way *Paris qui dort* thematizes not the constancy but the hysterical instability of its speed. As Michelson observes, the most obvious metacinematic gesture in Clair's film pairs the paralysis ray with the camera itself: when the professor and his friend are wrestling over the position of the ray's lever, they are effectively fighting over the camera speed, causing traffic to speed up, slow down, halt, or restart.[16] This pairing of motion-picture camera and paralysis ray is less counter-intuitive than it seems, given the causal relation between stasis and speed: once you freeze motion into still frames, you can control their playback velocity. Thus both camera and ray are speed-control devices by virtue of being paralysis devices. But the film no sooner establishes this pairing than it liquidates it. After the norm of 'real velocity' has been shown to be contingent on the speed of a hysterically variable camera, we see the camera's double in the film—the paralysis ray, which we might call the Bad Camera—go up in smoke. It's as if this Bad Camera had to be sacrificed in order for life to resume its normal pace as rendered by the Good Camera's constant velocity, even as the relativization of 'true' velocity by the Bad Camera leaves the viewer with a residual wooziness, a humoral perturbation. A question hangs in the air, a question about the second order of velocity: what, after all, is the proper speed *of speed*?

Cinema is only one of several technologies or technical wonders privileged by *Paris qui dort*. The aeroplane, the Eiffel Tower, and the wireless share an exemption from the effects of the paralysis ray, all of them by dint of some affiliation with altitude; the wireless is projected onto a vertical axis by its historical association with the tower, which was first used as a radio transmitter in 1904 and as the broadcast platform for the first round-the-world radio signal in 1913. One would expect the binding of these technologies around the armature of the tower to reinforce this historical connection between the vertical axis and high speeds: since 1901, when the aviator Santos-Dumont sped round it at a prize-winning 15 mph in his motorized balloon, the tower had become a standard axis in air races; and its role as a wireless transmitter meanwhile amplified its affiliations with speed in making it the emblem of the nascent global communications network, an icon of near-instantaneous worldwide connectivity. But in Clair's film, this fetish of speed and simultaneity is something else entirely; it is the crow's nest from which a languorous crew look out on a city that has become an ice floe, slowness gazing at stasis. Although reserved from paralysis, the tower and the technologies that converge in it work not as sites of intoxicating speed but as islands of englaciation from whose summits even the unfrozen city slows to a crawl. As with the film's metacommentary on cinema, technologies typically allied with speed get reaffiliated with silence and stillness. One effect of this rescripting is to make the viewer lonely for motion, an effect produced partly through the high-speed reveries of characters remembering the animated city and partly through the contrast between the antic pace and action-crammed frames of more conventional silent films and the ocular patience of *Paris qui dort*. After the encyclopedia of speed and stoppage effects produced by the battle over the lever-slash-camera, we long, as Albert does, for speed itself to move at the proper speed, which the film sets at the pace of Parisian street life in the twenties and finally resumes and locks in with the ray's destruction.

This longing for speed, however, does not result from the film's having turned the clock back to some bucolic or pastoral moment that makes us impatient to catch up to the 1920s present again. *Paris qui dort* is a castaway film, and the fact alone of its protagonists' being isolated in time rather than in space does not set it apart from other castaway narratives; the spatial peripheralization of shipwreck nearly always attends or even tropes an ejection into the political, theological, and technological past. *Paris qui dort* differs in that its castaways are ejected not into the past but into the future, their urban desert island limned by the technologies that incarnate the future's cutting edge—aviation, a wireless global communications network, cinema, and even X-rays (the inventor of the paralysis ray being called 'Ixe' in the film's Pathé cut, making his device the 'Rayon Ixe' or X-ray). But what sort of future is this, in which modernity's relentless acceleration seems to have produced slowness, and the teeming metropolis—teeming with people, vehicles, stimuli, realia—has been evacuated? Barthes's jet-man may not look much like Clair's castaways, but he is their descendant, sitting downstream in a flow at whose headwaters they stand. That flow has less to do, finally, with the speed of objects than with the speed of information; their high-altitude vantage is indifferent, finally, to the speed of bodies and conveyances at street level, can barely see the difference between stasis and motion. Such a space is insulated not just from paralysis but also from the whole question of the first order of speed, speed as 'the optical perception of points and surfaces' in Barthes's words. Its repose comes from the degree to which, and the speed at which, it seems to have superseded the whole question of moving bodies in optical space.

But as I indicated earlier, there is a term missing from Barthes's description of the new order of speed, yet prominent in *Paris qui dort*: capital. Remember that when the clock is stopped in the film, money becomes meaninglessly plentiful, so much so that the entertainment value of launching large banknotes off the top of the Eiffel Tower exceeds the exchange value of the now hateful paper. Yet because he has thrown away his meaningless fortune, the Albert who returns to clock time needs to stop the clock again in order to acquire money. Two things are happening here: first, money's function as a general equivalent is shown to depend on its temporal analogue, clock time, so that when the clock no longer provides a common and transactable reference for time and velocity, money loses its character as supermedium of exchange. Second, the acquisition and expenditure of money are assigned to mutually exclusive chronotopes. In other words, to acquire money *and* be able to deploy it meaningfully, you need to be able to manipulate time, or, more specifically, the social production of time—a notion that surprises no one acquainted with Fordism or Taylorism or, for that matter, with the work of the historian and political economist Moishe Postone.[17] In both the operations I have described, money is temporalized, made a function of time, a product of the manipulation of time. The reciprocal operation is implied as well, a monetization of time whereby various frames of temporal reference differ predominantly in the kinds of fiscal operations each can host; thus the felt velocity of time becomes a variable dependent on money's velocity, or at least on its particular function. Clair's crazy ray is not just the camera's on-screen avatar but also the materialization of capitalism as the ultimate speed technology, a means of modularizing the pace of experience for the sake of discrete economic operations. The film makes it impossible to think about camera speed without also thinking about the velocity of capital.

Paris qui dort contains a beautifully compact vignette about money, speed, and film. Early in his lone exploration of the sleeping city, Albert comes upon a motionless man clearly poised to hurl himself into the Seine (**Fig. 15.13**). 'Can't allow suicides!—People are too scarce!', say the English intertitles. Albert finds, at the man's feet, a note giving the reason for his intended self-slaughter: 'It's the terrible pace of modern life that has driven me to this. I cannot stand the rush and roar of this city.'[18] Frozen on the quay with arms outstretched, neither dead nor animate, he seems to have been granted his dying wish for stillness while being exempted

Figure 15.13. Albert runs to the aid of a would-be suicide on the quay. *Paris qui dort*, directed by René Clair (Kastor and Lallement, 1924).

from the death he thought must lead to it. In one of the film's few instances of gift giving, Albert returns the suicide note to its place and then plants a banknote in the figure's outstretched hand. (The act seems especially generous if we consider Clair's original scenario for the film, in which Albert is compelled to take his job as night watchman on the tower because he has lost everything, quite suddenly, in the stock market.[19]) When the quayside leaper is released from the ray's paralysis, his discovery of Jean's gift causes him, whether through gratitude or sheer surprise, to abort his fatal plunge (**Fig. 15.14**). Of course, most of the redistributions of wealth made possible by the ray are less altruistic (**Fig. 15.15**). But the point here is not that people will tend to redistribute wealth selfishly when given the chance. It's something darker: that the temporal conditions necessary for money's redistribution are mutually exclusive of money's value. Only the one who controls the means—which is to say, according to the logic of Clair's film, the (camera) *speeds*—of time's social production can redistribute wealth without causing it to evaporate. From the perspective of those who lack such means of control, money will seem to be approaching an infinite velocity, appearing (or, if you are the luckless Albert at the Bourse, disappearing) with the near instantaneity and dematerialized status of a telecommunications signal.

Barthes's analysis passes over another term, this time one that's absent in Clair's film as well: labour. Despite having exploited a wide range of scenarios, poses, and social types for its experiments with speed and stoppage, *Paris qui dort* exhibits

Figure 15.14. The would-be suicide 'wakes' to find his hands full of banknotes. *Paris qui dort*, directed by René Clair (Kastor and Lallement, 1924).

Figure 15.15. Albert stealing a pearl necklace from a sleeping diner to give to Hesta. *Paris qui dort*, directed by René Clair (Kastor and Lallement, 1924).

little interest in the labouring body or the production process, either in stasis or in motion. Unlike its cinematic cousins, the 'city symphony' films of the twenties and thirties—films that thrive on portrayals of labour, even if in the process they usually conflate the worker with the machine—*Paris qui dort* cannot imagine a credible site of production, can only imagine capital as coming from looted bank vaults and the picked pockets of the rich.[20] It is difficult to assign a valence to this omission— to say for certain whether the film avoids the sites and agents of production out of complicity with the new telecommunicative society or as part of its satire of that society. One could say, at least, that *Paris qui dort* symptomatizes in advance the information age's tendency to replace the narrative of production with the fetish category of 'flow'—to see capital as flowing from capital, and the commodity as spontaneously generated in shops, museums, and restaurants. There is one moment in Clair's film, however, that suggests that more may keep us from suicide than a fistful of francs that can travel at the speed of sound or light. Just as the castaways are reaching the depths of anomie, the distress call from the mad scientist's niece comes over the wireless (**Fig. 15.16**). 'At last there was someone else to live for', the title reads. Here the high-tech, high-altitude, globalized world of the castaways is revealed in its decadence and narcissism, and the ground-level world of the city as a world where one can live for the other; the awful generality of the panorama gives way, at last, to the specifics of the street address. For all that the 'terrible pace of modern life' can drive a man to attempt suicide, that same

Figure 15.16. Hesta, the pilot, and Albert receive a wireless plea for help from the mad scientist's niece. *Paris qui dort*, directed by René Clair (Kastor and Lallement, 1924).

world of first-order speed remains the space of ethical demands that may pull one back from the brink. Over against the solipsism of the second order of speed—the stratospheric repose described by Barthes and adumbrated by the film—the old order of jostled and hurtling bodies celebrated by Marinetti and other traditionalists remains the only order in which *Paris qui dort* can locate even the possibility of living for the other.

But for Albert and the mad scientist's niece, the question of living for the other is quickly replaced by the question of living with the other, as the two become engaged during the film's final frames. Although *Paris qui dort* shares certain formal and topical traits with expressionism and surrealism, its final investment in the marriage plot measures its distance from both, as well as its devotion to the Mack Sennett comedies that Clair adored. In the film's opening scene, Albert is a precursor to Barthes's jet-man in his high-altitude monastery, like a stylite hermit fasting atop a desert pillar. But it is hard to imagine that he and his fiancée will continue to live atop the tower; what we witness at the film's conclusion is surely Albert's first visit to the observation deck as a tourist, a visit to be followed by his shacking up in a proper street address with his beloved. In its move from bachelordom to marriage, and (implicitly) from lonely eyrie to cosy ground nest, *Paris qui dort* intriguingly points up the queerness of the position it abandons: as against the priapic straight masculinity of the aviator, the queerness of the jet-man in his monastic 'abstention and withdrawal from pleasures', in his 'glamorous singularity' and 'pure passivity' (these are Barthes's phrases), and in the 'sudden mutation' or 'metamorphosis of species' that bar him from reproducing with other humans (which is the definition, after all, of speciation).[21] More, as a figure of stillness-at-high-speed, the jet-man has his cinematic analogue in the still shot—not, that is, in an isolated still, but in a static shot like those freeze-frames in *Paris qui dort* where a stopped image is held before our eyes even as the film continues at sixteen frames-per-second (the rate at which Clair's film was shot). By mapping such shots onto the bacheloric altitudes and temporal capers its protagonist renounces in marriage, *Paris qui dort* associatively queers the still in the context of cinema, a gesture that Barthes's jet pilot, that celibate man out of reproductivist time, only helps us apprehend with greater clarity.

Yet for all that this final set of claims pushes the jet-man and the affianced couple apart along the axes of sexual and cinematic temporality, *Paris qui dort* would also lodge them together in at least one respect: whether you are moving at the speed of sound or at the speed of a bourgeois couple toward matrimony, you are also moving at the speed of money if you are moving at all. The old speed of 'exterior friction' and propeller-humankind at least had the virtue of wearing its mechanism, and hence its monetary dependencies, on its sleeve. The new speed produces the impression of repose to the extent that it fuses the body with the mechanism, making the jet appear a function of the pilot or, conversely, the pilot a feature of the cockpit; making the tower a prosthetic torso or the tower-top observer the crowning cell of a very tall sensory stalk. *Paris qui dort* insists, contra Barthes, that there is no separating the 'coenaesthesis of motionlessness' from the economic flows that undergird it utterly; that one name for those 'contractions, black-outs, terrors and faints'; for that 'inner devastation, [that] unnatural perturbation, [that] motionless crisis of bodily consciousness'; or just for that queer feeling in the pit of the stomach—is capital.

NOTES

1. I have in mind here particularly Enda Duffy's *The Speed Handbook: Velocity, Pleasure, Modernism* (Chapel Hill, NC: Duke University Press, 2009) and the rich lineage in which it falls. Some key works include Paul Virilio, *Speed and Politics: An Essay on Dromology*, translated by Mark Polizzotti (New York: Semiotext(e), 1986); Wolfgang Schivelbusch, *The Railway Journey: The Industrialization of Time and Space in the Nineteenth Century* (Berkeley, CA: University of California Press, 1987); Andrew Thacker, *Moving Through Modernity: Space and Geography in Modernism* (Manchester: Manchester University Press, 2003); and, most recently, Jonathan Grossman's *Charles Dickens's Networks: Public Transport and the Novel* (New York: Oxford University Press, 2012).
2. Roland Barthes, 'The Jet-man', in *Mythologies*, translated by Annette Lavers (New York: Hill and Wang, 1972), pp. 71–2; 71; emphasis in the original.
3. Barthes, 'The Jet-man', pp. 71–2.
4. Roland Barthes, *S/Z: An Essay*, translated by Richard Miller (New York: Hill and Wang, 1974), p. 110.

5. Barthes, 'The Jet-man', p. 71.

6. See Don DeLillo, 'Human Moments in World War III' (1983), reprinted in *The Angel Esmeralda: Nine Stories* (New York: Scribner, 2011), pp. 25–44.

7. *Paris qui dort*, directed by René Clair (Kastor and Lallement, 1924). Except where noted, the intertitles I quote are those in the sixty–minute English-language version.

8. Annette Michelson, 'Dr Crase and Mr Clair', *October* 11 (1979): pp. 30–53; 51. 'Crase' is what *The Crazy Ray*, the English-language version of *Paris qui dort*, calls the mad scientist, who was left unnamed in the original release.

9. Michelson, 'Dr Crase and Mr Clair', pp. 50–1.

10. Transcript of a 1973 interview by Armand Panigel with René Clair; quoted in Richard Abel, *French Cinema: The First Wave, 1915–1929* (Princeton, NJ: Princeton University Press, 1987), p. 380.

11. Celia McGerr, for example, finds Clair is continually 'diverted from... the film's mystery plot by the lure of the purely aesthetic', his interest 'wandering from the narrative to details of *mise-en-scène*' to the point where the narrative 'trips [him] up at inopportune moments': Celia McGerr, *René Clair* (Boston, MA: Twayne, 1980), pp. 34–5, 37.

12. See, for example, Raymond Bellour, 'Concerning "The Photographic"', in *Still Moving: Between Cinema and Photography* (Durham, NC: Duke University Press, 2008), pp. 253–76; 257. Garrett Stewart's brief but suggestive metacinematic treatment of the film does read it, finally, as a 'humanist parable' that warns against a consumerist model of time as an empty repository: 'Time may be money after all, and is spent in this case without pleasure or mental reward. No value accumulates, nothing of worth accrues.... Meaningful duration must, that is, like cinematic narrative itself, be not so much steadily consumed as disruptively produced.' Garrett Stewart, *Framed Time: Toward a Postfilmic Cinema* (Chicago: University of Chicago Press, 2007), p. 128.

13. On the surviving versions of the film and their relationship to the original release, now lost, see R. C. Dole, *The Films of René Clair, Vol. II: Documentation* (Metuchen, NJ: Scarecrow, 1986), pp. 8–11.

14. René Bizet, review of *Paris qui dort* in *La Revue de France* (December 1924); quoted in Dole, *The Films of René Clair*, pp. 21.

15. Michelson touches on the film's kinship with Eugène Atget's Parisian photographs, whose 'sense of imminence, of occurrences past or still to come' she finds *Paris qui dort* shares, and whose 'ecstatic' emptiness helps link Clair's film to surrealism's related emphasis on the ecstatic: Michelson, 'Dr Crase and Mr Clair', pp. 42–3.

16. Michelson, 'Dr Crase and Mr Clair', pp. 44–5.

17. See, especially, Moishe Postone, *Time, Labor and Social Domination: A Reinterpretation of Marx's Critical Theory* (Cambridge: Cambridge University Press, 1993).

18. In the recut French version of the film, the would-be suicide is holding an unopened envelope addressed to 'Monsieur le Commissaire de Police'; we are never shown the envelope's contents.

19. See Dole, *The Films of René Clair*, pp. 19.

20. On interwar city symphony films, see Laura Marcus, '"A Hymn to Movement": The "City Symphony" of the 1920s and 1930s', *Modernist Cultures* 5.1 (2010): pp. 30–46.

21. Barthes, 'The Jet-man', pp. 72–3.

16

Frame-Advance Modernism
The Case of Fritz Lang's *M*

Garrett Stewart

In this essay's original setting as a conference topic under the umbrella notion of 'moving modernism', I had trusted my title would ring a bell, or, better, throw a projector switch. Yet the case for the frame in this sense, as transparent photograph (or photogram) on the backlit spinning reel, is one that repeatedly needs advancing, rather than being taken as axiomatic. And all the more, I find, in the spreading intermedia landscape of New Modernist Studies, where, if I may put it this way, theory is going to the movies as never before.

Faced with the kinetic hypothesis of modernist mobility, certainly cinema comes to mind right away. Moving pictures. Not so-called at first, though. And for good reason. Too candid, that transferred epithet. What moves is indeed only the pictures, in order to picture movement. The *actual* moving of single transparencies, single backlit photograms, yields *virtual* movement. This is what people came for at first: the new magic, even before the specific attractions. In some of the earliest projection venues, in fact, the first image was held like a slide (made possible by water cooling) so as to highlight the wonder of its launch into action. Each screening thus served to bear forth the medium from its own genetic origin in the still.

Like moving pictures, the term motion pictures came later too: also true to the apparatus, at least in a roundabout way. The motion of anything on screen is what the projector's own *motion pictures*, pictures in the thrown beam of change itself. This transition per se between celluloid frames or increments is then transferred to spatial transit across the screen frame. The *real* advance (pun allowed) of the flickers was the frame advance. Which is what encourages Friedrich Kittler, in *Optical Media*, to go so far as to subordinate cinema to the digital. For him the necessary intermittence of the projected image in its syncopated pulsation of frame/[bar]/frame is thus discrete, binary, and in itself, though photographically composited, ultimately non-analogue in its motion effects.[1] This is what the early modernist philosopher of time Henri Bergson disliked about film, its simulation rather than capture of *durée*, as did chronophotographer Étienne-Jules Marey, objecting to cinema's non-analytic conflation of poses, its squandering of the properly discrete graphing of difference in the illusory spectacle of procession.[2] No anachronism is necessary to see this. I am therefore less concerned than Kittler to rethink cinema's material strip in the backward light of digital difference than to detect—in the narrative editing that exploits this original filmic micro-frame—one director's inadvertent forecast of an ocular mediation that characterizes the surveillance ethos of a whole (and now electronically implemented) rhetoric in contemporary cinema.[3] This is what we might call Fritz Lang's perpetual modernism, the weird currency of his camerawork. In the grips of his shot logic, the future is now.

Much depends on scale. With Lang's *M*, the issue of fixity versus motion is not just, as Jacques Rancière sees it in *Film Fables*, a tension—in its own right quintessentially modernist—between mimesis and diegesis.[4] While for Rancière this formative division of labour pits image against plot, each reciprocally 'thwarting' the other, a similar though invisible tension, one level down, is at work between photogram and frame line. What did Lang seem to know and to show about this underlying aspect of the image file—and its prehistory—at the very moment when, in his first sound film, he was double-timing silent cinema with his first audial track? What did the intermittent audial synchronizations he had budget for, or interest in, underscore about the fundamental intermittence of the strip? And how did he commandeer this apprehension for the pacing of narrative impact?

Premonitions aside, these are the historical questions that get this essay going—and that should open its eyes to images in the film that borrow their composition and framing from adjacent graphic arts of the period. The reasons for this are more than thematic. It's not just that Lang's montage aligns a time-based medium with the alternative pictorial formats it subsumes in the process. It does so with immediate technical as well as narrative repercussions, thus rendering inter-art comparisons less tangential than they often seem. Film is like sculpture in motion, like mobile panoramas, like large-scale narrative painting, and, increasingly in modernism, like dance, like cubism, like war and its mechanized sightlines, etc.—where the likeness serves to *keep* the very distance it would bridge. This is of course, for the most part, as it should be. With one medial exception. My previous work (concerning films previous, in turn, to the digital advent)—studying the relation of film to photomechanical imaging—could reasonably dispense with the framework of similes. Film isn't like photography. Film *is* photography (or was, until computerized imaging). And, within narrative films, some photographs, printed rather than transparent, figure that fact. Quite variously: now genealogically, now elegiacally, now ironically.

But when one speaks about a certain photographic style more broadly, rather than simply the fact of photography, the axis of comparison widens once again. This is the case when contemplating an entire Weimar art moment, *Neue Sachlichkeit* (New Objectivity), as it inflects a contemporaneous film like *M*. How might this aesthetic practice, in painting as well as photography, be more than just a cultural ambience in Lang's film? Or more even than just an explicit set of intertexts? How, that is, might on-camera satiric portraiture reminiscent of the canvases of Georg Grosz, for instance, alongside shots evoking still-life photographic treatments of urban industrial Germany and its merchandising displays in the interwar years—with their stringent geometries rejecting in every way the inward urgencies of expressionism—be seen as developing in *M* something, for want of a better term, more inframedial? This is to ask: without actual photographs on camera until the film's climactic scene—where the serial child murderer Beckert is confronted with implausibly enlarged prints of his victims in the neutral photographic mode of studio portraits—how, that is, building toward this, might the very different pictorial zeitgeist of the period find an impact *in*, rather than just on, Lang's narrative? An impact, that is—in this first (and perforce, in this respect, most experimental) of his sound films—on the narrative's own disclosures about the already 'mixed medium' of speeding photo-transparencies (picture plus motorized projection) under the pressure of the new hybrid mediation of audio/visual synchronicity.

This is a synchronicity only fitfully secured in *M*—and often against the separate tread of image. Sound triggers an independent graphic pattern in the film's very first sequence. Accompanying the forlorn mother's repeated shouting out of 'Elsie' in this anguished missing-person episode (the first scream we hear in Lang's cinema), we see a veritable *Neue Sachlichkeit* portfolio of photo allusions shuffled past in cinematically static (rather than optically frozen) fixed frames.[5] Much later, as if bookending this effect, we come upon serial images of the deserted corporate offices from which the killer has been removed—this, in another quasi-photographic dossier of depopulated and hence unmoving images redolent of the period's stripped-down, almost clinical aesthetic. These reveal the impersonal space, now ransacked, immediately recognized as typical of objectivist photography, including in the mix, this time, certain openly stop-action freeze frames. In this optical episode, the less sound, in fact, the better. Thus isolated, these shots come forward as the recognizable photographic icons, and intrinsically silent film frames, that in fact they are.

But more than that. For by this point Lang's spectator is wholly entailed, rhetorically, in the ocular articulation of plot that these images slow to a sprocket-driven crawl. So that what ultimately distinguishes the narrative's two phases of serial (photogrammatic) stasis, early and late—even while implicitly linking them at the level of allusive photographic composition—is the relation of the second series, by now, to a disembodied surveillance motif saturating Lang's work, before and after *M*, and everywhere implicit, as well, in a certain lineage of film theory ('the system of the suture') that repeatedly queries the relation of optic frame to an invasive and disavowed spectatorial gaze, masking narrative cinema's essential gaps in service to diegetic coherence.[6] Implicit in this theory is the overridden action of the track as well as of editing. For what happens from frame to frame, subliminally, is also denied in the shot plan and its spatial discontinuities—where one pattern above all is quintessential: the continuous reciprocal absentation of the shot/countershot.

In this construction of interpersonal space by its own denied intervention, camerawork eventually finds just the genres it needs for both the general massaging of spectation and its thematic ironies. Or, across genres, just the modes of optic apprehension required: voyeurism and surveillance. Each is a mode of heavily invested spectatorial licence (via presumed absence) that redounds to the recognized mediations of certain vexed screen moments—and to what I would term (naming indeed the method of this essay) the 'narratography' of their potential notice.[7] The main reason to call up again, in its full polemic extremity, the once dominant model of suture—explanatory paradigm for the lures and elisions of screen vision—is that its utopian backstory (the fall from the purity of image to the motivated and selectively framed act of sighting), mostly forgotten in its application as ideological critique, has tacitly resurfaced, though unnoted as such, in a revealing recent context. For suture theory's mythic prehistory and passive axiom— the lost primacy of vision despoiled by narrative scene—appears to inform a notable recent commentary on *M*, concentrating as that account by Rancière does, however, on the fixed-frame (and hence idealized) shot of a pivotal sequence whose ocular mood ends up wholly violated by the ensuing frame changes unexamined by Rancière, including the film's most aggressively sutured countershot. But before considering Rancière's attempt (contra suture) to extricate looking again from editing, ultimately vision from narrative, we need to explore the visual (rather than theoretical) preparation, indeed the inter-art context, for the scene on which he concentrates. This involves the broader skein of allusion to the motifs of contemporary photography and painting that this one scene participates in and explicitly foregrounds, both in its fixed-frame hold on a toyshop window (Rancière's defining moment) and in that same shot's *mise en scène* as mercantile display.

LANG'S *OBJECTIF*-ISM

Few directors have been less 'camera-shy', if you will, than Lang in exposing the cinematographic cast of their narratives. But in *M* he foregrounds the veritable lens (*objectif*) of his shots with, even for him, an unusual degree of pictographic self-consciousness. He does so precisely, I've started to suggest, by letting the image track revert by allusion to recognizable fixed-frame compositions in the contemporary art practice known as the New Objectivism. Cinema criticism has in fact already been quick to note, for instance, the allusion to the *Neue Sachlichkeit* photographic still life in the reflected shopfront cutlery of a passing shot in *M*—this, quite aside from the inevitable irony of knives as latent weapons in the homicide plot. But that's only the still-life tip of the iceberg in the cool if not chilling network of the film's fine-art intertexts from the *Neue Sachlichkeit* aesthetic. Under this new objectification, frontal images of buildings versus those of people show little difference in affect, including gleaming new industrial settings and post-war devastation alike. The depopulated office corridor from the architectonic vocabulary of *Neue Sachlichkeit* photography will turn up at a pivotal moment in *M*. So, too, the often listless window-framed cityscape, ubiquitous in this art style, as if in a kind of minimalist correction of German romanticism's view-from-the-open-casement.

Most obvious perhaps of all the inter-art checkpoints in this film, especially given a sense of the child murderer Beckert as standing in for a whole generation of shell-shocked victims grappling with their violent urges, is an Otto Dix lithograph from 1916 titled *Wounded Man* (**Fig.16.1**) that finds clear overtones in Peter Lorre's performance as Beckert (**Fig. 16.2**), whose traumatized expressionist gestures must be contained—stylistically as well as narratively—by the aesthetics of *mise en scène* and camerawork alike.[8] When not convulsed with trauma, however,

Figure 16.1. Otto Dix, *Wounded Man*, Lithograph, 1916.

Figure 16.2. Still from *M*, directed by Fritz Lang (1931).

humanoid forms in the New Objectivity tend, instead, to be reduced to mario-nettes, discarded dolls, or—in a related trope of spiritless form—the moulded egglike craniums of numerous automata in the works of painter Georg Grosz, an influence perhaps on the film's first ominous balloon shot (that anthropomorphic plaything caught in telephone wires after the murder of Elsie Beckmann), includ-ing the close match between this shot and an iconic *Neue Sachlichkeit* still life of high-tension wires by Albert Renger-Patzsch. This ongoing relation of kinetic nar-ration to fixed-frame plastic art saturates Lang's film and its manifest sense of its own serial celluloid medium even when there is no internal rear-projection, as sometimes there is, of the crime's indexical trace (the huge blow-up of the killer's fingerprint) nor any overt allusion to the death masks of his victims as single and serial photo images (also pending in those portraits of his pre-teen victims in the film's climactic scene). But what in particular do such earlier allusions to the New Objectivity import into (or impart to) Lang's narrative technique at this moment of his first venture into sound?

One possible answer lies fallow in an argument not concerned directly with *M* or Lang. For David Trotter, film's chief influence on modernist literature resides in the pre-narrative *actualité* as view, as sheer sighting, rather than anything associ-ated with its actualization of frame advance, so that the tactical blind spot in the gaze of recorded bodies before the camera is matched by the unblinking neutrality of their filmic capture.[9] On this showing, and in ways not unrelated to the origi-nary image before suture, cinema thus approaches more nearly than otherwise possible, by way of a modernist epistemology, to a stringent aesthetics of record without representation. In this sense, montage aside, the *Neue Sachlichkeit* aura of Lang's *mise en scène* might seem, along with objectivism in poetry, a definitive real-ization of modernist optics. But I'll be asking why, in the midst of this inter-art ambience, we are nonetheless reminded by Lang's montage not just of the predom-inantly still-life images from the latest Weimar art wave on which *M*'s set design and camera placement is based, but reminded as well—and partly by the same cross-medial inference—of the stilled life of the strip as it is openly and mechani-cally tracked into action, whether with or (as so often in *M*) without movement, but serialized nonetheless in its undertext. Or, put more succinctly, asking why—and how—Lang's film comes to disclose its unique reflexive objectivism as a matter not just of the image composed but of the image composited.

In broader intermedial terms, of course, as seen with the Dix image from over a decade before, it is this aesthetic of New Sobriety (an alternate designation for the *Neue Sachlichkeit* movement) from which Lorre's performance is a backsliding to the externalized torments of the expressionist soul itself. So that when he is not on screen, it is as if the fixed-frame, quasi-photographic shots that interrupt and sanitize his polymorphous gestures take an entire art moment as their antiseptic counterweight. To note at first merely those motifs of the *Neue Sachlichkeit* movement that appear in the film's opening episode, there is the window-ledge or dormer-view still life—just before, in the least romantic of moments, Mrs Beckmann calls out to (the evermore off-screen) Elsie out the framing window. Next, there is the emptied site of architec-tural symmetry, a mainstay of photographs in the period, in the overhead shot down the symmetrical stairwell, empty of the returning girl. Then there is the prevalent visual trope of the deserted attic room (about which several art historians comment apart from Lang's film—perhaps most famously illustrated in a 1926 work by Ernst Thoms called simply *Attic*). As such, it is a paradoxically domestic space of nonhabitation (complete in Lang's shot, further matching the painting, with the line-drying undergarments of the girl's absent body). And finally there is the tabletop still life, as well as the related framings of more abstract geometries, often spheroid, including more than one still life with ball influenced by René Magritte's *The Secret Life* from 1927. Such are the specific optical motifs that converge not only at the Beckmann kitchen table with the circular shapes of the child's plate and glass, never to be filled again, but also on the subsequent discovery of Elsie's absent body survived only by its rocking ball and overhead balloon figure, the latter's tubular torso and limbs animated by the wind alone, no marionette strings attached.

Apart from any direct connection to Otto Rudolf Schatz's 1929 painting of a male balloon vendor and two teen girls, this metonymy turned metaphor in Lang—with the breath-inflated object released by the dead body it lingers to figure—is thus very much of its visual moment. With Elsie's face-painted humanoid balloon form linked to that enigmatic doll and puppet motif of these same years—where, in the ultimate anti-expressionist gesture, the human form is reduced to mere curvatures of an unventriloquized objecthood, a hollow simulacrum—this topos of the *Neue Sachlichkeit* manner (prevalent a full decade before Hans Bellmer launched his ongoing work in the sculpting of doll forms) is related by Lang, as well, to a cut-out harlequin operated as a mechanical automaton at a pivotal later moment. Doing its deep-knee bends thanks to an unseen motor, this is the mobile object shot from behind in the toyshop display, a kinetic focal point of the brief scene that goes strangely unmentioned when Rancière deliberates over what he takes to be the placid respite it affords.

Centred there amid the immobilities of commercial presentation—and spoiling from within, one might well think, any utopian interregnum (Rancière's point) from the killer's homicidal intentions—is the flat mechanical underside of the puppet's involuntary spasms framed together with its onlooker, a robotic killer whose own strings are being pulled not by desire, he later explains, but by compulsion. 'Not want to, must; not want to, must', he repeats about his killing in his last frenzied monologue, as if speaking there for an entire generation sent to war, an inference as if confirmed by the mob's threat not, in so many words, to execute him for the police crackdown his violence has visited upon them, but to put him, in military parlance, 'out of commission'. This threat emerges in a final scene where the balloon has come back—in the hands of its original salesman, the blind beggar who identifies Beckert's habitual whistle—not only to taunt the killer but to mock his expressionist rant when his own tortured cranium keeps disappearing momentarily behind its inflated, vacant reminder of those lifeless bodies he leaves in his wake, but by whose guilt, in his own tacit cinematic metaphors for self-surveillance, he is 'shadowed' and 'tracked'.

At this point, there's no forgetting the opening instance of the balloon figure as simulated human form, taking up the ball's cancelled momentum when, after being caught momentarily in the overhead wires, it is released to invisibility in the ongoing flux of duration. In ways that obliquely anticipate the film's closure—when editing dismisses from view the apprehended killer without any judgment or extermination visited upon him beyond that of total displacement by plot and camerawork—death seems, in the earlier scene, almost brought to definition in optical terms. With the human body artificially imaged by toy figure to begin with, death takes graphically figured shape both as inanimate presence within frame and as removal from it—thus offering in résumé, as it happens, the filmstrip's own two motoring conditions in the artificial increments of its manufactured kinesis.

If we want to say that this early balloon image, perhaps the film's most famous shot—complete with its *Neue Sachlichkeit* overtones—comes back to haunt Beckert in the accusations of the blind man, it does so only after Lang has brought off a bravura panning shot that deliberately reduces the *mise en scène* it sweeps past to a quasi-photographic tableau. This unfolds, once more, by way of an intertext from Weimar graphic art, in this case large-format epic painting, where the film's underworld iconography seems crossed with the mass dissidence of leftist unrest as represented in the 1929 tableau of the Communist Internationale by German painter Otto Griebel. On view in that famous canvas is a wall of impassive faces like that which Beckert confronts in the criminal body of the kangaroo court. He is arraigned there in the deserted basement of bankrupt German industry—in particular a failed brewery cellaring (and fermenting) only resentment in a group portrait over which the camera edges left to right as if it were a scanned image in itself, the least ripple of human movement discernible only toward the end, and far right, of the travelling shot. Yet again at a critical narrative juncture in Lang, and with other two-dimensional media in mind, cinematography parses its own variable amalgam of framed stasis and motor advance.

IMAGE VIS-À-VIS (OR VS?) NARRATIVE

The pattern is as clear as it is cumulative. Time and again in *M*, from wide framing to tight, motion is either contrasted or reduced to stillness within a lens-conscious geometry of bracketing and capture, where the look of a shot often takes its intermedial bearings from plastic rather than kinetic art. The same is true, though unnoted in this respect, for that earlier scene of a supposedly recovered ocular utopia that sustains Rancière's attention as one of his cinematographic parables. Articulating his dichotomy between image and narrative in *Film Fables*, Rancière does not explicitly mention the fabular origin of suture theory in a primal and uncontaminated field of view, though, as I've suggested, his claims appear rooted—and less ironically, at that—in a similar strain of medial nostalgia for a more innocent optic field before its diegetic framing. This seems especially the case in his reading of *M*, where the plot-deferring toyshop idyll of pleasurable vision, almost haptic, but not prehensile—rather than an infantilizing identification with the displayed objects of desire—is analysed as a remission from motivation itself, let alone plot. For Rancière lays no stress on the way this scene of non-aggressive (however latently acquisitive) vision makes time for narrative to catch up with the specular agent—as stressed by Lang's editing in hyperbolically optical terms. The narrative effect is to submit any unfettered looking on the murderer's part, or on ours by association, to the concerted and unnerving scopophilia of the surveillance plot.

What Rancière wants from the scene is something else entirely, something for him definitive at this stage of Lang's career. In an essay mostly on the director's later 1955 film *While the City Sleeps*, where a murderer is climactically addressed in a private domestic space by the broadcast harangue of a TV reporter, Rancière introduces *M* by contrast, hailing as it does (and presumably hailing us by way of medial if not ideological interpellation) from a different 'age' of the image, a different 'apparatus of visibility'[10]—as Rancière rather cryptically puts it. Under this earlier aegis, otherwise undefined, the murderer is granted a 'moment of grace' understood 'in the strong sense of the term', the transient chance to 'be human' just before the 'hunt' closes in.[11] For Rancière, this is not a pocket of pleasure somehow naively free from narrative, but a moment intersected by a different modality altogether. It is a case, in his vocabulary, of *aisthesis* making autonomous room for itself within *mimesis*, where Beckert is allowed not only to 'delight in a spectacle' but also, in reciprocal specularity, to be liberated—in his own on-screen right—to an untrammelled 'image' of that delight. Looking is thereby valorized for him and for us at once. The 'issue is not one of narrative suspension, but of poetics', thus drawing on, and renewing, the perennial tension in film between optics and plot. Screen event opens at this moment, on Rancière's account, to an 'empty time' not of the post-WWII time image (Deleuze's emphasis elsewhere) but to the temporal rhythms of a more capacious *flânerie*, 'the time of goals held in abeyance'.[12] In any film exploring the boundaries of its own medium, its 'fable' will report in part on the uneven distribution of *opsis* and diegesis across the weave of sequence.

But how convincing is this claim for the counterplot of image over narration in *M*, especially in this particular narrative sequence? What could it really mean for Beckert to be 'nothing more than a peaceful image seen through a shop window'?[13] An image for whom, and by what means? The question might be idle if it weren't forced so soon, in more aggressive terms, upon exactly this optic idyll by its immediately following shots. If the look of sheer looking comes across as a poetic node resistant to the chase and quarry plot, our seeing of it transpires in context with a perhaps less serene poetic licence. From what covert vantage, for instance, are we meant to see 'through the window'? And if only, of course, by the invisible affordance of a camera stationed somewhere behind the toys, as if from a shopkeeper's absent viewpoint, what does it mean to recognize the film's own 'apparatus of visibility' in this unusually salient fashion?

Then, too, why isn't the supposed *poesis* of the moment thwarted by diegesis in our sensing, as well we may, that no matter where this already and literally marked man goes (with a chalked 'M' for *Mörder* (Murderer) recently pressed, though so far unnoticed, on the back of his overcoat), or wherever he looks, he's always—even from the most unlikely perspectives—being seen? The hiatus bracketed by this scene is indeed decidedly set off—though not *from* narrative so much as *by* it, and within its vice-like grip. The subsequent reactivation of the film's plot drive—including both its agent's despair over detection and capture and our genre-ingrained wish for it, later if not sooner—transpires when *opsis* can no longer remain detached from *muthos* (Rancière's Aristotelian dichotomy), image from plot, but must be expressly run down and overcome by it, not just 'thwarted' but terminally defeated.

LOOKING ESPIED

Like the pending crux of editing it is meant to evoke, the phrasing of this subhead goes both ways. Even just before this moment of sutured surveillance, in what Rancière sees as Beckert's temporary vacation from his own drives, the specular dispensation of sheer looking is not as safely barricaded from plot—least of all from its latent aggression—as it may seem. Nor, for that matter, from plot's socio-political context, since that commercial display of the toyshop window is certainly not cleansed of a commodity fetishism over its merchandised wares within an inflationary interwar economy and its black-market underbelly. Nor even suspended from plot's psychosexual violence. However much carved out from barbarity, the moment (barely more, sustained for only just over ten seconds) is one in which Beckert's gaze is only triangulated, rather than directly engaged, with any supposed purity of spectacle—this, through his staring at the girl's separate delight so as either to feed off it or actively manipulate it, or of course both.

Further, given the encroachment of the surveillance plot, it is surely no surprise that this ocular indulgence, turning his back momentarily on a world out to get him, would leave Beckert prey to detection. This spying is effected by one of the army of beggars recruited by the underworld, who has now caught up with him in the near distance—as we soon realize—and is stationed (with others in relay) to track his next and every move. For plot as well as for character, then, the optic stasis of this lull in compulsion, unable to shake off its context in any wholesale way, marks little more than a temporary *repression* of the violent drive rather than its intermission. A drive whose traces, it is important to stress, have already returned in mechanical travesty—the puppetry of action—from within the graphics of the episode.

And so the importance, yet again, of that *Neue Sachlichkeit* motif. For framed within the reframed scenic field of the plate-glass window, as we know, and nearest us, is the unrecognized double of the psychopath—jerked into violent gestures by impulses beyond his control (to say nothing of the screen actor impersonating them only by having his image yanked into action by the projector's tug on the sprocket-holed strip). The point can perhaps best be put negatively. To say that Lang here isolates a motif from the New Objectivity (puppets, automata)—and in the process brings to it, or it to, an artificial animation—is not so far to have singled this shot out from many another before and after it in *M*. The intertext is at this point a kind of prototype. Once again Lang's film remobilizes contemporary graphic art in the cinematography of secondary (and invasive) spectation. Hence, a double intermedial analogue. To the extent that this mechanically activated clownish cut-out calls up still images of emptied humanoid forms from the period, it places these similitudes under cinematic redescription as motorized images. To the further extent (*pace* Rancière) that the two-dimensional marionette's manic parody of the madman disturbs the dilated respite of this episode, it prepares for the further dynamization—just seconds away in the same scene—of a fixed framed image (in mirror rather than window this time) by the whiplash suture of a disruptive answering shot.

With Lang once more marking narrative juncture with optic disjuncture, this pending suture takes place, in its scopic displacement, when Beckert—looking over his shoulder into the toyshop entrance mirror and seeing suddenly the effect of his branding with the letter 'M'—also sees the closing in of his unrealized surveillance. Window shopping has given way, only a few feet away, to reflective scrutiny. But not without the mechanical mannequin having already mocked the Murderer time and again when its knees are bent by mechanical repetition into the flanking angles of an embodied mimic M. After such a compromised momentary spell before the transparent plane of fantasy, what follows is the opacity of self-recognition under almost immediate external siege. This is to say that the letter M, one of the few alphabetic characters identical with its own mirror reversal, accompanies a self-image coming to Beckert now from outside himself (but only at the near distance of the mirror at first, **Fig. 16.3**)—as if in the negative imprint of a

Figure 16.3. Still from *M*, directed by Fritz Lang (1931).

photograph: just that mode of visual identification which the police have never had in his elusive case.

Almost in that same instant, however, Beckert not only sees himself as marked man, as pariah, but sees himself *seen* as such by an illicitly deputized vigilance at one remove from his own doubled image. For over this same shoulder, along a slightly raised line of sight, Beckert stares into and through the camera into our own (soon replaced) gaze. A line of characteristically trenchant hyperbole from Roland Barthes comes to mind: 'If a single gaze from the screen came to rest on me, the whole film would be lost.'[14] When Barthes (in the epigraph) thinks to distinguish the legal look into the photographic camera from its transgressive status in the moving-image system of cinema, he means that the film would be "lost" if the "suture" were not finessed at a somewhat oblique angle. Lost because so directly found out. Lang's is the aggressive exception that secures the norm—so aggressive, in fact, that the discourse on suture singles out his practice (without mentioning *M* or this particular shot exchange) as a case of 'the deliberate terrorist intentions' on call in the shot/countershot design.[15] We are not so much hailed by the direct gaze as nailed by it.

Sutured in as the 'absent ones' of a yet undisclosed reverse shot, we return the horror of Beckert's recoil by disappearing into his glimpse of the underworld spy ducking behind a truck. Such is the anchoring look of a reseamed fissure performed by a looking (on the spy's part) there for only a split second longer than our look, in instantaneous erasure, had seemed to be. Thus has this pivotal moment in the chase plot pivoted in turn around its own 180-degree sight line, splicing in our avid narrative curiosity as one kind of assault on Beckert's already sundered specular autonomy before displacing us by another—and this time diegetic—threat. The displacement is never complete, however. As if pointedly to despoil in ironic retrospect the apparently benign context of that earlier shopfront looking, spectator and spy now pose (and, in cinematographic terms, posit) an equivalent danger to Beckert as character: the ratified paranoia of being seen.

Nor is the fact of our seeing, in turn, free of a lurking perturbation. An otherwise compromising chain of associations, once appeasingly delinked, would go like this. Concerning Beckert's world, this isn't life, isn't even theatre; it's film. We're not spies, not even ordinary live spectators; we're viewers. This isn't our surveillance; it's our strictly narrative apprehension of the prerecorded scene. But in these subliminal disclaimers, we would, according to the ideological critique implicit in suture theory, be protesting too much, denying in this case the very close thematic connection between our mass reaction to the child killer on screen and the modes of detection employed, within the plot, against the lone sociopath, both by bureaucracy and by the criminal mob alike. Imbricated in the eyeline stare, we are implicated perforce in its manhunt politics, whose juridical and dramaturgical satisfactions are not as easy to keep separate as a viewer might want to assume. With Beckert now on one side of a framing transparent plane where he doesn't notice us, now at the far focal point of a framed mirror image in which he momentarily (fantasmatically) does, this narratographic slippage allows no clean distinction at the level of plot between cinematic visibility and narrative's depicted invigilation. Precisely because of what Rancière notices but deflects by celebration at the opening of this episode—call it *opsis* isolated in crisis rather than arrived to alleviate it—all imaging in this sequence feels not just contrived but part of an unsettling media connivance.

With the result that invisibility emerges for the protagonist at a new premium. After hiding out over the course of the prolonged coming scene of illegal search and seizure in the urban office building, hounded down by the gang, caged like a trapped animal in an attic cubicle scanned by a torch as if it were the forensic equivalent of a projector's beam, Beckert is finally carried off in a body bag—his capital punishment already, by association, a foregone conclusion. Yet he is still to be exposed again to the melodramatic frame-up of mass derision in his underworld (and underground) show trial. Here is where the eventually convergent lines of parallel montage—Beckert on the sexual hunt and then the run, the cops in full dragnet mode, the mob closing in—must necessarily come to a head, according to Deleuze (with *M* his detailed test case), in the closural energies of a showdown.[16] This is the 'duel' that, borrowed with other genre overtones, is the required resolution of all pre-war films of the movement image, where parallel timelines (not released to the pure cerebration of the time image) must be roped in and tethered together by plot. This is the case even in a threefold montage like that in *M*, where Deleuze's SAS´ formula (Situation transformed by Action into new Situation) finds police pitted against mob even while each force is directed as well against Beckert.

But in *M* the final duel is in a sense abrogated, despite Deleuze's claim, when its inevitable loser is dispatched from the screen frame at the moment of his capture. The true showdown is not shown. Though Deleuze never articulates a revived formula for the modernist time image, we can nevertheless see a version of its reflexive modernism in the curtailed (and optically re-encompassed) movement image of *M*. Given the supervening role of image over action, image whether actual or virtual, in the post-WWII cinema of mentalized temporality, Deleuze notes (one of his central determinants) the conversion of narrative agents to 'spectators' in and on their own life. With Lang as pre-war benchmark, this later development might well be seen as the internalization of surveillance in the form of hermetic vigil. In any case, no clear distinction between duel and self-enclosed ocular circuit can be maintained in Lang when the revised situation (S' of the former paradigm) is displaced off-site and out of view. Here in Lang's pre-war experiment, and as inflected by his inter-art Weimar allusions, is a case of action—in and beyond the parameters of a surveillance plot—rendered inseparable from its prosecution as framed views. This is an action whose remorseless narrative drive is put at last into remission not by *opsis* but by a total release from it. What 'remains to be seen' is how completely this suspended sighting brought about by closure has been prepared for by an explicit escalation of forensic picturing.

STOP-ACTION IMPACT: INTERTEXT AS SUBTEXT

Well before that dispersion of the final duel, the mob has cornered Beckert not in a defunct industrial setting but in that bastion of modern capitalism, the office building, the space of public exchange and its commercial archives—on whose precincts these two manners of criminal, the thief and the child murderer, are equal trespassers. And to whose settings the photography of the period has been repeatedly drawn. Preoccupied not just with factory locales (exterior and interior)— with, that is, the dynamos and turbine halls that connect with the *mise en scène* of films from Lang's own *Metropolis* (1926) to Charlie Chaplin's *Modern Times* (1936)—the period's photography was as much concerned with industrial effects as with causes. Especially in the prolific work from the 1920s of Walter A. Peterhans, we see numerous imprint reproductions of (other) industrial copies, as for instance the frequent still lifes of mass-produced glassware, aluminium pots, hand tools, shoe trees, and the like.

At the same time, the New Sobriety gravitates as well to depopulated bureaucratic spaces in the new *moderne* mode of architectural symmetry, explicitly Bauhaus and otherwise, as for instance in Hans Finsler's *Central Corridor*— clean-edged and scrubbed impersonal spaces quite the opposite of another impinging ingredient of Lang's image repertoire (even when kept wholly off frame): the spate of (post-war) paintings and drawings showing the lacerated female victims of 'sexmurder'. The compensatory zone of the emptied, disinfected workplace (rather than bloodied bed) is the kind of orderly image evoked in *M* at a transitional moment of official inscription. This passing two-word lettering represents an aspect of urban signage beyond the wall of wanted posters and assorted advertising pillars featured in earlier scenes (and also common to *Neue Sachlichkeit* painting as well as photography, as in Georg Scholz's 1926 oil work, *Self Portrait in Front of an Advertising Column.* This later moment is one in which narrative lingers over an institutional address, a quasi-legal imperative, that puts the name Lang back into the command to 'Drive Slowly' (*Langsam Fahren*) as it appears prominently over the symmetrically framed and sleekly gated office garage to which the mob has tracked Beckert. This inscription might seem to generate an immediate if oblique fallout for the impetus of the cinematic strip itself. For the whole prolonged sequence to come puts the brakes on full animation and—after Beckert has been hounded down and found, bagged like animal prey, and hauled away—concludes with various shots of the aftermath like a litany of damage and casualties in war reportage.

Here begins a three-stage pattern of photogrammatic disclosure that taps the narrative's deepest sense, at exactly the building climax of its surveillance and manhunt plot, of its own narrative function as discretely articulated filmic nexus. In this first unexpectedly piecemeal sequence, after five quick-cut still images in a row (among them, the inhabited shots of dead or unconscious bodies involving apparent freeze-frames), we catch the slightest hint of motion in a lock still swinging in the immediate wake of forced entry and evacuation; and then, finally, a presumed still shot gradually animated by the beam not of a projector but of a torch as one abandoned criminal is brought literally to the surface of his underworld. Moreover, as if to remind us of the quasi-forensic images that have built up in this way towards the discovered thug's retrieval and arrest, when he arrives at the police station he himself is transfixed by the office directory, including major billing for the in-house police photographer.

Just before (stage two of the terraced photogrammatic parable), Inspector Lohmann has been handed a 'protocol'. It is a typed report on the attack whose pages are presided over in superimposition—in a trumping of police lab by film lab—by the precinematic spooling of a ticker tape that has either fed the information to them or will soon disseminate it further. These are pages he turns over as if they were private intertitles for a silent film being threaded through in his mind— or indeed an optical allusion to the protocinematic flick book of photo stills turned into a miniature thumbed movie and evoked here as such by the ongoing series of lap dissolves. Call it one version of modernist stream of consciousness, cinema-style. What happens is that we too leaf again through the images we've just seen, and then some, seventeen fixed frames in all, several in their architectural rigidity and balance calling up a further aura of the *Neue Sachlichkeit* manner. And all of them fused this time by the dovetailed bridgework of lap dissolve. This amounts to a page-like overfolding or shuffling of cinematic planes rather than the jump cuts of the previous and in some cases identical series, which the first time through was presented as sheer narration without the diegetic embedding of a read text and the associative links presumed by the investigative mind in perusing it.

I say mind deliberately. According to Deleuze, in his unacknowledged updating of Hugo Münsterberg's mentalist thesis about cinema, the point-cut and the relinkage, as Deleuze calls them—or, in other words, the overt edit and the marked bridge—when detached from the rational montage of a sheer sensorimotor continuum, are, along with the wholly blank screen, the three indices of cinema as thought.[17] Together here, cuts and ligatures collaborate in the noetic image, or what Deleuze calls the noosign, the sign in this case of a character's own mental imaging. My added point is that these spliced single frames, many of them freeze-frames, and borrowing all the more in this way as well from the analytic stasis and symmetry of the *Neue Sachlichkeit*, can best be said, in the Deleuzian sense, to take thought only by revealing at the same time the unthought of cinema so wholly elided in Deleuze's phenomenology: namely, the single frame in fragmentary or blurred transition, either one.

This run of images in *M* gives thought, therefore, not to the sensorimotor image, yet not just to the association of ideas either, but to the motor of all images in the rotated spool. Further, to single out the image in the eye of police inspection in this case is to link the photoframe, however decoupled from its typical, split-second sequence, to the spectatorial logic of evidentiary data rather than pure imaging— to detection, to spying, to the prying rather than privatized eye, to systems of image management and ocular control, in other words to a society of surveillance in a culture of the instrumentalized rather than the disinterested view; or, in one other word, to modernity. Narrative film seems acknowledging here, yet again, its descent from the lost utopia of unframed visibility under the theory of suture— before either the embodied or the openly equipmental look.

But back to the inspector's mental inspection of his teletext. Despite all the bodies discovered there by typescript, and envisioned as one reads—their virtual images soon to be accompanied (we can only assume) by forensic photos eventually incorporated into the report—it is only the missing body of Beckert that concerns

Inspector Lohmann. And when, pursuing his whereabouts, he moves to interrogate that one apprehended mobster hauled up to justice, the same subliminal mode of fixed-frame, quasi-photographic illustration (stage three in this sequence of fore-grounded mediation) accompanies the man's coerced confession of Beckert's where-abouts. In his immediately visualized mention of the old brewery that went 'belly-up' in the depression, it is as if the photo inserts representing what he describes serve so fully to visualize the site disclosed by the criminal's voice-over that they inherit and eclipse its authority by uncurtaining the cinematic scene itself.[18]

With no typescript intervening this time in the crook's oral admission, what we get is a sliding transition from an overvoiced subjective insert to an actual estab-lishing shot, the snitch's vocal signifiers replaced in process by photographic signi-fieds. This is an optical free indirect discourse representing not just what's in the speaker's own mind's eye, or what is transferred from it through the hideout's rec-ognition by Lohmann, but what is realized for us as well in transition from the photofixity of these manifestations to a fixed-frame, quasi-photographic shot, more in the New Objectivist manner of architectonic minimalism. It is a shot (of a spare stairway and railing) that opens upon the next and nearly final scene (when Beckert is dragged down it). But we arrive at this symbolic underground set for the underworld inquisition only after traversing those four entirely depopulated shots that seem operating as stand-ins for the blasted landmarks of national defeat.

If the mental slideshow (and photogrammatic subtext) of that decimated commercial space can't help but call up wartime photographs of bombed-out urban sites, this is the same wreckage and debris that have elsewhere, and program-matically, been won back for rationalized order by the sterile (because deliberately antiseptic and purified) forms of the New Objectivity. Here, too, is a sequence by which the movement image is so arrested at its source that it can seem to return us, by way of Walter Benjamin's famous remark, to Eugène Atget's unpeopled photo-graphs of urban settings as if they were evacuated crime scenes: in this case, not just via desertion and forensic revisitation but by way of a strategic cover, in their neglect and obscurity, for the scapegoating violence of a underworld mob jury.[19] This is a scapegoating that is later alleviated only by the victim's disappearance altogether from the frame—before his subsequent official sentencing (quickly cut away from) by a now legal tribunal. This second and equally abrogated judgment is a coda dispatched in a fixed shot whose architectural decor on the wall behind the judges recalls in the outlined scale of its moulding a screen's blank rectangle—an empty sector of the overall image plane sparing us this time, like the shot as a whole, any last frame-up of the narrative's long-surveilled murderer. This release from view comes, however, only after Beckert has been forced in the previous trial scene, in a jolting run of sutured shots across a focus-pulled display of reframed photographs, to confront serial photographic images of his serial victims (**Fig. 16.4**).

But well before and altogether aside from such individual photoprints in motion within the diegesis, what I've been suggesting, because I think Lang's editing tech-nique suggests it, is that the ongoing stream of intertexts from the New Objectivists, channelled in turn by the narrative flow, serves in its turn to objectify something about cinema that otherwise goes unseen but not unknown by early audiences.

Figure 16.4. Still from *M*, directed by Fritz Lang (1931).

This is its immediate generation from, as well as its genealogical relation to, the fixed framed photographic imprint. The intertextual oscillation becomes in this way an infratextual resonance, a kind of hypomediation, not observable but nonetheless operative from frame to frame, subliminal but felt—even when there are no inset images, though there sometimes are, to set back and so show forth, by association, this undertextual basis in the fixed trace of the racing frame line.

PANOPSIS AND PLOT

And all of this comes bearing down in Lang's conclusion, mine too, on the climactic shot where, by the symbolic long arm of the law—though never once, if I may put it this way, *seen* by the police—the outcast is finally and mercifully cast out from our own view. Part of what is so moving, if you will, about Lang's modernism, at least so inquisitively kinetic, is that more is apprehended by narrative process than just this criminal deviant in a dragnet plot. The surveillance story aside, we see here, mission accomplished, the equivocated optics of cinema's very prosecution in the frame advance of its own narrative frame-ups. Now you see it; now you don't. The 'duel' goes so wholly unresolved that Lohmann never even fires off so much as a look at his captive. In this way, almost paradoxically, the case study of a modern surveillance network, in its own partial cinematic coalition of image and sound, has taken the pinioned criminal off-camera just before the case can officially be brought.

But that's just a little too fast—noticeably on the film's part, as well as on the part of analysis. Apprehended and quarantined in that last close-up—his image isolated so as to be spared either two-shot or suture, yet as if imprisoned by framing alone—Beckert, in the last we see of him, is held before us in a privileged view, unshared by the lateral encroachment of the law. But that privilege hardly spares him, or us, from something deep in the mechanics of cinema into which few films before (or even after) *M* have driven so consistent a wedge. Call it the social norms of scopophilia, in and beyond the cinema. One thing this last shot may bring to mind, before cutting to Beckert's absence from the day and place of judgment, is Michel Foucault's insistence that the modern state, in its tacit parameters as a police state, was initially bolstered by the removal of corporal punishment from the public sphere, from mass view.[20] Taking hangings and beheadings off the communal stage helped to secure a panoptic regime in which a civilian 'vision' internalizes the edicts and interdicts of the law without having the satisfaction of the scapegoat through which to vent an anxious sense of rule and its cruelties. That anxiety becomes instead muted but pervasive under, again, the long arm of the law and its unseen impersonal gaze (Lang's tandem tropes). Not necessarily via stock or scaffold, but in many other equally implacable ways, movies in a sense return a communal (but not expressly legislated) violence to public view, even while generalizing the spectatorial bloodlust they solicit into a more neutralized scopic pleasure not in itself party to the violence under depiction, which is to say vicarious without being sacrificial. But potentially uncomfortable, nonetheless, in its curiosities, its voyeuristic thrills.

The near miss of physical violence at the end of *M* offers in effect the confirmation of its specular aggression. Though the verdict too goes off-screen and unread, leaving us only the mourning mothers in their call for further public vigilance—for more *over-sight*, as it were—there seems little doubt that violent retribution is to be meted out to Beckert, given the place of capital punishment in German criminal law of the period. Death literally goes without saying, let alone showing, wholly off-stage, ob-scene. But this is the least of it. Even as a sacrifice to a communal order that may well have betrayed him into violence in the first place (as trench victim), the issue is not so much that Beckert dies for our sins, or, with more historical specificity, for the sins of a war-ravaged generation. It is how we are 'spared' that death that interests Lang. His murdering protagonist would no doubt have been summarily executed by edict of the underworld court, but the law arrives just in time, all but invisible at point of capture, merely impinging on the culprit's cornered closeup. Here and at every earlier point of the film, Lang is at greater pains to manage how his audience responds to the images of detection than to the spectacle of violence, to the epistemological burdens of narrative than to the psychology of closure and extermination.

In *M*, taking the marked man at last out-of-frame has its symmetrical ironies. Leaving its own frame forever, too, Elsie's balloon, like Elsie, is there one moment, gone the next. So, comparably, punitively, with Beckert. In between, and with that one exception Rancière is so right to notice if wrong to isolate as the remedial counterpoint to plot, few characters have ever been more excruciated than Beckert by their time *in* frame, on camera, under surveillance, in view. We don't just look on at the pain and panic. With that one signal exception that Rancière might have gone on to notice as so drastically disbanded later in the same scene, our being invisibly sutured in as perceptual centre of Beckert's track-down, whatever we feel about it or him, stations our participation itself as a recurrent function of the plot, there at the outer envelope of its visible—and visual—transactions. And there, just there, is where the arrested visuals of those multiplying still images at the plot's forensic climax, locked down in their anti-cinematic stasis, go out of their way to break into the movement-image itself and derail its normal storytelling. Insisted upon for once, rather than taken invisibly for granted, is film's role, its rolling past, as a chain of studied images whose scrutiny, as graphic frames and as plot increments at once, entrains the real visual narrative beneath its manhunt scenario.

At this level, one story Lang's montage has had to tell is that of frame-advance modernism within a particular vision (and one uses the term vision advisedly) of modern state bureaucracy and its relentless instinct for the restraint of transgression—including, in an unusually prominent part of the story, those modernist visual forms from other media that have elsewhere worked to feature such institutional anonymities or satirize their sterility. In *M*, filmic process thus makes its precarious way within an expanded field not just of other optic media but of other scopic motives. In Lang's experiment, as we've seen, cinema moves one kind of picture while calling up the contravening fixity of other kinds of picturing, drawn, painted, or photographic. By such optical *allusion*, the filmic stream's illusory capture of motion is undermined by an insistence on its machinic reproduction of that movement instead. So far, a formalist disclosure. But so far from *merely* formalist is the cumulative effect of this in Lang's film that the graphic arts' evoked counterpoint to screen action serves to delimit precisely the Weimar social backdrop to that surveillance regime upon which the mounting inferences of arrested continuity, together with invasive supervision, finally converge: the scene itself as image file, all event evidentiary. By intertext as well as infratext, then, *M* is a film about the participation of its own surveillance ethos in the wider spectrum of modernist visual culture, including that culture's imperatives, its addictions, its queasy depletions. In one of its farthest reaching cognates, M stands not for Murderer, Marked Man, Manhunt, or even Montage, but rather for Modern itself under the sign of the seen.

NOTES

1. Friedrich Kittler, *Optical Media*, translated by Anthony Enns (Cambridge: Polity Press, 2010), where film as 'hybrid medium' operates only as it 'combines analogue or continuous single frames with a discontinuous or discrete image sequence', p. 162.
2. See Mary Ann Doane, *The Emergence of Cinematic Time: Modernity, Contingency, the Archive* (Cambridge, MA: Harvard University Press, 2002), pp. 33–68.

3. Though the approach of this essay, with its emphasis on single-frame forensics in rela-tion to the narrative frame line and its invasive optics, operates at a different scale from the sustained overview of Tom Gunning's *The Films of Fritz Lang: Allegories of Vision and Modernity* (London: British Film Institute, 2000), his extensively indexed remarks on 'surveillance' might well help his reader to assemble an entire stand-alone mono-graph on audiovisual surveillance as the narrative obsession (as well as historical des-tiny) of Lang's very medium, a book-within-the book that would lay its own apt claim to the subtitle of the whole.

4. Jacques Rancière, *Film Fables* (Oxford: Berg, 2006), pp. 1–19.

5. For the most widely available survey of this movement, see Sergiusz Michalski, *New Objectivity: Painting, Graphic Art and Photography in Weimar Germany 1919–1933* (Cologne: Benedikt Taschen, 1994); the images discussed in this essay have all, some quite recently, become available online.

6. Jean-Pierre Oudart, 'Cinema and Suture,' http://www.lacan.com/symptom8_articles/oudart8.html accessed 6 Feb. 2016. This text was published in French in *Cahiers du Cinéma* 211 and 212 (April and May 1969), its English version (translated by Kari Hanet) appearing almost a decade later in *Screen* 18 (Winter 1978).

7. This is the method defined in contrast with a medium-blind narratology both in my study *Framed Time: Toward a Postfilmic Cinema* (Chicago: University of Chicago Press, 2006) and, in respect to a different time-based (syntactic) medium, in *Novel Violence: A Narratography of Victorian Fiction* (Chicago: University of Chicago Press, 2009).

8. See *M*'s place in this post-WWI psychosocial paradigm, amid a fuller discussion of Lang, in Anton Kaes, *Shell Shock Cinema: Weimar Culture and the Wounds of War* (Princeton, NJ: Princeton University Press, 2009).

9. David Trotter, *Cinema and Modernism* (Oxford: Blackwell, 2007), pp. 4–13, where he distinguishes his approach from my own in *Between Film and Screen*, pp. 4–8.

10. Rancière, *Film Fables*, p. 48.

11. Rancière, *Film Fables*, p. 49.

12. Rancière, *Film Fables*, pp. 49–50.

13. Rancière, *Film Fables*, p. 49.

14. Roland Barthes, in the posthumously published essay 'Right in the Eyes,' *The Responsibility of Form: Critical Essays on Music, Art, and Representation*, trans. Richard Howard (New York: Hill and Wang, 1977), p. 242, where the same passage expands on this prohibition of the two-way gaze, as distinct from the legal 'address' of pho-tography: 'I am not far from considering this ban as the cinema's distinctive feature.' We may therefore see this protocol of the film camera warped and 'disfeatured' by the wrenching suture of *M*.

15. In Oudart's essay, Lang is so much the touchstone of suture's fullest and most aggres-sive dramatic force, including its scophophilic charge, that the director gets the last word in Oudart's closing sentence: 'The discovery that the cinema, in speaking itself, speaks of eroticism, and is the privileged space where eroticism can always be signified, should probably be credited to Lang; and although all the consequences are far from being drawn yet, this discovery engages the whole cinema' (n.p.).

16. Gilles Deleuze, *Cinema 1: The Movement Image*, translated by Hugh Tomlinson and Barbara Habberjam (Minneapolis, MN: University of Minnesota Press, 1986), pp. 155–6.

17. Together with the raw interruption of movement, it is thus 'the point–cut, relinkage and the black or white screen' that, comprising the three purely 'cerebral components' of cinema, form together a whole 'noosphere'. See Deleuze, *Cinema 2—The Time*

Image, translated by Hugh Tomlinson and Barbara Habberjam (Minneapolis, MN: University of Minnesota Press, 1989), p. 215.

18. This is one more example that Michel Chion, in *Film, A Sound Art*, translated by Claudia Gorbman (New York: Columbia University Press, 2009), might have tuned his ears to in discussing certain earlier moments in *M* when a sound bridge precipitates—by voice-over—a distant visualization so autonomous that 'the film will then "forget to close the quotation marks"' (pp. 70–1).

19. Walter Benjamin, 'The Work of Art in the Age of Mechanical Reproduction', where he paraphrases a going line on Atget's deserted streets: 'It has quite justly been said of him that he photographed them like scenes of crime' (see http://www.marxists.org/ reference/subject/philosophy/works/ge/benjamin.htm).

20. See Michel Foucault, *Discipline and Punish: The Birth of the Prison*, translated by Alan Sheridan (New York: Pantheon, 1978).

17

Perpetual Motion
Speed, Spectacle, and Cycle Racing

Deborah Longworth

'Bicycles and motorcycles are divine,' Marinetti declared in 'The New Ethical Religion of Speed' (1916).[1] Three years earlier he had included the bicycle as one of the new forms of technology (along with the telegraph, the telephone, the gramophone, the train, the motorcycle, the automobile, the ocean liner, the airship, the aeroplane, and the cinema) that were shaping the modern sensibility.[2] Yet this was a very different viewpoint from that expressed in 'The Founding and Manifesto of Futurism' in 1909, in the opening paragraphs of which he famously harangues a pair of cyclists who cause him to overturn his car and end up in a ditch. 'We affirm that the world's magnificence has been enriched by a new beauty: the beauty of speed,' Marinetti declaims in the Manifesto, but here the car, the locomotive, the steamer, and the aeroplane are eulogized as the modern machines par excellence, while the bicycle is set apart as a distinctly passé mode of transport.[3] Far from examples of the divinity of pure speed as the catalyst of Futurist creativity, the cyclists in the founding manifesto waver and dither along the road, 'wobbling like two equally convincing but nevertheless contradictory arguments', shaking their fists at the car speeding towards them. They appear to be touring cyclists, unsure of their skill, out for a day's leisure ride; the sort common to nineteenth-century images of cycling as a healthy recreational pastime. That cycling had experienced such a boom growth across Britain, Europe, and the United States in the 1890s, but by the 1910s had been superseded by the automobile as the preferable mode of transport, indeed made it a particularly resonant example of the belle époque that Marinetti was so loudly opposing in the founding manifesto.

What, then, brought about the sudden shift in Marinetti's attitude towards the bicycle, so that instead of an outmoded cultural icon of the later nineteenth century, it became one of the key metaphors for the Futurist religion of speed? And in what ways does a recovery of the history of cycle sport help us to understand the heavily masculine rhetoric of machine-like speed and endurance in the cultural iconography of the bicycle more broadly in early twentieth-century literary and visual representation? Marinetti's change of mind may have had something to do with the fact that several influential figures of the European avant-garde were as fanatical about racing bicycles as he was about roaring motor cars. In Paris in the early 1900s he met Alfred Jarry, whose fantastical tale of a ten-thousand-mile race between a train and a five-man tandem bicycle in *The Supermale* (1902), collapsed the division between man and machine. A novella about exceptional bodily endurance, *The Supermale* was an articulation of Jarry's 'pataphysics', but the set piece of the bicycle race in chapter five also owed much to the commercial promotion and massive public popularity of cycle speed records from the mid-1890s, as well as Jarry's own practice of racing the train between Paris and Corbeil on his elite Clément Luxe racing bicycle.[4] In the short story 'The Crucifixion Considered as a Bicycle Race' ('La Passion considérée comme course de côte'), Jarry presented a mocking parody of a rapidly burgeoning and sensationalist sporting press, as Jesus, a sprint racer on the difficult Golgotha course, punctures on a crown of thorns after an early lead and is forced to continue the race carrying his wood-framed machine on his back.[5] Jarry's bicycle obsession was characteristically idiosyncratic, but his understanding of the physics and aesthetics of cycling, as well as his knowledge of the contemporary scene of cycle sport, is obvious in both works.

Marinetti's debt to Jarry's absurdist avant-gardism is well-recognized, and his prose poem about a fantastical automobile race in which the drivers ultimately will their vehicles to flight into the sky, 'Death Holds the Steering Wheel' ('La Mort tient le volant', 1908), undoubtedly echoes the rhetoric of machine-like overcoming that also characterizes the ten-thousand-mile race in *The Supermale*, if without Jarry's qualifying mockery.[6] In this piece, however, it is still the automobile and the aeroplane that Marinetti favours as the machines by which man can realize the potential power of his will and overcome the normal limits of space and time. What perhaps contributed most to his sudden embrace of the bicycle sometime between 1909 and 1913 was the influence of Umberto Boccioni, whom he met in early 1910 and whose theories of 'plastic' or geometrical dynamism in art would give pictorial shape to Futurist axioms about speed as the defining quality of twentieth-century modernity. Boccioni's aim was to overcome the stasis of the captured image of a moving object, and instead to convey the continuous movement or dynamism of an object not so much against as in synthesis with the relative forces of its surroundings, as he outlined in the 'Futurist Painting: Technical Manifesto' (1910): 'The gesture which we would reproduce on canvas shall no longer be a fixed *moment* in universal dynamism. It shall simply be the *dynamic sensation* itself....To paint a human figure you must not paint it; you must render the whole of its surrounding atmosphere.'[7] Boccioni's *Dynamism of a Cyclist* (1913), an image of a competitive racer (he wears the competitor number 15 on his back), is one of a series of studies of movement that gave form to the ideas put forward in his lecture 'Futurist Painting', delivered at the Circolo Artistico in Rome in May 1911 (see **Fig. 17.1**). Modern life, Boccioni had argued, was no longer to be perceived in terms of the traditional representational models of panorama or perspective, both of which depended on assumptions of distance or depth that no longer applied in the new technological, quantum world of the twentieth century. Speed and movement were the sensations by which modern life was experienced, and that modern art was challenged with conveying. The 'pictorial dynamism' that Boccioni advocated would capture not merely movement but also the

Figure 17.1. Umberto Boccioni, *Dynamism of a Cyclist* (Dinamismo di un ciclista) (1913).

will to speed and latent energy of an object, its 'relative' but also 'absolute' motion. The example he gave for velocity as rendered by Futurism, was a racing cyclist:

> [I]n painting, for example, a man speeding along on a bicycle we shall try to reproduce the instinct for speed that determines the action, not the visible forward motion of the cyclist. It doesn't matter to us that the cyclist's head might touch the edge of the wheel or his body stretch out behind losing itself in vibrations to infinity with an obvious deception of sight, since it is the sensation of the race, not the cyclist that we wish to depict.[8]

As can be seen from the numerous preparatory sketches for the 1913 painting, however, it took some time to develop the pictorial representation of a man riding a bicycle at speed into a Futurist evocation of the sensory experience of the race. As Bernard Vere has demonstrated, moreover, Boccioni was not alone in his choice of the racing cyclist for an exploration of the formal possibilities of portraying velocity in art, and *Dynamism of a Cyclist* was in fact the latest in a series of avant-garde paintings of the competitive cyclist produced in or around 1911–13.[9] In Lyonel Feininger's *The Bicycle Race* (1912), the movement of the five competitors is conveyed by the way in which the lead rider's wheel pushes beyond the limits of the frame, and their speed by the angular elongation of their form, while *At the Cycle-Race Track* (1912) and *Racing Cyclist* (1912), by the cubist Jean Metzinger, employ techniques of fragmentation and kaleidoscopic reassemblage to represent movement but also capture the commercial interpenetration of sport, spectacle, the mass media, and advertising that was integral to the identity of professional cycle racing. Vere carefully establishes the specific settings and social, and national and artistic contexts of these works, noting that it is likely that Boccioni was aware of both Feininger and Metzinger's paintings, and suggesting that *Dynamism of a Cyclist* was indeed in part a Futurist reply to the Cubist depiction of speed, masculinity and popular sporting culture in *At the Cycle-Race Track*.

Common to all of Boccioni's preparatory pieces for *Dynamism of a Cyclist*, as well as the final image, is the evocation of extreme speed, the inward curve of the front wheel, the centripetal lean of the cyclist, and his low stance over his machine, all of which would suggest that the setting is a sprint on either an indoor or outdoor velodrome. If so the perspective is that from the track centre, where the spectator would experience the vortex of speed as created by the riders' 360-degree revolutions, and thus be incorporated into the sensation of the race in a literal translation of the absolute motion Boccioni was attempting to define. The final painting also seems to include spectators on the other side of the cyclist, their faces suggested in the yellow area to the left of the picture, on either side of the curving cerise line that possibly indicates a barrier or tiered seating around the bend. In several of the sketches, Boccioni uses sweeping pen strokes around the wheels, handlebars, and across the legs and hunched back of the cyclist, to convey the impression of speed against the perpendicular sweeping lines of the curving track. In another sketch the elongation and repetition of wheels and limbs suggest movement through space. Neither technique, however, conveys quite the interrelation of bicycle, rider, track, and air resistance achieved by the cones and waves of glinting colour that make up the final canvas. Yet despite the claims of his earlier statement on Futurist painting of the racing cyclist, Boccioni does not entirely subordinate the individuality of the rider to the sensation of the race, and indeed the red, white, and blue of his jersey, along with the number 15 on his back, tempt efforts at identification (see **Fig. 17.2**).[10] It is possible that Boccioni, noting the commercial nature of cycling registered in Metzinger's image, was willing to hint at the celebrity culture that was already a prominent feature of the modernity of early twentieth-century cycle sport, while still retaining the formal interpenetration of 'lines of force' to convey the absolute motion contained in the relationship of cyclist, race, and spectators.

Given that the bicycle seems to have entered Marinetti's Futurist vocabulary at some point between the publication of the founding Manifesto in 1909 and the 'Words in Freedom' manifesto of 1913, it seems plausible to suggest that he was influenced at least in part by Boccioni's association of the racing cyclist and Futurist representations of dynamism from at least 1911. It would certainly seem to be the racing cyclist, rather than the pair of touring cyclists from the founding manifesto, that Marinetti has in mind when he identifies the bicycle as one of the technologies to be reshaping the modern psyche. For when he goes on to list the significant characteristics of this reshaping, alongside a horror of slowness and love of speed, he also includes, 'A horror of the quiet life, love of danger, and identification with everyday heroism', 'Man greatly extended by machines', and 'Sport pursued with passion, art and idealism. The concept and love of achieving "records"'.[11] Moreover, many of the axioms of 'The Ethical Religion of Speed' are suggestive of bicycle racing rather than the automobile or the aeroplane, as I hope to show. That the context for these ideas lies in no

Figure 17.2. François Faber, 1913.

small part within the scene of professional cycle racing has gone largely unnoticed. With the exception of Vere, cultural historians have typically expressed surprise at early twentieth-century avant-garde fascination with the bicycle, an object that has more frequently been explored by literary and art history scholars as a social phenomenon of the late nineteenth century, associated with images of 'New Women' in radical dress.[12] Yet this is to overlook the fact that all of the works noted above, as most of their titles indicate, focus on the phenomenon of the *racing* cyclist, and to fail to recognize the extraordinary prominence, and commercial and political significance, of the sport and spectacle of professional cycle racing and speed records within the mass culture of Europe and the US from the 1890s up until at least the 1940s. If, by the

1910s, the bicycle had been superseded by the automobile as a means of functional travel, it had taken on a new and widespread significance as a racing machine. When ridden fast, particularly in the context of competition, it could still outstrip the average car in speed. A strong racing cyclist could be expected to achieve around 35 mph in a sprint, and almost double that in a 'paced' sprint behind a tandem (triplets and quints were also common) or powered vehicle. The fastest finisher of the 'first' motor race, Paris–Bordeaux–Paris in 1895, averaged 15 mph. Four years later in 1899, the American Charles Murphy set a cycle speed record of a mile in 57.8 seconds, reaching 62 mph riding in the slipstream of a train on wooden cycle boards laid between the railway tracks (see **Fig. 17.3**). Set against the top speed of Ford's first mass-produced Model T motor car engine in 1909 of 40–5 mph, and that of the Blériot XI used by Louis Blériot in July 1909 to make the first flight across the English Channel, at 47 mph, the racing cyclist possessed a highly competitive human engine. Moreover, the cyclist arguably experienced a more immediate and active sensation of physical exertion and dynamism than the driver of the automobile, generating his speed himself, and more exposed to the forces of resistance that play on the moving object. Powering his machine by muscular force against the pedals, and battling air resistance, the clock, the terrain, the fatigue of muscles, and the pain of limbs, the racing cyclist offered a focal example of Futurist ideals of the mechanical extension of human effort and the articulation of vital masculine energy.

Figure 17.3. Charles Murphy, 1899.

It is worth pausing at this point, to briefly return to a tongue-in-cheek portrayal of the late nineteenth-century popularity of the bicycle that nevertheless points tellingly towards the speed culture of the early twentieth century, H. G. Wells' novel *Wheels of Chance* (1896). Wells, a staunch advocate of the bicycle, imagined a utopia in which cycle tracks for daily travel would be laid alongside major roads, as well as meandering through the countryside for more recreational riding. *Wheels of Chance*, subtitled *A Holiday Adventure*, was written at the height of the bicycle craze, when the 'safety bicycle', with its chain drive and same-size smaller wheels, had replaced the high-wheeled penny-farthing. The invention of the pneumatic tyre in 1888 had made for a smoother and less bone-shaking ride, and a dramatic fall in cost was making the bicycle accessible to a mass market. The protagonist, the suggestively named Hoopdriver, is the kind of rider that Marinetti swerves to avoid, a *very* wobbly novice cyclist who devotes his annual ten-day holiday from the drapery shop in which he works to a cycling tour of the English south coast. He embarks upon his adventure with a mixture of fear and enthusiasm but only a little skill. 'There is only one phrase to describe his course at this stage', writes Wells, 'and that is – voluptuous curves. He did not ride fast, he did not ride straight, an exacting critic might say he did not ride well—but he rode generously, opulently, using the whole road and even nibbling at the footpath.'[13] Wells nevertheless associates even Hoopdriver's timid recreational riding (he resolves to dismount whenever he sees a vehicle coming the other way) with an articulation of masculinity, albeit mockingly. Introducing his otherwise unremarkable protagonist at the start of the novel, the narrator is intrigued by his bruised and battered legs. Further investigation reveals the secret of his nightly cycling lessons, at which the narrator bursts into eulogy:

> Thus even in a shop assistant does the warmth of manhood assert itself, and drive him against all the conditions of his calling, against the counsels of prudence and the restrictions of his means, to seek the wholesome delights of exertion and danger and pain. And our first examination of the draper reveals beneath his draperies—the man![14]

Exertion, danger, pain. These are the characteristics that identify 'the man', and with which the bicycle endows even the pallid Hoopdriver. The plot advances by means of his various encounters with two other cyclists: a 'Young Lady in Grey', who wears bloomers and owns an expensive bicycle with pneumatic tyres, and another male cyclist, in pursuit of the would-be 'New Woman', whom the reader discovers he has enticed into eloping under the pretence of helping her to make an independent life through writing. It is this other male rider, Bechamel, who provides something of a jolt in Wells's otherwise conventional satire of the Victorian love of the bicycle. Hoopdriver first observes him in a pub, where he loudly berates himself for the violent yet seemingly instinctive manner of his riding:

> I came out for exercise, gentle exercise, and to notice the scenery and to botanise. And no sooner do I get on that accursed machine than off I go hammer and tongs; I never look to right or left, never notice a flower, never see a view—get hot, juicy, red—like a grilled chop. . . . I've reservoirs and reservoirs of muscular energy and one or other of

them is always leaking. It's a most interesting road, birds and trees, I've no doubt, and wayside flowers, and there's nothing I should enjoy more than watching them. But I can't. Get me on that machine and I have to go. Get me on anything and I have to go. And I don't want to go a bit. WHY should a man rush about like a rocket, all pace and fizzle? Why? It makes me furious. I can assure you, sir, I go scorching along the road, and cursing aloud at myself for doing it.[15]

At this he downs a glass of lemon squash and returns to his bicycle, pedalling furiously away and almost out of sight by the time Hoopdriver has followed him to the door. What is interesting about Bechamel, who is only a minor figure in the plot and disappears once the girl, Jessie, escapes from him with Hoopdriver, is that he seems to be driven more by the pure sensation of racing his machine than actually meeting up with his quarry or later pursuing her after her flight. His bicycle has become an autonomous machine that awakens the latent force of his muscular energy, and with which he seems to fuse, as if a rocket, propelled forward, unable to reduce its speed or pause to look at the scenery around him. *Wheels of Chance* offers perhaps a predictable celebration of the widening horizons promised by the bicycle, as well as a topical jibe at the bicycle as emblematic of the self-assertively independent and energetically athletic ambitions of the New Woman, but it also identifies a new image of the cyclist as a figure of muscular dynamism, driven by a modern instinct for speed.

The commercial organization and professionalization of cycling as a sport in the 1890s was largely engineered by the combined forces of the bicycle and wheel industry, which saw in cycle races an opportunity to demonstrate their products to a mass audience, and a rapidly emerging sporting press, which not only advertised the manufacturers but promoted, publicized, and reported cycle races as a means of increasing circulation in a competitive market. The first organized cycle race took place at the Parc de Saint-Cloud in Paris in May 1868, organized by the Olivier brothers, partners in the Michaux bicycle company that first manufactured the 'velocipede', the first type of bicycle with pedals. The first long-distance road race, from Paris to Rouen, in November 1869, was organized by the Oliviers and the fortnightly cycling magazine *Le Vélocipède Illustré*.[16] Both were won by the English-born James Moore, and in their promotional strategies and commercial interest set the example for the organization of the first races on safety bicycles from the 1890s. The 1890s were a period of rapid technological innovation in bicycle manufacture, and races both tested and promoted bike reliability and performance. Andrew Ritchie argues that 'Bicycle-racing was sponsored by the bicycle industry and by the media in a way which was strikingly "modern" in its social and economic organisation and impact.'[17] Sports press barons assumed the role of impresarios, promoting long-distance, endurance, and sprint events, on the road and the track that encouraged public appetite for bicycle racing as entertainment.

It was this commercial control that made bicycle racing the dominant sport in Continental and US sport at the turn of the century (the UK remained resolutely committed to cycling as an amateur sport). As cycling historian Andrew Ritchie writes, 'In this sense, cycling can be said to have been expressive of modernity, of modern patterns of consumption and of modern modes of presenting a dynamic, exciting, technology-based sport to a general public hungry for novelty, sensation and speed.'[18] Other than in national championships, the best riders typically rode for manufacturers rather than their nation, and raced for a cash prize. In May 1891 the inaugural Bordeaux–Paris race, the longest-ever route at the time, at 600 km, was organized by another leading cycling journal *Véloce Sport*, vying for its readership with the Paris daily *Le Petit Journal*, and keen to associate itself with what was intended to be the longest annual race in the French cycling calendar. To increase the profile of the race, a record-breaking long-distance English rider, George Pilkington Mills, holder of the world record for cycling between Land's End and John O'Groats was invited to take part. Mills duly won in a little over twenty-six hours, having opted to ride the distance continuously and throughout the night, without sleeping and stopping for only minutes at a time for food. In November of the same year, Pierre Giffard, editor of *Le Petit Journal*, countered with a return Paris–Brest–Paris race, which at 1,200 km was twice the length of *Véloce Sport*'s 'longest race'. Giffard was a canny promoter. He limited the race to French riders, thus ensuring a French champion, and promoted the race through editorials that emphasized the event as a test of phenomenal human endurance. The race was won by Charles Terront, who finished in 71 hours and 35 minutes, to be greeted in Paris by a crowd of ten thousand people. Two years after his Paris–Brest–Paris victory, in 1893, Terront rode 3,000 km from St Petersburg to Paris in fourteen days.[19]

Alongside long-distance road races were races and records for speed and endurance, such as the hour record for the longest distance cycled in one hour, and the Paris Bol d'Or, an annual tandem-paced, twenty-four-hour race. By far the most punishing yet sensational of the endurance events were the six-day races, a particularly popular feature of the US racing calendar, in which riders battled to cover the farthest distance and the spectators could bet on their favourites to win or place as well as put up prize 'purses' for points. Initially six-day racers rode for 142 hours, resting and sleeping when they chose by the side of the track, although few did this very often, until a law passed in 1898 limited individual competitors to riding no more than twelve hours a day, resulting in two-man teams.[20] For these kinds of races, which quickly became major urban entertainment spectacles, promoters invested in outdoor and indoor velodrome tracks. The first purpose-built cycle tracks had appeared in the 1870s, but the 1890s witnessed the organization of track racing into a popular mass spectator sport. Velodromes were typically multipurpose venues, with cycle tracks of shale, concrete, or wooden boards built around sports arenas and athletics tracks, and held significant commercial advantages for promoters; they were free from the logistical difficulties of road races, could sell advertising on the track hoardings, levy an entry charge, serve food and drink, and let the space for other events on non-race days. One of the earliest opened at Herne Hill in London in 1891, directed by George Hillier, editor of the British *Bicycling News* but a firm opponent, at least in theory, of professionalism. In the US, velodromes included the Springfield in Massachusetts, the Nutley in New Jersey, and Madison Square Garden in New York, home to the first six-day race (again in 1891). The major velodromes in Paris were the Vélodrome Buffalo (see **Fig. 17.4**)

Figure 17.4. Vélodrome Buffalo, 1913.

by Tristan Bernard and opened in 1893 on the site used by Buffalo Bill's European tour, the Vélodrome de la Seine, also managed by Bernard, and the Stade-Vélodrome Parc des Princes, opened in 1897, and managed by Henri Desgranges. Desgranges was himself a cyclist, and had set numerous track cycling records, including the first hour record at the Buffalo track in 1893. In 1900 he became editor of *L'Auto-Vélo*, a fledgling daily sports paper set up by the anti-Dreyfus automobile manufacturer, the Comte Jules-Albert de Dion, to rival Giffard's overtly Dreyfusard *Le Vélo*. *Le Vélo* was by far the leading sports paper of the period, with a circulation of around 80,000 copies a day. A battle for readers ensued, resulting most famously in Desgranges's conception of the Tour de France at the end of 1902. With an eye to an urban public's appetite for sporting spectacle, however, in the same year he also commissioned the conversion of the vast space of the Galerie des Machines, the grandiose iron and glass exhibition space built for the Paris Exposition Universelle of 1889 and at the time the longest interior space in the word, into an indoor velodrome with a banked oval track surrounded by tiered seating for spectators. The new Vélodrome d'Hiver (see **Fig. 17.5**) opened in December 1903, with capacity for 20,000 spectators (price of entry ranged from 1 franc for the cheapest standing space to 7 francs in the track centre), more than six times that of the Parc des Princes.[21]

Speed records from the 1890s and 1910s demonstrate the extraordinary human capacity for speed and endurance on the bicycle that contextualizes Jarry and Boccioni's

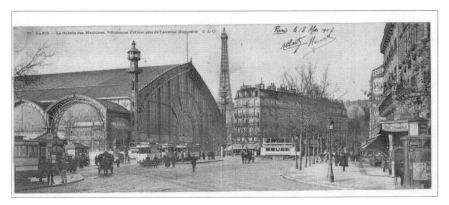

Figure 17.5. Vélodrome d'Hiver, 1907.

fascination with the racing cyclist. Improvements in bicycle technology and increased understanding of the physics and tactics of pacing, moreover, resulted in rapid performance leaps over the turn of the century. Desgranges recorded 35.325 km for the hour record in 1893. By 1900 the record had risen to 40.781 km, and between August 1912 and August 1914 was broken five times in a continuing battle in Paris between the French Marcel Berthet and the Swiss Oscar Egg that finally ended with Egg's achievement of a distance of 44.247 km. Over the same period, the record distance for the tandem-paced twenty-four-hour Bol d'Or increased from 736.946 km in 1894 to 951.750 km in 1912, the latter at the Vélodrome d'Hiver. Sprint records created star names of the fastest riders. In the early 1890s the quickest cyclist over short-distance sprints was the American national champion Arthur Zimmerman, who trained on the Herne Hill track and whose records included a 100-m 'flying start' in 5.4 seconds (just over 66 km/h or 41 mph).[22] Officially an amateur, Zimmerman quickly assumed a celebrity status that effectively made him a semi-professional, and in 1893, in front of a home crowd in Chicago, won the first amateur world sprint championship. In 1899 Marshall (Major) Taylor established a record time for the mile of 1 minute 41 seconds, at an average speed of close to 36 mph that stood for twenty-eight years.[23] In 1912 the fastest cyclist in the world was Frank Kramer, the highest-paid athlete in America at the time, and winner of the one-mile sprint professional world championship, held in Newark.[24] While the rhetoric of the sporting press lauded the heroic strength, energy, and perseverance of the riders battling in competition, the reality was, however, rather different. With the professionalization of cycle sport, it was the role of the riders to produce speed and spectacle for financial reward, and riders and their managers had various strategies for doing so, particularly in the longer endurance races. In the early road races it was not unheard of for riders to leap onto trains for part of the route, as the first Tour de France winner Maurice Garin did, for example.[25] More prevalent, however, was the use of a combination of stimulants to reduce pain and overcome flagging muscular power. Caffeine, alcohol, sugar cubes dipped in ether, cocaine and strychnine, often together, were common, and implicitly sanctioned in a period before banned doping.[26]

Jarry's imaginary 'ten-thousand mile race' looks rather less like literary fantasy when viewed within the context of the 1890s racing scene's obsession with feats of speed and endurance, and indeed it is plausible that he drew heavily on the commercial, social, and political nature of bicycle racing, as well as a number of its most celebrated exploits, for *The Supermale*. Perhaps the most notable speed event in this regard was Charles Murphy's hitherto equally unthinkable one-minute mile behind a steam train at Maywood, Long Island, in 1899, widely reported across the US and Europe, only two years before the publication of *The Supermale*. As Ritchie writes, Murphy's extraordinary ride 'was symbolic of a period when racing cyclists were setting more and more spectacular goals for themselves, paced by whatever machine could push up their speed'.[27] Far more than a feat of muscular power, it also required skilful bike handling, as the conditions were dangerous in the extreme. Murphy was riding at 60 mph on a track only three and a half feet wide. While the slipstream of the train could provide a great advantage by minimizing air resistance, the turbulence, if he fell too far behind, would almost certainly lead him to crash. The train had been fitted with a rear structure to partially shelter him, and provide a platform for his support team and officials. When the mile was up the near-unconscious Murphy had to be dragged, still attached to his bike, onto the rear platform. The *Chicago Tribune* reported that

> The spectacle was a most fearful one to those on the rear of the pacing train....As gently as possible Murphy, who had collapsed, was dragged over the rail. He sank unconscious but safe on the platform. The climax was too much for the official and spectators. Those in the pacing car were rushing about or sinking down, all with blanched faces, cheering madly or nervously trying to get at Murphy.[28]

Considerably less sensationalist was *Scientific American*, which noted that 'Without disparaging in any degree the persistence and pluck of the bicyclist, the most interesting feature of the ride is the impressive object lesson it affords as to the serious nature of atmospheric resistance on moving bodies'.[29]

The reporting of the race *against* a train in *The Supermale* mimics both the sensationalism of the popular press and the detached tone of the scientific journal. The novel opens with a debate between millionaire automobile and aeroplane manufacturer Arthur Gough, leading chemist William Elson, famed for his toxicological discovery that 'the only hygienic beverage was pure alcohol', Doctor Bathybius, a persistent opponent of Elson's theories, and thirty-year-old André Marcueil, a seemingly weakly man, with a pale face and slight stoop, who asserts that 'Human capacities have no limits.'[30] When Gough declares that even automobiles run out of fuel, Elson mentions his recent invention of 'a fuel for the human machine that could indefinitely delay muscular and nervous fatigue, repairing it as it is spent'.[31] Called 'Perpetual Motion Food' (and in English in the original French text), its exact ingredients remain secret, although Elson reveals that it contains both strychnine and alcohol. When the doctor expresses his disapproval, and Marcueil suggests that the infinite nervous and muscular power of the human physique should mean chemical stimulant is unnecessary, Elson invites them to judge the effects of his invention at its launch; he and Gough know each other well, Elson producing the fuel that propels Gough's vehicles to explosive speeds, and have organized a ten-thousand-mile race from Vladivostok to Paris between Gough's fastest locomotive and a five-man bicycle team sustained with no other food or drink than Perpetual Motion Food. 'In America, from the last few years of the nineteenth century, five- and six-man bicycle teams had many times beaten express trains over one or two miles,' Jarry's narrator notes, 'What was unheard of, though, was the claim that the human mechanism was superior to the machine *over long distances*.'[32]

The race itself is portrayed via the report given afterwards by one of the members of the team, Ted Oxborrow, to the *New York Herald*:

> Lying horizontally on the five-man bicycle—standard 1920 racing model, no handle bars, fifteen-millimeter tires, development 57.34 meters—our faces lower than our saddles, sheltered behind masks from wind and dust, our ten legs joined on either side by aluminum rods, we started off down the interminable, 10,000 mile-long-track that had been prepared alongside the lines of the great express. At first we were towed by a bullet-shaped car at the provisional speed of 120 kilometers per hour.[33]

The riders are strapped onto the bicycle so they cannot fall off, and at regular points over the day the leader, Corporal Gilbey, passes back a cube of Perpetual Motion Food, 'small, colourless, crumbly, and bitter-tasting'.[34] The speed is constantly measured, although alongside each other the tandem and the train appear static, as their relative speeds are the same. At the start of the second day the starting car is replaced by a pacing vehicle, a 'trumpet-shaped flying machine', and their speed increases to 250 kilometres per hour, the train and the bicycle still seemingly immobile relative to each other. On the morning of the third day, however, Oxborrow notices a stiffening in the pedal motion of the rider in front of him, Jewey Jacobs, and the express train starts to pull ahead. As he breathes 'the cadaverous odour of an incomprehensibly rapid decomposition',[35] which Elson later puts down to 'the secretion of an extraordinary abundance of muscular toxins', he realizes that the man is dead. The other riders pick up the pace, forcing Jacobs's legs, which are still harnessed to the pedals, to move, 'acting as a flywheel', as the corporal exclaims. Otherwise, Oxborrow observes, he would have been a 'dead weight', holding them back. Jarry was a passionate cyclist (see **Fig. 17.6**) and knowledgeable about bicycle racing, but he was also an astute critic of the culture of the sport:

> Jacobs was under contract to be fourth man in the great and honourable Perpetual Motion Food Race; he had signed a paper that would have set him back twenty-five thousand dollars for non-performance, payable on his future races. If he were dead he could no longer race, and would be unable to pay. So he had to race, then, alive or dead.[36]

The Supermale is futuristic, projecting the bicycle-racing culture and speed records of the 1890s into the 1920s in the manner of science fiction rather than fantasy. Jarry had already perceived the possibilities of the bicycle as a subject for science fiction six years previously in his comment on the pioneering French science-fiction writers 'J.-H. Rosny' in *Cyclo-guide Miran illustré* (1896). 'The Rosny brothers have already designed the cycle as a new organ,' he notes. 'More than anything else it is an extension of our skeletal system, and, being born of geometry, is perfectible.'[37] *The Supermale* clearly owes much to the novella of the

Figure 17.6. Alfred Jarry in Alfortville, Paris (n.d.).

older brother, J.-H. Rosny aîné, *Un autre monde* (Another World) (1895), from its use of the plot technique of the mad scientist demonstrating his latest invention to a group of credulous professional contemporaries, to its mutant protagonist, whose main form of sustenance is alcohol, and who lives at such a heightened speed, that his speech and writing are unintelligible. References to the contemporary scene and science of bicycle racing, moreover, abound in the novel: mention of the Dreyfus affair, the sponsorship of the race by the manufacturer Gough, the open acknowledgement of stimulants, the pacing machines, the English- and American-named riders, the explicit mention of Terront and the Paris–Brest race the homage to Terront's St. Petersburg–Paris ride in the Vladivostok to Paris route, and the hallucinations of Oxborrow in the final days of the race as a result of extreme fatigue and drunkenness. The 'Negro' Sammy White, 'well known from his record-breaking mile and half-mile races on the hairpin tracks of Massachusetts', is almost certainly a reference to Major Taylor, who battled racial hostility in America but was far more widely accepted in France.[38] The death of Jacobs is possibly inspired by English rider Arthur Linton's death two months after winning the Bordeaux–Paris race in 1896, officially due to typhoid fever, but heavily rumoured to be the result of 'trimethyl' or strychnine. It also seems plausible to suggest that Murphy provides something of a model for the 'supermale' Marcueil himself, the hunchbacked rider that Oxborrow sees in the train's slipstream. For Jarry's race is not only that between the train and the five-man bicycle team, but also between the train and Marcueil, who is determined to prove that a man can win against a train without the support of either pacing machines or chemical enhancement.

Throughout the course of the race, Oxborrow is perplexed to see this single cyclist pedalling behind the train, at the same speed as the five-man team. At first he thinks it must be a reflection in the side of the train carriage, or a hallucination resulting from the Perpetual Motion Food, as he cannot believe that an individual man could keep up with their current speed, which has risen to 300 kilometres per hour and continues to increase. At this point the quint has reached such a speed that it lifts briefly into the air. 'It is known', Oxborrow comments, 'that a body in motion, moving at a high speed, rises in a glide, its speed overcoming its adherence to the ground. It will, of course, fall back again, if it is not provided with some organs designed to propel it through space'.[39] Extraordinarily, the shadowy rider, who seems to be riding an early boneshaker, dressed in belle époque attire complete with frock coat, top hat, and pince-nez, continues to keep up with the race, strewing red roses at various points, and at the turning point even seems to clash on the bend with the train, before pulling ahead. Oxborrow determines he must be dreaming, but in the last moments of the race he sees the rider in what he describes as the return of a sober yet strangely visionary clarity:

> The swelling of his extensor muscles had torn his shorts over his thighs! His bicycle was a racing model the like of which I had never seen, with microscopic tires and a development greater than that of our machine; he was pedaling with the greatest of ease... The muscles of his calves were palpitating like two alabaster hearts'.[40]

The caricature of the early nineteenth-century leisured cyclist has given way to a muscled athlete on a scientifically innovative racing bicycle, whose physical system operates without limits and without fuel requirements, and who can achieve the same speeds as a train or aeroplane. The five-man bicycle officially wins the race, the locomotive engine giving out when Gough, in a final effort to win, demands that alcohol be poured into its boiler. The riders are inconsolable, however, recognizing that the red roses at the finishing post mean that Marcueil has arrived before them.

From Jarry's seemingly superhuman bicyclist, we can return to Marinetti, his vision of the 'extended man', a 'nonhuman, mechanical species, built for constant speed', and his sudden elevation of the bicycle to a 'divinity' in 'The New Ethical Religion of Speed'.[41] 'Sportsmen are the first neophytes of this religion,' he proclaims in the latter piece.[42] Had Marinetti read Jarry more closely in the interval since 1909? Certainly the 1916 piece celebrates the bicycle with a passion hitherto unseen in his celebration of modern technologies and the machine-like capacities of man. Marinetti hopes to see the Danube 'running in a straight line, at 300 kilometres an hour', and speaks of 'the sanctity of wheel and rail track'.[43] He makes an implicit reference to speed records in his observation that 'Kilometres and hours are not equal, they vary in length and duration for the man of speed',[44] and to the relationship of weight and speed, more significant for the bicyclist than the driver of the motor-powered cycle or automobile, in his observation on the necessity of a 'Victory of the self over the treacherous intrigues created by our Weight which seeks, through betrayal, to murder our speed, dragging it down into a pit of immobility'.[45] If, more overtly, the automobile and the aeroplane still remain pre-eminent, the call 'Let us *imitate* the train and the motorcar' (my italics) is a telling one. Marinetti asserts:

> Race along race along race along fly fly. Danger danger danger danger to right and to left below and above inside and out scent breathe drink in death. Militarized revolution of gears. Precise concise lyricism. To enjoy more coolness and more life than in rivers and seas, you have to fly in the ice-cold slipstream at full speed.[46]

The racing bicycle, in its fusion of man and machine, its *extension* of the dynamism of man, offered something close to this imitative possibility. As 'Mile-A-Minute Murphy' had demonstrated, the racing bicyclist could approximate to the speed of a train, and as Jarry had imagined, could equal the speed of flight.

NOTES

1. Filippo Tommaso Marinetti, 'The New Ethical Religion of Speed', in *Critical Writings: New Edition*, ed. Günter Berghaus (New York: Farrar, Strauss, and Giroux, 1916), pp. 253–9; 256.
2. 'Destruction of Syntax—Untrammeled Imagination—Words-in-Freedom', in Marinetti, *Critical Writings*, pp. 120–32; 120.
3. 'The Foundation and Manifesto of Futurism', in Marinetti, *Critical Writings*, pp. 11–17; 13.
4. Alastair Brotchie, *Alfred Jarry: A Pataphysical Life* (Cambridge, MA: MIT Press, 2011).
5. Alfred Jarry, 'The Crucifixion Considered as a Bicycle Race', in *The Selected Works of Alfred Jarry*, edited by Roger Shattuck and Simon Watson Taylor, translated by Roger Shattuck (New York: Grove Press, 1965), pp. 122–4.
6. F. T. Marinetti, 'La Mort tient le volant', in *La Ville charnelle* (Paris: E. Sansot, 1908), 228. See also Luca Somigli, *Legitimizing the Artist: Manifesto Writing and European Modernism, 1885–1915* (Toronto: University of Toronto Press, 2003), p. 108.
7. Umberto Boccioni, 'Futurist Painting: Technical Manifesto', in *Manifesto: A Century of Isms*, edited by Mary Ann Caws (Lincoln, NE: University of Nebraska Press, 2001), pp. 178–82; 179.
8. Quoted in Flavio Fergonzi, *The Mattioli Collection: Masterpieces of the Italian Avant-Garde* (Milan: Skira Editore, 2003), p. 180.
9. Bernard Vere, 'Pedal-Powered Avant-Gardes: Cycling Paintings in 1912–13', in *The Visual in Sport*, edited by Mike O'Mahony and Mike Huggins (London: Routledge, 2011), pp. 70–87.
10. Vere suggests that the cyclist may be the Luxembourg rider François Faber, who in 1913 won the Paris–Roubaix road race, as well as two stages of the Tour de France. This would certainly be consistent with his theory that *Dynamism of a Cyclist* was in part a response to Metzinger's painting, which depicts the 1912 Paris–Roubaix winner Charles Crupelandt at the finish of the race on the Roubaix velodrome. Faber was a well-known professional cyclist, known as 'the Giant', winner of the 1909 Tour de France, runner up in 1910, and winner of the Bordeaux–Paris road race in 1911. If Faber was the model for the cyclist in Boccioni's painting, then the number 15 is intriguing, as Vere notes that he did not wear 15 in the 1913 Tour. He did come third in the final stage of the Tour, stage fifteen, which ended in Paris on 27 July at the Parc des Princes velodrome. Four days later he also took part in a six-hour race at the

Buffalo velodrome, wearing a track jersey that resembles the bolder colour divisions of the jersey of the Boccioni cyclist. Boccioni was almost certainly in Italy in late July, but may have seen race reports. The number may have been an allusion to the Tour stage, or the number Faber wore at the Buffalo six-hour race. It is also disconcertingly premonitory; Faber died in May 1915 at the Battle of Artois.

11. Marinetti, *Critical Writings*, p. 122

12. See for example Patricia Marks, *Bicycles, Bangs and Bloomers: The New Woman in the Popular Press* (Lexington, KY: University Press of Kentucky, 1990).

13. H. G. Wells, *The Wheels of Chance* (London: Dent, 1896), p. 22.

14. Wells, *The Wheels of Chance*, p. 11.

15. Wells, *The Wheels of Chance*, pp. 44–5.

16. Hugh Dauncey, *French Cycling: A Social and Cultural History* (Liverpool: Liverpool University Press, 2012), p. 29.

17. J. A. Mangan, ed., *Reformers, Sport, Modernizers: Middle-Class Revolutionaries* (London: Frank Cass, 2002; London: Routledge, 2012), p. 262.

18. Andrew Ritchie, 'Amateur World Champion 1893': The International Cycling Career of American Arthur Augustus Zimmerman, 1888–1896', in *Modern Sport: The Global Obsession*, edited by Boria Majumdar and Fan Hong (London: Routledge, 2009), pp. 63–81; 65.

19. See Dauncey *French Cycling* and Andrew Ritchie and Rudiger Rubenstein, 'Mostly Middle-Class Cycling Heroes: The Fin de Siècle Commercial Obsession with Speed, Distance and Records', in Mangan, *Reformers, Sport, Modernizers*, pp. 91–133.

20. Ibid.

21. See Dauncey, *French Cycling*.

22. See Ritchie, 'Amateur World Champion 1893'.

23. See Andrew Ritchie, *Major Taylor: The Extraordinary Career of a Champion Bicycle Racer* (Baltimore: Johns Hopkins University Press, 1988).

24. Michael C. Gabriele, *The Golden Age of Bicycle Racing in New Jersey* (Charleston, SC: The History Press, 2011), p. 53.

25. Hugh Dauncey, 'French Cycling Heroes of the Tour: Winners and Losers', in *The Tour de France 1903–2003: A Century of Sporting Structures, Meanings and Values*, edited by Hugh Dauncey and Geoff Hare (London: Frank Cass, 2003), pp. 175–202; 178.

26. John Hoberman, *Mortal Engines: The Science of Performance and the Dehumanization of Sport* (New York: The Free Press, 1992), p. 112.

27. See Ritchie, *Major Taylor*, p. 119.

28. Ritchie, *Major Taylor*, p. 120.

29. Ritchie, *Major Taylor*, p. 120.

30. Alfred Jarry, *The Supermale*, translated by Ralph Gladstone and Barbara Wright (New York: New Directions, 1964), pp. 49, 7.

31. Jarry, *The Supermale*, p. 7.

32. Jarry, *The Supermale*, p. 50.

33. Jarry, *The Supermale*, p. 51.

34. Jarry, *The Supermale*, p. 52.

35. Jarry, *The Supermale*, p. 56.

36. Jarry, *The Supermale*, p. 58.

37. Quoted in Jill Fell, *Alfred Jarry, an Imagination in Revolt* (Madison, NJ: Fairleigh Dickinson University Press, 2005), p. 49.

38. Jarry, *The Supermale*, p. 64.

39. Jarry, *The Supermale*, p. 61.

40. Jarry, *The Supermale*, p. 70.
41. Marinetti, 'Extended Man and the Kingdom of the Machine', in *Critical Writings*, pp. 85–8; 86.
42. Marinetti, *Critical Writings*, p. 255.
43. Marinetti, *Critical Writings*, p. 255.
44. Marinetti, *Critical Writings*, p. 257.
45. Marinetti, *Critical Writings*, p. 258.
46. Marinetti, *Critical Writings*, p. 257.

18

A Desire Named Streetcar

Julian Murphet

For a figure to migrate from everyday life into aesthetic form, there needs to be an everyday life in the first place. More than that, there must be a crisis in the legitimacy of its reproduction, such that the figure can emerge—like Heidegger's hammer[1]—in its conspicuous Thing-being, and thus be exposed to second-order critical reflection.

> It happens that the stage sets collapse. Rising, streetcar, four hours in the office or the factory, meal, streetcar, four hours of work, meal, sleep, and Monday Tuesday Wednesday Thursday Friday and Saturday according to the same rhythm—this path is easily followed most of the time. But one day the 'why' arises and everything begins in that weariness tinged with amazement.[2]

Here in Camus's 'weariness tinged with amazement' is the condition of attention in the aesthetic regime.[3] With it, the everyday decomposes into its elements, each now discerned in its routine abstraction as a mode of Sisyphean torment. Of these elements, the streetcar (the American English equivalent of the British English 'tram') emerges as perhaps the most emblematic shorthand for the very reproduction of daily life: a figure of movement in which nothing moves, yet the stage set of the quotidian is woven of its repetitive shuttles to and fro across the urban surface. Articulating the Scylla of home with the Charybdis of labour, the streetcar was perhaps modernity's privileged chronotope of the everyday, and as such, alive with contradictions. To map, however briefly, its appearance in aesthetic forms, is to seize hold of an unreconciled antagonism between dystopian and utopian energies.

In what follows, I would like to develop a provisional framework for conceptualizing the historicity of the aesthetic—and especially the transformation of cultural 'dominants'—by way of a focused consideration of this single figure. In brief, I will want to put specific pressure on Fredric Jameson's recent reconsideration of Western realism as a force field in which the narrative order of the *récit*, and the affective intensities of phenomenological embodiment, are held in compact by the conventions of authority specific to the realist novel as a form, before unravelling in the anomie of modernism.[4] It is my contention that the shift from a realist to a modernist cultural dominant can be observed with peculiar clarity in the widespread repurposing of 'realist' figures for 'modernist' ends—a process that entailed a relative demotion of the cognitive or didactic function of those figures, and a promotion of their sheerly affective capabilities. Singling out the streetcar as a figure already loaded with cognitive energies by the realists, we can observe (as in a laboratory situation) the kinds of aesthetic work then undertaken to transpose the figure from a realist to a modernist constellation; without, however, sacrificing that cognitive content altogether. In fact, my claim is that modernism can be understood as a clandestine fidelity to the cognitive achievement of the realists, such that, relatively ironized and muted, it can undergird a frenzy of formal experimentation with its figures.

But perhaps the best way to test this hypothesis is from the other side, for postmodernism can be grasped as a situation in which the cognitive dimension has finally been dispensed with altogether, that grim ballast gaily shorn away, so that the motley affects can float free like Barthelme's great balloon.[5] Hollywood tends to register this new-won affective autonomy within the rigid constraints of nostalgia film, so that a codified emotion immediately coordinates the available phenomenological intensities—witness the melancholic ruminations out the streetcar window of Angelina Jolie in Eastwood's *Changeling* (USA, 2008); or the giddy comedy of the red cars in *Who Framed Roger Rabbit?* (USA, 1988); both efforts to register LA's annihilated Pacific Electric streetcar system by way of residual cinematic affects. Meanwhile, Miyazaki's haunted trolley ride of ghosts and phantoms in *Spirited Away* (Japan, 2001) conjures up a posthumous memory of a once mighty Japanese trolley grid reduced now to a handful of irregular lines; once again, the affect outstays the referent, and channels the response inward. But no contemporary 'postmodernization' of the streetcar figure quite matches the one in Sokurov's *Father and Son* (Russia, 2003). 'This is a strange city. Where are you taking me? Somewhere in the past'. With these words, spoken in gravelly Russian, begins the greatest trolley sequence since Murnau, disclosing what is indeed a 'strange city', Eliotic in its unreality. A film set in St Petersburg is displaced cryptically into Lisbon—Lusophone street signs, pale sandstone buildings, and darker-skinned passengers all make clear the radical shift in locale. Sokurov raises the stakes on nostalgia by pushing through its image, and into its affect: made material by delicate yellow filters, fetishistic close-ups of chrome handles and wheels, and above all the gentle canting of the trolley around the pitched streets. By making this luminous journey the central event of his film, Sokurov suggests that the streetcar is today the privileged vehicle for the nostalgia affect, since the vehicle itself has the quality of converting quotidian drift into aesthetic experience.

Nostalgia for the modern: Werner Sollors is perfectly right to point out that 'electric streetcars, once a prime symbol of modernity, have now assumed an aura of nostalgic quaintness after their literal disappearance from most American cities'.[6] But another, less understood reason for that nostalgia is that, already for the moderns themselves, the figure was ensnared in a structure of feeling somewhat antiquated and perishing. It was above all an *inherited* figure, whose remarkable success and centrality to the late realists rendered it suspicious and ripe for refutation and rebuke. 'Trams and dusty trees./Highbury bore me.' Eliot's lines point to a *genealogy* for the Thames daughters, a dusty heritage to be contested by the post-Wagnerian satirist, as much as affirmed. Modernism constructs its effects within a set of coordinates already jingling to the sound of the trolley bell. The schoolgirls going abroad in 'Suite Clownesque'—'Each with a skirt just down to the ancle'—are hardly the flappers of a later moment; their pubescent jaunt is felt as perfectly Edwardian: 'Here's a street car—let's jump in.' It is only the final line that clinches the satirist's acerbic point: "'Where shall we go to next?"'[7] With one foot in the nineteenth century, and one in the next, this early poem shows up the streetcar as a figure of sterile, superannuated repetition and circulation, even as it opens up a hitherto unsuspected existential void at the point of maximal 'fun'.

In the St. Louis where Eliot stored up such memories, and which was later commemorated in full-blown nostalgia mode by the Oscar-winning 'Trolley Song' in Minnelli's *Meet Me in St. Louis* (USA, 1944), the streetcars were in fact animated by altogether darker energies—energies that fed a distinct and antithetical aesthetic dominant. By 1903, the St Louis streetcar system was in a state of crisis. The process of private monopolization in Missouri had been unprecedentedly rapid and radical. During the 1890s, a few giant companies consolidated the various extant traction companies, cut back on services, avoided almost all their taxes, and bribed the Missouri legislature to legalize a full monopoly. Lay-offs, cutbacks, and the degradation of services led the Amalgamated Association of Street Railway Employees to strike for weeks on end, bringing the city to a standstill, until the board sent in a posse of armed thugs and a troop of strike-breakers. By the actual date of the fictional 'Trolley Song', twenty public officials were being convicted of traction bribery.[8]

This kind of material, typical of its time and recalled obliquely in another Hollywood song—the 'Charlie Kane' number with its account of 'traction magnates on the run'—provided the primary diet of US Naturalist *engagement*.[9] The streetcar systems that transformed dozens of sleepy horse-drawn towns into modern cities at the turn of the century offered the crusading late realists a suitable topic for their reformist zeal; since the overnight transformation of the city's roadways by tracks that ran out into rapidly developing suburbs, and regulated social movement to the tune of vast corporate profits, was clearly a definitive episode in the consolidation of private capital over daily life. If the city was a microcosm of the social whole, then the streetcar installed itself as the privileged figure for thinking the totality as a dynamic system. More than any other technology, it drew together the city's radial bands and rings into a retail hub, stimulated new cycles of turnover and speeds of accumulation, and made palpable the hand-in-glove relationship between city administrations and speculative finance. Moreover, it was a stage on which class struggle flared into social visibility; the St Louis streetcar strike was only one of many dozens that fomented unionizing activities and a new spirit of solidarity among the urban proletariat at the turn of the century. The skilled men who worked the lines were well aware of their value to the giddy pace of development. They are recalled in the great final sequence of Dreiser's early masterpiece, where Hurstwood first sympathizes with their cause before joining the ranks of scabs to meet his fate:

The men complained that this system was extending, and that the time was not far off when but a few out of seven thousand employés would have regular two-dollar-a-day work at all. They demanded that the system be abolished, and that ten hours be considered a day's work, barring unavoidable delays, with two dollars and twenty-five cents pay. They demanded immediate acceptance of these terms, which the various trolley companies refused.[10]

Grasping the streetcar as a lightning rod for class antagonisms, Dreiser built his enterprise on that of William Dean Howells, whose *A Hazard of New Fortunes* (1890) had similarly drawn its portrait of New York against the spectacle of a streetcar strike in the novel's climax. There, the son of the capitalist Dryfoos, the German socialist Lindau, and the journalist protagonist March all converge tragically over a violent contestation of the rights of labour against the predations of streetcar capital on the lines of New York. Till then,

> The strike seemed a vary far-off thing, though the paper he bought to look up the stockmarket was full of noisy typography about yesterday's troubles on the surface lines. Among the millions in Wall Street there was some joking and some swearing, but not much thinking, about the six thousand men who had taken such chances in their attempt to better their condition.[11]

Meanwhile the temporary absence of streetcars has altered the very physiognomy of the city, as well as its rate of profit. The humble trolley car was a vehicle of prodigious consequence.

Nor was that consequence simply economic; its impact on urban planning and the texture of daily life was equally profound. This was particularly marked in Boston, where after fifteen years of an integrated electric trolley service and a consequent trebling of population, three determinate urban rings had materialized. In the words of Sam Bass Warner, 'By 1900 the interaction of the growth of the street railway and class building patterns had produced class-segregated suburbs. As the bands of new construction moved ever outward they impressed upon the land their own special architectural and social patterns.'[12] The inner suburbs, initially home to the lower-middle class, soon opened up into what observers called the 'zone of emergence': places where immigrant families moved from their original inner-city locales. In Boston, the Irish, Jews, Canadians, and Germans all migrated to the inner suburban ring of Roxbury in the 1890s. As a result, any typical ride in a trolley car was one of extraordinary proximity to otherness, routinized by daily commuting. Employers and employees; natives and aliens; men and women; adults and children: the streetcar was the single most instrumental factor in habituating the modern urbanite to the touch and the glance of the Other.[13] 'The carful, again and again, is a foreign carful; a row of faces, up and down, testifying, without exception, to alienism unmistakable, alienism undisguised and unashamed.'[14] But Henry James's xenophobia in the streetcar's close space is effectively counterposed by the patriotic sociability of Gertrude Stein's Helen (in the late-realist *Q.E.D.*), who, while wandering in Boston, 'revelled in the American street-car crowd with its ready intercourse, free comments and airy persiflage all without double meanings which created an atmosphere that never suggested for a moment the need to be on guard'.[15] For the streetcar was itself a powerful instrument of civic reform, as any number of contemporary General Electric advertisements will attest. While it brought the alien, it also brought suburban distance from industrial pollution, made available the beach, and encouraged weekend hikes—as well as Stein's healthy intercourse of cultural equals.[16]

> Great industries were moving in. The huge railroad corporations which had long before recognized the prospects of the place had seized upon vast tracts of land for

transfer and shipping purposes. Streetcar lines had been extended far out into the open country in anticipation of rapid growth. The city had laid miles and miles of streets and sewers through regions where perhaps one solitary house stood out alone—a pioneer of the populous ways to be.[17]

Dreiser's inaugural image of the spreading Chicago of modernity discloses the centrality of infrastructure—sewers, streets, lines, cables—to the realists' conception of the real. Their 'real' is not the immediate surface of things, but their underlying networks and subterranean hardware. And this infrastructural domain is configured as the realm of bourgeois desire as such, the diabolical animus of their aesthetic and world view. Bourgeois desire works under the surface of things, 'seizing hold' of land, 'laying out' miles of cable and bitumen, in order to co-opt the wishes of those caught in its mediating web—to create one seamless circuit of desire. The *flâneur* may have been the ironic hero of high capitalism; but in the period of monopoly capital, that class of pedestrian was usurped by the straphanger. Young Carrie Meeber, who takes her place along the streetcar line, speaks for millions when she stands of an evening on her front steps and simply watches:

> Carrie was...looking at the lights in the stores about, the people passing, and the street cars jingling merrily past toward the heart of the city or out toward the suburbs,—directions which to her were interesting mysteries.... She never wearied of wondering where the people in the cars were going or what the enjoyments were which they had.[18]

This is the priceless passive correlative of the formative desire of the speculators in finance[19]—one desire stimulates another, and another, in an infinite network of envious acquisitive energy, all intimately connected to the electric currents illuminating the shopfronts and the 'merry' passage of the cars. The desire named streetcar was the spirit of monopoly capitalism itself.

Frank Norris, who likewise deployed the naturalist convention of the streetcar strike in his *McTeague*, coined the image of the 'octopus' to account for the infrastructural web of energy monopolized by Pacific Electric during its years of boom.[20] The metaphor was advised; for we are given, by naturalism, to perceive the financial linkage of streetcar systems with railway conglomerates, electrical companies, steel magnates, developers, and real estate speculators, as one great devouring organism of capital.[21] It was this organism that Dreiser himself, Norris's most illustrious cadet, set himself to mapping anew in his 'Trilogy of Desire'—a distended *roman à clef* about the notorious streetcar speculator Charles Yerkes. Even prior to their electrification, Yerkes's alter ego Cowperwood grasps the Chicago streetcars as the very key to the secret of modern capital:

> He surveyed these extending lines, with their jingling cars, as he went about the city, with an almost hungry eye. Chicago was growing fast, and these little horse-cars on certain streets were crowded night and morning—fairly bulging with people at the rush-hours. If he could only secure an octopus-grip on one or all of them; if he could combine and control them all! What a fortune!... He forever busied himself with various aspects of the scene quite as a poet might have concerned himself with rocks and rills. To own these street-railways! To own these street-railways! So rang the song in his mind.[22]

But here, too, we sense the limits of the naturalist aesthetic, and specifically of its illustrious streetcar figure. For although the narrator can inform us brusquely that a song rang in Cowperwood's mind when his reveries took to 'becoming-octopus', we never hear that song itself. The simile with the poet is a clunky satire, not meant to elicit any actual aesthetic frisson.

That is to say, of course, that the naturalist figure of the streetcar is above all a *cognitive* one. Its was a chronotope whose very form was also its content—the web of tracks facilitating intricate topological coverage and deft transitionality, the sociological *combinatoire* of the daily commute making for intriguing moments of characterological encounter, the well-known public stories of traction corruption fuelling the engines of narrative exposure, and the infamous strikes allowing for climactic scenes of totalizing conflict. Condensed into this figure, too, were the trillions of electrons per second travelling at light speed through the new urban grid; the billions of commuters per year making up the industrial and retail workforces of the second machine age; the billions of dollars prestidigitated into capital by complex brokering systems; the thousands of tonnes of steel and coal that powered the whole; the countless thousands of man-hours from which surplus value was squeezed; and so forth. The figure moved, but it moved in such a way as to congeal the surface of the city into a 'representation'. It was a palpable mode of public mystification—a public service in private hands—and for the naturalists, that mystification consisted in a reification of the economic dynamics of daily life, which must be *exposed*. The peculiar quality of the streetcar, as an artistic chronotope, was that it could be interrupted at any point—a wildcat strike, a hiccup in the flows of capital investment, an access of sheer hysteria or rage on board, an accident—to provoke the system around it momentarily to reveal its interrelated consistency, its *totality*. Or even better, with a slight '*détournement*', its allegorical potential could be brought to light, as in Upton Sinclair's vision of the slaughter yards as a nightmare mirror image of Chicago in *The Jungle*:

> It was near to the east entrance that they stood, and all along the east side of the yards ran the railroad tracks, into which the cars were run, loaded with cattle. All night long this had been going on, and now the pens were full: by tonight they would be empty, and the same thing would be done again.
>
> ...
>
> There were two hundred and fifty miles of track within the yards, their guide went on to tell them. They brought about ten thousand head of cattle every day, and as many hogs, and half as many sheep—which meant some eight or ten million creatures turned into food every year.... it was quite uncanny to watch them, pressing on to their fate, all unsuspicious—a very river of death. Our friends were not poetical, and the sight suggested to them no metaphors of human destiny; they thought only of the wonderful efficiency of it all.[23]

The streetcars that deliver Jurgis to the yards, and Ona to her own exploitative fate at work, are felt to be continuous with these conveyor belts of butchery. The streetcar permits the daily mass consumption of labour by that 'Great Butcher...the spirit of Capitalism', of which Sinclair's narrator writes that 'It divided the country into districts, and fixed the price of meat in all of them.... With millions of dollars a week that poured in upon it, it was reaching out for the control of other interests, railroads and trolley lines, gas and electric light franchises.'[24]

Again, the internal artistic frustration with the purely epistemological status of the streetcar figure is again dangerously close to erupting. Just as Cowperwood's octopus trances leave no poetic trace, so Sinclair's witnesses 'were not poetical' either. If Tommy Hinds can gather dozens of Midwestern workers around him and 'paint little pictures of "the System"',[25] satisfying their class craving for enlightenment, the sense increasingly was that the streetcar itself—as one such picture—had really only been half-illuminated. Whatever the figure's indicated 'poetry', it was not registering in these crude naturalist diagrams of the totality.

That the strong cognitive flavour of the streetcar as a figure for thinking the totality persisted into the period of high modernism, however, is attested by any number of instances. Think of Ulrich's meditation on a brief political skirmish in Vienna:

> You cannot step into the street or drink a glass of water or get on a streetcar without touching the balanced levers of a gigantic apparatus of laws and interrelations, setting them in motion or letting them maintain you in your peaceful existence; one knows hardly any of these levers, which reach deep into the inner workings and, coming out the other side, lose themselves in a network whose structure has never yet been unravelled by anyone.[26]

The streetcar, humble appurtenance that it is, still resonates to the epistemological clang of the Whole, connected synecdochically to this 'network' managed by 'levers' by which modern life is driven. Only note the new accent of unknowability as the free indirect discourse follows Ulrich into the baffled cul-de-sac of this network's excess over subjective cognition. Cognition is thus reduced to a desperate game of catch-up through arbitrary 'technical' snapshots of the elusive totality:

> He saw people climbing in and out of the cars, and his technically trained eye toyed distractedly with the interplay of welding and casting, rolling and bolting, of engineering and hand finishing, of historical development and the present state of the art, which combined to make up these barracks-on-wheels that these people were using.[27]

Indeed, rather than 'plunging' us knowledgeably 'into the earth through the wires of an electric trolley',[28] the cars as figures recede from cognition, their best effect now reduced to supplying the privileged modernist trope of 'epiphany', as when Ulrich, 'peering out from the body of modern transportation and still an involuntary part of it', catches sight of a baroque stone column in 'optical collision' with its modern setting.[29] The epistemological is thus eclipsed by the epiphanic, where, absurdly, 'everything had in effect come to nothing'.[30]

Alfred Döblin echoes this existential note in his *Alexanderplatz*, whose great opening sequence on board the no. 41 car that brings Biberkopf home from prison ends with this brief summary: 'He got off the car, without being noticed, and was back among people again. What happened? Nothing.... Outside everything was moving, but—back of it—there was nothing! It—did not—live!'[31] The experience itself is rendered in a kind of hysterical impressionist shorthand:

the car raced on with him along the tracks, and only his head was left in the direction of the prison. The car took a bend; trees and houses intervened. Busy streets emerged, Seestrasse, people got on and off. Something inside him screamed in terror: Look out, look out, it's going to start now.[32]

The car-ride is an apt occasion for the narrative voice to confer verbal privileges on the object world; the passive mood dominates to the extent that the trolley car orchestrates the flood of phenomenal experience; appositive conjunctions proliferate. This is not to say that the cognitive dimension is effaced, since the car lines continue to radiate strong epistemological signals:

> Car No. 68 runs across Rosenthaler Platz, Wittenau, Nordbanhof, Heilanstalt, Weddingplatz, Stettiner Station, Roselthaler Platz, Alexanderplatz, Straussberger Platz, Frankfurter Allee Station, Lichtenberg, Herzberge Insane Asylum. The three Berlin transport companies—street-car, elevated and underground, omnibus—form a tariff-union. Fares for adults are 20 pfennigs, for schoolchildren 10 pfennigs.[33]

The passage continues in exaggerated, bullet-point naturalist mode, shoring up knowledge with a blithe confidence that is structurally compromised by its distance from Biberkopf's 'terror'. Towards the end of the novel, Döblin arrives at a stylistic solution to this now radically bifurcated mode of apprehending the city's movements.

> And then what does he do? He starts little by little to go about the streets, he walks around Berlin.

> Berlin: 52° 31′ North Latitude, 13° 25′ East Longitude, 20 main-line stations, 121 suburban lines, 27 belt lines, 14 city lines, 7 shunting stations, street-car, elevated railroad, autobus service. There's only one Kaiser Town, there's only one Vienna. A Woman's Desire in three words, three words comprise all a woman's desire. Imagine it, a New York firm advertises a new cosmetic which gives a yellowish retina that fresh bluish tint only possessed by youth. The most beautiful pupil, from deep blue to velvet-brown, can be got from our tubes. Why spend so much on having your furs cleaned?[34]

It is here as if the syntax mirrors the base-and-superstructural logic of commodified urban consciousness itself: in order to be able to 'see' through the eyes of the generalized and feminized desire that emanates from consumer capitalism, there needs to be incessant, regularized traffic. The infrastructure of such sensory attunement and alienation is a massive, electrified transport system, which is (as Döblin presents it) nothing less that the soul of contemporary Berlin itself—a quantifiable network of lines, interchanges, transfers, and stations, without which 'Berlin' would not exist, let alone its phenomenological intensities. So, the cognitive dimension persists as a kind of noumenal aesthetic infrastructure to what is effectively the text's new-found concern, namely, the rise of surcharged affective materials within the urban field constituted by modern transport systems. Here, at last, the 'poem' of the streetcars begins to be heard.

What is Biberkopf's 'terror', exactly? The 'isolated body begins to know more global waves of generalized sensation,' writes Fredric Jameson, introducing his account of 'affect' as a binary other to the narrative armoury of the *récit* in the force field of realism.[35] What Biberkopf is experiencing here, it seems, is not 'terror' as such (a narrative cliché formulated and elaborated by the Gothic novelists, if not the august spirit of tragedy itself), but something without a name or a face—'*Something* inside him screamed in terror' [my emphasis]. The streetcar immerses the ex-convict into a riptide of contingency so overwhelming as to disorder his frame of reference, unhinging words from things. Döblin thus commits his text to a series of syntactical and grammatical experiments devised to stimulate an experiential mode without any stable identity, a 'structure of feeling' abandoned to the present and measurable vertically only in volumes. Affect as such, writes Jameson, is 'an eternal present,... an element which is somehow self-sufficient, feeding on itself and perpetuating its own existence'.[36] And in that sense, the affective 'poem' of the streetcar is an experimental verbal approximation of this kind of distended perpetual present, from which must be divorced every trace of the epistemological, whose dimension is horizontal, in time, and enframed by conventional means–ends rationality. But only in as much as, with its flanged wheels still nestled hard against the sunken rails, the trolley remains engaged in scheduled propulsion through the urban network—the poem of affect can only be heard while the streetcar goes unconsciously about its business.

It is worth reminding ourselves at this junction that Marx's metaphor of base and superstructure was a railway analogy, to the 'superstructure' of rolling stock that can only move along lines prescribed by the 'real foundation' of the tracks themselves. It was an analogy meant to suggest determinate limits to the apparently autonomous dynamisms of the superstructure—of culture, ideology, and the state apparatus—in the sense that, for all the variability of speed and bidirectionality available to the individual car, without the system of tracks it wasn't able to move at all. We can develop the metaphor apropos the modernist appropriation of streetcar figuration: the new formalist privileging of phenomenological affectivity is made possible precisely by residual late-realist cognitivist contents serving as its base. The epistemic function dwindles in aesthetic prestige—for other historical reasons, as we shall see—but without disappearing altogether; in other words, the modernist attention to affective contingency and flux is underwritten by an inherited cognitive content that is ironized without being evacuated. In testament to the perdurable 'realism' of the figure, even in the giddiest heights of modernist play and exuberant surrealism, recall the climax to the first act of Bulgakov's *Master and Margarita*, where, signally failing to heed the warning signs ('Caution Tram-Car!'), Berlioz meets his grisly fate:

> The woman driver tore at the brake, the car dug its nose into the ground, then instantly jumped up, and glass flew from the windows with a crash and a jingle. Here someone in Berlioz's brain cried desperately: 'Can it be? ...' Once more, and for the last time, the moon flashed, but now breaking to pieces, and then it became dark.

> The tram-car went over Berlioz, and a round dark object was thrown up the cobbled slope below the fence of the Patriarch's walk. Having rolled back down this slope, it went bouncing along the cobblestones of the street.

> It was the severed head of Berlioz.[37]

This memento mori slyly chastises the impulse to veer off into sheer postmodern affectivity through a crude 'return to the base'.

The reasons for the decline and exhaustion of this figure's cognitive load are not purely internal. Of course, to the degree that it had served the preceding generation as a veritable epistemological mother lode, the figure was rendered vulnerably conspicuous and muted as an aesthetic matter of course into a more opaque, ambiguous, affective image by the generation of 1914. But the extrinsic reasons for this decline were more powerful still, and concerned a radical challenge to the electro-capital monopoly over everyday life circa 1910—the sudden tearing apart of the integrated 'web' that electro-capital's mass transport, department stores, amusement parks, and commuter belts had hitherto spun over the quotidian, symbolically represented by the rolling out of Ford's Model T from Detroit's Piquette Park plant in 1908. The impact of petro-capital upon the electrical monopolies was decisive, and forever altered the nature and trajectory of mass transport, nationally and internationally. The massive investments in roadways that ensured the irreversible hegemony of the private motor car were levied by municipal, state, and federal agencies, but their spearhead was, as usual, private capital: rubber distributors, tyre manufacturers, car dealers, 'parts suppliers, oil companies, service-station owners, road builders, and land developers',[38] all of whom recognized the greater rate of profit in cheap automobiles as against efficient streetcar systems. 'By 1920,... most urban residents and virtually all highway engineers saw streets primarily as arteries for motor vehicles',[39] as they remain to this day.

As an aesthetic figure, the private motor car waxed apocalyptic. Personal speed, bought at the cost of public safety and pursued in a manner that was a priori antisocial, led to a newly 'unknowable' trace work of aleatory high-speed vectors scrawled across the city grid and beyond. Where the streetcar was tethered as a utility to known schedules and the fixed trackwork of the 'base', the motor car exceeded cognition by the power of the atomized multitude, which took to the streets now freed from that testing proximity to the Other that had defined the sociology of the first mass form of transport. Beside the now endlessly proliferating roadways themselves, there was no infrastructure—no flow of electricity, no network of passenger stops, no industrial workforce, no track maintenance—to petrol-driven mass transport beyond the private maintenance of the vehicle itself. As a figure, then, the motor car was always and already predisposed to a disproportionately 'affective' aesthetic logic, as Marinetti's great 'Manifesto' will consistently remind us (not to mention Fitzgerald's hurtling deathtraps, let alone poor Toad of Toad Hall)—having jettisoned any burdensome cognitive cargo in a private subsumption of 'movement' itself. This is the context in which, elegiacally and with an acutely anachronistic sense of imminent archaism, modernism seized hold of the streetcar image as precisely 'dated' and cognitively depleted. The streetcar 'stage set', Camus's 1947 image of a wobbling everyday presence-to-hand, was already 'collapsing' by 1914. The relative shift to affective tonalities and moods is not simply an aesthetic reaction to overtly didactic figuration, but a movement internal to aesthetic cognition itself: an implicit recognition of the rapid decline of the figure's use value, and an adaptive quest for other values, urgently, in what was now visibly an endangered species of social mobility.

Nowhere is this process better exemplified than in that immense exercise in studious anachronism, *Ulysses*, which can be read, productively, as the greatest streetcar novel of them all. For Joyce's epic is both a compendious summa of the available uses of naturalist streetcar figuration, circa 1904, and their belated modernist subsumption, circa 1922, after the motor car had swept the world's streetcar systems into cognitive irrelevance. Just as *Ulysses* itself can be seen as 'the sardonic catafalque of the victorian world', so too its ubiquitous streetcars must be understood as participating centrally in the work's prevailing dialectic, which Wyndham Lewis grasped so economically:

> that stage of fanatic naturalism long ago has been passed. All the machinery appropriate to its production has long since been discarded, luckily for the pure creative impulse of the artist. The nineteenth-century naturalism of that obsessional, fanatical order is what you find on the one hand in *Ulysses*. On the other, you have a great variety of recent influences enabling Mr. Joyce to use it in the way that he did.[40]

The observation is richer than it knows; for the point is surely that the thrilling 'recency' of Joyce's aesthetic work is entirely predicated on the sheer mass of 'fanatical' naturalism on which it goes to work. It is not that the 'machinery' of naturalism is discarded; it is that modernism consists in a radical reframing and defamiliarization of that machinery, which continues to carry within it the cognitive radiation whose half-life the freeloading 'recent influences' can happily take for granted.

Beginning near the end, Bloom's engulfment in 'Circe's' phantasmagoria is initiated by the near-death incident he has with a monstrous 'sandstrewer' trolley car:

> *(He looks round, darts forward suddenly. Through rising fog a dragon sandstrewer, travelling at caution, slews heavily down upon him, its huge red headlight winking, its trolley hissing on the wire. The motorman bangs his footgong.)*

THE GONG

Bang Bang Bla Bak Blud Bugg Bloo.

...

THE MOTORMAN

Hey, shitbreeches, are you doing the hat trick?[41]

As in Bulgakov, the accent here is on the residual 'effect of the real' retained by the streetcar within a newly modernist aesthetic space; the similarly curt encounter, between a responsible working-class figure, and the 'dreamy' petit bourgeois, encodes class conflict; and the further this colossal chapter descends into sheer fantasy, reverie, and nightmare, the more the note of the streetcar is sounded, as an aide-memoire of the naturalist blueprint. The note is inscribed in the very setting: '*The Mabbot street entrance of nighttown, before which stretches an uncobbled tramsiding set with skeleton tracks, red and green will-o'-the-wisps and danger signals*'.[42] Bloom recalls another altercation with a pre-electric trolley—'I scolded that tramdriver on Harold's cross bridge for illusing the poor horse with his harness scab. Bad French I got for my pains. Of course it was frosty and the last tram';[43] but that is only a dry run on the phantasmatic revival of his rare social triumph in the funeral carriage that morning with Power, Cunningham, and Dedalus. Magnified into an alderman by his warm memory of Cunningham's 'Quite right. They ought to', Bloom reiterates his reformist 'scheme to connect by tramline the Cattle Market (North Circular road and Prussia street) with the quays (Sheriff street, lower, and East Wall)...[etc.]':[44] 'better run a tramline, I say, from the cattlemarket to the river. That's the music of the future. That's my programme'.[45] And with that nod to Lewis's *Jungle*, the full-scale naturalist 'desire named streetcar' returns, mock-triumphal in its zealous indictment of the robber barons:

BLOOM

(*impassionedly*) These flying Dutchmen or lying Dutchmen as they recline in their upholstered poop, casting dice, what reck they? Machines is their cry, their chimera, their panacea. Laboursaving apparatuses, supplanters, bugbears, manufactured monsters for mutual murder, hideous hobgoblins produced by a horde of capitalistic lusts upon our prostituted labour. The poor man starves while they are grassing their royal mountain stags or shooting peasants and phartridges in their purblind pomp of pelf and power. But their reign is rover for rever and ever and ev ...[46]

A gobbledygook redaction out of Dreiser, Norris, Sinclair, and Howells, this lampooning of the naturalist octopus gutters out into Luddism pure and simple. Bloom's alderman rattles off cliché after cliché, in a tongue-in-cheek satire of populist political discourse that has the supplementary function of gainsaying the *engagement* of the naturalist aesthetic itself. The hand of the 'arranger' contrives for Joyce to have his cake and eat it as regards this perdurable figure: insisting on its realism vis-à-vis the contextual *Walpurgisnacht*, while watching it vanish into puffs of anachronistic hot air.

And so it goes. Bloom's day and world view is sustained by that 1904 structure of feeling that saw in the public streetcar an eternal image of efficiency, reform, and the flows of exchange. The final petit-bourgeois utopian image of chez Bloom concludes with the specification: 'situate at a given point not less than 1 statute mile from the periphery of the metropolis, within a time limit of not more than 15 minutes from tram or train line'. But Bloom's boosterish ideological infrastructure is contradicted by its aesthetic realization on the day itself, where trams tend to block saucy views ('A heavy tramcar honking its gong slewed between'[47]), threaten life and limb, mask farts ('Tram kran kran kran. Good oppor'[48]), and disappear from consciousness altogether—as does the only tram he rides on Bloomsday, cost '0.0.1',[49] out to the grieving Dignams to arrange for their insurance. Indeed, Bloom himself needs to be rudely displaced from the centre of attention in order for Joyce to engineer his book's first astonishing structural tour de force with the inauspicious words 'Father Conmee turned the corner and walked along the North Circular road. It was a wonder that there was not a tramline in such an important thoroughfare. Surely, there ought to be.'[50] 'Wandering Rocks' is predicated on the utopian formal possibilities of an integrated urban transport system, its inward- and outward-bound trams serving as the not-so-secret 'motivation of the device' of that chapter's gleeful narrative autonomies and criss-crossing of synchronous paths. Indeed, the chapter is unthinkable in either a purely pedestrian or a fully automobilic frame of reference, but fully dependent in its balletic sociability and formal irony upon the streetcar system in which everyone can pass everybody else, in full view, without having to say a word. Here, the affect of the streetcar is felt as a thrilling formal subsumption of late-realist totalities into a new and hitherto unimaginable aesthetic suffusion of simultaneities; a sublation whose thrilling writerly *techne* is redoubled in the technology of which it was, in 1922, already a nostalgic recollection.

NOTES

1. See Martin Heidegger, *Being and Time*, translated by John Macquarie and Edward Robinson (New York: Harper Collins, 1962), pp. 102–70.
2. Albert Camus, *The Myth of Sisyphus and Other Essays*, translated by Justin O'Brien (New York: Knopf, 1955), pp. 12–13.
3. Jacques Rancière, *Aisthesis: Scenes from the Aesthetic Regime of Art*, translated by Zakir Paul (London and New York: Verso, 2013), pp. ix–xvi.
4. Fredric Jameson, *The Antinomies of Realism* (New York and London: Verso, 2013), pp. 15–77.
5. Donald Barthelme, 'The Balloon' (1966), in *Sixty Stories* (London: Penguin, 1993), pp. 46–51.
6. Werner Sollors, *Ethnic Modernism* (Cambridge, MA: Harvard University Press, 2008), p. 36.
7. T. S. Eliot, *Inventions of the March Hare: Poems 1909–1917* (Orlando, FL: Houghton Mifflin Harcourt, 1996), p. 32.
8. Andrew D. Young, *The St. Louis Streetcar Story* (Glendale, CA: Interurbans Press, 1987)
9. The US focus of this part of the chapter is explained by the fact that American naturalists simply had the jump on the rest of the world. It was they who laid down the ground rules for representation of this critical technology. 'In 1890...the number of passengers carried on American street railways...was more than two billion per year, or more than twice that of the rest of the world combined.' Kenneth T. Jackson, *Crabgrass Frontier: The Suburbanization of the United States* (New York and Oxford: Oxford University Press, 1985), p. 111.
10. Theodor Dreiser, *Sister Carrie* (New York: Penguin, 1986), p. 409.
11. William Dean Howells, *A Hazard of New Fortunes* (*Project Gutenberg* eBook #4600, 2006), http://www.gutenberg.org/cache/epub/4600/pg4600.html accessed 1 Oct. 2015.
12. Sam Bass Warner, *Streetcar Suburbs: The Process of Growth in Boston (1870–1900)*, 2nd ed. (Cambridge, MA: Harvard University Press, 1978), p. 64.
13. 'The convenience of electric traction also helped segregate neighborhoods by class, ethnicity and race, and made it possible for all kinds of people to ride together democratically—and at times uncomfortably—on the same streetcar.' Scott Molloy, *Trolley Wars: Streetcar Workers on the Line* (Durham, NH: University of New Hampshire Press, 2007), p. 2.
14. Henry James, *The American Scene* (London: Chapman & Hall, 1907), p. 126.
15. Gertrude Stein, *Q.E.D.*, in *Writings, 1903–1932*, Vol. 1 (New York: Library of America, 1998), p. 239.
16. It is worth remembering that the capital fund that made Stein's various aesthetic labours possible in the first place, her father's fortune, was amassed in speculation on Oakland's streetcar system.
17. Dreiser, *Sister Carrie*, p. 16.
18. Dreiser, *Sister Carrie*, p. 51.
19. 'It was the streetcars that delivered the hordes of shoppers to the huge selling spaces, and the streetcars that took them home again. The department-store owners learned to locate at the intersection of the busiest transit lines.' Jackson, *Crabgrass Frontier*, p. 114.

20. 'The symbol of a vast power, huge, terrible, flinging the echo of its thunder over all the reaches of the valley, leaving blood and destruction in its path; the leviathan, with tentacles of steel clutching into the soil, the soulless Force, the iron-hearted Power, the monster, the Colossus, the Octopus.' Frank Norris, *The Octopus: A Story of California* (New York: Doubleday, Page and Co., 1901), p. 32.

21. In the USA, 'the "robber barons" of the street railways—Peter Widener, Henry and William Whitney, Charles Yerkes, Borax Smith, and Henry Huntington—made immense fortunes…involved in subdividing and selling land near their routes. As the streetcars proved fast and profitable, with 800 street railway lines established in the US by 1902, much wider areas were opened up to subdivision.' Dolores Hayden, *Building Suburbia: Green Fields and Urban Growth, 1820–2000* (New York: Vintage, 2004), p. 76.

22. Theodor Dreiser, *The Titan*, Ch. 21 (*Project Gutenberg Australia* eBook, n.d.), http://gutenberg.net.au/ebooks/fr100299.txt accessed 1 Oct. 2015.

23. Upton Sinclair, *The Jungle* (New York: Penguin, 1985), pp. 41–2.

24. Sinclair, *The Jungle*, pp. 376–7.

25. Sinclair, *The Jungle*, p. 383.

26. Robert Musil, *The Man Without Qualities*, translated by Sophie Wilkins and Burton Pike (London: Picador, 1997), pp. 165–6.

27. Musil, *The Man Without Qualities*, p. 943.

28. Musil, *The Man Without Qualities*, p. 65.

29. Musil, *The Man Without Qualities*, pp. 946–7. The passage is analysed by Alan Thiher in *Understanding Robert Musil* (Columbia, SC: University of South Carolina Press, 2009): 'Street-side epiphanies seem to be part of Musil's essayistic strategy to allow ideas to contest ideas', p. 293.

30. Musil, *The Man Without Qualities*, p. 947.

31. Alfred Döblin, *Berlin Alexanderplatz: The Story of Franz Biberkopf*, translated by Eugene Jolas (New York: Continuum, 1996), p. 5.

32. Döblin, *Berlin Alexanderplatz*, pp. 4–5.

33. Döblin, *Berlin Alexanderplatz*, p. 53.

34. Döblin, *Berlin Alexanderplatz*, pp. 625–6.

35. Jameson, *The Antinomies of Realism*, p. 28.

36. Jameson, *The Antinomies of Realism*, p. 36.

37. Mikhail Bulgakov, *The Master and Margarita*, translated by Richard Pevear and Larissa Volokhonsky (London: Penguin, 2000), p. 46.

38. Jackson, *Crabgrass Frontier*, p. 164.

39. Jackson, *Crabgrass Frontier*, p. 164.

40. Wyndham Lewis, *Time and Western Man*, edited by Paul Edwards (Santa Rosa, CA: Black Sparrow Press, 1993), p. 90.

41. James Joyce, *Ulysses* (London: Penguin, 2000), p. 567.

42. Joyce, *Ulysses*, p. 561.

43. Joyce, *Ulysses*, p. 581.

44. Joyce, *Ulysses*, p. 846.

45. Joyce, *Ulysses*, p. 601.

46. Joyce, *Ulysses*, pp. 601–2.

47. Joyce, *Ulysses*, p. 90.

48. Joyce, *Ulysses*, p. 376.

49. Joyce, *Ulysses*, p. 836.

50. Joyce, *Ulysses*, p. 283.

Selected Bibliography

Abel, Richard. *French Cinema: The First Wave, 1915–1929*. Princeton, NJ: Princeton University Press, 1987.

Ackerman, Robert. *The Myth and Ritual School: J. G. Frazer and the Cambridge Ritualists*. London and New York: Routledge, 2002.

Acocella, Joan and Lynn Garafola, eds. *André Levinson on Dance*. Hanover, NH: Wesleyan University Press, 1991.

Adams, Robert Martin. *Surface and Symbol: The Consistency of James Joyce's Ulysses*. New York: Oxford University Press, 1962.

Adorno, Theodor. *The Jargon of Authenticity*, translated by Knut Tarnowski and Frederic Will. London: Routledge and Kegan Paul, 1973.

Adorno, Theodor. 'Notes on Kafka'. In *Prisms*, translated by Samuel and Sherry Weber, 260–1. Cambridge, MA: MIT Press, 1981.

Agamben, Giorgio, 'Notes on Gesture', in *Means Without Ends: Notes on Politics*, 49–62. Minneapolis, MN: University of Minnesota Press, 2000.

Alexander, Neal, and James Moran, eds. *Regional Modernisms*. Edinburgh: Edinburgh University Press, 2013.

Allsop, Kenneth. *The Angry Decade*. London: Peter Owen, 1958.

American Psychiatric Association. *Diagnostic and Statistical Manual of Mental Disorders 1* (Washington, DC: American Psychiatric Association Mental Hospital Service, 1952).

Appadurai, Arjun. *Modernity at Large: Cultural Dimensions of Globalization*. Minneapolis, MN: University of Minnesota Press, 1996.

Arendt, Hannah. *Eichmann in Jerusalem: A Report on the Banality of Evil* (1963). Harmondsworth: Penguin, 1994.

Arendt, Hannah. 'Truth and Politics'. In *Between Past and Future: Eight Exercises in Political Thought*, 223–60. London: Penguin, 2006.

Ashbery, John. 'The Impossible: Gertrude Stein' (1957). In *Selected Prose*, edited by Eugene Richie, 11–15. Ann Arbor, MI: University of Michigan Press, 2004.

Atherton, James. *The Books at the Wake*. Mamaroneck, NY: Paul P. Appel, 1974.

Auden, W. H. *The Age of Anxiety: A Baroque Eclogue*. Princeton, NJ, and Oxford: Princeton University Press, 2011.

Auden, W. H. *The English Auden*, edited by Edward Mendelson. London: Faber, 1977.

Badiou, Alain. *L'Être et l'événement*. Paris: Seuil, 1988.

Badiou, Alain. *L'Hypothèse communiste*. Paris: Lignes, 2009.

Bakhtin, M. M. *Problemy tvorchestva Dostoievskogo* (1929). In *Sobranie sochinenii. Tom 2*, 5–175. Moscow: Russkie slovari, 2000.

Bakhtin, M. M. 'Slovo v romane'. In *Sobranie sochinenii. Tom 3, teoriia romana (1930–1961)*, 9–179. Moscow: Iazyk slavianskikh kul'tur, 2012.

Bakshy, Alexander. 'The Road to Art in the Motion Picture'. *Theatre Arts Monthly*, 11 (June 1927): 456.

Baldick, Chris. *The Modern Movement*, vol. 10 of *The Oxford English Literary History*. Oxford: Oxford University Press, 2004.

Banes, Sally. *Dancing Women: Female Bodies on Stage*. London and New York: Routledge, 1998.

Barth, John. 'The Literature of Exhaustion'. *Atlantic*, 220 (1967): 29–34.

Barthelme, Donald. 'The Balloon' (1966). In *Sixty Stories*, 46–51. London: Penguin, 1993.

Barthes, Roland. *Mythologies*, translated by Annette Lavers. New York: Hill and Wang, 1972.

Barthes, Roland. 'Right in the Eyes'. In *The Responsibility of Form: Critical Essays on Music, Art, and Representation*, translated by Richard Howard, 242. New York: Hill and Wang, 1977).

Barthes, Roland. *S/Z: An Essay*, translated by Richard Miller. New York: Hill and Wang, 1974.

Beard, G. M. *American Nervousness, Its Causes and Consequences*. New York: G. P. Putnam's Sons, 1881.

Beckett, Samuel. *Complete Dramatic Works*. London: Faber, 1984.

Beckett, Samuel. *Molloy, Malone Dies, The Unnamable*. London: Calder and Boyars, 1973.

Beckett, Samuel. *Murphy* (1938), edited by J. C. C. Mays. London: Faber, 2009.

Beckett, Samuel. *Watt* (1953). London: Calder, 1970.

Bellour, Raymond. 'Concerning "The Photographic"'. In *Still Moving: Between Cinema and Photography*, edited by Karen Beckman and Jean Ma, 253–76. Durham, NC: Duke University Press, 2008.

Benjamin, Walter. *Illuminations: Essays and Reflections*, edited by Hannah Arendt, translated by Harry Zohn. New York: Schocken, 1969.

Benjamin, Walter. *Selected Writings: Volume 4. 1938–40*, edited by Howard Eiland and Michael W. Jennings, translated by Edmund Jephcott et al. Cambridge, MA, and London: Harvard University Press, 2003.

Benton, Tim. *Modernism 1914–1939: Designing a New World*. London: V&A Publications, 2006.

Bergson, Henri. *Creative Evolution*, translated by Arthur Mitchell. New York: Henry Holt, 1911.

Bergson, Henri. *The Creative Mind: An Introduction to Metaphysics*. New York: Philosophical Library, 1946, rpt. New York: Dover, 2007.

Bergson, Henri. *Matter and Memory*, translated by Nancy Margaret Paul and W. Scott Palmer. London: Swan Sonnenschein; New York: Macmillan, 1911.

Bergson, Henri. *The Meaning of the War: Life and Matter in Conflict*. London and Edinburgh: Ballantyne Press, 1915.

Bergson, Henri. *Time and Free Will: An Essay on the Immediate Data of Consciousness*, translated by F. L. Pogson. London: George Allen and Unwin, 1910.

Berman, Jessica. 'Imagining World Literature'. In *Disciplining Modernism*, edited by Pamela L. Caughie, 53–70. Basingstoke: Palgrave Macmillan, 2009.

Berman, Jessica. *Modernist Commitments: Ethics, Politics, and Transnational Modernism*. New York: Columbia University Press, 2011.

Berman, Marshall. *All That Is Solid Melts Into Air: The Experience of Modernity*. London: Verso, 1983.

Bishop, Janet, Cécile Debray, and Rebecca Rabinow, eds. *The Steins Collect: Matisse, Picasso, and the Parisian Avant-Garde* (touring exhibition, San Francisco Museum of Modern Art, 21 May–6 September 2011, Grand Palais, Paris, 5 October 2011–13, January 2012, Metropolitan Museum of Art, New York, 1 February–3 June 2012). New Haven, CT: Yale University Press, 2011.

Blake, Casey Nelson. *Beloved Community: The Cultural Criticism of Randolph Bourne, Van Wyck Brooks, Waldo Frank, and Lewis Mumford*. Chapel Hill, NC: University of North Carolina Press, 1990.

Boccioni, Umberto. 'Futurist Painting: Technical Manifesto'. In *Manifesto: A Century of Isms*, edited by Mary Ann Caws, 178–82. Lincoln, NE: University of Nebraska Press, 2001.

Boothman, Derek. 'Gramsci's Interest in Language: The Influence of Matteo Bartoli's *Dispense di Glottologia* (1912–13) on the *Prison Notebooks*'. *Journal of Romance Studies* 12 (2012): 10–23.

Bourne, Randolph. 'Trans-national America'. *Atlantic Monthly* 118 (July 1916): 86–97.

Bowen, Elizabeth. *The Heat of the Day* (1948). Harmondsworth: Penguin, 1962.

Bowen, Elizabeth. *The Last September*, introduced by Victoria Glendenning. London: Vintage, 1998.

Bowles, Paul. *The Spider's House*. New York: Random House, 1955.

Bradbury, Malcolm. *No, Not Bloomsbury*. London: Arrow Books, 1989.

Bradbury, Malcolm, and Alan McFarlane, eds. *Modernism: A Guide to European Literature*. Harmondsworth: Penguin, 1976.

Bréal, Michel. *Semantics: Studies in the Science of Meaning* translated by Nina Cust. New York: Dover, 1964.

Brennan, Teresa. *Exhausting Modernity: Grounds for a New Economy*. London: Routledge, 2000.

Breton, André. *L'Amour fou* (1937), translated as *Mad Love* by Mary Ann Caws. Lincoln, NE: Bison Books, 1987.

Brooker, Peter, Andrzej Gasiorek, Deborah Longworth, and Andrew Thacker, eds. *The Oxford Handbook of Modernisms*. Oxford: Oxford University Press, 2010.

Brooker, Peter and Andrew Thacker, eds. *The Oxford Critical and Cultural History of Modernist Magazines: Volume II, North America 1894–1960*. Oxford: Oxford University Press, 2012.

Brotchie, Alastair. *Alfred Jarry: A Pataphysical Life*. Cambridge, MA: MIT Press, 2011.

Brown, Richard. 'Molly's Gibraltar: The Other Location in Joyce's *Ulysses*'. In *A Companion to James Joyce*, edited by Richard Brown, 157–73. Oxford: Blackwell, 2008.

Bru, Sascha, and Dirk de Geest. 'What Modernism Was and Is'. In *Modernism Today*, edited by Sjef Houppermans, Peter Liebregts, Jan Baetens, and Otto Boele, 1–10. Amsterdam: Rodopi, 2013.

Bulgakov, Mikhail. *The Master and Margarita*, translated by Richard Pevear and Larissa Volokhonsky. London: Penguin, 2000.

Burgess, Anthony. *Re Joyce*. New York: W.W. Norton, 1965.

Burke, Kenneth. 'Appendix: Revolutionary Symbolism in America. Speech by Kenneth Burke to American Writers' Congress, April 26, 1935'. In *The Legacy of Kenneth Burke*, edited by Herbert W. Simons and Trevor Melia, 267–73. Madison, WI: University of Wisconsin Press, 1989.

Burt, Ramsay. *The Male Dancer*. London and New York: Routledge, 1995.

Butler, Judith. *Precarious Life: the Powers of Mourning and Violence*. London and New York: Verso, 2006.

Cabanne, Pierre. *Dialogues with Marcel Duchamp*, translated by Ron Padgett. New York: Viking, 1971.

Caillois, Roger. 'Mimicry and Legendary Psychasthenia'. In *The Edge of Surrealism: A Roger Caillois Reader*, edited by Claudine Frank, translated by Claudine Frank and Camille Naish, 89–107. Durham, NC, and London: Duke University Press, 2003.

Callaway, Frank. 'Hal Collins and the Warlock Connection'. In *Peter Warlock: A Centenary Celebration*, edited by David Cox and John Bishop, 242–7. London: Thames, 1994.

Camus, Albert. *The Myth of Sisyphus and Other Essays*, translated by Justin O'Brien. New York: Knopf, 1955.

Canetti, Elias. *Crowds and Power* (1960), translated by Carol Stewart. London: Victor Gollancz, 1962.

Cangueilhem, Georges. *Knowledge of Life*. New York: Fordham University Press, 1988.

Cannon, Walter Bradford. *Bodily Changes in Pain, Hunger, Fear and Rage: An Account of Recent Researches into the Function of Emotional Excitement.* New York: Appleton, 1915.

Carlucci, Alessandro. *Gramsci and Languages: Unification, Diversity, Hegemony.* Leiden: Brill, 2013.

Casanova, Pascale. *The World Republic of Letters*, translated by M. B. DeBevoise. Cambridge, MA: Harvard University Press, 2004.

Cassirer, Ernst. *Language and Myth*, translated Susan K. Langer. New York: Dover, 1946.

Cassirer, Ernst. *The Myth of the State.* New Haven, CT: Yale University Press, 1946.

Cassirer, Ernst. *The Philosophy of Symbolic Forms, Volume Two: Mythical Thought*, translated by Ralph Manheim. New Haven, CT: Yale University Press, 1955.

Chion, Michel. *Film, A Sound Art*, translated by Claudia Gorbman. New York: Columbia University Press, 2009.

Clair, René, dir. *Paris qui dort.* Kastor and Lallement, 1924.

Cocteau, Jean. 'Preface: 1922' to *The Wedding on the Eiffel Tower* (1921). In *Modern French Plays: An Anthology from Jarry to Ionesco*, edited and translated by Michael Benedikt and George E. Wellwarth, 96–7. London: Faber, 1964.

Cocteau, Jean. *The Wedding on the Eiffel Tower.* In *Modern French Plays: An Anthology from Jarry to Ionesco*, edited and translated by Michael Benedikt and George E Wellwarth, 101–15. London: Faber, 1964.

Conquest, Robert. 'For the Death of a Poet'. In *The Book of the P.E.N.*, edited by Hermon Ould, 131–7. London: Arthur Barker, 1950.

Conrad, Joseph. *The Secret Agent: A Simple Tale.* Harmondsworth: Penguin, 1980.

Coupe, Lawrence. 'Jack Lindsay: From the Aphrodite to Arena'. In *Jack Lindsay: The Thirties and Forties*, edited by Robert Mackie, 46–60. London: Institute of Commonwealth Studies, 1984.

Craig, Edward Gordon. *Designs for the Theatre.* London: Heinemann, 1948.

Craig, Edward Gordon. *The Mask*, Vol. 4. Florence, 1911.

Crary, Jonathan. *24/7: Late Capitalism and the Ends of Sleep.* London: Verso, 2013.

Cuddy-Keane, Melba. 'Modernism, Geopolitics, Globalization'. *Modernism/Modernity* 10 (2003): 539–58.

Curnow, Wystan. 'An Interview with Len Lye'. *Art New Zealand*, 17 (Spring 1980) http://www.art-newzealand.com/Issues11to20/Lye09.htm accessed 1 Feb. 2016.

Darwin, Charles. *The Expression of the Emotions in Man and Animals.* London: John Murray, 1872.

Dauncey, Hugh. *French Cycling: A Social and Cultural History.* Liverpool: Liverpool University Press, 2012.

Dauncey, Hugh. 'French Cycling Heroes of the Tour: Winners and Losers'. In *The Tour de France 1903–2003: A Century of Sporting Structures, Meanings and Values*, edited by Hugh Dauncey and Geoff Hare, 175–202. London: Frank Cass, 2003.

Day, Dorothy. 'Poverty and Precarity'. *The Catholic Worker* (May 1952), pp. 2, 6, http//www.catholicworker.org/dorothy day/articles/633.pdf accessed 6 Feb. 2016.

Delay, Jean. *The Youth of André Gide*, translated and abridged by June Guicharnaud. Chicago: University of Chicago Press, 1963.

Deleuze, Gilles. *Cinema 1: The Movement Image*, translated by Hugh Tomlinson and Barbara Habberjam. Minneapolis, MN: University of Minnesota Press, 1986.

Deleuze, Gilles. *Cinema 2: The Time Image*, translated by Hugh Tomlinson and Barbara Habberjam. Minneapolis, MN: University of Minnesota Press, 1989.

Deleuze, Gilles, and Felix Guattari. 'Percept, Affect, Concept'. In *What Is Philosophy?*, translated by Hugh Tomlinson and Graham Burchell, 163–99. New York: Columbia University Press, 1994.

DeLillo, Don. 'Human Moments in World War III' (1983). Reprinted in *The Angel Esmeralda: Nine Stories*, 25–44. New York: Scribner, 2011.

Dimock, Wai Chee. *Through Other Continents: American Literature Across Deep Time.* Princeton, NJ: Princeton University Press, 2006.

Doane, Mary Ann. *The Emergence of Cinematic Time: Modernity, Contingency, the Archive.* Cambridge, MA: Harvard University Press, 2002.

Döblin, Alfred. *Berlin Alexanderplatz: The Story of Franz Biberkopf,* translated by Eugene Jolas. New York: Continuum, 1996.

Dole, R. C. *The Films of René Clair, Vol. II: Documentation.* Metuchen, NJ: Scarecrow, 1986.

Doyle, Laura. 'Toward a Philosophy of Transnationalism'. *The Journal of Transnational American Studies* 1 (2009), http://escholarship.org/uc/item/9vr1k8hk accessed 1 Feb. 2016.

Doyle, Laura, and Laura Winkiel, eds. *Geomodernism: Race, Modernism, Modernity.* Bloomington, IN: Indiana University Press, 2005.

Dreiser, Theodor. *Sister Carrie.* New York: Penguin, 1986.

Dreiser, Theodor. *The Titan,* Ch. 21. *Project Gutenberg Australia* eBook. n.d. http://gutenberg .net.au/ebooks/fr100299.txt accessed 1 Oct. 2015.

DuBois, W. E. B. *Correspondence of W. E. B. DuBois: Selections, 1944–1963,* edited by H. Aptheker. Amherst, MA: Massachusetts University Press, 1997.

Duchamp, Marcel. *Affect-Marcel: The Selected Correspondence of Marcel Duchamp.* French–English edition, edited by Francis M. Naumann and Hector Obalk. London: Thames & Hudson, 2000.

Duffy, Enda. *The Speed Handbook: Velocity, Pleasure, Modernism.* Chapel Hill, NC: Duke University Press, 2009.

Duffy, Enda. *The Subaltern Ulysses.* Minneapolis, MN: University of Minnesota Press, 1994.

Duncan, Irma, and Allen Ross MacDougall. *Isadora Duncan's Russian Days.* New York: Covici-Friede Publishers, 1929.

Duncan, Isadora. *Art of the Dance.* New York: Theatre Arts Books, 1928.

Duncan, Isadora. *My Life.* New York: Liveright, 1927, reprinted 1996.

During, Simon. 'Modernism in the Era of Human Rights'. *Affirmations: Of the Modern* 1 (Autumn 2013): 139–59.

Durkheim, Emile. *Suicide*: *A Study in Sociology* (1897). London: Routledge Classics, 2002.

Dworkin, Craig, *Reading the Illegible.* Evanston, IL: Northwestern University Press, 2006.

Dydo, Ulla E. *Gertrude Stein: The Language that Rises 1923–1934.* Evanston, IL: Northwestern University Press, 2003.

Eliot, T. S. *Inventions of the March Hare: Poems 1909–1917.* Orlando, FL: Houghton Mifflin Harcourt, 1996.

Eliot, T. S. *Poetry and Drama.* London: Faber, 1950.

Eliot, T. S. *Selected Essays.* London: Faber, 1951.

Eliot, T. S. 'Tradition and the Individual Talent'. In *The Sacred Wood,* 2nd ed., 47–59. London: Methuen, 1920.

Eliot, T. S. '*Ulysses,* Order and Myth'. In *Selected Prose of T. S. Eliot,* 175–8. London: Faber, 1975.

Eliot, T. S. *The Waste Land* (1922). In *Collected Poems 1909–1935,* 67–98. New York: Harcourt, Brace and Co., 1936.

Ellis, David, and Howard Mills. *D. H. Lawrence's Non-Fiction: Art, Thought and Genre.* Cambridge: Cambridge University Press, 1988.

Engels, Friedrich. *Selected Writings*, edited and introduced by W. O. Henderson. Harmondsworth: Penguin, 1967.

Esty, Jed. *A Shrinking Island: Modernism and National Culture in England* (Princeton, NJ, and Oxford: Princeton University Press, 2003.

Evans Letters, Lawrence Durrell Collection, Vol. LII, British Library Add MS 73143.

Evans, Patrick, Lawrence Durrell, Ruthven Todd, Edgar Foxall, Oswell Blakeston, and Rayner Heppenstall. *Proems*. London: Fortune Press, 1938.

Fell, Jill. *Alfred Jarry, an Imagination in Revolt*. Madison, NJ: Fairleigh Dickinson University Press, 2005.

Fergonzi, Flavio. *The Mattioli Collection: Masterpieces of the Italian Avant-Garde*. Milan: Skira Editore, 2003.

Field, Henry M. *Gibraltar*. New York: Scribner's, 1888.

Fiori, Giuseppe. *Antonio Gramsci: Life of a Revolutionary*, translated by Tom Nairn. New York: Schocken Books, 1973.

Ford, Mark. 'Nicholas Moore, Stevens and the Fortune Press'. In *Wallace Stevens across the Atlantic*, edited by Bart Eeckhout and Edward Ragg, 165–85. Basingstoke: Palgrave, 2008.

Foucault, Michel. *Discipline and Punish: The Birth of the Prison*, translated by Alan Sheridan. New York: Pantheon, 1978.

Freud, Sigmund. 'Psychoanalytic Notes on an Account of a Case of Paranoia' (1911). Republished as *The Schreber Case*, translated by Andrew Webber, introduced by Colin MacCabe. London: Penguin, 2003.

Friedman, Susan Stanford. 'Definitional Excursions: The Meanings of Modern/Modernity/Modernism'. *Modernism/Modernity* 8 (2001): 493–513.

Friedman, Susan Stanford. 'Periodizing Modernism: Postcolonial Modernities and the Space/Time Borders of Modernist Studies'. *Modernism/Modernity* 13 (2006): 425–43.

Friedman, Susan Stanford. 'Planetarity: Musing Modernist Studies'. *Modernism/Modernity* 17 (2010): 471–99.

Friedman, Susan Stanford. *Planetary Modernism: Provocations on Modernity Across Time*. New York: Columbia University Press, 2015.

Gabriele, Michael C. *The Golden Age of Bicycle Racing in New Jersey*. Charleston, SC: The History Press, 2011.

Galsworthy, John. 'What the PEN Is'. *P.E.N. News*, 48 (June 1932): 4.

Germino, Dante. *Antonio Gramsci: Architect of a New Politics*. Baton Rouge, LA: Louisiana University Press, 1990.

Gibson, Andrew. *Joyce's Revenge: History, Politics, and Aesthetics in Joyce's Ulysses*. Oxford: Oxford University Press, 2002.

Gide, André. *Morceaux choisis*. Paris: Gallimard, 1921.

Gifford, Don, and Robert J. Seidman. *Notes for Joyce: An Annotation of James Joyce's Ulysses*. New York: Dutton, 1974.

Giles, Paul. *The Global Remapping of American Literature*. Princeton, NJ: Princeton University Press, 2011.

Ginneken, Jaap van. *Crowds, Psychology, and Politics, 1871–1899*. Cambridge: Cambridge University Press, 1992.

Golding, William. *Pincher Martin*. London: Faber, 1956.

Gordon, W. Terence. *C. K. Ogden: A Bio-Bibliographical Essay*. Metuchen, NJ: Scarecrow Press, 1990.

Gramsci, Antonio. *Cara compagna. Lettere amorose a Giulia Schucht*, edited by Emma Chimenti. Milan: Kaos edizioni, 2012.

Gramsci, Antonio. 'I dolori della Sardegna'. *Avanti*, 16 April 1919. Reprinted in *Scritti sulla Sardegna*, edited by Guido Melia, 74–5. Nuoro: Illiso edizioni, 2008.

Gramsci, Antonio. *Gramsci, Language, and Translation*, edited by Peter Ives and Rocco Lacorte. Lanham, MD: Lexington Books, 2010.

Gramsci, Antonio. *Lettere 1908–1926*, edited by Antonio A. Santucci. Turin: Einaudi, 1992.

Gramsci, Antonio. *Letters from Prison*, edited by Frank Rosengarten, translated by Raymond Rosenthal. New York: Columbia University Press, 1994.

Gramsci, Antonio. *Prison Notebooks*. Volume II, edited and translated by Joseph A. Buttigieg. New York: Columbia University Press, 1996.

Gramsci, Antonio. *Prison Notebooks*. Volume III, edited and translated by Joseph A. Buttigieg. New York: Columbia University Press, 2007.

Gramsci, Antonio. *Selections from Cultural Writings*, edited by David Forgacs and Geoffrey Nowell-Smith, translated by William Boelhower. London: Lawrence and Wishart, 1985.

Gramsci, Antonio. *Selections from Prison Notebooks*, edited and translated by Quintin Hoare and Geoffrey Nowell-Smith. London: Lawrence and Wishart, 1971.

Gray, Richard T. *Constructive Destruction: Kafka's Aphorisms. Literary Tradition and Literary Transformation*. Tübingen: Niemeyer, 1987.

Green, Henry. *Party Going*. In *Loving Living Party Going*, introduced by John Updike. London: Picador, 1978.

Green, Henry. *Surviving: The Uncollected Prose Writings of Henry Green*, edited by Matthew Yorke. London: Chatto and Windus, 1992.

Grossman, Jonathan. *Charles Dickens's Networks: Public Transport and the Novel*. New York: Oxford University Press, 2012.

Gunning, Tom. *The Films of Fritz Lang: Allegories of Vision and Modernity*. London: British Film Institute, 2000.

Habermas, Jürgen. *The Structural Transformation of the Bourgeois Public Sphere*, translated by Thomas McCarthy. Oxford: Polity Press, 1989.

Hamilton, Patrick. *Hangover Square* (1941), introduced by J. B. Priestley. London: Penguin, 2001.

Hassan, Ihab. *The Dismemberment of Orpheus: Towards a Postmodern Literature*. New York: Oxford University Press, 1977.

Hassan, Ihab. *The Postmodern Turn: Essays in Postmodern Theory and Culture*. Columbus, OH: Ohio State University Press, 1988.

Hayden, Dolores. *Building Suburbia: Green Fields and Urban Growth, 1820–2000*. New York: Vintage, 2004.

Hegglund, Jon. *World Views: Metageographies of Modernist Fiction*. New York: Oxford University Press, 2012.

Heidegger, Martin. *Basic Writings: From Being and Time (1927) to The Task of Thinking (1964)*, edited and introduced by David Farrell Krell. London and Henley: Routledge and Kegan Paul, 1978.

Heidegger, Martin. *Being and Time*, translated by John Macquarie and Edward Robinson. New York: Harper Collins, 1962.

Heidegger, Martin. 'The Thing'. In *Poetry, Language, Thought*, translated and introduced Albert Hofstadter, 163–86. New York; Hagerstown, MD; San Francisco; London: Harper and Row, 1975.

Hemingway, Ernest. *A Moveable Feast* (1964). London: Arrow, 2011.

'Hengist' [Edwin Muir]. 'Epistles to the Provincials'. *The New Age* (18 March 1920–).

Henry, Michel. *Marx: II. Une Philosophie de l'économie*. Paris: Gallimard, 1976.

Heppenstall, Rayner. *The Intellectual Part*. London: Barrie and Rockliff, 1963.

Heppenstall, Rayner. *Master Eccentric: The Journals of Rayner Heppenstall*, edited by Jonathan Goodman. London: Allison and Busby, 1986.

Herod, Andrew. *Scale*. London: Routledge, 2011.

Herring, Phillip. *Joyce's Uncertainty Principle*. Princeton, NJ: Princeton University Press, 1987.

Hoberman, John. *Mortal Engines: The Science of Performance and the Dehumanization of Sport*. New York: The Free Press, 1992.

Horrocks, Roger. *Len Lye: A Biography*. Auckland: Auckland University Press, 2001.

Howells, William Dean. *A Hazard of New Fortunes*. Project Gutenberg eBook #4600, 2006. http://www.gutenberg.org/cache/epub/4600/pg4600.html accessed 1 Oct. 2015.

Hurwitz, Harold. 'Ezra Pound and Rabindranath Tagore'. *American Literature* 36 (1964): 53–63.

Huxley, Aldous. *Brave New World* (1932). New York: Harper Perennial, 2006.

Huyssen, Andreas. 'Geographies of Modernism in a Globalizing World'. In *Geographies of Modernism: Literature, Cultures, Spaces*, edited by Peter Brooker and Andrew Thacker, 6–18. (London: Routledge, 2005).

Huyssen, Andreas. *Miniature Metropolis: Literature in an Age of Photography and Film*. Cambridge, MA: Harvard University Press, 2015.

Iriye, Akira. *Global Community: The Role of International Organizations in the Making of the Contemporary World*. Berkeley, CA: University of California Press, 2002.

Jackson, Kenneth T. *Crabgrass Frontier: The Suburbanization of the United States*. New York and Oxford: Oxford University Press, 1985.

James, Henry. *The American Scene*. London: Chapman and Hall, 1907.

James, William. 'What is an Emotion?'. *Mind* 9 (1884): 188–205.

Jameson, Fredric. *The Antinomies of Realism*. New York and London: Verso, 2013.

Jameson, Fredric. *A Singular Modernity: Essay on the Ontology of the Present*. London and New York: Verso, 2002.

Jameson, Fredric. '*Ulysses* in History'. In *James Joyce and Modern Literature*, edited by W. J. McCormack and Alistair Stead, 126–41. London: Routledge and Kegan Paul, 1982.

Jameson, Storm. *Journey from the North: Autobiography of Storm Jameson*. New York: Harper and Row, 1970.

Jarry, Alfred. 'The Crucifixion Considered as a Bicycle Race'. In *The Selected Works of Alfred Jarry*, edited by Roger Shattuck and Simon Watson Taylor, translated by Roger Shattuck, 122–4. New York: Grove Press, 1965.

Jarry, Alfred. *The Supermale*, translated by Ralph Gladstone and Barbara Wright. New York: New Directions, 1964.

Jones, Susan. *Literature, Modernism and Dance*. Oxford: Oxford University Press, 2013.

Joyce, James. *Finnegans Wake*. London: Faber, 1939.

Joyce, James. *Letters of James Joyce*, edited by Stuart Gilbert and Richard Ellmann, 3 vols. London: Faber, 1957–66.

Joyce, James. *Poems and Shorter Writings*. London: Faber, 1991.

Joyce, James. *Stephen Hero*. London: Jonathan Cape, 1956.

Joyce, James. *Ulysses*, edited by Jeri Johnson. Oxford: Oxford University Press, 1993.

Joyce, Stanislaus. *My Brother's Keeper*. New York: Viking, 1958.

Judovitz, Dalia. *Drawing on Art: Duchamp & Company*. Minneapolis, MN: University of Minnesota Press, 2010.

Judovitz, Dalia. *Unpacking Duchamp: Art in Transit*. Berkeley, CA: University of California Press, 1995.

Kaes, Anton. *Shell Shock Cinema: Weimar Culture and the Wounds of War*. Princeton, NJ: Princeton University Press, 2009.

Kafka, Franz. *The Basic Kafka*, edited by Erich Heller. New York: Simon and Schuster, 1979.

Kafka, Franz. *The Blue Octavo Notebooks*, translated by Ernst Kaiser and Eithne Wilkins. Cambridge: Exact Change, 1991.

Kafka, Franz. *The Great Wall of China and Other Short Works*, translated and edited by Malcolm Pasley. New York: Penguin, 1973.

Kafka, Franz. *Letters to Friends, Family and Editors*, translated by Richard and Clara Winston. New York: Schocken, 1977.

Kafka, Franz. 'Unmasking a Confidence Trickster', translated by Willa and Edwin Muir. In *The Complete Stories*, edited by Nahum N. Glatzer, 397. New York: Schocken, 1971.

Kantorowicz, Alfred. *P.E.N. News* 62 (March 1934): 4.

Kenner, Hugh. 'The Making of the Modernist Canon'. *Chicago Review* 34 (1984): 49–61.

Kenner, Hugh. *A Sinking Island: The Modern English Writers*. London: Barrie and Jenkins, 1988.

Kermode, Frank. *Continuities*. London: Routledge, Kegan, and Paul, 1968.

Kermode, Frank. *The Genesis of Secrecy: On the Interpretation of Narrative*. Cambridge, MA: Harvard University Press, 1979.

Kermode, Frank. *History and Value: The Clarendon and Northcliffe Lectures*. London and New York: Oxford University Press, 1989.

Kern, Stephen. *The Culture of Time and Space, 1880–1918*. New edition. Cambridge, MA: Harvard University Press, 2003.

Kildal, Arne. 'Speech: Welcome at the Oslo Conference'. *P.E.N. News* 13 (September, 1928): 2.

Kinkead-Weekes, Mark. *D. H. Lawrence: Triumph to Exile, 1912–1922*. Cambridge: Cambridge University Press, 1996.

Kittler, Friedrich. *Optical Media*, translated by Anthony Enns. Cambridge: Polity Press, 2010.

Kodama, Sanehide, ed. *Ezra Pound and Japan: Letters and Essays*. Redeling Ridge, CT: Black Swan Books, 1987.

Koestler, Arthur. *Darkness At Noon*, translated by Daphne Hardy. Harmondsworth: Penguin Books, 1972.

Lawrence, D. H. *The Letters of D. H. Lawrence, Vol. 3: Oct. 1916–June 1921*, edited by James T. Boulton and Andrew Robertson. Cambridge: Cambridge University Press, 1984.

Lawrence, D. H. *P.E.N. News*, 20 (April 1929): p. 5.

Lawrence, D. H. 'Preface to *The Mother* by Grazia Deledda'. In *Phoenix: The Posthumous Papers of D. H. Lawrence*, edited and introduced by Edward D. McDonald, 263–4. New York: Viking Press, 1972.

Lawrence, D. H. *Sea and Sardinia*, edited by Mara Kalnins, introduction and notes by Jill Franks. London: Penguin, 1999.

Lawrence, D. H. *Selected Literary Criticism*, edited by Anthony Beal. New York: Viking, 1956.

Leblanc, Maurice. *Voici des ailes!* (1898). Quoted in Stephen Kern, *The Culture of Time and Space, 1880–1918*, 113. Cambridge, MA: Harvard University Press, 2003.

Le Bon, Gustav. *The Crowd: A Study of the Popular Mind*. New York: Macmillan, 1896.

Lefebvre, Henri. *The Production of Space*. Oxford: Blackwell, 1991.

Lessing, Doris. 'The Small Personal Voice'. In *Declaration*, edited by Tom Maschler, 11–29. London: MacGibbon and Kee, 1959.

Lewis, Wyndham. *The Revenge for Love*. Harmondsworth: Penguin Books, 1982.

Lewis, Wyndham. *Time and Western Man*, edited by Paul Edwards. Santa Rosa, CA: Black Sparrow Press, 1993.

Lindsay, Jack. *Franfrolico and After*. London: Bodley Head, 1962.

Lindsay, Jack. *The Roaring Twenties*. London: Bodley Head, 1960.

Lindsay, Jack, and P. R. Stephensen, eds. *The London Aphrodite*. London: Franfrolico Press, 1928–9.

Lodge, Oliver. *The Ether of Space*. New York and London: Harper and Brothers, 1909.

Lye, Len. Len Lye Archive, Govett-Brewster Art Gallery, New Plymouth.

Lye, Len. *Figures of Motion: Selected Writings*, edited by Wystan Curnow and Roger Horrocks. Auckland: Auckland University Press, 1984.

Lyr, René. 'Resolution'. *P.E.N. News*, 56 (June 1933): 5.

McGerr, Celia. *René Clair*. Boston, MA: Twayne, 1980.

Mackinder, Halford. 'The Geographical Pivot of History'. *The Geographic Journal*, 4 (April 1904): 421–37.

Mangan, J. A., ed. *Reformers, Sport, Modernizers: Middle-Class Revolutionaries*. London: Frank Cass, 2002; London: Routledge, 2012.

Mao, Douglas, and Rebecca L. Walkowitz. 'The New Modernist Studies'. *PMLA*, 123 (2009): 737–48.

Marcus, Laura. '"A Hymn to Movement": The "City Symphony" of the 1920s and 1930s'. *Modernist Cultures*, 5 (2010): 30–46.

Marinetti, Filippo Tommaso. *Critical Writings: New Edition*, edited by Günter Berghaus. New York: Farrar, Strauss, and Giroux, 1916.

Marinetti, Filippo Tommaso. 'La Mort tient le volant'. In *La Ville Charnelle*. Paris: E. Sansot, 1908.

Marks, Patricia. *Bicycles, Bangs and Bloomers: The New Woman in the Popular Press*. Lexington, KY: University Press of Kentucky, 1990.

Marx, Karl. *Capital: A Critique of Political Economy. Volume 1*, introduced by Ernest Mandel and translated by Ben Fowkes. Harmondsworth: Penguin, 1976.

Marx, Karl. *Surveys from Exile. Political Writings: Volume 2*, edited and introduced by David Fernbach. Harmondsworth: Penguin, 1973).

Marx, Karl, and Friedrich Engels. *The German Ideology, including Theses on Feuerbach and Introduction to the Critique of Political Economy*. Amherst, NY: Prometheus, 1998.

Mazower, Mark. *Governing the World: The Rise and Fall of an Idea*. London: Allen Lane, 2012.

Mazower, Mark. *No Enchanted Palace: The End of Empire and the Ideological Origins of the United Nations*. Princeton, NJ: Princeton University Press, 2009.

Mellow, James. *Charmed Circle: Gertrude Stein & Company*. New York: Avon, 1974.

Meyer, Steven. *Irresistible Dictation: Gertrude Stein and the Correlations of Writing and Science*. Stanford, CA: Stanford University Press, 2001.

Michalski, Sergiusz. *New Objectivity: Painting, Graphic Art and Photograph in Weimar German 1919–1933*. Cologne: Benedikt Taschen, 1994.

Michelson, Annette. 'Dr Crase and Mr Clair'. *October*, 11 (1979): 30–53.

Miller, Tyrus. *Late Modernism: Politics, Fiction and the Arts between the Wars*. Berkeley, CA, and London: University of California Press, 1999.

Mitter, Partha. *The Triumph of Modernism: India's Artists and the Avant-garde, 1922–1947*. London: Reaktion Books, 2007.

Mohler, Olga, *Francis Picabia*. Turin: Ed. Notizie, 1975.

Molloy, Scott. *Trolley Wars: Streetcar Workers on the Line*. Durham, NH: University of New Hampshire Press, 2007.

Monro, Craig. *Inky Stephenson: Wild Man of Letters*. Melbourne: University of Melbourne Press, 1984.

Moore, Harry T. *Poste Restante: A Lawrence Travel Calendar.* Berkeley, CA: University of California Press, 1956.

Moretti, Franco. 'The Long Goodbye: *Ulysses* and the End of Liberal Capitalism'. In *Signs Taken For Wonders,* 182–208. London: Verso, 1988.

Morin, Edgar. *On Complexity*, translated by Robin Postel. Cresskill, NJ: Hampton Press, 2008.

Mosso, Angelo. *Fear*. London: Longmans, Green, and Company, 1896.

Moyn, Samuel. *The Last Utopia: Human Rights in History.* Cambridge, MA: The Belknap Press, 2010.

Musil, Robert. *The Man Without Qualities*, translated by Sophie Wilkins and Burton Pike. London: Picador, 1997.

Naumann, Francis M. *Marcel Duchamp: The Art of Making Art in the Age of Mechanical Reproduction.* New York: Harry Abrams, 1999.

Nead, Lynda. *The Haunted Gallery: Painting, Photography, Film c.1900*. New Haven, CT and London: Yale University Press, 2007.

Nietzsche, Friedrich. *Ecce Homo*. In *Basic Writings of Nietzsche*, translated by Walter Kaufmann. New York: Random House, 1968.

Nietzsche, Friedrich. *Thus Spake Zarathustra*, translated by R. J. Hollingdale. Harmondsworth: Penguin, 1969.

Norris, Frank. *The Octopus: A Story of California*. New York: Doubleday, Page, and Co., 1901.

Ogden, C. K. 'The Power of Words'. *Cambridge Magazine*, 11 (1923): 50.

Ogden, C. K. 'Word Magic'. *Psyche*, 18 (1938–52): 9–126.

Ogden, C. K., and I. A. Richards. 'Words of Power'. In *The Meaning of Meaning: A Study of the Influence of Language on Thought and of the Science of Symbolism,* 32–100. (London: Kegan Paul, Trench, Trubner, & Co.: 1923).

Ortolano, Guy. *The Two Cultures Controversy: Science, Literature and Cultural Politics in Post-War Britain.* London and New York: Cambridge University Press, 2011.

Orwell, George. *Coming Up for Air.* London: Victor Gollancz, 1939.

Orwell, George. *Keep the Aspidistra Flying.* Harmondsworth: Penguin Books, 1975.

Oudart, Jean-Pierre. 'Cinema and Suture', translated by Kari Hanet. *Screen*,18 (Winter 1978), http://www.lacan.com/symptom8_articles/oudart8.html accessed 6 Feb. 2016.

Ould, Herman. *P.E.N. News*, 56 (June 1933): 5.

Overy, Richard. *The Morbid Age: Britain and the Crisis of Civilisation, 1919–1939*. London: Penguin, 2010.

Palumbo-Liu, David, Bruce Robbins, and Nirvana Tanoukhi, eds. *Immanuel Wallerstein and the Problem of the World: System, Scale, Culture.* Durham, NC: Duke University Press, 2011.

Parry, Benita. 'Aspects of Peripheral Modernism'. *Ariel*, 40 (2009): 27–55.

Parvulescu, Anca. *Laughter: Notes on a Passion*. Cambridge, MA: MIT Press, 2010.

Penton, Brian. 'Note on the Form of the Novel'. In *Scrutinies* II, edited by Edgell Rickword, 255, 257. London: Wishart, 1931.

Perloff, Marjorie. 'Of Objects and Readymades: Gertrude Stein and Marcel Duchamp'. *Forum for Modern Language Studies*, 32 (1996): 137–54.

Perloff, Marjorie. 'Poetry as Word-System: The Art of Gertrude Stein'. In *The Poetics of Indeterminacy: Rimbaud to Cage* (1981), 67–108. (Evanston, IL: Northwestern University Press, 1999).

Perloff, Marjorie. *21st-Century Modernism: The 'New' Poetics*. Oxford: Blackwell, 2002.

Picasso, Pablo. *Poèmes*, edited by Androula Michaël. Paris: le cherche midi, 2005.

Picasso, Pablo. '21 december xxxv'. In *Writing Through: Translations and Variations* by Jerome Rothenberg, 66. Middletown, CT: Wesleyan University Press, 2004.

Postone, Moishe. *Time, Labor and Social Domination: A Reinterpretation of Marx's Critical Theory*. Cambridge: Cambridge University Press, 1993.

Potter, Michelle. 'Designed for Dance: The Costumes of Léon Bakst and the Art of Isadora Duncan'. *Dance Chronicle*, 13 (1990): 154–69.

Potter, Rachel. 'Modernist Rights: International P.E.N. 1921–1936'. *Critical Quarterly*, 55 (July 2013): 66–80.

Potter, Rachel. *Obscene Modernism: Literary Censorship and Experiment 1900–1940*. Oxford University Press, 2013.

Pound, Ezra. 'Cavalcanti'. In *Literary Essays of Ezra Pound*, edited by T. S. Eliot, 149–200. New York: New Directions, 1934.

Pound, Ezra. *Pisan Cantos*, edited by Richard Sieburth. New York: New Directions, 2003.

Pound, Ezra. 'Provincialism the Enemy'. *The New Age* (12 July 1917–).

Pound, Ezra. 'Rabindranath Tagore'. *Fortnightly Review*, March 1913: 571–9.

Prendergast, Christopher. 'The World Republic of Letters'. In *Debating World Literature*, edited by Christopher Prendergast, 1–25. London: Verso, 2004.

Preston, Carrie. *Modernism's Mythic Pose: Gender, Genre and Solo Performance*. Oxford: Oxford University Press, 2011.

Rabinbach, Anson. *The Human Motor: Energy, Fatigue, and the Origins of Modernity*. Berkeley, CA: University of California Press, 1992.

Rabinowitz, Rubin. *The Reaction against Experiment in the English Novel 1950–60*. New York: Columbia University Press, 1967.

Ramazani, Jahan. 'A Transnational Poetics'. *American Literary History*, 18 (Summer 2006): 332–59.

Rancière, Jacques. *Aisthesis: Scenes from the Aesthetic Regime of Art*, translated by Zakir Paul. London and New York: Verso, 2013.

Rancière, Jacques. 'The Archaeomodern Turn'. In *Walter Benjamin and the Demands of History*, edited by Michael P. Steinberg, 24–40. Ithaca, NY: Cornell University Press, 1996.

Rancière, Jacques. *Film Fables*. Oxford: Berg, 2006.

Rawls, John. *A Theory of Justice*. Cambridge, MA: Harvard University Press, 1971.

Reizbaum, Marilyn. *James Joyce's Judaic Others*. Stanford, CA: Stanford University Press, 1999.

Richards, I. A. 'Some Recollections of C. K. Ogden'. In *C. K. Ogden: A Collective Memoir*, edited by P. Sargent Florence and J. R. L. Anderson, 96–109. London: Elek Pemberton, 1977.

Richardson, Brian. 'Remapping the Present: the Master Narrative of Modern Literary History and the Lost Forms of Twentieth Century Fiction'. *Twentieth Century*, 43 (Autumn 1997): 291–309.

Ritchie, Andrew. 'Amateur World Champion 1893: The International Cycling Career of American Arthur Augustus Zimmerman, 1888–1896'. In *Modern Sport: The Global Obsession*, edited by Boria Majumdar and Fan Hong, 63–81. London: Routledge, 2009.

Ritchie, Andrew. *Major Taylor: The Extraordinary Career of a Champion Bicycle Racer*. Baltimore, MD: Johns Hopkins University Press, 1988.

Roberts, Neil. *D. H. Lawrence: Travel and Cultural Difference*. Basingstoke: Palgrave, 2004.

Rood, Arnold, ed. *Gordon Craig on Movement and Dance*. London: Dance Books, 1977.

Rosanvallon, Pierre. 'Inaugural Lecture, Collège de France'. In *Democracy Past and Future*, edited by Samuel Moyne, 31–58. New York: Columbia University Press, 2006.

Rosenquist, Rodney. *Modernism, the Market and the Institution of the New*. Cambridge: Cambridge University Press, 2009.

Russell, Bertrand. 'The Philosophy of Bergson'. *Monist*, 22 (1912): 321–47.

Ryle, Gilbert. *The Concept of Mind*. London: Hutchinson, 1949.

Said, Edward. 'Traveling Theory'. In *The World, the Text, and the Critic*. Cambridge, MA: Harvard University Press, 1983.

Salmon, Louis. 'Gabriel Tarde and the Dreyfus Affair: Reflections on the Engagement of an Intellectual'. *Champ Pénal/Penal Field*, 2 (2005). http://champpenal.revues.org/7185 accessed 6 Feb. 2016.

Salten, Felix. 'Spoken by Felix Salten'. *P.E.N. News*, 16 (December 1928): 7.

Sansom, William. *The Body* (1949), introduced by Anthony Burgess. London: Robin Clark, 1990.

Saussure, Ferdinand de. 'Notes on Whitney'. In *Writings in General Linguistics*, edited by Simon Bouquet and Rudolf Engler, translated by Carol Sanders and Matthew Pires, 140–56. Oxford: Oxford University Press, 2006.

Schechter, Darrow. 'Two Views of the Revolution: Gramsci and Sorel, 1916–1920'. *History of European Ideas*, 12 (1990): 637–53.

Schivelbusch, Wolfgang. *The Railway Journey: The Industrialization of Time and Space in the Nineteenth Century*. Berkeley, CA: University of California Press, 1987.

Scott, Bonnie Kime. *Refiguring Modernism, Vol. 1: The Women of 1928*. Bloomington, IN: Indiana University Press, 1995.

Scott, C. A. D. 'The First International Club of Writers'. *Literary Digest International Book Review*, 1 (November 1923): 47.

Seidel, Michael. *Epic Geography*. Princeton, NJ: Princeton University Press, 1976.

Selye, Hans. *The Stress of Life*. New York: McGraw-Hill, 1956.

Serres, Michel. *Récits d'humanisme*. Paris: Le Pommier, 2006.

Sheppard, Eric, and Robert B. McMaster, eds. *Scale and Geographical Inquiry: Nature, Society, and Method*. Oxford: Blackwell, 2004.

Simmel, Georg. 'Fashion'. In *On Individuality and Social Forms*, edited by Donald N. Levine, 294–323. Chicago: University of Chicago Press, 1971.

Sinclair, Upton. *The Jungle*. New York: Penguin, 1985.

Slaughter, Joseph. *Human Rights, Inc.: The World Novel, Narrative Form, and International Law*. New York: Fordham University Press, 2007.

Sloterdijk, Peter. 'The Last Hunger Artist'. In *You Must Change Your Life*, translated by Wieland Hoban, 61–72. Cambridge: Polity Press, 2013.

Smith, Neil. 'Homeless/Global: Scaling places'. In *Mapping the Futures: Local Cultures, Global Change*, edited by Jon Bird, Barry Curtis, Tim Putnam, George Robertson, and Lisa Tickner, 87–119. London: Routledge, 1993.

Smith, Timothy D'Arch. *R. A. Caton and the Fortune Press*. London: Bertrand Rota, 1983.

Snaith, Anna, and Michael H. Whitworth. 'Approaches to Space and Place in Woolf'. In *Locating Woolf: The Politics of Space and Place*, edited by Anna Snaith and Michael H. Whitworth, 1–28. Basingstoke: Palgrave Macmillan, 2007.

Sollors, Werner. *Ethnic Modernism*. Cambridge, MA: Harvard University Press, 2008.

Somigli, Luca. *Legitimizing the Artist: Manifesto Writing and European Modernism, 1885–1915*. Toronto: University of Toronto Press, 2003.

Sontag, Susan. *Illness as Metaphor*. New York, Farrar, Straus, and Giroux, 1978.

Sorel, Georges. *Reflections on Violence*, translated by T. E. Hulme. Cambridge: Cambridge University Press, 1999.

Spark, Muriel. *Memento Mori*. Harmondsworth: Penguin, 1961.

Spengler, Herbert. *The Decline of the West, vol. 2*, translated by Charles Francis Atkinson. New York: Knopf, 1926.

Squires, Michael, and Lynn K. Talbot. *Living at the Edge: A Biography of D. H. Lawrence and Frieda von Richthofen*. Madison, WI: University of Wisconsin Press, 2002.

Stein, Gertrude. *The Autobiography of Alice B. Toklas* (1933). New York: Vintage Books, 1990.

Stein, Gertrude. *Dix Portraits*. Bilingual edition with French translations by Georges Hugnet and Virgil Thomson. Paris: Éditions de la Montagne, 1930.

Stein, Gertrude. *Everybody's Autobiography* (1937). New York: Vintage, 1973.

Stein, Gertrude. *Geography and Plays* (1922). Introduction by Cyrena Pondrom. Madison, WI; University of Wisconsin Press, 1993.

Stein, Gertrude. *Gertrude Stein on Picasso*, edited by Edward Burns, afterword by Leon Katz and Edward Burns. New York: Liveright, 1970.

Stein, Gertrude. 'The Making of the Making of Americans'. In *Selected Writings of Gertrude Stein*, edited by Carl Van Vechten, 257–8. New York: Viking, 1945.

Stein, Gertrude. *Picasso* (Paris: Librairie Floury, 1938).

Stein, Gertrude. *Picasso*, translated by Gertrude Stein with Alice B. Toklas (London: B. T. Batsford, 1939).

Stein, Gertrude. *Q.E.D.* in *Writings, 1903–1932*, Vol. 1 (New York: Library of America, 1998).

Stein, Gertrude. *Stanzas in Meditation, The Corrected Edition*, edited by Susannah Hollister and Emily Setina (New Haven, CT: Yale University Press, 2012).

Stein, Gertrude. *A Stein Reader*, edited and introduction by Ulla E. Dydo. Evanston, IL: Northwestern University Press, 1993.

Stein, Gertrude and Carl Van Vetchen. *The Letters of Gertrude Stein and Carl Van Vechten, 1913–46*, edited by Edward Burns. New York: Columbia University Press, 1986.

Stewart, Garrett. *Between Film and Screen: Modernism's Photo Synthesis*. Chicago: University of Chicago Press, 2000.

Stewart, Garrett. 'Cinécriture: Modernism's Flicker Effect'. *New Literary History*, 299 (1998): 727–68.

Stewart, Garrett. *Framed Time: Toward a Postfilmic Cinema*. Chicago: University of Chicago Press, 2007.

Stewart, Garrett. *Novel Violence: A Narratography of Victorian Fiction*. Chicago: University of Chicago Press, 2009.

Stravinsky, Igor. *The Firebird* and *Les Noces*. Directed by Ross MacGibbon, performed by the Royal Ballet. London: BBC/Opus Arte, 2001. DVD.

Stravinsky, Igor, and Robert Craft. *Expositions and Developments*. London: Faber, 1962.

Tarde, Gabriel. *On Communication and Social Influence: Selected Papers*, edited by Terry N. Clark. Chicago: University of Chicago Press, 1969.

Taxidou, Olga. *Modernism and Performance: Jarry to Brecht* (Basingstoke: Palgrave Macmillan, 2007.

Taylor, Richard. *The Drama of W. B. Yeats: Irish Myth and the Japanese No*. London and New Haven, CT: Yale University Press, 1976.

Terry, Walter. *Isadora Duncan: Her Life, Her Art, Her Legacy*. New York: Dodd and Meade Company, 1963.

Thacker, Andrew. 'The Idea of a Critical Literary Geography'. *New Formations*, 57 (Winter 2005–6): 56–73.

Thacker, Andrew. *Moving Through Modernity: Space and Geography in Modernism*. Manchester: Manchester University Press, 2003.

Thiher, Alan. *Understanding Robert Musil*. Columbia, SC: University of South Carolina Press, 2009.

Tichi, Cecelia. *Shifting Gears: Technology, Literature, Culture in Modernist America*. Chapel Hill, NC: University of North Carolina Press, 1987.

Tomkins, Calvin. *Duchamp*. New York: Henry Holt, 1996.

Tourette, Gilles de la. *Études cliniques et physiologiques sur la marche*. Paris: Bureaux de progrès, 1886.

Trotter, David. *Cinema and Modernism*. Oxford: Blackwell, 2007.

Tufte, Virginia. *Artful Sentences, Syntax as Style*. Cheshire, CT: Graphics Press, 2006.

United Nations. *Universal Declaration of Human Rights*, 1948, Article 19, www.un.org/en/documents/udhr accessed 1 Feb. 2016.

Upward, Edward. *Journey to the Border*, introduced by Stephen Spender. London: Enitharmon Press, 1994.

Valois, Ninette de. *Come Dance with Me*. London: Faber, 1957.

Vattimo, Gianni, and Pier Aldo Rovatti, eds. *Il pensiero debole*. Milan: Feltrinelli, 1987.

Vere, Bernard. 'Pedal-Powered Avant-Gardes: Cycling Paintings in 1912–13'. In *The Visual in Sport*, edited by Mike O'Mahony and Mike Huggins, 70–87. London: Routledge, 2011.

Virilio, Paul. *The Art of the Motor*, translated by Julie Rose. Minneapolis, MN: University of Minnesota Press, 1995.

Virilio, Paul. *Speed and Politics: An Essay on Dromology*, translated by Mark Polizzotti. New York: Semiotext(e), 1986.

Walkowitz, Rebecca L. *Cosmopolitan Style: Modernism Beyond the Nation*. New York: Columbia University Press, 2006.

Warner, Sam Bass. *Streetcar Suburbs: The Process of Growth in Boston (1870–1900)*. 2nd ed. Cambridge, MA: Harvard University Press, 1978.

Watson, Steve. *Strange Bedfellows: The First American Avant-garde*. New York: Abbeville Press, 1991.

Wellek, René. *Concepts of Criticism*, edited by Stephen G. Nichols. New Haven, CT: Yale University Press, 1963.

Wells, H. G. *The Autocracy of Mr Parham: His Remarkable Adventures in this Changing World*. London: William Heinemann, 1930.

Wells, H. G. *The Outline of History: Being a Plain History of Life and Mankind*. New York: Doubleday and Co., 1971.

Wells, H. G. 'Republic of the Human Mind'. *P.E.N. News*, 56 (June 1933): 2–3.

Wells, H. G. *The Wheels of Chance*. London: Dent, 1896.

White, Patrick. *The Aunt's Story*. London: Vintage, 1994.

White, Patrick. *Happy Valley*. London: Harrap, 1929.

White, Patrick. *The Letters of Patrick White*, edited by David Marr. Chicago: University of Chicago Press, 1996.

White, Patrick. *The Living and the Dead* (1941). Harmondsworth: Penguin, 1967.

Wilde, Oscar. *The Picture of Dorian Gray*. In *The Portable Oscar Wilde*, edited by Stanley Weintraub. New York: Viking Penguin, 1977.

Wilford, R. A. 'The PEN Club, 1930–50'. *Journal of Contemporary History*, 14 (1979): 99–116.

Williams, Raymond. *Marxism and Literature*. Oxford: Oxford University Press, 1977.

Wilson, Angus. *Diversity and Depth in Fiction: Selected Critical Essays*, edited by Kerry McSweeney. London: Secker and Warburg, 1983.

Wittgenstein, Ludwig. 'Notes for Lectures on Private Experience and Sense Data'. *Philosophical Review*, 77 (1968): 275–320.

Wollaeger, Mark, with Matt Eatough, eds. *The Oxford Handbook of Global Modernisms*. New York: Oxford University Press, 2012.

Woolf, Virginia. *The Diary of Virginia Woolf*, vol. 2, 1920–1924, edited by Anne Olivier Bell. Harmondsworth: Penguin, 1981.

Woolf, Virginia. *The Essays of Virginia Woolf*, vol. 3, 1919–1924, edited by Andrew McNeillie. New York: Harcourt Brace Jovanovich, 1988.

Woolf, Virginia. *The London Scene*. London: Snowbooks, 2004.

Woolf, Virginia. *Mrs Dalloway*. Oxford: Oxford University Press, 1992.

Woolf, Virginia. *Orlando*. London: Hogarth Press, 1928.

Woolf, Virginia. *A Room of One's Own* and *Three Guineas*. Oxford: Oxford University Press, 1992.

Woolf, Virginia. *The Waves*. London: Triad/Granada, 1980.

Woolf, Virginia. *A Writer's Diary: Being Extracts from the Diary of Virginia Woolf*, edited by Leonard Woolf (London: Triad/Granada, 1981).

Woolf, Virginia. *The Years*. Oxford: Oxford University Press, 1992.

Yeats, W. B. 'Among School Children'. In *Selected Poems and Two Plays of W. B. Yeats*, edited by M. L. Rosenthal, 115. New York: Macmillan, 1962.

Young, Andrew D. *The St. Louis Streetcar Story*. Glendale, CA: Interurbans Press, 1987.

Young, Robert C. 'Il Gramsci meridionale'. In *The Postcolonial Gramsci*, edited by Neelam Srivastava and Baidik Bhattacharya, 17–33. New York: Routledge, 2012.

Index

Printed and bound by CPI Group (UK) Ltd, Croydon, CR0 4YY